The WALKER, the DRIVER, and OTTO

Published 2024 by Price Creek Press
Printed in the USA
Cover by Daniel McIntosh. Blue heron image modified from an image provided by Adobe Stock Photos (AdobeStock_627166156.png).
First paperback edition

ISBN: 979-8-8692-8219-4

The WALKER, *the* DRIVER, *and* OTTO

Wayfaring Strangers on a Continental Roundabout

Frances A. McIntosh

PRICE CREEK PRESS

DEPOE BAY, OREGON

Dedication

Contents

Part Four

Part Five

Part Six

Part Seven

Part Eight

Part Nine

Part Ten

Part Eleven

Part Twelve

Prologue

"No man is quite sane," writes Ralph Waldo Emerson. "Each has a vein of folly in his composition, a slight determination of blood to the head, to make sure of holding him hard to some one point which nature has taken to heart." Knowing myself and something of the others I live with, not to mention a few friends that come to mind, I cannot argue with Ralph Waldo.

Don, a forty-four-year-old man, sets out to walk the perimeter of the United States in a year's time at a thirty-mile-a-day pace. Fran, once Don's wife—though not for the past twelve years (at the time of the walk)—volunteers to drive the support van and accompany Don on his year-long trek. David, her husband, gives his blessing to the adventure by volunteering to keep the home fires burning, take care of the bills, print and circulate the newsletter Fran writes about Don's progress, and in general provide home support when needed. Plenty of evidence right there of Emerson's insight into human nature.

The questions that these introductory remarks will raise in the reader's mind—as, in truth, they once did in my own mind—undoubtedly begin with the word "Why." There are no quick and easy answers to these questions. The answers are contained within the story of the journey—which is an unfolding, a revealing, an unveiling.

In a less personal vein, there is one question I would like to address before the story begins. When a friend asked me before I left on this journey what places in the country I was most looking forward to seeing, I recall not knowing what to say. Don and I had driven across the country several times together in our previous life as a married couple, but it somehow seemed pointless to me now, when I thought about it, to be looking forward to any one particular place. I could not think, before we set out, how any passing glimpses of a place could be sustaining. Somehow the idea of creeping around the country's perimeter at a walking pace could hardly sound promising in that respect. And yet, in many ways it turned out to be the land itself—with *all* its particular places—that most sustained us. The ever-changing details of the country were a constant source of unexpected wonder. It was exactly what was *not* available to the eye, the ear, the nose, and all the various human sensibilities—when a person goes careening about the land at high speeds—that came to us vividly on a daily, hourly basis. One did not even have to be an enthusiastic fan of Nature, as I was, to be moved by what Nature gave. One did not have to know the names of exotic plants and animals in our path (however eager we were to learn them) to delight in what was seen and heard and felt and smelled and tasted.

Don's every step of a ten-hour walking day was *on the land*. And most of my time waiting was as if from behind a blind. Nature was unafraid. Indeed, it seemed the more we became aware of it, the more Nature—that is, the land, sky, water, and what grew or walked or lived within—reached out to us in consolation for the loss of other company, if not, as it often seemed, out of its own helpless curiosity.

And there, alone (as the driver usually was and as the walker usually was), out in the middle of nowhere and everywhere, each felt safe, somehow comfortable, and part of the whole. It was in towns and cities, which were not our own, that we often felt awkward, like strangers, unsure of the customs of a place, and therefore "out of place." We were never in a town long enough to find a way of fitting in. We were painfully aware of forever "passing through."

Although each state made its boundaries clear to us, its separation from the state before, the country itself was seamless—connected. It was the connections that we both became intimately aware of, so that even the people we met along the way seemed more of a piece, more of a spirit, more of one small, human community than so many widely scattered and unrelated individuals.

It was in the connectedness of things that we saw something that could be read and learned from. Aside from any isolated facts about a particular area, which might be gathered more thoroughly from books, we could read the land for what it said to each of us personally. There was something to appreciate and be grateful for in what the land offered, even beyond what it was—that is, for how the land played its part in one's own story.

"Once in a life," writes N. Scott Momaday, "a person ought to concentrate on the remembered earth. He ought to give himself up to a particular experience—look at it from many angles—wonder upon it—dwell upon it. He ought to imagine he touches it with his hands or feet in every season and listens to the sounds upon it. He ought to imagine creatures there and all the faintest motions of the wind. He ought to recollect the glare of the moon and the colors of the dawn and dusk." Indeed, I think what follows in these pages is my own heartfelt rendering of our adventurous journeying in a very tangible and reflective manner, as described by Momaday. It is my hope that the reader will find some companionable reward in coming along with us.

Part One

JUNE 1987

Vermont, New York, Ontario

Chapter 1

A Man on the Road

The first reward of the journey was one I did not anticipate. It came of seeing a man walking a long road—alone, vulnerable, determined, unburdened. I thought it an uncommon sight: someone walking a road hours from any town without a pack on his back or any visible sign of having provided for himself or his journey—no jacket tied about the waist, no water bottle, no watch upon the wrist even. All the man bore in deference to the day, besides his light clothing, was a baseball cap and a pair of visor-like sunglasses.

Who was this? I suddenly had to ask myself. As I watched the man approach, it was as if I saw him in a waking dream. Was it my dream, or his?

The sun was high and did not shine directly on the man's face, but I could see that he was fair-skinned under a perpetual tan from a life lived much out-of-doors. There was nothing sad nor worried about this face. Though it was middle-aged, lean, and hardened, it was also open and youthfully aglow.

The body beneath the face was sturdy like a young oak—not tall but compact, muscular, light, ready to spring. It did spring: The man's step was lively; he hardly let his heel touch the ground. He wore a red T-shirt with something written across the front in white; gray, pocket-less running shorts; white socks stretched over the tanned calves; and a pair of new, navy-blue running shoes.

I speculated on what a passing motorist might think of this man. He might be a hitchhiker, but no, he didn't walk that side of the road or ever turn to face the traffic. If he had a vehicle somewhere that had broken down, he was making no appeal to the occasional passing car or truck for help. Indeed, he projected an air of self-sufficiency and looked to know what he was doing—where he was going. His focus, the position of his head, the carriage of his whole body seemed to be fixed on something in the far distance. And, in spite of the visible energy in each step, it was plain that he was not really in a hurry.

I could see that the man fit into the setting, and that it was even possible to tell that he liked the fit. He walked up a steep slope, and mountains framed him—not rough and craggy peaks but ones variously treed, broad leaf and evergreen. In a wet ditch, for accent, the wild iris sprang—blue flags trembling in the steady breeze. Daisies, buttercups, and the orange hawkweed blossomed along the roadside. In the distance below and behind, the landscape closed over a gleam of bright lake waters reflecting the sun's dazzle. It was, in the main, a green world under a blue and gold sky—not lush, exactly, but rather keener than that; and, I thought, somehow something like the man himself.

Now I reached for the camera willingly, forgetting it was one reason why I was there. I wished I could get it all in, but I settled for what I could get and hoped that it would turn out to be a significant part of the whole. There was something to see here, and it was what I meant to be witness to—what I would eventually write about if I could. I wanted it to be enough. How gracefully the mountain road curved and rose beneath the man! And while he was alone upon it, I saw that it was all his. And I was glad for him.

"What time is it?" he called out to me as he came within hearing.

When I told him, he frowned and said that he really ought to be further along by now—there, even.

While I put the camera away, I reflected that that was the one thing I couldn't have guessed about Don, seeing him walk the road or even knowing what he was up to—how impatient he was! Why such an impatient man would choose to *walk* the perimeter of the United

States, I would never fully understand. But then there was much about this man that was hard for a woman like me to understand.

The moment he reached the Volkswagen camper-van, which was anchor to us both, I could feel the atmosphere change, as if things must suddenly and noisily run wild for a while where before all had been still and holding. When Don was gone again, the calm would gradually return. Often enough I preferred the calm, but I could hardly mind the stir when I knew it would not last long.

"You want something to eat? I forgot to tell you, I got some good cookies at the last little store I stopped at."

"No, not right now. When I go, maybe. Mostly, I'm thirsty." He grabbed some ice out of the cooler, dropped it into a large, plastic mug, and without sitting down, filled it from a jug on the counter. After a long drink he added, "I think it would be great to get to Long Lake before anyone else does. Not that I'm going to run to get there, but I'd like to be stretched out on the beach and look as if I'd been there all day—especially when Patty and Vinny arrive. It'll make me mad if they pass me on the road. You haven't seen them, have you?"

No, I hadn't seen them. Vinny and Patty were biking together that day the eighty-three miles from Middlebury, Vermont. It was sort of a joke as to who was going to arrive first at the hamlet of Long Lake in the Adirondacks of upper New York State. Don had issued a challenge to all the Team Ross members—friends who liked to compete with one another in various athletic events: citizen cross-country ski races, triathlons, road races, golf games, planned or impromptu games of all sorts. It was mostly for fun because members of the team were of various ages, both sexes, and varying states of fitness or skill. The one major requirement of membership, or so the team laughed and pretended, had to do with whether or not you were willing to cheat in order to win. Besides competing among themselves, they also competed as a team at times.

Don estimated Patty and Vin were liable to arrive in Long Lake by five in the afternoon. Don would be hard pressed to get there much sooner. The hottest rivalry among Team Ross members was between Vin and Don. Patty Ross, an Olympic cross-country skier, became the team leader when the members originally decided to compete with one another at cross-country skiing. Naturally, everyone wanted to take advantage of Patty's Olympic expertise, so she became coach and the team was named after her. Nearly everyone on the team was currently a coach of some sport themselves, not to mention working out regularly and keeping up an interest in all manner of professional sports besides.

The race to Long Lake was for all Team Ross, but only a handful, those closest to Don, took up the challenge. And because of job commitments and other reasons, those who were coming would be leaving for Long Lake at different times and traveling in different ways. All but one were coming from Middlebury: Patty and Vin by bike, Luke by motorcycle, David and Dan by car. Debbie was coming by car from Virginia. The real purpose was not "the race" but simply to wish the walker goodbye and good luck one last time. The *big* farewell party had already been.

Meanwhile, Don, the forty-four year old walker, was on his third day's walk—of a walk he hoped would ultimately take him ten thousand miles. He wanted to average thirty miles a day. His first day out he hiked nineteen. That was June 18, and he had had to teach a full day of school. It was the last school day of the year, and all the Middlebury Junior High teachers and students were lined up to see him off at the end of it. He left directly from his job teaching physical education. He strode out the gym door and passed between lines of cheering students clear out to the parking lot. He was hugged and kissed and patted and blessed and kidded. It had been four years getting to that point, and tired as he was, after all the hoopla attending the wind-up of the school year, his departure, and the getting ready for the adventure besides—Don was full of fresh energy to be off. His focus was forward.

I watched the walker guzzle mug after mug of ice water and juice pacing between cups. I thought Don looked mighty tired.

"Aren't you going to sit down and put your feet up even once today? You've been going since six this morning and you look beat."

But he shook his head, handed me his mug, and said he would take a couple of those cookies now. He was already walking off when he bit into the first one.

"These *are* good," he yelled back at me. And then, "Fran, why don't you go all the way to Long Lake now—it can't be much more than seven miles. I'm psyched."

"Okay!" I called after him and breathed a long sigh as the air settled about me and the quiet returned.

What the year ahead of us held I did not know, but I knew some of the story of the man I was watching. This was a man I was once married to for twelve years—just about twelve years previous—father of our two sons, a man I still loved, but a man I had left for another long ago.

Between Don and myself was a world of differences. He was far more content and far simpler in most ways than I was, yet harder to capture in words. Somehow for things and people more complex, moody, scarred, unhappy, haunted—and especially for the exaggerations of these and other character traits—humankind has uncounted words, endless descriptions, and no surfeit of appetite. For what is genuinely good we have much less to say and, somehow, little that is adequate.

I watched Don move on into the distance. Now, he was beginning to disappear over the crest of the hill. He did not look back.

Chapter 2

A Woman on the Road

It was more like nine miles to Long Lake, I noticed. I estimated it would take Don another two-and-a-half hours. I scouted the town for some sign of the others and found none. I parked next to the old log inn opposite the lake's public beach, where any arrivals would easily spot the brown VW camper, then got out to stretch and take in the resort setting.

It was early in the season yet, and though the day was as bright as they come, and the sun penetratingly warm in the cool air, the small beach was not crowded. I had never been to Long Lake, and I was taken with the arm-like stretch of the calm lake waters reaching north and opening a vista between mountains that seemed to call for a different adventure entirely; one by canoe, chiefly—birch bark canoe. I would have wished the town away and the wilderness returned, but I saw that a wild land beckoned not far off, where the mountains piled upon mountains in the remote blue haze and where the silvery water fingered its way into the distant valleys among them.

It took me only about ten minutes to walk out of the main section of town, leaving the stores, gift shops, restaurants, inns, and ice cream stands behind. It would take probably another hour to meet Don, but the idea of a bit of a hike seemed good to me. I hadn't meant to wait all day to take one, but in the morning the black flies were bad, and even now, if one stood still, they hovered and bit. I was pleased to pass a little chapel on my way out, St. Henry's, where I could attend church later, if I got back in time.

Meanwhile, I walked—a woman alone upon the long road—vulnerable, determined, but not exactly unburdened. Something bore down upon me, something invisible, but something with weight. It may have taken the spring out of my step, but it did not break my stride. I had born it too long and was accustomed to the weight of it.

A middle-aged woman, small but not slight, I wore a pair of high-waisted, loose fitting, army-green pants made of cotton, held up by suspenders. Tucked into these pants was an off-white, high-necked, billowy-sleeved cotton blouse. The shoes on my feet were new—off-white, leather, well-cushioned. I carried a pair of binoculars on one shoulder and walked with my hand in my pocket to help keep them there.

If someone could have seen me then, or any time, they might have said my face was a strong one, the jaw set. My nose—how would they put it?—distinctive. They might also add, "She walks in another world, even while trying to observe and find her way in this one."

Once out of town, I, too, felt myself fitting into the setting. At first, I looked about often and did not maintain a steady forward focus. I stopped at times, risking the pesky flies, to catch a glimpse of something on the wing in my field glasses. I could just about name all I saw of bird or flower or the commoner grasses, and sometimes did, to myself, when something struck me, so that I would remember to jot it down later in my little black book of nature notes. The book was in my back pocket, a pencil clipped inside it.

After a while, though, my attention wandered from the immediate scene to my mind's eye view of the mountains I was just then walking among. Back home, in Vermont, I often hiked to certain places to see these very Adirondacks, which lay beyond the wide valley and just the other side of Lake Champlain. I liked to look off to them. I liked especially to measure the year's progress by where the sun went down behind them. Every day of the year, the sun goes down in a slightly different place, except at the solstices, when the sun would seem to go down in the same spot for days. But often it appeared to me that the sun did not sink behind the Adirondacks so much as it slipped in among them. And that's where I imagined I was now—among them, among the silhouettes where the sun went sliding slightly sideways and down in slow motion--a gold coin into a silver slot between the flattened peaks.

But tomorrow, I thought with a sudden thrill, I would be flying south with David, the man I had married more than ten years before. We would fly to an exotic clime, to a place that was nothing at all like the place where I was now. Not that I would rather be in Florida than where I was now, but it would be good to be with David and put the obligations for the coming year behind me, if only for a week. It was a week David and I might not have had at all if it hadn't been for a lucky raffle drawing. I was glad. It had helped to take the edge off the first goodbye.

There, on the boulder, where I liked best to watch the sun go down, looking off into these very mountains, David and I said our first farewell. It was odd. It was almost the only time we had been to the boulder at midday. It was hard. A year was a long time—too long to see the end of. We could not bring ourselves to linger; better to think about the Long Lake reunion only three days away. Better to be quickly gone.

When I caught up to Don, he asked me again if I'd seen any sign of Patty or Vin. I hadn't. And then for one triumphant moment Don thought he was definitely going to win the race to Long Lake. He mistakenly thought the town was only a few minutes away. He was not too happy to learn that I had been walking over an hour to meet him. Don was nearing the end of his second thirty-two mile day, and a three-day total of eighty-three miles. I could tell he was feeling it. As fit as Don was, he had not really had the time to do much training in terms of long-distance walks; he figured the adventure itself would get him into "walking" shape readily enough. But this was the beginning, and at this point he felt the pain in every step.

I hadn't been walking with Don for much more than a half hour when Patty and Vin suddenly went whizzing past us on their bikes. The bikers did not slow down, say hello, or give any sign that they noticed either of us. In a flash they had disappeared round the bend.

"That's them!" Don fairly shouted, adding a few curses under his breath.

"Darn it all, Don, you almost beat them. But why didn't they stop?"

"They were pretending not to see us, I bet." Don said this with noticeable frustration. "Let's pretend we already got there ourselves and got bored waiting and came out to search for them."

"Right, but do you think they even saw us?"

"They saw us," Don muttered, shaking his head.

A short while later, two leisurely bikers came peddling back toward us. They were smiling and laughing together as they advanced. Patty's straight dark hair was pulled back into two small ponytails. She was the rosy picture of youth and health, hardly looking as if she had just biked eighty miles. Vin was the picture of youth and health, too, only not so rosy; he was a curly-headed Italian who looked as if he knew how to take care of himself. A devilish twinkle in both their eyes let me know Don was in for some hazing.

"Hey, Walker, been on the road long?" Patty called, giving Vinny a conspiratorial glance.

"Last one to Long Lake is a..."

But Vinny did not have a chance to finish because Don butt in with, "Hey, we've been walking all over looking for you guys! Where have you two been?"

And that was how it went for a while, but everyone knew perfectly well who had won. Patty and Vin and I jollied the walker along. The talk was animated and full of exchange about the hazards and hardships of biking or walking such a distance; the dangers of speeding logging trucks on the mountain roads with their sometimes empty flatbeds and their heavy chains loudly rattling, threatening to break loose and brutally knock a walker or biker off the face of the earth; the swarms of insects in places; the steepness of the hills; the heat at times; the wind; the beauty of the land—flowering meadows, hovering mountains, shining lakes and streams—the entire way.

Having been on the road longer, Don and I had a few stories to tell—Don, of being interviewed on the road by a New York State radio station, of the *long* shortcut via Johnson Pond Road, of meeting Bill Jennings at the North Hudson Post Office where Don was soaking his feet in a bucket of spring water—I, of losing Don, locking the keys in the camper, and strange noises in the night where we had camped out. And all this talk was repeated time and again—variations on a theme of adventure—as the others arrived.

Next came Debbie: fair, long blonde hair, athletic, not officially a Team Ross member because no longer living in Middlebury, but close to Don, who was for four years her swim coach at Middlebury College. Then, big, husky Luke, who still liked to throw discus and shot, arrived on a huge motorcycle which it seemed only someone the size of Luke could handle. And last, David arrived with Dan.

When Don and I were married, we had two sons—Dan was the younger. Andy, the older of our two sons by eleven months, would have come to Long Lake too, except he was already at his summer job at a camp on the eastern side of Vermont. Andy had been at the big farewell party; this reunion was really only an afterthought. Dan was of a stockier build than his father and was blonder, but he had the open glow Don had. And from his mother? Well, people said that Dan had something of my eyes when he smiled. He was the youngest present, and like his brother Andy, would be a senior in college while his father, Don, would be walking the perimeter of the country, and while his mother would be going along to drive the support vehicle.

The party kept to the public beach to start. Every time someone arrived I got out the camera and took pictures. I got Debbie fresh from her run, which Debbie took almost immediately to wake herself up after the long day's drive from Virginia. And I got Debbie with Patty and Vin and the walker—smiles and bodies beaming from the exhilaration of the day. I got Luke, and his motorcycle, and Dan and David into the pictures when they arrived. And David got me, arm around the walker and son.

Everyone dove into the lake at some point to shed the heat and dust and sweat of the day, reviving in the cold, clear waters. I even had a chance to squeeze in a visit to St. Henry's before things really got going—while the others went to look up Bill Jennings' grandfather at his Long Lake store just to say hello. Don had promised Bill Jennings he would stop in and tell Bill's grandfather about The Walk. There was such a freshness and a newness to this long walk, it seemed rather momentous. And anyway, Bill Jennings, a perfect stranger, had wanted to shake Don's hand and wish him all the best when he had learned of it. It was the sort of attention Don thrived on, drew energy from.

The gathering of friends was what Don thrived on, too. Once Don was through walking for the day and the party had begun, he did not seem to remember his tired legs and aching feet. He seemed to have forgotten about having to set out on The Walk again the next day; and he celebrated with all present as if it was the end of The Walk already; as if Long Lake, New York, had been *the* destination all along.

But what no one knew then was that everyone who had come to Long Lake would find their separate ways to meet up with Don and me again on the journey.

Chapter 3

Another Farewell

Two days later, while Don was trekking through upper New York State toward the Canadian border, David and I were checking into a hotel outside Orlando, Florida. The raffle I had won in late May, thanks to David throwing my name into a barrel at least a month earlier, included round-trip airfare for two, rental car, hotel accommodations, and some cash. The cash was supposed to contribute toward meals, gas for the car, and tickets to Epcot or Disney World; but after one visit to Epcot in the searing, day-long heat, we decided to head out in the relative comfort of the air-conditioned rental car and explore other parts of the state.

Besides, we both realized that, to us, the gift of the trip was in the time it gave us to be together. We did not need the entertainment of amusement parks, however grand. We appreciated instead the uncrowded beaches we found on the Gulf and the Atlantic, and went as far afield as the old city of St. Augustine and were glad we did.

But though this time was a genuine gift to a married couple about to be voluntarily, if reluctantly, separated for the better part of a year; fate gave it one royal twist. It happened shortly after we had checked into our hotel. David disappeared into the bathroom with his barber scissors and shaving kit. I browsed through Epcot literature in the adjoining room.

"I don't know, David," I called teasingly to him, "I've always said—and heard it confirmed in court—shaving off beards and mustaches is grounds for divorce."

David did not respond. I could tell he was busy looking into the mirror and taking stock of himself. *Should I or shouldn't I?* He must have been debating.

I thought David's straw-blonde hair and somewhat darker beard and mustache gave him a rather distinguished look. Yet how would he look without his beard? Even David couldn't have said. He hadn't seen his face without hair since he first decided to grow a beard in the late sixties—nearly twenty years ago. I had only seen him without his beard in pictures.

David was not often an impulsive man. He was known more for his thoughtful, dependable, sober, and hard-working ways. He was an active, behind-the-scenes volunteer in his community, served on various boards, and was co-owner with Vin (who was also a good friend of Don's and had come to Long Lake) of a successful sporting goods business in Middlebury. David had earned the respect of his fellow townspeople on all these counts and others. He was also known for his sense of humor, which was as quick as it was dry, so people who didn't know him might look at him a little odd and wonder how to take him.

I guess it was David's good-humored appreciation for the element of surprise that lured him on now, when he reached for the barber scissors and began cutting into his beard with abandon.

"I wish you wouldn't, you know," I called in again, "even though I agree that if any time's the right time, this is it. Still...I *really* wish you wouldn't."

David did not answer. I heard him put the scissors down. He applied shaving cream to the stubble on the right side of his face and picked up the razor.

A while later, I heard him chuckling out loud. He held the towel over the shaven half of his face and walked into the room where I waited expectantly.

"Oh dear, let's see what you've done," I said, still hoping he hadn't done it. "Remove the veil." And then, when he did my mouth fell open with a little shriek.

He laughed and went back into the bathroom to finish the job. "It's not that bad, is it?" he called good naturedly back to me.

But he was beginning to see for himself that my response was not entirely uncalled for. By the time he was fully clean shaven, even he was a little stunned. He realized he was looking at someone in the mirror he would never have expected to see staring back at him. I had merely seen it first.

I stepped into the bathroom and came up behind him now, pointing at his reflection in the mirror. "You know who you look like, don't you?"

And then together, we both said it, "Captain Kangaroo!"

The ridiculous truth spoken aloud broke us both down into hysterical fits of laughter until our stomachs ached and the tears came.

Yet, especially to me, the tears were not all light-hearted ones. I had fully expected our love to be tested in the separation over the coming year, but I had not expected the tests to begin so soon.

Every time I looked at David over our week together in Florida I was surprised again. I could not get used to it. It was the double chin. His beard had beautifully camouflaged a double chin. And though David was not in any sense "fat" otherwise, he took on a softened look from this extra chin that was not in the least flattering. In addition, all of his natural facial mannerisms and expressions were suddenly transformed: They were not his own but those of someone I did not recognize, or else they were Captain Kangaroo's, I couldn't always be sure which. But to me, at any rate, the face was definitely and heartbreakingly not quite David's.

David himself was not happy with my response to him, but then since he did not walk around in front of mirrors all day long, he could more or less forget his awkward transformation. He was reassured, however, when I did not withdraw from him or reject him physically. It was just annoying to him to know too often from my own expressions that I could not quite get used to his. He was already determined to grow the beard back; but however quickly it was likely to grow, he, too, saw that the year rushing toward us had already begun. Things were already different. Something already had been lost. The ground beneath us both had been shaken.

Yet as the week progressed, the approaching "goodbye" and all that it represented made the silliness of a missing beard and mustache just that—sheer silliness. Things might be different, but surely he was the same David. I was the same Fran. Ours was the same close-knit relationship. True, for the coming year our lives would be very different from what they had been. No one could predict the outcome. And people *do* change, even when their appearance seems to stay the same. And sometimes people don't change, even when their appearance does. But the fact is—and this we both felt strongly but could not bring ourselves to acknowledge openly—there is always change.

Meanwhile, the sultry days; the warm, gentle waters of the Gulf, which felt hot to the face; the cooler and rougher Atlantic with the rocking waves; the leaping marlin and high-diving pelican; the cackling gallinule and the silent lizard basking in the sun, the mimosa and crape myrtle in fragrant bloom along the old, cobbled streets of St. Augustine—all—were too soon behind us, as in a dream. Our plane flew into darkness; we had one night at home; and it was time to say farewell again.

One of the last things we did together on the mountain was to go to Lucky Seven, the mountain spring, and fill the camper van full with a supply of fresh water. There was something like a small miracle in the way the frigid water poured forth year-round, tumbling out of a small pipe, overflowing a big iron tub, spilling out into the wayside. Banded purple butterflies fluttered all about the wet road in the cool, forested shade.

When I climbed into the driver's seat, I worried about the extra weight of such a generous water supply. "Otto" suddenly felt different. I had named the ten-year-old, brown-and-white VW camper because I wanted it to be a friend and not fail me. As I drove Otto away, it seemed to have come jigglingly to life and felt more like a horse than a machine. I tried to sit lightly in the saddle.

David followed me down the mountain in his car. We stopped to picnic at Crown Point Bridge, next to Lake Champlain. The bridge crossed the lake, the border between New York and Vermont. We tried to eat leisurely, to pretend we had all day, to put off the sense of the inevitable. We might as well have tried to grow his beard back by tugging on the whiskers.

Then finally—suddenly—the moment could not be ignored. It was getting late and I had a long, uncertain drive ahead of me. Maybe it helped that David did not look like himself at that moment. Maybe it helped that my vision blurred and I looked somehow past him. We kissed and parted.

David wrote to me later describing how hard it was to watch me go, to let me go; how he stood unwilling to move until the brown camper was lost to his sight. He said he was thankful, when I was gone, that he had plenty of work to go to, that he did not have to dwell on that moment.

I kept my eyes on David in the rearview mirror as long as I could. But soon, however reluctantly, I had to shift my focus forward. The journey had begun—my journey. I was now "the driver." I had some reckoning to do. The long road led on ahead, and to me it seemed as if everything was laid out ahead of me—even, somehow, the life I had already lived.

Chapter 4

Catching the Walker

I did not know what a long time it would take to catch up with the walker. There was no interstate to hum along on. I was unable to drive very fast through the Adirondacks anyway. For one thing, when I took the mountain curves, Otto felt as if he could almost tip over. For another, he took the hills reluctantly, displaying little power or enthusiasm for getting up the long, steep slopes. And though Otto had been thoroughly checked over, I was not sure how much confidence to place in his brakes when heading down these same slopes. He was, in my restless imagination, an unproven beast. The strong winds that had come up buffeted the camper at times with such force that Otto seemed even more to me like something alive—something wild and difficult to control.

I have a bad habit of birdwatching while driving, but I worried about taking the wrong turns and getting lost, so I tried to resist this temptation and concentrate on the road. More than once, though, I was distracted by deer fleeing into the mountain forests—struck by how exactly their color recalled the Flagler Beach sands near St. Augustine. My mind wandered as I drove even when my eyes didn't.

I thought how unlikely it was that I was doing what I was doing. Who would have thought that eight months ago, when David found this VW camper advertised in the newspaper, and Don decided to go ahead and buy it in hopes of it becoming a support vehicle for The Walk—that I would end up being the one to drive it! For some dumb reason we all thought there would be lots of drivers, not just one. It seemed likely that Andy and Dan might each want to take a semester off from school to drive for their father. But as it turned out, both were eager to finish their senior years in college and to put their undergraduate work behind them. Others did express interest in being drivers for Don's walk, particularly Team Ross members, but no one was really free enough from job and career commitments to do it. And then, too, no one was quite *that* committed to Don. Of course, Don did not officially get word from the school board that his sabbatical was granted until a few months before he was to leave, so there wasn't much time left for finding a driver.

I wondered for a moment why I had ended up being driver. But in the same instant, I knew full well *exactly* why—I had volunteered. It's just that it was still rather sudden-seeming and hard to grasp. What I really didn't know yet was what, exactly, I had volunteered *for*. What would "being driver" really amount to? And in the *long* run, what would it require of me? It was too early to tell.

I had volunteered and David had let me go. That was what was amazing. Was it out of guilt, or gratitude? Probably something of both, yet at that point, before I knew what the journey was all about, I simply could not have said. I definitely felt I had owed a debt to Don— but David? I wasn't sure to what extent he felt this indebtedness, but I guess we were both going to find out. I was surprised to learn that Don was a little worried about owing David and me when the year was over. It was at the end of the first day's walk, when we were camped on the edge of Lake Champlain, that I first learned of Don's concern.

I was in the upper bunk under Otto's popped top. It was very like a tent up there, I thought, with canvas sides and a small, screened window that could be zipped closed. I called this bunk "the little observatory," after the loft in which I sleep at home, under tall windows facing south where I can watch the sun, moon, and planets move through the ecliptic plane. Now I could look through the little canvas window to the night of stars outside Otto. Later, if I was still awake, I could watch the moon set behind the Adirondacks. Sounds came easily through the canvas; and that first night I listened to the gentle lapping of the lake and to the low, contented cackling of a pair of domestic geese. I felt I had complete privacy in Otto's upper bunk. No one could see me up there. I also felt safe with Don more visible and on guard, so to speak, in the bunk below.

It could not help but seem a little strange to us both—that first night—just the two of us. Don and I hadn't been alone together like that in many years, but we were both tired and talk was scarce.

"You know, a year is a long time," Don said when we had both been lying quietly on our separate bunks for a while.

"Too long, really, to see to the end of," I agreed, and then added, "I was just saying that very thing to David earlier today."

"Now, Fran, I want you to understand something. This favor you're doing me—that you and David are doing me, I mean. Well, it's an awfully big favor, I know, and I'm worried about…well, when the year is over…" he paused.

When I saw what he was getting at, I laughed. "Don't worry, Don, both David and I feel that we owe you or we wouldn't be doing this. I'm just hoping that by the end of the year we can call it "even"—or at least maybe then I won't feel I owe you so much. Anyway, don't worry about owing David and me anything, okay?"

"Well, I don't know. I'm not sure you're right. I'll have to think about it. Anyway, I'm too tired right now. I guess there will be plenty of time to think on the road."

"For both of us," I agreed.

I pulled into the town of Long Lake. It was the second time I'd ever been there. I was retracing Don's walking route, and I would have to pay closer attention now because I had never driven the roads beyond Long Lake. I was interested in seeing the route Don walked, but even when the roads were new to me, I found my mind wandering. I had been so busy and preoccupied the last several weeks I had not had much time to think. And now that I was alone, odd realizations came to me.

I thought how ironic it was that it would mostly just be the two of us—Don and me—on this journey. When I was married to Don years earlier, I recalled how often I used to wish just the two of us could do things together. Every time we went anywhere, we were always in a group—usually a big group, and often we were acting as chaperons. It seemed as if Don liked to have a party going on around him, whatever we did. Not only that, but when we were together some twenty-six years earlier, while I was still in high school, we had had plans of going off on a big adventure when I graduated—just the two of us. We were going to go to England, or some other far-off place. I got pregnant instead. So now, though we hadn't been married for a good twelve years, and though neither of us would have changed the way things had turned out, here we were suddenly going off—together! What was this journey going to be for us?

Well, *I* called it a journey. Don liked to call it an adventure. That was our family motto from the very beginning—"adventure." Don had reminded me of this when he first brought up the idea of The Walk to me four years ago. I questioned him thoroughly about this new idea for nearly a year before I began to go along with it, somehow knowing it was not as simple as Don tried to make it out. He was so sure then that he could just walk off with a pack on his back and no one would have to worry about him.

Don was good at dreaming up adventures. One idea, which had a longer life than most, was for the four of us (Don and I and our two then-grade-school-age sons) to sail around the world together. Never mind that we lived landlocked, smack in the middle of the continent at the time, or knew anything about sailing, or could hardly afford such a thing as a sailboat. True, a short while later, we lived a year in the Virgin Islands on St. Croix keeping that dream in mind. But then, when Don got horribly seasick on a deep-sea fishing expedition, he quit dreaming of sailing anywhere at all.

Definitely this was going to be an adventure. In *Blue Highways*, William Least Heat Moon said, "There are two kinds of adventurers: those who go truly hoping to find adventure and those who go secretly hoping they won't." As to which I was? I really wasn't so sure anymore. Anyway, I liked to think of the adventure mostly as a "journey"—a long, roundabout journey home.

By the time I arrived at the Ogdensburg Bridge, the sun was well on its way toward setting. The crossing of this bridge over the St. Lawrence Seaway, from the U.S. into Canada, nearly made my heart stop. The waters were unexpectedly huge, the bridge unexpectedly high, and the sky in the foreign country ahead now ominously dark and threatening.

I thought of Don walking this bridge and how it must have been an exciting moment for him—a milestone. He would love the lofty views the bridge gave in all directions. To him it would be a fantastic two-mile stroll across the far-reaching waters below, but to me there was something fearsome in the way the bridge seemed to loom up all at once out of nowhere. Even the border crossing was somehow more significant than I had thought it would be. Though I was barely two hundred miles from home, it felt suddenly much further than that. Entering another country made it seem further still.

I would not have been going into Canada at all if Don had not decided to cut across Ontario above the Great Lakes. It was a more direct route for him, and by going that way he could avoid the industrial cities of the Midwest. He liked the idea that it would get him into less-familiar territory more quickly. It was not the *exact* perimeter of the country he was shooting for, anyway, and thus he did not mind this shortcut taking him to the other side of the U.S. boundary.

I drove on. The night came quickly—a great darkness compounded by a brooding sky. The clouds lowered and the fog turned homely lights into weird, glowing islands. Traffic got bad. My progress slowed considerably.

I started looking for public phones when I drove through a town. I stopped more than once to consult the map and see if I was still going in the right direction. I was supposed to call David at home to find out if Don had checked in to confirm his whereabouts. The last one to see Don was Patty, who had driven up to Ottawa to meet the Walker for a day off on the town a few days earlier. The message from Patty was that I should meet Don at a place called Haley Station. I saw by the map that it was still a long way off. Both Don and I had expected to meet up *before* it got dark. The drive was taking much longer than planned.

Finally I spotted a phone. It was an unfamiliar-looking public phone, which reminded me where I was and that I had no Canadian money. I tried an American quarter and sighed with relief when it worked.

No, David had not yet heard anything from Don—must be he was waiting somewhere at Haley Station. Surely he'd call in to say "where" any minute, David thought.

David's voice sounded far away and disappointingly matter-of-fact. I climbed back into Otto and drove on.

There seemed to be fewer towns now and fewer public places to phone. I worried about whether Don would call in as planned. When I finally came to another town and spotted a phone, I called home again.

Yes, David had heard from Don, but Don was not at Haley Station. It turned out to be only a defunct railroad crossing without a gas station, restaurant, or any place where Don could get out of the weather and wait comfortably for the Driver to show. He was now at a place beyond there. I estimated I was still a couple of hours away. David told me to check in again later because Don wasn't sure how long he could wait where he was. I was glad David asked me to call again.

But now it began to storm. I had to drive even more slowly. The visibility was poor and the reflections of car lights and other lights on all the wet surfaces strained my eyes. At half past ten I found a phone in another town. The rain was pouring hard and I did not feel safe on the shabby street. The phone booth offered little shelter with its broken glass. I got through to David, though, and somehow this time his voice sounded closer and more reassuring.

Yes, he had heard from Don again. Don had had to move on again. The place where he was waiting closed. He was now outside a town called Cobden, and the diner where he was waiting would be open only another hour. I figured I could just about make it.

On I drove. Don was out there, up ahead, somewhere in the dark, wet night. I began to have visions of some sort of super-walker who would somehow always manage to keep just ahead of me. It began to seem impossible that he had walked all that way—even in a foreign land. How things had changed! Florida and hot sunny beaches existed in some other world. David was distant, too. I tried to picture him but couldn't. I didn't want to remember him without his beard and mustache, but now I couldn't seem to picture him at all. And where was Don?

When at long last I spotted the Walker, it was nearly midnight. The rain had stopped and Don was just stepping out of a diner where the lights were only half on. The owners had kindly let him linger after closing hours while they were cleaning up.

The Walker was as glad to see me as I was to see him. Then, after getting directions to a place in the town of Cobden, beside Muskrat Lake, where we could park Otto, we drove off together to camp. We were each too tired that night to say much, but Don made it clear that the week he had been on his own with a pack on his back had not been easy. If ever he was going to average a thirty-mile-a-day pace, which he hadn't yet, he would need my support in the camper. And that was good to know, I thought, otherwise what was I doing there?

JULY

Ontario, Michigan, Wisconsin, Minnesota

Chapter 5

I'm Not Doing This for a Whole Year

There was the rumbling and clacking and hooting of trains in the night. Don slept soundly and did not seem to hear them, but I knew them to be penetrating my dreams and carrying me further yet from home. They took me to my childhood home, recalling my past and even the country's past. I had ridden the train on childhood adventures. And once even as a child I had run away to a distant city by train. I half wondered in my sleep whether I wasn't running away again. I had not heard trains on the edge of my dreams in many years. I imagined I was in a time machine and then shrunk to the size of a matchstick, riding a toy train in its repetitive rounds on top of the pool table in the basement of my childhood home. I could still feel the rhythmic jostling of the rails beneath me when my eyes opened to the morning; and when the movements did not cease, I had to wonder suddenly what was going on in the bunk below.

"What in the world are you doing down there, Don?"

"Sit-ups. I've got to do these sit-ups—and some stretching afterwards. I've found it helps. I do this every morning now," he said between gasps.

"Good grief, you mean walking thirty miles every day is not going to be enough? You have to do exercises besides? Sounds crazy to me. By the way, there's milk in the cooler and cereal in the cabinet down there," I offered.

"Good. It'll be a lot easier to eat breakfast here and get on the road early. I spent too much money, got too much bad food, and nearly died of thirst while you were gone. It was hot here, and I bet it was even hotter in Florida."

I told him about the Florida heat, about David shaving his beard and mustache, about the wildlife I saw. And then I asked Don what he had thought of walking the Ogdensburg Bridge.

"It was amazing—only I *almost* couldn't talk the customs officials into letting me into Canada on foot. If I hadn't told them you would be coming along in a van to meet up with me, I don't know if they'd have let me in. I don't think they much believed me about The Walk."

And then, while doing his stretching exercises below, Don told me about walking through storms; about running out of water and fainting from heat exhaustion in a motel lobby; about trying to treat his blisters, his aching feet, and throbbing Achilles tendons; about getting sick from a bad steak sandwich; and getting kicked out of a diner in North Gower for being too wet from the rain.

"How long did Debbie stay with you?" I asked, knowing Debbie had driven up from Virginia partly to help Don out and partly to walk some of the miles with him.

"She really only could stay two days—two full days. We camped the night after you and David left at Wolf Pond. She hiked twelve miles with me that day, but the next day it rained the whole time so she stayed in the car and read. I hope she had some fun. I was really glad she was there—hey, you know what those other guys did before they left Long Lake?"

"What other guys?" I asked, beginning to crawl out of my sleeping bag to get dressed on the upper bunk.

"You know, Luke and Patty and Dan. They rented a seaplane and had the pilot buzz me while I was heading toward Tupper Lake. They buzzed Vinny and Debbie, too, while they were swimming. And then the whole gang brought me a Father's Day lunch on the road—of guess what? And I thought I could get by with eating anything on this trip—a pint of ice cream, three different kinds of candy bars, and a big bag of sour-cream-and-chive potato chips, which I washed down with a quart of orange juice—yuck! Did my stomach hurt later!"

I laughed, and Don continued between munches of cereal.

"But you know what turned out to be a lot of fun was taking a day off with Patty in Ottawa. She met up with me in Richmond, and we drove in together. Only I think I walked almost as far touring Ottawa on my day off as most the other days. But at least at the end of it I got to soak in a whirlpool. We got a great deal at a hotel there downtown and ate that night at a great Japanese restaurant—you know, one of those places where the chef twirls knives an inch from your nose while he's cooking dinner on your table? Fran, I think you would really like Ottawa—you and David'll have to go there sometime. All the parliament buildings and the old bell tower there are really neat— oh, and we even watched the changing of the guard, like in England, you know."

By the time Don had finished breakfast, cleaned up, and was outside on the grass doing pushups, I was dressed, putting my bunk away, and pulling Otto's top down. I was not interested in any breakfast but was hoping for a hot cup of tea somewhere. Maybe in Cobden I could find a place near a laundromat; most of Don's clothes were mildewed, wet, or mud-splattered and he had asked me to wash them. He was worried about getting his waterproof rainsuit cleaned before the weather turned bad again. And then, with a wave of the banana he had grabbed as he started off, he was gone. He had hardly been still an extra minute.

I met up with Don at intervals throughout that day…and the next…and the next…and the next…

I could see soon enough that Don had hardened to the road considerably since his first days out, and I really admired his continuing eagerness to be out there walking. I envied him his steady daily achievements. Every day the total number of miles would swell—and this was, for Don, a reward in itself. It was a reward to some extent for me too, simply to watch him do it. But though I knew things were a little easier for the Walker now that he didn't have to carry the hated pack, and now that he knew Otto and I would always be seven or eight miles down the road with refreshments—such as cool drinks, sandwiches, snacks, a soft seat, shade, and some company—still, after a week or so on the road, I couldn't see how he could keep it up, and especially how he could be doing it without breaking down the way I was.

It wasn't that Don was a stoic or that he didn't have things to complain about. There *were* things and he *did* complain. The road he was walking through Ontario, Canadian Route 17, was less than ideal. It was dangerously narrow, without passing lanes, and had horrendous numbers of wildly speeding trucks on it—the typical heavy logging trucks and other huge cruisers. The breakdown lane where Don walked was often round-shouldered and always gravelly. By the end of the day, he could feel every sharp-edged stone underfoot, or his hip and ankle joints might ache from the slant he'd had to walk. And somehow, no matter what he did, the balls of his feet ached awfully the last five or more miles of the day. He thought he could remedy this by using different inner soles or by experimenting with various sorts of padding, but almost nothing he tried seemed to make much difference.

It was probably even the way he walked, Don thought, since he knew he landed and rolled off the balls of his feet without putting much of his heel to the ground. But when he did experiment with changing the way he walked, he began to have trouble with his Achilles tendons. Still, whatever the pain or hardships to his physical being, Don never put off getting back out there on the road.

But what amazed me even more than Don's energy, physical stamina, and fortitude was the mental adjustment he had made to life on the road. Here was a man who was accustomed to being around people the livelong day: teaching gym to class after class of junior high students; being school trainer for a variety of sports teams after school; coaching the Middlebury College Swim Team in the evening, and working out swimming himself; not to mention dashing around to squeeze in courses at the University of Vermont for a second master's degree—and still finding time for friends? Here was a "people person" if ever there was one. I knew that as well as I knew the weight of my own head. So how could he suddenly be spending all those hours alone—and be doing it cheerfully, for the most part? It boggled my mind.

Was it because he was living his dream—actually making real, day by day, what had been for so long merely an idea in his head? I simply could not know the full power of this by my present experience because it was not, in the same sense, true for me. I was there of my own volition, but I was also there somewhat reluctantly—even somewhat accidentally. Had another driver surfaced, I might not have been there at all. And I had definitely never once dreamed beforehand of going off on an adventure that did not more directly include David.

For his part, I could tell that Don was rather baffled by me in those early weeks on The Walk. I don't think he knew how to account for my seeming misery. And I was miserable. I quietly wept above him on my bed at night. When I sniffed loudly now and then, I blamed it on allergies, but Don must have known better.

But worse, I was too readily reduced to tears during the day. Time and again, the stupidest things would upset me, like losing track of the pliers needed to open one of Otto's louvered windows or driving off in Otto forgetting to put things away, thus causing something to spill or break. It didn't help one bit that I seemed to be constantly cracking a knee, elbow, or head while trying to get used to the confining dimensions of Otto. And many times I would crack my head when something else was already going wrong. I just could not seem to adjust. I was too homesick. I had envisioned the physical hardships to some extent, but I had completely underestimated those of the heart.

And, I did miss David, and I was alone an awful lot. But being alone so much couldn't really be getting to me, I didn't think. After all, for the past five years, since I had quit teaching, I spent nearly every day alone anyway—writing. I thrived on solitude—or so I had often said. So why wasn't I thriving now? I loved to write and I was writing now—day and night. I wrote in my journals, I wrote David every day, I wrote friends and relatives, I was even writing a newsletter once a week, which I sent home to David to share with anyone who was interested in following "The Walk."

Well, it would help, I thought, if I could only get some mail. Don wouldn't have minded a little mail either, though because of something called a Canadian mail "slow down," neither of us was likely to get any.

I know Don thought I was making myself miserable by thinking too much. And maybe I was—I certainly had plenty of time to think. And I did think about home, and I knew I would suffer from homesickness—but I never dreamed how deeply I would feel the ache of it in every fiber of my being.

But when the Walker caught up to the parked camper one afternoon and saw me in fresh tears again, I guess he finally had to voice some concern. He sat down in Otto, took off his shoes to air his feet, and began dressing a small blister.

"Well, Fran, what *is* wrong?"

"Oh, nothing. You want something to drink? How's it going with you?" I had to turn away because his sympathetic tone was only evoking more tears.

"Things are good with me. I'll get myself something in a minute. But right now I'm wondering about you. I mean, what's going on—don't you think you're going to be able to *survive* a year without David looking after you, is that it?"

I glanced at him and felt my face redden. I answered glumly, "I don't know."

He continued taking care of his feet, set the pair of shoes he'd been wearing aside, and reached for another pair. "I think it's best to change shoes pretty often. Makes my feet feel better. Gives them some variety."

"Gosh, Don, don't *you* miss anyone? You *must* miss being around people?"

"Well, yes and no—I mean, sure I miss people, but this isn't going to last forever, you know."

I looked at him. He'd walked nearly five hundred miles in eighteen days and had taken only one day off. He'd never walked so far in his life. He looked fit, but he also looked weary.

"But Don, a year can seem like forever, you know. What do you think, can *you* keep this up—day after weary day—for a whole year?"

"I don't know," he said. But then, after looking up and staring off into space for a time, he added brightly, "Nope—I'm not going to."

"You're not—what?" I said, taken aback.

"I'm not going to do it," he repeated. And then, after the silence that followed he said, "I'm not going to do it for *a whole year*, I'm just going to do it today."

I watched him head out and disappear around a bend in the road. I was beginning to see what he meant. Maybe I was somehow trying for too much at once. And the more I thought about what he had said and the way he had said it, the more I could see it as something of a challenge. If he can keep on keeping on, I guess I can, too. Quit looking ahead, I told myself. One day only…yes, I think I might manage that. One day at a time. Anyway, it was, it suddenly occurred to me, the manner in which most big debts are paid—that is, not all at once but little by little—with interest.

Chapter 6

It's a Big Country

Once the Walker got onto Canadian Route 17 at Corkery, west of Ottawa, he followed it all the way to Sault Ste. Marie, where he re-entered the U.S. Nearly half of that distance Don walked in close proximity of the Ottawa River.

Chalk River, Deep River, Rapide de Joachims, Stonecliffe, Bissett Creek, Deux Riveres—places along a three-hundred-mile river stretch and countless, nameless places between—beckoned to the walker. He could almost hear the echoing footfalls of explorers, trappers, loggers, and miners sounding before him, and underlying these, going back six thousand years, the softer tread of the Indians themselves. Don said that he could imagine himself making the sort of progress the earliest explorers might have, and he felt, in spite of having to keep to a well-trod route, that he, too, was something of an explorer. He was not seeking the canoe route to the Northwest as so many had who went before him, nor was he looking for fur-bearing animals, or sources of lumber, or precious metals. He was after something less tangible, but something he could keep. He would know it when he saw it.

Signs designated the area Don walked as "the near north," not to be confused, I supposed, with "the far north." It wasn't the far north of Canada, but it was pretty far north for comparable places in the northern U.S. For some reason, we had both expected it to be cooler than it was. Mornings and evenings did tend to be cool, but days

40

when the sun beat down out of a cloudless sky were brilliantly hot; and when the atmosphere clouded over, which it did frequently, the searing sunlight was replaced by a steam-bath humidity—an even greater trial to the Walker.

We were grateful for the many clear, cold, swift, and still waters. These made the hot days bearable. The Ottawa River often seemed to be swift one moment and still the next. Sometimes it transformed itself into wide, lake-like openings embraced by graceful hills and river bluffs. Once on foot, I followed a downward-plunging dirt road through a forest that came out onto the Ottawa, where the serenity of the water was so great it appeared not to flow at all.

I did not wait for an invitation to swim, even though I knew I ought not swim alone in unfamiliar waters; I simply could not resist. I stripped to my swimsuit on the rocky beach and waded out into the cool, shallow water. The familiar call of a phoebe nearby seemed to encourage me.

The smooth, sandy bottom was etched by squiggly lined mussel trails. The river looked to be at least a mile wide. It was July first, Canada Day, a big holiday. A pair of canoeists paddled effortlessly past on the far side; sailboats a few miles downstream white-dotted the glittering water; a white seaplane circled the blue sky upstream; and a few motorboats scored the water's surface with short-lived designs, very like the river bottom's mussel trails, one pulling a water skier. And there I was—one lone, somewhat frightened swimmer.

The water was shallow and pale-golden-clear for a good distance out. When it reached my thighs, I dove in and swam. Shortly thereafter I was startled by an underwater view of an immediate, pitch-dark deep, signifying a great and sudden fall in the river's depth. I swam out over this chasm anyway, my heart matching the thrumming speed of a distant motorboat.

Later I convinced the Walker it would be worth his while to hike the extra distance to swim in the river here. There were so many places to swim, however, he was hard to persuade. And yet it turned out to be, and the Walker agreed, one of the most memorable of all our swims in the Ottawa.

Another time, Don sent me scouting ahead west of Webwood, Ontario, where we had left the Ottawa River far behind; there didn't seem to be any obvious swimming holes in sight. Yet we still hoped to find waters somewhere about on this miserably hot day.

I got a lead to a swimming hole from some kids selling bags of blueberries (the local equivalent of the neighborhood lemonade stand). Once on the back roads, however, I became uncertain of the way and had to hail a passing truckload of teenage boys to ask if they knew of this swimming hole. They turned out to be headed for that very place and said I could follow.

They soon left me in a cloud of dust. And though the dusty trail was easy enough to track, I began to have doubts as to whether I should continue to do so. The road narrowed, and narrowed again, until it had the quality and dimensions of a stony mountain path, sharply winding every which way and steeply falling and rising. Finally, after one last, long climb, it dead-ended at Birch Lake Dam.

I saw at once that it was worth the trouble. On my left hand lay the graceful cove of a beautiful, birch-lined lake; on my right, a precipitously pitching stream cascading hundreds of feet out of it and down into a boulder-strewn, whirlpooling ravine. The place to swim was off the small dam, but at the moment it was all men and six-packs of beer. I thought it best to retreat and return at day's end with Don.

When we did return, not a soul was there, and not a six-pack, either. The small spillway made for a great shower, and the glassy lake for a bath. Don stretched and exercised and even swam a short workout. I showered and swam and reveled in the fortunate discovery of this place, reminded of what so often lay hidden to a traveler, thankful we had been led to what we never could have found on our own.

We camped next to unknown streams by night and sometimes had a sea to swim in by day. The first big body of water was Lake Nipissing, which seemed huge and scary when I first came upon it at North Bay. The big ships at anchor there made it seem like an ocean. I did not know then that these ships could, by way of the French River, get to Georgian Bay on Lake Huron. The Great Lake

Huron was even more oceanic in its expanse, but the swims in it seemed odd because the water lacked the taste of salt. The waves were gentle too and made lovely parallel ripple marks on the sandy bottom through the clear waters in the shallows.

In this part of the country, water was the saving grace of nearly every day. Don bodysurfed in the rapids of the Serpent River, and bathed with gulls in the Mississagi and loons in the St. Mary's. Once, in the oppressive, humid heat building before a storm, I swam alone in a small river that flowed into George Lake. There was nothing great about the place, but the heat drove me in—off a black, cindery beach beneath and between a highway bridge and a railroad underpass. I didn't stay in long.

While making my way back to Otto, I looked up to find—literally within arm's reach and pressing down upon me—the black belly of a monster storm cloud hovering in a yellow sky. I ran to Otto, scrambled in, and began to batten down the hatches. I wondered where Don was, but there was no going to his rescue at that point. Having grown up in the Midwest, I recognized the telltale makings of a tornado. No sooner did I get Otto's top un-popped than the sky fell with one great ear-shattering crack of thunder. Otto rocked at the blow, his louvered windows rattled like a sack of dry bones, he groaned. Shortly thereafter, with slightly less impact, the contents of the storm cloud came crashing down on top of us.

Don, too, had been lucky. He found all the protection he needed in the shelter of a roadside stand—and just in time. Crouching under what little cover there was, he could even take pleasure in the storm raging about him—lightning coloring the clouds like roses, electrifying the hot, moist air in jagged cracks of gold breaking a steel-blue sky. When the worst of the hoopla was over, Don brushed a little wet sand off his rear and walked on. Sault Ste. Marie was practically within smelling distance. The rain pouring down on top of him as he went was a blessing.

But storms were infrequent on Don's Canadian trek, and all-day rains nonexistent. The main hardships for him were the heat and the road itself—ill-banked and bothersome, dangerous when the traffic was bad. Don tried to make eye-contact with oncoming drivers. He saw too much going on behind the wheel that made him nervous—drivers writing things down, reading maps, hunting for things, grooming, and even what looked like napping. Don did not nap. But any peaceful moments on the road he savored.

In many respects, the Canadian terrain was reassuringly familiar. It seemed to me to be composed of all the elements of home, yet oddly scrambled. Echoes of the Green Mountains came to me when we neared the foothills of the Laurentians, such as at Mattawa, or when we skirted the wilds of Algonquin Provincial Park. Echoes of the Champlain Valley came to me when the land took a tame, pastoral turn, opening up into rolling hayfields of timothy, red clover, daisies, and the purple vetch.

The season did seem somewhat more advanced than at home, which I thought must be because we were that much further north. Wild blueberries were being picked much earlier; and jewelweed was already coming into flower, often with a ruby-throated hummingbird in still-flight nursing the nectar from the dangling blossoms.

I cherished such tastes and glimpses. Small discoveries could smooth an otherwise rugged day, as once did the finding of a song sparrow's nest beside the St. Mary's River. I was preparing to swim when I flushed the singer from its wild nursery in a tangle of bank-side roots. A closer look revealed a deftly woven cup containing four small, slightly greenish, brown-speckled eggs. It was a gift—as was the mystery of a small raft of assorted foliage inexplicably plying a backwater swamp below a railroad embankment. Hidden, I finally saw it transformed into a muskrat carrying weeds. The creature used its booty to make repairs on its lodge. And two wayside flowers, which I rarely saw at home, made abundant displays—Canada thistle and Huron tansy—palest lilac and deepest gold.

I shared my discoveries with the Walker, who shared his discoveries with me. He solved the riddle of the strange wheezing, snorting, and stomping that we had both heard at night in the Adirondacks and more than once in Canada. Don woke one morning and saw the whole thing—a deer—caught in the middle of its tantrum. It was apparently upset at Otto for blocking one of its trails.

And there were loons throughout Ontario, which seemed, more than anything else, to speak the truest things in their eerie, wailing cries: something about the strangeness of life and its loneliness, too. And one day Don discovered, and I later went to see also, a pair of loons on one of the lake-like openings of the Ottawa. On the back of one of the parent birds rode one tiny loonling. But after watching for quite a while, I saw the parents let the little loon down to swim a bit on its own. They took turns disappearing under the water to fish and to bring back tasty tidbits to their offspring. And once, both parents disappeared, and there, in what must have seemed oceanic waters, the little bird bobbed—alone, barely still, perhaps afraid. And that, I thought, was the big lesson: Ultimately you're on your own.

I wasn't sure whether to be thankful or not for all the reminders of home. Every reminder tugged painfully at my heart. I wondered if I wasn't becoming unconsciously adept at transforming what I saw into the familiar. But the green-treed lands and rolling fields and meadows *were* familiar. I tasted home in the wild strawberry and heard its unmistakable ring in the song of the hermit thrush. The hermit's ethereal music was the most familiar of all. I knew it well from my own mountain habitat. It rang forth from a dark hemlock wood as if wrought from the finest crystal, though sent to the ear from a few ounces of feathers and flesh. Once I thrilled to hear what seemed a great competition of these thrushes. It was as if each master singer sang to its own young not only to show how it must be done, but to demonstrate how not to be outdone. The living wood was transformed into a great hall of marble, with the delicate and complex strains of these otherworldly songs—as if heaven lay somewhere in that very wood, yet ever and always deeper in.

That was the thing about Nature—it could hint at heaven, whereas the daily trials of the journey could often hint at something else. Toward the end of The Walk in Canada, after hiking some seven hundred miles, Don began noticing a weird numbness along his thighs and in the balls of his feet—a numbness that yet did not diminish the pain he felt in his feet at the day's end. Also, when he swam to cool off, his feet throbbed at times with an excruciating ache after just a short while in the water. Sometimes massaging his feet and doing some stretching before he went in helped, sometimes it didn't.

The empty mail drops in various towns, where David was supposed to be forwarding mail, were not cheering, either, thanks to the continuing Canadian mail slowdown. Every post office promised to send on anything that came later, but it was not very hopeful.

Still, we travelers were thankful we had not yet run into any *big* trouble. When Don was tempted to brag about the weather or our luck, I would remind him, "A year is a long time."

"True," he would agree. And once, "Too bad they couldn't make softer roads." And then, as an afterthought, the Walker added, "It's a big country."

Chapter 7

The King of the Walk

If the land was somehow the sustaining chord in our life on the road, it was the people of an area who often gave the land its warm or neutral or chilling overtones. How far a friendly greeting or smile could go toward making us feel at ease in a place! Since our encounters with people were infrequent, thanks to the ever-pressing need to move on and gain the miles, we each made an effort to share what encounters we had. Sometimes the walker was stopped by someone, or he met up with someone, whom he would then send on to meet the driver. More often I would meet people and introduce the Walker when he caught up. Sometimes we met people together at a café or diner.

I was usually hoping for a diner in the mornings, since that was when I most relished a hot cup of tea. Otto's built-in gas stove had broken beyond safe use or repair, so the search for a hot cup of tea was a strong and continuing incentive for me to get out among the people. Both of us appreciated a morning café stop for the available restrooms.

It was when I drove ahead one morning west of North Bay, Ontario, that I met the Moermans. I might have turned back and driven into North Bay, where I was much more likely to find the supplies I needed as well as a choice of diners, but I hated any sort of backtracking. Don did, too. Besides, I had gotten lost in North Bay the day before and did not have fond memories of the place.

I drove west. The day looked as if it was going to heat up quickly, so I did not want to get too far ahead of the Walker. When a place came into view, and when I liked the looks of the old man sitting on the front stoop sipping his coffee, I pulled over. The man reminded me of my maternal grandfather; he had a broad forehead, a craggy jaw, and a stern look.

The place itself looked like it *might* be a store. A row of old gas pumps graced the broken asphalt out front. It had definitely seen better days. After an exchange of nods, the old man followed me in.

Well, if it is a store, I thought, it has meager provisions and strange offerings. I noticed some old books, a few odd hunting and fishing supplies, hats and T-shirts yellowed with dust and age, among other things. But a gray formica-topped table stood in the middle of the place with three chairs, a few newspapers scattered on top, and a help-yourself-to-coffee setup.

I asked the old man if he had any tea. He said he didn't have tea, but he'd be happy to boil me up some water if I had the tea bags, so I decided to stay a while. I went back to Otto for my stash of tea, teapot, and writing materials. I set up at the little table, sipped tea, and began finishing a letter to David. I did not write for long.

After a few fishermen came and went, and while I was writing, the old man sat down opposite me and introduced himself. Rene (pronounced "Rainy") wanted to know what I was writing about, so I told him about Don and The Walk. A little while later, his wife Jeanette, a slight woman with a frizz of reddish hair done up behind, younger looking than her husband, came down from their upstairs apartment in her bathrobe and slippers. Soon Jeanette and Rene's thirty-eight-year-old son, George, arrived from his house on the property, and finally their grandson, Brian, romped in.

Rene and Jeanette Moerman were the proprietors of the place— Laronde Creek Lodge—and had been for forty years. I hadn't noticed it was a lodge. There were some cabins lined up out back along a small watercourse. Jeanette showed me two different postcards of their place in former, better times. The Moermans talked for a while about how a new highway had taken away a lot of business and about how tourists these days liked to be closer to Lake Nipissing than their lodge was.

Before she went back upstairs to get dressed, and before her son arrived, Jeanette spoke about George and his failed marriage and of his young wife who had run off because nothing would make her happy. George spoke of his wife, too, when he came along. Brian wanted to show me the newly minted Canadian coin—a dollar recently issued in honor of Canada Day. It was a remarkable piece of money—lightweight, twelve-sided, and looked to be pinkish gold, while in reality it consisted largely of aluminum from recycled cans. The coin bore the queen's head on one side and the loon on the other and was referred to as "the loony dollar."

Rene talked of other travelers who had come through. Just a month earlier, Rene watched a man bearing a heavy cross, the foot of which rolled by on small supporting wheels, but the cross-bearer did not stop in.

But in the late sixties there was Elzear Duquette, who was traveling on foot from Montreal to Vancouver. "He was," Rene recalled, chuckling to himself, "jogging along like a young pony, wearing a harness, and pulling behind him—a coffin on wheels!" Rene went on to describe how the man kept his various supplies in the coffin and even slept in the thing at night.

I wasn't even sure I could believe this strange tale, but Rene produced a five-by-seven glossy, black-and-white photograph of the man kneeling in front of his coffin on wheels. Elzear was dressed a little fancifully, I thought, rather like a circus performer; and he was holding a large and ornate cross, perhaps three feet in height. The coffin, too, was gaily ornate and was displaying various cardboarded news clippings about the man and his successful journey. The photo was titled and signed by Elzear himself, who wrote under his signature, "Le Roi De La Marche." Rene could not explain the whys and wherefores of the man's trip, because the man could speak only French and Rene could speak only English. Elzear had sent the photo back to the Moermans at the completion of his walk.

Rene, and George too, recalled Terry Fox stopping by, who had bone cancer, and who was running from Canadian coast to Canadian

49

coast. When Terry did not make it, having died in the attempt, Steve Fanya took up his cause, and this man also stopped in at Laronde Creek Lodge. And so, by some odd chance, Don and I happened along, following in this rather picturesque tradition, adding our crazy tale to the others.

I shared a story the Walker and I had heard from a man at a tiny grocery in Deux Riveres. A couple in their seventies had stopped in for supplies a few weeks earlier. They were doing a bike-auto-row down the Ottawa River to the St. Lawrence, out the Gulf of St. Lawrence to Nova Scotia, and down the coast of Nova Scotia via the Atlantic to the Bay of Fundy. They would stop at a place, launch their rowboat and tie it up; drive up the road a fair piece and park their car; bicycle back to their boat, load the bikes into the boat; and row down river to where they had left their car! Rene shook his head in wonder when he heard this tale, and the others laughed.

When the Walker caught up, the Moermans treated him royally. Though they were not set up to serve meals, Jeanette went into her own kitchen to fix something for Don, while the rest of the family gathered round to hear from the Walker himself what he had to say about his adventures so far.

Later, I insisted we all go out front for a picture-taking session. Jeanette kept joking, "If I get into the picture, I'm liable to bust the camera, eh?"—a remark that turned out to be disappointingly prophetic, through no fault of Jeanette's. I was to find out later I did not have the film properly engaged, and thus did not get these pictures after all. The idea was to send another "King of the Walk" photo back to the Moermans at journey's end—with the Moerman family included.

Just as I was climbing into Otto and the Walker was getting his hat, Jeanette had a little conference with Brian, George, and Rene. She then approached the two of us.

"We, uh," Jeanette cleared her throat, "we want you to have this for good luck on your journey, eh?" It was the brand-new loony dollar in its little cardboard and cellophane frame. Jeanette had written around the outside, "R&J Moerman Family 1987 dollar." She might as well have been handing out letters from home, the way the gift touched us both. We thanked the Moermans heartily for everything, promised to let them know how the trip went, and headed on.

It was only a little while later I realized I had forgotten to get the supplies I originally stopped for—ice, gas, and a few groceries. But I decided not to turn around. The Moermans didn't have groceries anyway, and the journey was—to move on.

Chapter 8

Bridge to the U.S.A.

Don walked through dozens of little towns and the fair-sized city of Sudbury, but we both began to realize more and more that, because of the way we were traveling, opportunities for something like meeting the Moermans were going to be rare. Yet the friendliness of the Moermans did cast a warm glow over our experiences—a glow that did not quickly wear off.

Near Sudbury the land seemed to break or was broken into. This was nickel- and copper-mining country. But in some places, I thought that if you didn't know what had been going on since the late 1800s, you would have to wonder what careless giants had come through to ravage the place. Don and I recalled passing through the Sudbury region once years before, and thought we could tell efforts had been made since to soften the look of the territory. Nonetheless, certain sections laid waste conjured up visions of nuclear disaster. There was a noticeable increase in the truck traffic, too, which did not help us to appreciate the area more. Don did a truck count at one point and came up with eighty trucks per hour.

The last hope for mail in Canada was at Thessalon. But in spite of checking on two different days, I collected nothing. This discouraging news coincided with my discovery that the camera was acting funny. I noticed I was getting a lot of extra shots beyond the number the roll of film allowed for. I inquired of the postmaster as to whether there was a camera shop in town, but he said there wasn't. Then, after a moment's thought, he added that I might be able to get help from a man named Roger Mulligan, who did a lot of camera work and had a darkroom in his house. The thoughtful postmaster even gave me the man's phone number.

When I got hold of Roger, he said he was just getting ready to depart on a hunting trip. "But if you can come right away, I might be able to help you out," he added.

I had to backtrack and then go miles in another direction to get to his place, but fortunately Roger was still in the process of packing his car when I got there. He took the film out of my camera in his darkroom and then told me I probably had loaded the camera incorrectly. I readily admitted that I was a novice. He gave me a fresh lesson, and, as if to soothe the discovery that my last thirty-six pictures were nonexistent, he also gave me a couple rolls of film. He said that he appreciated the fact I was chronicling a once-in-a-lifetime event, and that he understood my frustration. He asked me to pass on his good wishes to the Walker.

It was the briefest meeting, and I could hardly express my thanks. I hated to think of the pictures I had lost, but I felt lucky to have had Roger's help. His kindness made up in part for the disappointment in myself.

Don made Sault Ste. Marie on July 13. He thought the sign "Bridge to the USA" might as well have said "Bridge to Home," the way his heart reacted when he saw it. He loved walking bridges, and this was going to be a big bridge and a big moment.

I was excited, too, and went ahead to scout the bridge. When I got there, I noticed a small sign saying, "No Pedestrian Traffic Allowed." I wondered what Don could do about that. I knew he was a fanatic about walking every inch. If I let him out even a few feet past the place where he had ended the day before, he would actually walk back to the exact spot before beginning. Somehow he had talked his way onto the Ogdensburg Bridge across the St. Lawrence, but could he do it here?

When the Walker caught up to the bridge, the Canadian Customs Officials gave him an emphatic "No!" It was a busy bridge with heavy traffic and there was no real place for pedestrians to walk it safely.

They said they would not discuss it further and that they did not have the authority to change the rule in any case. As for who did have the authority to make an exception? Don wangled a name from one of the more sympathetic officials. Then the Walker immediately tried to get the man on the phone—a Mr. Dell—but alas, he was out to lunch.

I then called back to Middlebury to David and Vin's sports store. After I talked to David, Don talked to Vin and then also to Patty, who happened to be working at the store that day. Don kept pacing as he talked, as if to emphasize with more than words that nothing was going to keep him from walking that bridge. David, Vin, and Patty all expressed their sympathetic concern and wished the Walker luck.

Don called Mr. Dell's office three more times before he finally got the man himself. The Walker's phone-pacing steps picked up as he talked more and more animatedly to Mr. Dell about The Walk. He gestured energetically with his arms, and I was discouraged to hear Don using the word "but" so often. It did not sound promising.

All of a sudden Don stood motionless. He wasn't saying anything. And then a little while later I watched a smile slowly break over his face. When I heard the walker begin to express profuse thanks to Mr. Dell, I smiled, too, and was glad for Don. He would be crossing the Bridge to the U.S.A. on foot after all. I climbed into Otto alone and drove ahead.

However, the Walker did not walk the bridge alone. For safety's sake, he was escorted by James A. Parr, a bridge maintenance worker, who rode alongside Don in a tiny, orange bridge vehicle with flashing lights. Triumphant, Don carefully made his way in a narrow catwalk and took in the view below of industrial Sault Ste. Marie, extensive railyards, and later the St. Mary's River. But Mr. Parr proved to be no mere bridge worker. The portly man also happened to be the bandleader-singer of a group called The Moody Blue Country Band. He even sang for Don as they went along together.

When I later asked Don what it was the man sang, Don said, "Well, it was hard to catch *all* the words because of the traffic and the way the wind was blowing, but it was a song Mr. Parr said he wrote himself. Something about missing his mother when he was in the Navy, and about a blind man on the corner who must've had a mother, too…and I don't know what all, but I thought it was great."

A few miles later, at the Michigan Welcome Center, the Walker checked in briefly to use the facilities and was awarded two large jars of bread-and-butter pickle chips made in Michigan. Most visitors, we were informed, receive only one jar. It was a rather grand re-entry, we had to admit. And though The Walk through Canada had had its fine moments, we were both glad to be back in the U.S.A.

Chapter 9

You Ought to Take a Picture of That

Neither Don nor I knew exactly where we had gotten, when we began the journey across the Upper Peninsula of Michigan. We did not know the territory. By the map we could see we were caught between Great Lakes—Superior above us, Michigan and a bit of Huron below. On a big map of the United States, this peninsula did not stand out as particularly big, and yet almost immediately it began to *feel* big.

For the Walker, the road itself, Michigan's Route 28, gave a welcome sense of expanded room, thanks to a significantly wider breakdown lane. This was clearly an improvement over Ontario's Route 17. These generous road margins were also better banked, even flat sometimes; the type of gravel in them different too, more consolidated, if not always easier on Don's feet. But in all respects it was a roomier route to walk—the sense of roominess enhanced by remarkably less truck traffic as well as less traffic of other sorts. And besides the quieter road, there was an uncanny emptiness, yet as if it had not always been so.

Long stretches of road had little to speak of in the way of services— few diners, gas stations, laundromats, working phones, and the like. "For Sale" signs were rampant in places; many restaurants and motels stood closed or even abandoned. We learned later that this evidence of economic decline had mostly to do with layoffs, factory closings, and mining shut-downs in the iron ore and copper industries. Yet we thought it was a lovely land even so, and found it hard to imagine it would not make a comeback.

This was the Upper Midwest. Hundreds of miles south, outside St. Louis, Don and I had both done a lot of growing up, so if the Upper Peninsula of Michigan was not particularly familiar territory, something about it was more like what we had once known than it was like the Northeast. The land was changing. The earth was flattening, the road was straightening, and at times the wind was becoming a new hardship. When the wind aligned itself with a ruler-straight road out of the west, it put tough demands on the Walker. He felt then as if he was walking uphill yet was constantly being cheated out of the downhill side. And to look down a long road without a bend— without the lure of wondering what's around the next bend—well, it was a new experience for Don.

The straight way often led through forests, chiefly thick stands of assorted evergreens, which cut off any view but could also cut the force of any crosswind having to make its way through the density of needle-trimmed branch. And while there may have been a scarcity of logging trucks, there certainly seemed no scarcity of potential logs.

The Walker was still cutting up pieces of foam rubber and other materials to try to further cushion his shoes and ease the pain in his feet at day's end. In twelve miles or less, a piece of quarter-inch closed-cell foam rubber would be pounded to the thinness of a postage stamp. A certain rubbery pad he tried did not compress, but it warmed beneath Don's feet, felt heavy, and caused extra friction, hence more blisters. The Walker was beginning to suspect that unless his feet toughened more on their own as a result of more miles, there wasn't much he would be able to do to soften the blows to them. It was mainly the last five miles of the day that really hurt, anyway, yet Don did not want to give those five miles up.

Since Cobden, Ontario, the Walker had been achieving a thirty-mile-a-day average (or better), and this was an important goal to him. If he could keep to this goal, by his figuring, he could take time *off* The Walk when he felt the need or inclination—and still complete the perimeter within the year. He was already looking ahead to taking time to make a fraternity brother's reunion in Idaho, in late August.

Meanwhile, he had walked nearly a month with only one day off. And yet, the new terrain, the generous road space, the quieter road, the miles already stretching out far behind him—he felt like singing. He *did* sing. No need to be quite so alert on *this* road; and he reported to me that he was working his way through all his favorite Broadway musicals, and even making a few up.

The first day in Michigan, the weather had changed dramatically— from a heart-wilting heat to a rain-whipping cold. It was a wet, chilling forty degrees the morning of July 14, and I was not singing. Otto had no heat, a fact I'd known from the start. We had planned to do without. The theory was: Don would walk the cold, northerly parts of the country in the summer and the warm, southerly parts in the winter. I bundled myself in heavy sweat clothing and a down vest, prayed for sun, and thought *This cold won't last.*

We had camped the night before in a park on Whitefish Bay on Lake Superior. First glimpses of this greatest of Great Lakes revealed a face of dark, maddened, storm-driven waters. Wild waves roared the night long and hacked at the shore. I thought a canoe I watched the next morning was going to be battered to bits as two canoeists battled the froth and fury to bring it in. But Don's path led away from the wild lake, and we did not see it again until Munising, where it wore a different face entirely.

The penetrating chill convinced me to stop at the earliest opportunity for heat if nothing else. I soon came upon a place called "TeePee Cone" advertising only its ice cream, which did not sound terribly hopeful. But I suspected this might be all I'd come across for a while, so I stopped at the little place built in the shape of a tepee.

To my surprise, the décor within did not suggest an ice cream stand at all—or a tepee. Small as it was, it was not only warm and welcoming, it was downright homey. Someone had lavished on the place real red-checkered tablecloths (as opposed to the commoner plastic); fresh, frilly cotton curtains, and china. Tea was served to me in a genuine bone-china teacup of the forget-me-not rose pattern. Lots of things can take away from a good cup of tea, but to sip it from real china is to have something put into it that can hardly be described.

Soon the Walker caught up, noticed that I had stopped, and also was not sorry to get out of the chill rain for a break. Before he sat down, though, he went to use the restroom. A while later, he came out exclaiming with boisterous enthusiasm, "Wow! What a bathroom!"

Everyone in the place laughed. A group of regulars sitting at the counter turned as they did to give the Walker a long, bemused look. The owner-cook behind the counter proclaimed with pride that his wife was the one responsible.

"You've got to go in there, Fran," Don announced.

Well, it was about time for me to go in there anyway, but I felt my face flushed with embarrassment. I soon saw what Don meant.

The place was more like a cozy living room than a bathroom, rather spacious considering the size of the restaurant. A braided rug warmed the floor; polished mahogany shelves with quaint, old-fashioned knickknacks tidily arranged on lace doilies stood near the commode; flowered wallpaper graced the walls—all dustless, spotless. I can't recall now whether there were embroidered linen hand towels, but if there weren't, that's all that was missing. A neatly framed sampler declared "Cleanliness is next to Godliness." And compared to what facilities we were used to seeing on the road, this little room did seem a good cry nearer to heaven.

"You ought to take a picture of that," Don said when I came out, still unable to control his enthusiasm. But I thought it was enough simply to have been there.

Chapter 10

Joy in Little Things

The first chance for mail since several tries in Canada was at Eckerman, Michigan. When the day dried out and began to look more hopeful, I decided to go scouting ahead for mail and groceries. I stopped on the way at a dot on the map called Strongs, but there was not exactly a grocery. What was there was a gas-station motel overflowing with trash. I noticed an American flag flying over the place in perfect tatters; it continued to unravel in the wind before my eyes. I hoped this did not mean anything.

Eckerman was a mile or more off Route 28. A huge official sign announced the tiny post office there with a big arrow pointing in its direction. They must know how desperate I am, I thought. The only other thing Eckerman boasted, its only apparent business establishment, was also announced by a great and outlandish sign— "King Tut's Bar and Grocery." Feeling nervous about the possibility of finding mail, I stopped first at King Tut's.

Inside, the place was murkier than a tomb, dominated by a gigantic, boxy bar rather like a monster's sarcophagus. My eyes adjusting to the gloom, I noticed there weren't any other customers about. *That's all right with me*, I thought. I had to hunt for the groceries, which turned out to be displayed on a small bookshelf—a few tuna fish cans among other goods, but much less than what I might keep on hand at home. I picked up a dusty can of tuna and went to pay for it.

60

There, at the cash register at the end of the cumbersome bar, it was plain that old King Tut himself presided.

"You wouldn't have any bread, would you?" I asked the short, fat, bald man.

He said he might just happen to have one last loaf left in the freezer. Then he disappeared into the deeper darkness. But when he returned, a long while later, he was swearing to himself and accusing his wife of selling it out from under him.

"Any other grocery stores about?" I asked.

"Not for twenty miles," he said.

I paid him for the tuna and left. On to the post office, where I hardly dared hope I'd have better luck.

When the postmaster actually handed over a packet of mail, I was shaking all over. I might have hugged the man if he hadn't been standing behind a counter. Aside from welcome letters from friends for both of us, the main prize for me was a twenty-four-page letter (written in compressed computer type) from David. He had given up on getting anything through to Canada when his first envelope came back to him, and so had saved up three weeks worth for Eckerman in care of general delivery.

David's letter was full of love and concern, good wishes for the Walker, and news of son Andy at camp and son Dan at his summer school course, among other things. David also passed along details of home, which he knew I would savor, such as the phoebes nesting over the back porch light. These were the sorts of details I kept track of in my nature journal and almanac, and now David meant to do something of the same *for* me. But the best news was David confirming his plans to come visit. Estimating by the map, he thought he could meet us somewhere in North Dakota in early August. The only sad note was learning that my own letters from Canada had not gotten through to him, either, until recently.

I read and re-read his letter. I laughed and cried at his words. But I felt how quickly—how greedily I had devoured them even so. I realized belatedly, in spite of my joy, that it was going to be hard rations living on letters. There was the phone too, thank goodness, but hoping for phones, for David to be able to be reached by phone (to be never reached myself), for privacy to talk at both ends of the line, for a good connection, for a place without interfering traffic, without harassing insects, for a safe place, even for a *working* phone—well, it hadn't proved to be as simple or as satisfying as I once might have thought.

The distance was there. It was increasing every day. I did not like the way this felt. I could sense home, and all that home stood for, receding behind me. The very earth seemed to be slipping away beneath me as I drove. I saw again the unraveling flag and knew something inside myself was unraveling—my sense of place, of belonging. Where was I? Here, there, everywhere…nowhere.

All was somehow fleeting. The Michigan towns, even—Hulbert, Newberry, Laketon, Seney, Walsh, Creighton—were not always there. Some were off Route 28, some were disappearing, and some, like Walsh and Creighton, had disappeared. The simple, unavoidable newness of each day was a continuing bewilderment. I searched for signs that all was well, but there seemed so many signs and the messages conflicting.

I rescue a nestling killdeer near North Manistique Lake from a pestering dog and cry when it dies in my hand. I chuckle to see a troop of wild turkeys sauntering through the tiny village of Hulbert at dusk as if they own the place. I smile at cliff swallows sweeping the air of insects and feeding young in their bottle-nosed mud nests. Once I listen intently to a whippoorwill repeating its name all night long, as if I can learn what it means by it. I do not get it. And worse, I think there is something to get. I write to David:

"Oh dear, every day has so much in it—so much of the unknown, the unpredictable. I am constantly grateful for all the littlest things—a place to camp, to brush my teeth, or wash my hair, or bathe—food, Otto continuing in good stead, Don reporting on something he saw, any familiar bird song or flower, a stranger's friendly greeting. It's funny how all the little things mean so much. The more I think about it, the more I think it is the little things that count most in life, in this world. Or to put it another way—the little things are the big things, and the big things are really the little ones. Does that make any sense?"

The Walker was finding joy in little things, too: one three-inch, plastic, red and yellow skateboard in mint condition; odd rocks; a paper Canadian flag on a stick; a Wade Boggs baseball card; one small rubber lizard, jaws agape; two pairs of pliers; ninety-five cents worth of change gleaned here and there in nickels, dimes, quarters along the way.

"Don, are you going to save everything you see on the road from a year's walk?"

"Don't worry, I'm not picking everything up. Just a few choice items."

"Well, I doubt we need another pair of pliers."

"Don't worry about it, Fran. Hey, did you see that rainbow back there? It was so broad, and then it just seemed to get sucked up into the clouds. Oh, and I found another quarter. So what's the total so far?"

"Let's see, that makes a dollar twenty."

"Hmmm—after eight hundred miles, that's something a little better than a tenth of a cent a mile. Another bonus. I hadn't counted on earning money as I go."

"Right," I said and had to laugh in spite of myself.

Chapter 11

Two Cinnamon Buns, Please

"I think I have fallen, like Alice, down some crazy rabbit hole. Or anyway, my mind has. My mind feels totally boxed in. All is dark ahead—or blank, the road an unwinding scroll yet to be written upon. And all feels dark and blank behind as well—as if what has happened has been too quickly erased because too quickly and unexpectedly lived. Why should I be surprised at anything that happens? Why should I not concede that I have somehow gotten into Wonderland?"

Writing down such entries in my journal, as well as recording all that occurred, helped me to look outside "the box" of my mind— or away from the confining "now-ness" that seemed to hem us in. Like Wonderland, the journey had the discontinuous, arbitrary, unpredictability of dreams.

Why should either of us have smiled to discover, when Don was walking through Luce County, Michigan, that Paul Bunyan had been born there—supposedly, not far from the old McNerney farm site near the Tahquemon River? In 1849, no less. If we had already breathed deeply of the air of exaggeration at such places as King Tut's or TeePee Cone, why not here?

Late one evening, Don trudged wearily and hungrily through the tiny crossroads town of McMillan. The few buildings there were closed for the night, or closed down; it was hard to tell which. But Don could not fail to notice there, as I had also, what was painted in huge, brown letters on the tall, windowless, concrete-block side of a yellow building: "Poor Boy Restaurant—Famous, Hot, Homemade Cinnamon Buns." The next morning, Don reported that he had dreamed about cinnamon buns all night long. But since there was no way to be certain the restaurant was still operating, neither of us dared get our hopes up as we headed back to McMillan.

But to our surprise, the Poor Boy *was* open. We were the first customers in the door; some of the help arrived after us. Don was hungry and ordered a full breakfast of eggs, toast, home fries, and two cinnamon buns on the side.

The waitress just laughed at him and stood there, waiting.

Don laughed back and said, "I'm really hungry and, well, you don't know how far I've walked to get here."

The waitress smiled indulgently and said, "I don't care how far you've walked, Mister; the last guy to eat two cinnamon buns with breakfast in this place was Paul Bunyan himself."

Don thought this over a minute and reluctantly shaved one cinnamon bun from his order, much to the apparent relief of the waitress. When she was gone, he muttered under his breath that he could always order another one later.

While the eggs and home fries were cooking, the cinnamon bun arrived. Well, in truth, we weren't sure what it was at first. It fairly overflowed the tray it was carried out on and had to be hoisted onto the table with considerable care. It was big as a two-layer birthday cake—as rich, as gooey, and with the added delight of being fresh from the oven—hot!

I thought this definitely worth recording on film so I went for the camera. It wasn't easy getting eater and bun into the same picture. But delicious as it was, eggs and home fries too, and hungry as the Walker was, he couldn't polish off the bun—even with my help. We happily carted off the bulky remains and feasted on it for the rest of the day.

July 17, I ran errands in the big little town of Munising, Michigan. It was beautifully situated on the Great Lake Superior. In town, Route 28 suddenly spread like melting butter into four lanes, not to mention angled parking lanes on both sides of the four-lane street.

This was Main Street. The open space it contained seemed enough to swallow a football stadium. Perhaps the town fathers had had Paul Bunyan's stride in mind when they laid out the streets.

I felt lucky to find Otto's favorite brand of oil here, which I had been unable to find elsewhere. I got a generous supply as a matter of security only; so far Otto had not lost any oil between changes. I also collected mail at the post office, so that if the town had already seemed a fine one, the acquisitions of oil and mail merely added to its luster.

But the real jewel of Munising, if something so expansive could be called that, was the great lake itself. Its colors were gem-like— deep, clear, bright. In the main it was a royal sapphire blue, but in places this blue shaded exquisitely into a dark, glassy turquoise. For a while in the morning the water was as still as a stone, but later the wind picked up, quivering over it from the south, bringing it to life, changing its color to a peacock blue and feathering its surface with a light froth.

Even the weather was being driven to extremes—had we really once been cold in Michigan? The heat of the day was now sweltering, in spite of a strong wind. But since Don was keeping steady company with the lake, it seemed good fortune to think that refreshment could not be far off. It was unpleasant waiting in Otto, and with long, empty stretches of white, sandy beach at hand, I thought I might as well be first to test the waters of this inland sea.

I climbed down a high bank of dunes and was just walking into the water, when I was brought up short by the sudden clasp of cold iron about my ankles. Was this water? How dense it felt—what a bitter, body-aching cold—more solid-seeming than any water I had ever stepped into. And though I was accustomed to bathing in frigid mountain streams at home, whatever I did, I could not get used to the Superior cold—even with the incentive of the steamy, tropical heat. Coming up out of the shocking wet into the suffocating breath of the wind, I could discover no happy medium. I was almost instantly dry and, too soon somehow, sticky and hot.

When I thought to sit on the beach, I was bothered and bitten by flies. At last I retreated up the sandy bank to Otto, but made the mistake of leaving Otto's sliding door open while I packed up and brushed the sand off me.

When I climbed in and slammed the door shut, I found I had at least a hundred beach flies as companions. I tried everything to encourage them to depart, and then began swatting. But the flies were devilishly quick, and I ended up hurting myself more than them. I aligned the camper with the strong wind in an effort to blow them out, but they would not be moved. Later I saw others of these determined creatures, able to cling to the outside of Otto's windshield at fifty-five M.P.H.!

When Don caught up, he wanted to cool off by swimming too, yet was even less successful at braving the water than I was. The cold seemed to crush his poor feet with pain. He did not appreciate the flies on the beach or in Otto, either, and after a minuscule break decided he might as well keep walking. It wasn't until we were camped later that night that we had the time and the motivation to swat (maybe ten swats for every kill) until there wasn't one living fly—an exhausting workout after a long day.

So maybe that's why the beaches were deserted on such hot days. We'd seen only one fat-insulated woman actually staying in the water long enough to swim, and one lone water skier braving both the hot air and the cold water in full wet suit. Locals did say it was a particularly bad year for flies. As for the lake temperature? It was the warmest it had been in ages.

But if the glacial feel of the lake did not attract many swimmers, the warmer waters feeding into it often did. And once, when Don was about to pass out from the heat, he caught sight of a small waterfall cascading over the mouth of a shallow cave, not far off the road opposite the lake. The height and flow of a generous bathroom shower, it tumbled its cool blessing over the Walker standing under it— clothes and all. And since I had somehow missed it, Don persuaded me to go back so that I, too, might gratefully revive beneath it.

At Marquette we turned away from Lake Superior and did not meet it again in Michigan. I was sorry to leave it, if not for the feel of its waters, then for its blue of all blues. The color alone was a physical refreshment, like a clear sky but more meaty, solid. I saw many monarch butterflies against the Superior blue, and a number of ruby-throated hummingbirds. I saw mergansers upon it and wild orchids beside it. Light alone—as caught in a monarch's wing or glancing from the iridescence of hummingbird feathers—is arresting, but against the Superior blue, the impact of these colliding colors was stunning.

Chapter 12

What Day Is It, Anyway?

Don ended his thirty-first day of The Walk putting in his nine-hundredth mile. For both of us, the period of time that had been covered seemed much longer than what was measured by the calendar. A month on The Walk had in it something of geologic time—or maybe "dream" time. And I was reminded how different time was on the road than it was at home when I would talk to David.

"Yikes, is it Wednesday already? The weekend'll be here before you know it," he might say.

And though I recognized the comment as a familiar one I once might have made myself—I never found myself saying anything like it on the journey. And neither did Don. We couldn't see ahead. We were far more likely to say, "What day is it, anyway?" And "Good grief, it seems like yesterday was at least a year ago." Or "Friday? Are you sure it's Friday? I thought yesterday was Friday." We had to actually look at the calendar to get any sense that time was passing.

And time proved—again and again—its own private theory of relativity. By this late in July—nearly a month after the summer solstice—I expected to be noticing the days getting shorter as they would have been at home. But they weren't getting shorter. They were actually lengthening. Don and I both noticed that the sun was setting later and later. I eventually figured out that this had to do with our thirty-mile-a-day pace westward toward the next time zone. I mean, there *was* a rational explanation. But somehow it is one thing for the mind to grasp this, and another for the whole being. The sun—seeming to hang longer and longer up there in the sky—and our outrunning the spin of the earth at a *walking* pace—was disorienting, to say the least.

"Doesn't it ever get dark around here?" Don would ask.

"I don't know," I would answer, "What day is it, anyway?"

So how did we celebrate the nine-hundredth mile and the end of the first month on The Walk? We took hot showers at Northern Michigan University and found a place to camp roadside just before a big storm hit—a storm that really did frighten me as I lay awake staring into the darkness at the all-too-insubstantial roof of Otto protecting me from the hammering blows of thunder and the electrifying spears of lightning. Later when the rain fell I envisioned flood waters washing us off "Wetmore's Landing" where we had parked. Later still, I heard a pickup truck pull in, and I worried about what was going on when its occupants went marching off into the woods in the wee hours on such a night. When the truck eventually drove off, I prayed no skullduggery had been afoot.

After Don got on the road the next morning, I drove back to the Cathedral of St. Peter in Marquette. Then, as the skies must have been slowly breaking out of doors, penetrating shafts of sunlight suddenly reached through the lofty, stained-glass windows to touch the dark heads of the congregation far below, while the choir sang "Amazing Grace." And my heart did, too.

There was another bad storm in Michigan, but by day. And though I warned Don, because I could see it coming where I had been desperately doing some laundry in a bucket of red-gold waters I had fished from Tioga Creek, for want of a convenient laundromat, he insisted he keep walking. By luck, he caught up to the shelter I had found at the Cozy Inn just before the storm hit. We met a biker there, Jim from Seattle, who was on his way to Boston—the first of many cross-country bikers we met. And we heard news of another couple who had done a perimeter walk like Don's, but in seven years' time. I silently prayed our journey would keep to schedule.

July 20, at Michigamme, I wrote to David:

"I have been at Skytta's Gas and Grocery going on two hours now—Otto's rug is draped on top of a dumpster overflowing with garbage, and Otto is open and turned to let the sun in to dry him out. Wet dirty laundry is strewn about drying too. We've had a flood—a subtle one, not one to swim in. Somehow Otto's cooler drain opened in the night and the rapidly melting ice seeped into everything on the floor… Good grief! Now the ants are attacking me, the camper is filling up with flies and I have just had to move everything to make way for the garbage truck. I guess, I will be glad enough to move on— though the lady that owns this place has been nice to talk with—not that we did much more than exchange complaints about the heat. And last night while searching for a camp site, Otto got stuck in some deep, rich, red Michigan mud. If I don't find a laundromat soon, we'll have to pitch a tent for the laundry in order to have enough room to sleep in Otto."

And days later I did find a laundromat—Nordene's Launderette at Bruce Crossing, but I locked the keys inside Otto. And since Don had gone on ahead of me on the road, I had to beg a kind old man to give me a ride out to Don to get the extra key. The man's wife watched over my laundry and typewriter while we were away. Ray and Marge Tulppo were good luck making up for bad.

But perhaps the best luck of all in Michigan was meeting Nathan Avedisian west of Trout Creek. I was at a rest area on the Middle Branch of the Ontonagon River, which I had already scouted for a possible swimming hole and decided there couldn't possibly be a safe one. I had followed a sign pointing out a treacherous walk to a view of Agate Falls. At the end of the fenced walkway a small Niagara, perhaps fifty yards wide and rather far below, roared and spilled in a series of vertical terraces, finally falling off out of my sight. I returned to Otto disappointed.

Then later, while I was writing a letter, I noticed a boy coming from the direction of the look-off absolutely dripping wet. He had a towel draped around his neck and was pushing a bicycle. And just as he was mounting up to ride off, I yelled to him. "Hey there, have you been in swimming?"

The sweat was dripping onto my letter even as I spoke, and I waited with envious longing as the boy came closer to Otto to see who had yelled at him. Well, yes, he said, he had been in swimming.

So I told the boy about Don and his walk and that Don would be at this place about 4:40. And I asked him if he'd be interested in returning then to show us where his swimming hole was. I gave him one of Don's cards. I could tell he was getting interested.

After staring at the card a while, he said he would come back later. Then I asked him his name and the directions to the nearest post office, and after obliging he disappeared.

When he was gone, I somehow doubted he would come back. But I was wrong. Nathan arrived about fifteen minutes after Don, when Don had just about decided to get back out on the road and get the last of the hot, grueling miles behind him for the day. But when Nathan showed, the idea of a swim was too good to pass up.

We followed Nathan, who walked ahead of us pushing his bike along the narrow walkway I'd been down earlier. I wondered what we were in for. When we came to a place where there was a break in the railing, Nathan leaned his bike against a tree and said we'd have to climb down the bank there to get to the river.

"Down there?" I shouted over the noise of the waters. "But how?"

"Just follow me." Nathan shouted back with utter confidence.

But I stood there unable to imagine doing what he asked. The dirt bank was too vertical and the river was roaring its own warnings at the bottom. Yet Nathan demonstrated with careful agility how we were to lower ourselves down with a hand on a sapling here, a foot to a rock crevice there, a mad slide to the next handhold, and so on, until we all, one way or another, managed to make it down. I was last and earned a few scrapes in the process.

Nathan did not hesitate at the rushing brink, but advised us to keep on our shoes and follow him in. The river was so fast here that, though I could see it was shallow, I feared slipping and being swept away by the current as I tried to keep my balance in it. But since Nathan and Don seemed to be having no trouble, I went in after them.

The rocks underfoot were surprisingly flat, brittle, and sharp-edged. I was glad I had my shoes on. We were moving out onto one of the terraces between the cascading falls. There was some cushiony moss under the water in places, but the footing did not seem particularly slippery. It was a thrill to stand in the river's flow with the thunder of falls on either hand, and for a moment I loved it. But I also figured enough is enough. Not Don. He shouted over the deafening waters to Nathan, who was further out, "I thought you said there'd be a place we could swim, Nathan!"

At that, Nathan smiled a little knowing smile and pressed on toward the middle of the river, where it was still only knee deep. Then suddenly, he took a small preparatory leap and dove out of sight. After another moment, I watched Don do the same. From my perspective it looked as if they had both dived into a deadly maelstrom below one of the biggest falls. When I waded out far enough and could see that they were still alive, I took my fears with me and jumped into the swirling depth after them.

It looked far worse than it was. The current did not sweep us away. Nathan did, however, caution us not to go any further into the main stream, because apparently there on the far side was where the real force of the river was.

In the chilling, churning hole below the falls where we swam were two views. One: up river you could see the water crashing toward you and down from the higher terraces. Two: down river, at eye level, you could see only the near edge of the next terrace below, beyond which were the distant tops of trees, where you assumed the river found level ground again, but it looked to be in another world.

I swam toward Nathan and Don and shouted, "Nathan, are the waters ever coming over the falls so strong that you *can't* swim here?"

And Nathan shouted back, "Only when they open the dam!"

Chapter 13

The Debt

"Oh dear, I hope my letters aren't too dull—and I do apologize for saying anything bad about yours. You should punish me by not writing at all and refusing to do the newsletter. I just know what I might really want of letters cannot be. And I don't think my letters can be much to you either—except I can report on what it's like in this life of being a nomad—well, it's not even really like being a nomad because a nomad takes his whole family and world with him—right down to the last goat. This feels more fugitive—or like being in exile—self-exile. Oh, I don't know what it's like. I suppose all my talk about wanting to grow spiritually, as if Otto were some rolling hermitage, was nothing but idle words and stupidity. The spirits who watch out for vain and empty boasts must be laughing up a storm. It is as Emerson said: Beware of what you want for you will get it, or something like that."

But even as I wrote to David of having gotten something I thought I wanted, I had to ask myself what I was doing on this journey. It was somehow not a question that would let itself be answered once and for all. Instead, it was one of those questions I was tempted to answer differently depending on the kind of day it was. On a good day I knew I was there for Don. I felt as if I owed him this.

When Don and I had first gone our separate ways, he went with the boys, who were in fourth and fifth grade at the time, to a teaching job in Middlebury, Vermont; I went to graduate school in Cambridge,

Massachusetts. I little understood then how close to a cliff edge I was going to be walking. We had parted as friends and with the understanding that each would be adventuring independently, yet because of our two sons we would also try to remain close. We would not complain of one another or dwell on past failures and hurts.

I was thrilled to be on my own, I thought—as I had never yet been, having married Don at seventeen and having had both boys before I was twenty. Looking back, I can see now that at some point I was bound and determined to get that independence. I can clearly see in retrospect a certain reckless bent propelling me away from bonds I found limiting—perhaps at any cost. I did not or would not see it at the time, however.

And then David came into my life—a story worth a book of its own—and whatever craving for independence I once had seemed to evaporate as if I had never really wanted that at all. Something between David and me was better than independence—and yet I saw too, with a rather sudden clarity, that I was going to be without my children. I mean, when I left graduate school, I did not feel I had the right, since I was the one who wanted my independence in the first place, to wrench the boys away from their father, who had established a new life with them apart from me.

We visited back and forth, of course—David and I to Middlebury, Don and the boys to Boston. The boys accepted David, and Don did, too. David accepted the fact that Don and I had no hateful feelings toward one another and that we both wanted to work together as much as possible to be decent parents. David and I lived and worked at a boarding school that had longer and sometimes different vacations than those Don and the boys had, so we had lots of time to visit them in Vermont and they to visit us. But those few years were hard, and I was haunted by an awareness of my own selfishness—a selfishness that had ultimately separated me from my children.

I determined then to be, at least, a good friend to Don, if not wife—and to be the best parent for the boys I could be, if at a distance. Toward this end for those four years, which included the year of graduate school, most every day began with my writing three letters—one to Don, one to Andy, and one to Danny. By this means they would know for a certainty that I thought about them every day—and cared—and that I did love each of them even so…even if I could not change the circumstances or undo what I had done. But it wasn't that anyone would have necessarily changed the circumstances if they could have.

David understood my commitment to the boys. He could see for himself that I had promises to keep and would not be the woman he loved if I did not try to keep them. But it must have been hard for him too to know how my heart was torn to be away from my children.

We all thought it would be better if we could live closer. Then David and I landed teaching jobs in the Middlebury area and were going to move up to Vermont. But who was the most surprised when I proposed that the five of us share one house? Both Don and David thought I was crazy. The boys hardly knew what to think. I certainly didn't have much in my favor, until I suggested we three teachers pool resources and buy a place big enough for everyone to have their own space. Together we could afford a place that none of us could afford alone. I think the main reason Don and David finally consented was because each knew how badly I wanted to be with my sons, Andy and Danny. The boys must have known, too. And because it seemed such a crazy thing, we all agreed we would not even pretend it could work, but we would simply try it for one year. At the end of the year, we would decide whether to continue in one household or not.

Well, that year had its awkward, uncomfortable, even painful moments. And yet, it wasn't without its good side, too, so that when we talked about whether to continue or not, at the end of that year, we all voted to stay together.

There were some advantages and disadvantages for everyone. The most obvious disadvantage for all of us was how the situation looked to outsiders—as if some sort of freewheeling sexual arrangement might be going on between the woman—that is, myself—and her ex-husband and current husband. No one who really knew any of us thought this, and whoever else might have thought such a thing must have respectfully kept their silence when any of us were about, so we simply put that false view of things out of our minds. Don was busy with teaching and coaching and did not spend much time at home anyway. By the time the boys were through with their sports and extracurricular commitments in the evening, Don would come home with them to a dinner David and I had prepared. Dinner was the main event for which we all gathered. We felt it was important to do so. Otherwise, we felt freer than ever to go our separate ways. Now every vacation did not have to be spent getting mother and sons together—and they weren't. In summers Don and the boys would go off to camp. We were together, but there was sufficient space to bear our togetherness.

Still, it was an unusual situation and was something to live with. It was confusing to some extent to all of our families—mine, Don's, and David's. It required sacrifices of each of us, Andy and Danny too. I think a certain oblivious momentum carried us along. It was easier to keep going as we were than call a halt because of some little incident, or because some more-distant family member didn't understand. Little by little, and often after a visit to stay with us for a short time, our families came to accept that what we were doing wasn't so bad after all. There was even some recognizable good in it.

I know I felt immense gratitude to Don that he had been willing and able to share a household with David and me, so that I could be with Andy and Danny. It was with this in mind that I signed on as driver. David understood my feeling of indebtedness (undoubtedly mingled with a certain amount of guilt) and to some extent its power over me. Anyway, this was how it all looked ahead of time—in reality it was proving harder than I had imagined. When I would wail to myself, *What am I doing here?* I meant, sometimes, *What is a person like me even doing on this earth?* or, *What have I gotten myself into now?* as much as I meant, *What am I doing on this journey?*

Chapter 14

Blessed One Moment, Cursed the Next

All the time I had to think! All the strange places we found ourselves! How wayward and contrary things could seem! How easy to feel blessed one moment and cursed the next! How symbolic these trials and blessings, such as when we came upon The Sunshine Cafe in Sidnaw, Michigan. I'll remember Sidnaw for an additional detail besides its cafe—a picturesque, wrought-iron fence running down one side of its main street. How often it was, when passing through a place, that one such distinguishing detail could come to stand for the whole.

The Sunshine Cafe had two old, slightly tilted gas pumps out front and a big sandwich board sign with hand-scrawled letters saying, "Lunches." I was there at breakfast.

Inside was as run-down looking as outside—old, stained, dirty-looking linoleum floor; three mismatched dinette sets and odd chairs; two refrigerators—one old, one newish sitting the wrong side of the counter near the tables; a bit of a low bar with patched and taped, plastic-covered stools; cardboard cases of crackers, tomato juice cans, and other supplies stacked on the floor in corners; bulletin board with local events—most of which had gone by; some dusty fishing supplies—hooks, bobbers, and lead sinkers advertised as made in the U.P.; and a coat rack that consisted of a piece of clothesline strung against one wall with a few hangers on it.

And yet, whatever the looks of the place were, the cafe's atmosphere was bright as the sunshine in its name and friendly. The service was good, the food delicious, and the proportions generous to overwhelming. Eggs, toast, and home fries were served on platters large enough to carve a Thanksgiving turkey on—full to the brim! I know I didn't have to eat again that day.

Our last night in Michigan, July 22, we camped beside the Presque Isle River. It was a small, deep river full of iron like Tioga Creek and made my skin shine golden when I swam in it. The day had been a hot one, and Don and I hoped it would be cool to be camped by the water. After our swim it seemed unusually buggy, so we quickly took shelter in Otto. Because there was almost no breeze, we left Otto's back window open. There was a screen, which snapped on from the outside, so we felt protected. Ordinarily we closed this window at night.

It was amazing, once we were inside, what hordes of mosquitoes whined at the outside of every screen. We killed a few inside too, which we figured got in when we were opening and closing the doors. And then darkness fell and sleep came…for a while.

Don woke fully sometime after midnight. I had heard him earlier in the night occasionally lash out at an attacker in his sleep. But now, it was clear, he had given up on sleep and was openly declaring war on every mosquito in the place. I could hear him cursing and swatting and complaining as he did that somehow *they* were getting in.

I had noticed them, too, and in spite of the warm, sticky air, I had burrowed under a sheet for protection. When Don began his rampage below me on his bunk, I burrowed deeper, thinking I could ignore it. Finally, though, I realized I could probably get back to sleep sooner by helping.

We fought a good fight, yet it seemed no matter how many we slew, there was always one more mosquito to get. Eventually we had to agree that they had a way to get in—probably through Otto's back window, which did not have a perfect seal about the screen and its snaps. When Don shined his flashlight on the screen, he saw advancing hordes, but he also realized that to close the back window he would have to get out of Otto to do it.

Still, he dressed in what armor he could find and went out to close it, letting in more mosquitoes in the process, which had been ready to take advantage of just such an opportunity. But then after Don did this, there were battalions of trapped mosquitoes caught between the back window screen and the shut window. These hordes were so maddened that they continued to find ways in anyway. The war raged on.

Finally, it was my turn to offer a solution. I ordered the breaking of camp. We pulled down Otto's top, put beds away, and went speeding down the highway, hoping to leave the wild raiders behind. But still, there were all those trapped mosquitoes at the back window. In desperation I pulled over, got out, opened up the back window again and then remounted Otto. I ordered Don to thrash at the back screen as I got back up to speed. When Don said he thought they were all off, I screeched to a halt, ran out to slam shut the back window again, and then drove to scout another campsite. When I couldn't find anything perfectly legal or out of the way, I simply drove into an open field. Maybe we could at least catch a breeze before we were arrested. But at last, in the hour just before dawn, after a few final skirmishes, we celebrated the peace by laying down arms and getting back to sleep.

It was the good and the bad of the journey that one could be taken by surprise so easily—pleasantly or unpleasantly—a morning at The Sunshine Cafe, a night fighting the great mosquito war. Nearly all events had a momentous feel to them, a sense of exaggerated importance. Indeed, I had the feeling, even after weeks on the road, that anything could go wrong at any time. I didn't feel afraid so much as I felt unprepared, doubtful of my ability to cope with what might befall us, uncertain of what, exactly, to try to be ready for.

And while I had a flighty and heightened wariness, Don displayed a calm sureness of purpose physically grounded in each step. It was always steadying to me to see him approach the camper after hours of being alone with my thoughts. In my mind, almost anything could happen, but when I saw Don I thought, no, the earth is beneath us, the sky is overhead, and The Walk is a reality. It was a good realization that must have occurred countless times, and yet never without a sense of relief. I was reassured that my presence on the journey was as full of purpose as Don's steps. I was needed. It was good to be reminded.

The exasperating thing to me is how often any of us need to be reminded of what is given. It seems we need this about as often as we need to breathe to keep our hearts going. Maybe too, it is only natural to stave off this insatiable need by immersing ourselves in the activities of life. That's Don's approach, I know. Too much time to think can be undermining. It's good to be brought down to earth by concrete concerns.

"Don, what in the world are you doing with that dish towel pinned to the leg of your shorts? Where did you get it? And that handkerchief pinned to your sleeve? And that bandanna pinned to the back of your hat?"

"Don't you see, it's the sun. It's always beating down on me, but it's too hot to cover up completely. It's a way of making my own shade. I found this dish towel back there on the road, and then I got the idea. I had these safety pins in my fanny pack. And it's working. I can move the dish towels as the sun moves, and I can still feel the breeze when there is one, but man, is it hot on the asphalt! Phew!"

"Well, now I get it, but it sure is a strange-looking outfit. You might stop traffic if you weren't on such a lonely road. Guess what?"

"What?"

"You just walked your thousandth mile and we're about to enter the Central Time Zone. The sun will set an hour earlier and feel more normal, I think. But I want to leave Otto's clock as is. On home time. Back there at Bingo's gas station, when I asked the woman what time it was, she wanted to know if I wanted Michigan time or Wisconsin time—well, I realized then what I really wanted to know was home time. What do you think: I'll change my wrist watch, but Otto will stay on home time?"

"It's okay with me. Now, if Mike and Lorraine do catch up with us on the road, we can celebrate the first thousand miles. One-tenth of the journey. Hmmm, how long has it been since we've seen them?"

"It's got to be twenty years—or more, even. I can't really remember. I'm glad you called them, but for them to drive eight hours from Chicago just for one night with us and then eight hours home again—well, I just hope it's worth the trouble, though I can't imagine it will be."

"Don't worry about it, Fran. It was their idea to try to meet us. I can't wait to see them. We have lots of catching up to do."

"I know," I said. Don told me he had already explained a few pertinent things to them on the phone, like we were together on this adventure, but we really weren't together any more. Well, maybe that was one reason they were coming. "It'll be interesting." I said.

"Hey, look what I found." And Don whipped out a fresh-looking dollar bill. "You know, I bet I could double my earnings if I could walk both sides of the road at once."

"Right, Don."

Chapter 15

But What Do Your Neighbors Think?

At Wakefield, Michigan, Don stepped onto Route 2, a road the Walker planned to follow clear to the West Coast. Twelve miles past Wakefield, he walked out of Michigan and into Wisconsin. He had walked the Upper Peninsula in ten days. He would get through the northern reaches of Wisconsin in four-and-a-half.

The first we saw of Wisconsin was little different from what we'd been seeing of Michigan. But then it got hilly for a while and Don's legs ached with the difference. In some high places, looking south, we could see far vistas of a mounded, lush green—hills upon hills upon hills. It was still iron-producing country, and the lands seemed to speak of it. When I saw a cornfield tall and green, within a vista that looked off toward the Gogebic Iron Range, I realized how long it had been since I had seen such a pastoral detail. There hadn't been much farm country. Lands had mostly been too wet—marshy, swampy, boggy; and forested—cedar, spruce, larch. The roadside ditches were rampant with reeds and rushes looking rather like tangled brown hair. There were lots of deer tracks, sometimes deer themselves, and too frequently dead deer in the ditches—obvious casualties of the speeding traffic.

More and more, there were animals I never saw back home—like gophers and strange snakes. And there were some I wasn't sure what they were—wolverines? Road kills were one source of learning the changing wildlife, gruesome as it was. When speeding along in a car, a person may notice only the larger animals killed, but since Don was on foot, he saw how many of the smaller animals also meet their end by inadvertently crossing paths with a car or truck.

I learned new butterflies in this way, when I would walk the road to meet Don. The great spangled fritillary, the question mark angle-wing, the pink-edged sulphur, among others. I would show them to Don and he would say he had seen dozens of them dead beside the road. Lots of birds, too.

But I would make Don really look at whatever perfect butterfly specimen I had found, because whether there were hundreds of them or only one, the details of such delicate things were often astonishing to behold at close hand. The metallic spangle on the great spangled fritillary was like a great jewel the butterfly bore, a kind of earring, a lavish detail clearly meant to dazzle. I could see no other purpose. The almost unnoticeable pink trim on the yellow sulphur was also an exquisite addition—one that could so easily have been left off. I had to wonder that it was there at all, as if such things could only be dreamed up in a universe where there was a great excess of playtime. Don simply humored me at first, I think, but soon came to treasure such things in his own way. He certainly saw things on the road he had never had much opportunity to see before.

I was learning new wildflowers by the day like the purple bush clovers, the pink wild bean, the deeply magenta marsh thistle, and the lavender wild bergamot. I still found familiars too—Queen Anne's lace, the buttery gold St. Johnswort, the rampant pink knapweed, the gangly yellow evening primrose. But these were springing from a broader, more open expanse of land, a new setting. Forests did not grow up the sides of mountains as they did back home, but marched off in every direction under a sky of reaching dimensions.

Besides doing errands and chores, taking photographs, writing up the day in letters and journals, trying to get in some good walks—I drew, and sometimes played a wooden flute. I drew from bouquets of wildflowers I picked. I thought my drawings another way of sharing the journey with David. I had a piece of music I long wanted to master on the recorder, Bach's "Jesu, Joy of Man's Desiring." I practiced. Maybe by the end of the journey I would be able to play it halfway decently. But it was amazing how time, even in its new strained dimensions, could get eaten up by the routine of the road; I did not get to draw or to play the recorder nearly as much as I would have liked.

It was near the end of the first day in Wisconsin that our friends Mike and Lorraine caught up with us. We had been half expecting them all day. They only roughly knew our whereabouts and ended up arguing among themselves about which way to turn when they intercepted Route 2 in order to find us. Finally, when they didn't find us, they stopped at a state trooper's headquarters to see if they could get help there. We had been noticed—Otto camped illegally in a field (the night of the great mosquito war) and Don walking the road. So then Mike and Lorraine headed west on Route 2 and discovered the Walker putting in the last miles of his thirty-mile day. And soon after, they found me. The three of us waited together for the Walker to finish up.

I made what use I could of the hour or so to catch Mike and Lorraine up with some of the details about why Don and I were together but really weren't together anymore. It certainly wasn't the first time I had tried to explain about "us."

I glance at Mike and Lorraine from time to time to note their reactions, which alternated between fascinated stares and sympathetic gestures. But I never feel that I am putting things quite right. I am aware that each of us, including Andy and Dan, would have somewhat different things to say. I do not fully understand myself how or why things worked out exactly the way they did. It's partly conscious effort, partly who all of us are, partly even luck, I suppose. It's also alive; it's nothing fixed. I mean, it does not exist completely in the past. It is subject to change, as well as to be seen in changing light. The journey, it seemed, had a way of shedding new light upon it—from time to time.

Because of this, as I talked with Mike and Lorraine, I was somewhat aware of the clumsiness of my words. I looked to them to catch any glimpse of understanding I could, in order to know whether I was getting through at all.

"You mean, Franny, that you all live together in one house?" Lorraine asked, incredulous. "Gosh, I always knew you would go your own way in life, but it does seem far-fetched, Franny, even for you."

Mike was speechless.

"Well, I don't know what else to say about it, Lorraine. Somehow it works. I guess one sign that it works is that the bills get paid, the chores get done, and we don't have much to argue about. David and I take care of the house, but then we are the ones who spend the most time there. Everyone helps with the bills, and when there's a big job to be done, like stacking five cords of wood, everybody pitches in. We've never even had an argument over the finances of the place. If David is running short of money and can't pay a bill, then Don pays it or vice versa. There's a lot of trust and respect—and I guess if it didn't work, we wouldn't still all be together. It's going on ten years now.

"When both boys went off to college, we agreed that they ought to still have one household to come home to. I don't know what will happen after they graduate in May. I guess we'll have a meeting then and decide."

"But, Franny, what do your neighbors think of you all?" Lorraine asked.

Mike was still speechless.

"Well, they're friendly enough, and I suppose they've simply come to accept us as they've gotten to know us. If they don't approve, they keep it to themselves. I don't know. Probably a lot of people don't approve, but I suspect that they see that each of us is hardworking and sober and leave it at that. There *are* some funny stories. I know I found out once that a lot of people just assumed that Don was my brother. And the truth is if someone asks for Mrs. So and So on the phone, I say, "This is she," whatever last name they use. It's too confusing to try to stop and explain, so I don't."

"Well, you have a big house, right?" said Lorraine.

Mike still hadn't said anything.

"Yeah, it's an odd place—rambling, sort of. There's a small, barn-like attachment that is very much like a separate apartment, and that's where Don and the boys are. David and I have a loft above another part of the house. I guess it's partly the layout of the house that made it all seem possible, though we have improved it since we bought it.

"I don't know, Lorraine. I'm not saying it would be a good thing for anyone else to do, or that it's right, or that it's wrong—it's just the best thing we could think of for ourselves. That's all. You know, if at some point you really botch up your life and suddenly see that you have, and there's no going back, you just have to go on—make the best of it."

At this point the tension of not knowing how Mike was receiving all this began to get to me. I started to choke up. Mike was a fraternity brother and good friend of Don's since before Don and I met. I couldn't help but wonder as I spoke whether Mike would not think I had failed Don miserably,

I am an idealist of sorts, and moments like these—when one faces another human being, acknowledging in various ways how one has not come up to one's own ideals—well, they are killing. They ought to cure a person forever of his or her idealism. Why they do not in my own case testifies to my stubbornness, I guess. If I give up my ideals, what have I got? They are a sort of shining standard, and even if I am but dung by comparison, I think they ought to stand.

But Mike, seeing me begin to break, simply reached out, put his hand on my shoulder, and said gently but teasingly, "Hey, Franny, I don't believe a word you're saying!"

And then we all laughed, and Don walked up shortly thereafter, and a new round of reminiscences began in which we all talked nonstop and at the same time, and in the spirit of old and good friends forgave one another all past and future failings.

This kept up through dinner and afterward, and then began all over again at breakfast. Then Mike walked the first miles of the day with Don while Lorraine and I talked. Later we all took pictures of one another, and then Mike and Lorraine headed back on their eight-hour drive home.

It was a boost to both of us that they had come so far. Don walked that day with a lighter step and renewed vigor. People he knew and cared about had seen what he was up to—and were impressed. We were both happy and grateful to have renewed an old friendship. Indeed, renewing friendships with people we had lost track of and who had lost track of us became one of the recurring themes of the journey.

Chapter 16

Not Exactly a Vacation

At Ashland, Wisconsin, we saw Lake Superior again and camped beside it for the night. Here in Chequamegon Bay, the lake was fairly shallow and not so fiercely cold. Neither was it so beautifully clear, though we were glad enough to swim in it anyway. From Ashland it was a turn away from the lake and a day's walk to Iron River, where I was happy to retrieve mail for us.

One item: a postcard David forwarded from a friend of mine and former teaching colleague—a teacher who had traveled across Canada by train and was then vacationing in Vancouver. The tone of this card, the thought of vacation, as well as the quickness with which he had covered the entire continent—all made me stop and think. Our journey was anything but vacation-like. There might be light-hearted moments, such as with Mike and Lorraine, but I never would have described what we were doing as a vacation. Don might have thought of The Walk as a refreshing break from teaching when he was planning it, but I dare say he had to be off his feet when he thought so now.

At Superior, Wisconsin, we met Lake Superior again and for the last time. It was late in the day when we drove out to Wisconsin Point to camp, but Don was determined to swim. There was a strong, cool breeze coming off the water, and that was enough for me. Besides, the lake surf was rough. It looked like an ocean out there, with the waves wild and rolling and breaking against a rocky shore. The lake was also ruddy from the iron in its waters and from a crimson sunset light upon it. I hoped it was not red from the bodies bloodied by it. I was relieved when Don did not stay in long. Across a finger of the lake, upon and against a high ridge, sparkled the lights of Duluth, Minnesota. Tomorrow Don would walk into another state.

I stayed behind the next morning to let Don get through the city of Superior and then the outskirts of Duluth. I would catch up with him later on Route 2, when the roads would be less confusing. I had another post office run to make, anyway. To Wentworth.

When I found the sign that said, "Wentworth," there was another sign nearby saying, "abandoned." I was told at a gas station that Wentworth no longer existed and to check for my mail at South Range.

At the tiny post office in South Range, I was curtly informed that I had no mail waiting for me—even though I could see that they were still sorting the morning's mail. I said I would wait around anyway and check later. So I went to sit in Otto and finish a letter to David. The thought of no mail was too gloomy to dwell upon, and I couldn't give up the hope. I tried to write something cheerful while I waited. And then, before I could finish my letter, I was interrupted three times. The postmaster sent out my mail special delivery, with apologies each time, as the letters popped up in the sorting process. I was glad I had waited.

When I finished my letter, I mailed it at South Range, thanked the postmaster enthusiastically, and went to catch up with the Walker. Driving through Superior and Duluth, I realized with some alarm that Don must have had to walk the Bong Bridge over St. Louis Bay illegally—and part of an interstate, as well. He confirmed this when I found him climbing a long, shadeless hill on the outskirts of Duluth.

Maybe because I was feeling fat and happy with the mail, it suddenly hit me how thin Don was. His face was drawn, and there was a hollowness to him I hadn't noticed before. Both Mike and Lorraine had thought Don looked underweight, but then they hadn't seen him in years; and since he had shaved and dressed up a bit for our dinner out, I thought he looked rather fresh and healthy. Yet now I could plainly see that the miles were taking their toll.

Doctors back home who were interested in Don's walk had put him through a battery of tests before he left and would do so again at his return, but they also advised Don to put on some extra weight before he started his round-the-country marathon. This Don had done. He walked out of school at 160 pounds, which was a good ten pounds heavier than his average weight. He now looked closer to 140 pounds, and much less than that, I knew, could not be considered healthy for him.

I had not exactly been spoiling Don with lavish meals. Neither of us was interested in cooking on this journey, and Otto's stove was broken, anyway. Restaurants, when they happened to be within reach, were not much of a temptation at day's end, because we were both tired and Don did not want to go where he couldn't take off his shoes and socks and elevate his feet.

Don typically ate cold cereal and bananas in the morning; peanut butter sandwiches, bananas, and various snacks by day; and tuna fish sandwiches or cold spaghetti out of a jar by night. If I came upon a good grocery, I might get sliced turkey or beef, and if I came across any other interesting foods I bought them. Don ate tortieres in Canada and an American version of this homemade meat pie, when I could find it, across Michigan, where it was called a "pasty" (pronounced to rhyme with "nasty," only it wasn't).

Part of the problem was the heat. It was hard to eat a heavy meal when the weather was so hot. Lately Don had done a lot more drinking than eating—fruit juices and ice water. But I could see he was not really getting enough—especially if he expected to keep up his pace.

"Heavens, Don, I think Mike and Lorraine were right. You're beginning to look like a scarecrow. You're going to have to eat more. Your ribs are showing. Whatever happened to that stomach roll you had at Long Lake?"

"Long gone, I guess." Don climbed into Otto to take off his shoes. "You know, Fran, by now I have learned one thing for sure. It came up when I was talking to Mike the other day."

"What's that, Don?" I asked, getting out some makings for lunch.

"Well, before I left Middlebury, I was sure that The Walk was going to be mainly a mental challenge—like how to deal with long, boring hours walking roads and all. I figured I would easily get in *walking shape* as I went, and that physically The Walk would be a piece of cake." Don took the sandwich I handed him and went on. "Well, it's just the opposite. It turns out there's plenty to see and think about and be alert to out on the road—but I begin to seriously doubt that I'll ever walk the last miles of the day without a lot of pain."

"Well, I know one thing—I couldn't do what you're doing," I said. "The question is—can you keep doing it?"

"One day at a time, anyway. But I hope I don't have to walk by any more ice cream stands without being able to get a shake or something. There was one back there a few miles, but I had no money. I left my fanny pack in Otto. Fran, you wouldn't want to…"

"Yeah, I'll drive back and get you something ice cold and fattening. You've got to have a richer diet, somehow. At least, ice cream sounds good in heat like this. What do you think, is this heat going to keep up?"

"I don't know," Don sighed. "What day is it, anyway?"

Chapter 17

You Don't Find Happiness
at the End of the Road

All things are not the same from state to state, and the invisible lines that draw a border can make a person wonder about where the real differences lie. Are the people somehow different? Are the rules? How will a traveler be received?

The first day in Minnesota was another long, hot one. At the final stretch, I pulled over to wait for Don in a place barely off the main road. It was all I could find. When a state trooper pulled up behind me, after I had been there a good while, I braced for a lecture.

But no, he was just checking to see if I was having car trouble. When I told him about Don and The Walk, the friendly trooper hung around to find out more from the Walker himself. Later he gave us permission to camp where it wasn't strictly legal—at a canoe put-in on the St. Louis River. He also warned us that the waters were high and that we'd have to be careful if we swam.

The St. Louis was as the trooper warned. But it was also roiled and reddened by the iron-laden soil it carried, and thickly strewn with insect cases of some species similar to a mayfly, not to mention other bits of debris racing along. There were insect swarms dancing above the river, too, including plenty of over-sized Minnesota mosquitoes. But however dangerous and unappealing it was, we were too hot and grubby not to get in.

I could just hold my own against the strong current. And yet there was something more to the river. We could both sense that we really ought to keep only to the surface of the thing. Deeper down, somewhere in its hidden depths, was a stronger, swifter flow with a pull that could well drag us under and tow us away. My heart raced to think how much more there was of the river than of us. Afterwards, I knew we had braved it successfully only because it had let us.

Later still, well after dark, the trooper drove down to check on us. He didn't stop. He cruised slowly through our campsite and then went on about his duties. It was a thoughtful gesture and it gave me the feeling we were being watched over. It gave me a good feeling about Minnesota, too. The ice on a new state had been broken.

We heard the train that night, crossing the river by trestle. We were glad it was still with us, rumbling and clacking and hooting—close at hand and into the far distance. If we didn't hear it for a day or so, Don or I might mention the fact. We liked the wistful sounds of the train, and we thought we could not tire of hearing them. It seemed the farther the towns spread apart as we headed west, the more the train was with us.

But as the distance between towns increased, the more concerned we became with what a dot on the map might mean. We had learned already that a dot was no guarantee of a town or even services. Sometimes we found there was more hope of finding a grocery or gas station at a major crossroads, whether there was a dot on the map or not.

At the end of our second day in Minnesota, Don sent me ahead to scout the junction of Routes 2 and 200. We didn't particularly need gas or groceries, but we were desperate to cool off, and I wanted to ask where the closest swimmable waters were. Nothing much showed on the map, nor had I noticed any ponds, lakes, or streams as I drove along.

But at Routes 2 and 200 there was nothing either, and no place to inquire. Discouraged, I drove back, scouring the road. I thought I had passed a house where I might ask. And then, when I came to it and saw a sign out front saying, "fire warden," my hopes revived.

I knocked on the door. It was a screen door and I could see into the small house some distance. An elderly man came out from the back at my knock, and without approaching the door, he asked in a gruff voice what I wanted. I asked him if he knew of any places to swim in the area. He came closer to the door, peered hard at me through the screen, and wanted to know where I was from. When I told him, he came out the front door and onto his front step. Now he looked me over so closely I wondered if I had said I came from Mars. But then he warmed up a bit, and the next thing I knew we were talking like old friends.

His name was Milton Copt, and he said that he did know of a perfectly good "pothole" within a mile of his house, and that we were welcome to swim in it, as far as he was concerned. He said he used to swim in it himself not so many years back. I wasn't sure what he meant by a pothole, but I thought when Don caught up we could at least check it out.

When I told Milton about Don's walk, he was interested, but it reminded him that I wasn't the only cross-country traveler to knock at his door. Recently, he said, he was preached to by a man going cross-country on foot who was dressed up like Jesus, lugging a heavy cross on wheels. Milton said he did not much like being preached to by this man; he was sure he had read in the newspaper that the cross-bearer had been jailed in Duluth, though Milton wasn't sure what for. He seemed to recall reading that friends of the man from California had bailed him out. I told Milton that Don and I had also heard of the cross-bearer, and I wondered to myself if we might not be closing in on him.

Without much of a pause, Milton went from this tale to others. His eagerness to talk was matched by my own to listen. He spoke touchingly and at length about his wife of over forty years who had died two years back. He claimed he was in his late sixties, had grown up in the area, and had only once wandered very far from home—to Aberdeen, South Dakota (a couple hundred miles away), where he worked on a pipeline one summer. And though he had not cared much for travel, he said his life's philosophy was something he saw on a sign once and knew it to be true the second he saw it:

"You don't find happiness at the end of the road, you find it along the way."

Bound up in his talks he had all sorts of advice—how to save yourself from drowning without swimming a stroke, how to get out of a car underwater, how to get back onto ice after you fell through, how to grow sweet corn in northern Minnesota. This last, the sturdy old man with a twinkle in his eye expounded upon as he toured me about his extensive garden where his corn grew a vibrant green— tall and tasseled. He also bent down to dig with his hands a half dozen healthy red potatoes, which he later gave me. Pretty soon he was offering his side yard for our campsite, and unlimited use of his garden hose besides.

When Don found me parked in Milton's side-yard, Milton was gone for the evening—off to a dinner date with one of the local ladies. We scouted the "pothole"—in actuality a small, weed-choked, cattail-trimmed pond—and enjoyed a swim. For once I wanted to stay in longer than Don. The Walker did not find the pond appetizing. But to me the cool waters had in them the very taste of my grandfather's pond on his farm in rural Missouri. I savored my swim. Later we also took advantage of Milton's garden hose, the stream of which rivaled the cold of Lake Superior and made my head ache when I washed my hair under it.

That night I couldn't sleep. North Dakota was on my mind— now only the width of Minnesota away. North Dakota would bring David; David would bring a change in routine; and a change in routine meant company, at least for me. There was a lot we could catch up on that I never could find adequate words for in my letters, and I thought it would be good for David to know firsthand what it was really like on the road. It would save words later. I thought of Milton's philosophy, and I felt how glad I was that I was not just going to find David at the end of the road but also along the way.

When I still couldn't sleep, I went out to the stars. Disappointed to see what I thought were clouds moving in, I watched and saw them changed to something else before my eyes. Gradually the sky became all shimmer and wave tinted with pastels—a wild ribbon of rose here, a pale lavender flicker there, a red-violet vapor shooting between. The Northern Lights. I called to Don to tell him what was up and he, too, came out.

Together we watched what seemed like ghostly vapors, creating and uncreating an ethereal architecture against a starry canvas, parts of which were occasionally underscored by a shooting star. When the mosquitoes found us, though, we were forced to retreat. Still, I hadn't had enough, so I bundled up to try again.

But though I wore heavy sweat clothing, thick socks, rubberized rain shoes, and a hat with mosquito netting on a night that was already uncomfortably warm and without a breeze; and though I did my best to peer through the netting and the swarm of mosquitoes whining beyond; I wasn't entirely enchanted as I lay in the damp grass looking up. When a mosquito managed to creep under my sleeve and suck the blood from the palm of my hand, I thought I'd seen enough.

I read a day later in a local paper about a woman who saw the aurora and described green tongues of flame licking the bowl of the big dipper, and I knew then I had missed something. Not meant for me, I guess; and I thought how mosquitoes might well guard the way to the tree of life in place of the cherubim with the flaming sword.

The next morning Don met Milton, who invited us in for coffee and showed off pictures of his grandchildren. He gave me a butterfly poster, and I could tell that he wanted to give Don some sort of helpful advice. Don was describing to Milton how much the bottoms of his feet hurt the last five miles or so of every day. Milton looked at Don with sympathetic concern, shaking his head. For the moment, Milton was stumped. But after Don thanked him, said goodbye, and headed out to begin the day's hike, Milton suddenly had an idea. He shouted after the Walker.

"I know, Don, when the pain in your feet really starts to feel bad, then just put 'em down real soft."

We all laughed. And then Don called back, "Good idea, Milton. I'll remember that—put 'em down soft."

Chapter 18

A Backward Glance

Route 2 cut across Minnesota heading west but also heading more northerly, as well. Grand Rapids, Swan River, Warba, Blackberry, La Prairie—the heat continued. The northerly incline of our path did not seem to make a difference. Sometimes the only way I thought it was possible for the Walker to keep going in the heat was by clinging to the hope that somehow thirty miles down the road things might be different.

I was parked near a railroad crossing on the Leech Lake Indian Reservation at Bena, Minnesota, waiting for Don to end his day. For no good reason, we were half expecting a break in the weather. We were also half expecting Luke. Either one seemed farfetched. Luke had come to the Long Lake reunion on his motorcycle, but David had announced to me the night before on the phone that Luke was now heading on his bike to Minnesota. I had thought of Luke many times in Michigan, where it seemed half the state was vacationing on motorcycles, but now we were so far from home that such a ride seemed positively punishing.

But sure enough, a familiar roar alongside Otto eventually produced Luke. He had ridden two fourteen-hour days to catch us. He said he had seen but one walker the entire way—Don, about a mile back. Twelve hundred seventy-two miles—Don had walked it in forty-two days. Luke rode the same route and did it twenty times faster.

Somehow I found it very hard to believe we were close enough for anyone from home to catch us so quickly. The distance had been distorted by time.

At dinner that night at The Big Fish, where we all feasted on fresh walleye and celebrated the Walker's and the Biker's journeys, Luke pulled out a package of photographs.

"Oh, no," I exclaimed, "look at these—the Long Lake reunion!" Gazing at them, I felt as if I was looking back a hundred years in time. In one picture we were all bundled up because of the morning chill. It seemed another world.

"When was the last time we had to dress like that, Don?" And there was David—beard intact. Gosh, I thought, even Florida came between then and now. I couldn't take my eyes off the pictures.

"It's okay, Fran, you can look all you want," Luke said kindly. "I brought those for you guys to keep."

When Luke had to head back the next morning and duplicate his feat in order to get back to his job on Monday morning—well, if I hadn't had the photos in hand, I might have thought I dreamed Luke's visit.

"Gosh, aren't these pictures terrific, Don?"

"Dinner was great, too. And, Fran, I'm glad we found a place for Luke to stay. I don't know where we could have fit him in Otto and I doubt he would have been happy in our tent."

"But pictures, Don. I'd almost forgotten there were such things. I could have brought pictures of home."

"Yeah, and been more homesick even." Don stepped onto the road and turned in the opposite direction that Luke had flown on his motorcycle.

"I guess you're right," I agreed. "I sure hope Luke makes it back okay. It was something, wasn't it, Luke coming all that way. One crazy journey seems to inspire another."

Because of the relentless heat, relieved in Minnesota by two mornings' worth of drizzle and only occasional freshening breezes, the major blessing of each day continued to be the finding of water in which to swim or bathe. We could still see plenty of water on the map in the land of ten thousand lakes, so we didn't worry yet about running out.

Still, it was pretty plain to both of us that the waters were changing. We hesitated longer before getting into them. At Lake Winnibigoshish, at Denny's Resort, where we camped with Luke, Luke refused to get in at all. The greasy-looking waters had washed a flotilla of dead fish onto shore. Don and I went in anyway. Later we were told that "Winnibigoshish" was Ojibwa for big, dirty waters.

Clear, cold, deep water was getting harder to come by. When I scouted places on the map, the names did not inspire—Leech Lake, Midge Lake, Sucker Lake, Mud Lake. Signs advertising leeches at eight dollars a pound gave me pause to wonder. We saw the Mississippi three times. Near Bemidji, before we left it behind, Don swam across and back. It was not the wide, muddy giant here some thirty miles from its source, but was fairly swift and carried the Walker along with it. We swam in Bemidji Lake and Midge Lake the last day of July. We swam in Lake Lamond at Bagley, Minnesota, August 1.

Then, rather suddenly, not far west of the Mississippi, waters for swimming ran out. There was an obvious change in the land that went with this. Instead of wetland forests, swamps, and marshy areas, there began the drier, more open prairie. Extensive farmlands opened out as far as the eye could reach. A sign, where it all seemed to begin, summed it up perfectly: "Welcome to Fosston, Minnesota—where the prairie meets the pines." And that was about it. The change was abrupt. The wet, lakey flats of Minnesota with the closed-in feeling, due to the evergreen trees cutting off one's view, gave way to wide-open prairie agriculture. The scruffy wildness was being exchanged for something trim and tame. Wheat, corn, sugar beets, beans, potatoes, and hayfields were laid out before us in graceful sweeps clear to the horizon.

And here, where trees became scarce, the sun showed no mercy. Seeing the dramatic changes in the land, we hardly dared hope for a swimming hole. The last real swimming hole I found was on the Ball Club River, where kids had fixed a plank to the low highway bridge over it. All the time I waited beside it for Don to catch up, troops of boys came and went—some doing daredevil stunts off the bridge. When Don came along, we did not follow their example, though we did swim.

Yet even before such places disappeared altogether, a warning dried up our urge to bathe in natural waters. In Fosston, we were warned of a plague called "swimmer's itch" caused by some microorganism burrowing in under the skin—a creature abundant in lake and pond waters of the region in August, not to mention leeches. At Erskine, Minnesota, on August 2, we swam in Cameron Lake only because a portion of it was dammed off, with its water recirculating by fountain, supposedly making it safe for swimming. Even so, at 7:30 in the evening with the temperature at 103 degrees, we were the only ones in.

We were amazed how late in the day the peak of the heat came. And again we were surprised to find the sun, as we crept steadily westward through the Central Time Zone, beginning to set later and later. But as for the heat, we weren't the only ones complaining. Locals were saying it was as hot a summer as ever they could remember.

Part Three

AUGUST

Minnesota, North Dakota, Montana

Chapter 19

McIntosh Times

As the land opened out, the road stretched with it. West of the Mississippi, the width of Route 2 expanded with no corresponding increase in traffic. Otto loved it; he had a lane to himself. The Walker loved it too; his margin of safety doubled.

Towns we came to on the farmed and fertile prairie seemed more prosperous. Though natural waters for swimming had run out, the prairie towns often offered an alternative, like campgrounds with showers or town swimming pools. Don even discovered a town named after him—well, not really. But it was spelled the same and it was as neat and prosperous a tiny prairie town as any we saw—McIntosh.

On a Sunday afternoon, McIntosh was quiet and mostly deserted. By luck, the door of "Village Variety" was ajar and I got to speak with the proprietor, Garnet Aarnenson, who just happened to be in to do some cleaning up after a big Saturday sale. She told me the town got its name from a lone Scotsman in its history who married an Ojibwa woman and settled there—otherwise the people were of Swedish, Norwegian, and German descent more typical of the prairie. When I commented on the sudden openness and amazing flatness of the land, she laughed and said, "Yep, they say the land is so flat here and the road so straight, you can see all the way from McIntosh to Grand Forks, North Dakota." When I left Garnet I chuckled at a detail of the little town I had not noticed before—a long awning running across the face of one building with words labeling either end. At one end it said "library"; at the other end, "bar."

Thanks to Garnet, Don was interviewed by the *McIntosh Times*—the first newspaper of the journey to do so. The reporter, Elin Pederson, caught Don on the road the next day, fifteen miles west of McIntosh. She was a kind, soft-spoken, elderly woman who was lots of fun to meet. She took notes, I took notes, and we both took pictures. Sure enough, weeks later, David forwarded the results: we'd all made the front page—the Walker, the Driver, and Otto—with a fine article, to boot. It was a funny thing, though: long before this, Don had run into people now and then who would insist that they had read about him in some newspaper.

I guess we more or less expected the heat to continue; we had entered a new realm of the sun. But what we didn't expect, when Don walked into the shadeless open, was the continuing company of mosquitoes. True, the land was by no means a waterless desert. Still, to us the mosquito looked out of place. On the other hand, it was a new kind of mosquito.

If the wetland mosquito was big and a little slow, the prairie mosquito was quick and clever. Also wind adapted! However strongly the wind blew, the moment Don stepped into a patch of grass, the mosquitoes would get into his wind-draft and stay with him. Once I saw a cloud of them leap up from the grass in a forty M.P.H. headwind and cling easily to the hair on the back of Don's legs. We soon learned to steer clear of the grass. When we came to Crookston, Minnesota, we noticed men on tractors spraying. The local papers said mosquitoes were the worst they'd had in years.

A big sign outside the town said, "Crookston—population 8,900–ten thousand friendly people." It was the first of many town billboards we were to come to claiming "friendliness" as a town trait. And Crookston did seem a fine and friendly place—a college town situated on the Red Lake River.

We camped at a road construction site after swimming and taking advantage of showers at the town pool. Meanwhile, I had two parting glimpses of Crookston that stick fast in my memory.

One was of the world's largest oxcart. This Paul Bunyan-sized wooden wagon did not seem real to me, it was so big. I looked up to it from below as to a two-story building. At first I thought it had been built oversized simply to lure tourists, but not so. The sign beside it testified to its authenticity and claimed it was typically pulled by a single ox (Babe the Blue?). Scanning even the empty bulk of it, I had new respect for the size and strength of the ox, once a common sight in pioneer times. But, of course, the cart would be loaded down with tons (literally) of goods—piles of heavy furs among them, and would follow the Pembina Trail to St. Paul from Canada. The sign said that the creaking of the cart's wheels could be heard six miles off and was like no other sound you'd ever heard before, sending chills up your spine. The completion of the railroad in 1871 quickly put this means of hauling freight out of business. But as I stood there, admiring the thing, I imagined I could hear the eerie sound of it echoing across the century that stood between us.

The second thing I won't forget, I saw in a Crookston shopping center parking lot. It was early morning, the stores were not yet open, and several elephants were milling about like so many impatient shoppers. The circus had come to town.

In East Grand Forks, Minnesota, August 4, on the threshold of North Dakota, Don emptied his pockets: one luminescent, inch-high, plastic toy soldier; a white plastic shoe, five times the size of the toy soldier's foot; a screwdriver; something in a heavy plastic bag labeled "one-half inch drive ratchet renewal, parts enclosed"; a big Harley Davidson belt buckle made of brass; a newish bumper sticker (which Otto refused to wear) saying, "Answer my prayers—steal this car"; and two quarters.

"Don, that brings your road earnings to $4.45. But really, I'm beginning to worry about all this junk you're collecting. It's getting to be a nuisance. I mean, it's not like we have tons of extra room in Otto, you know. I guess getting some of the litter off the road is not a bad idea, but...hmmm. What are we going to do with it all, anyway?"

"I don't know. I can't pass some things up. Something catches my eye, and once I've gone to the trouble of bending over and picking it up...well, I do toss some things back down again."

"This, I find hard to believe," I said, not hiding my exasperation.

"We could box it up and send it home and decide later what to do with it," Don offered. Then he deftly changed the subject. Wasn't it time for me to head to Fargo to pick up David? It was.

Chapter 20

An Extra Pair of Eyes

Fargo—to me, the name was practically synonymous with the ends of the earth. I loved the sound of it—even the faraway sound of it. It conjured up a wild and rustic place and all sorts of brutal weather. As I drove through North Dakota the ninety miles from Grand Forks to Fargo, it wasn't hard to imagine that Otto was a stagecoach and I was rumbling across the prairie to the next outpost. I was surprised to enter the city of Fargo and the twentieth century at the same time. It was far more sophisticated and refined than I was prepared for. But soon, too, it was bound up with a personal joy, so that even much later on the journey I could say the name "Fargo" and renew a whole realm of happy associations, including all that the name originally stood for.

Since I was taking Otto to Fargo, and since we had to be careful of our expenses, Don was hoping, as cross-country walker, to wangle a deal at a motel. He wanted to relax, watch some TV, and maybe even swim in a pool. But he was nonetheless surprised when Lou, the manager at the new Regency Inn in East Grand Forks, offered the Walker not only a free room but dinner on the house, as well. Knowing Don was all set, I left for Fargo with a merry heart. In case David's plane was late, I wouldn't have to worry about the Walker: we could catch up with Don on Route 2 early the following day.

David's plane *was* late, and his luggage even later, arriving on a second plane sometime near midnight. We saw more of Fargo because of this than was originally planned. Once David landed, we headed downtown, and over dinner continued the sometimes awkward process of readjusting to each other's presence. The initial rush of wondrous disbelief and joy was ebbing—being checked by the reality of flesh and blood and personality. Not that there wasn't still plenty of joy; there was. It was later, when the luggage arrived, that the joy was temporarily replaced by something else.

"David, what in the world is all this?" I asked with a suddenly sinking heart and undisguised frustration as I scanned not only David's luggage, which certainly seemed a reasonable amount for his visit, but some large and cumbersome cardboard boxes besides.

"Well, some of it's a surprise, some of it's shoes for Don and other things you guys asked for, and well, don't worry, you'll be glad for it all."

"No, I won't." I said with utter surety. "You have no idea how cramped it is in Otto already, David. I was even wondering how you and your luggage were going to fit. This just looks awful." And I proceeded to moan and groan ungratefully, paying little attention to David's pleas to relax and not worry and he'd take care of everything and he'd find room for it all.

"But there is no room!" I protested. "And Don has been collecting stuff, and I can hardly find room for groceries as it is, and I really can't imagine where you are even going to sit in Otto when Don takes a break, much less find a place for all this...oh dear." Which is when I started to cry.

David sighed. And then he frowned unsympathetically. He knew the problem could be solved and was angry that I was spoiling the long-awaited and once-joyful reunion. He glared at me with great, eloquent silence.

Through my tears I glared back. But I began to think as I did that we were both tired and the hour was late and...not many thoughts later, I was able to get a grip on myself because I did see in David's expression what was at stake. Not that I felt any better about the baggage, but I could see that until *he* saw how things were, there was no use in my being so ugly about it. All I said in response was, "You'll see."

David said nothing. Together we hauled the baggage and heavy boxes out to the parking lot. It was too dark to rearrange things at the airport, so we just threw everything in a big pile inside Otto. This left as little room as I had feared, but I did my best to postpone worrying about it and said nothing.

David and I camped that night in Otto, sharing the upper bunk. David took up the space next to me that was usually piled with notebooks and journals I wrote in at night—a happy exchange.

The next day, I knew better that finding places in Otto for all the junk was the least of my worries. I began to be more concerned that time might play some cruel trick on me and suddenly begin to fly because of David's presence.

Early morning, before the wind was up, on the drive north back to Route 2, the world was heavy with dew. I was excited to share this new land with David, who had never before traveled west or seen the prairie. But it was David, a keen observer of nature himself, who soon pointed something out to me, simply saying, "Look!"

And I saw what he saw: dozens of spokey spider webs were woven between the taller roadside weed stalks, at right angles to the prevailing winds. The webs were all aglitter with the early sunlight entangled in the chainlike drops of dew. A stunning crop of fairy wheels, it seemed. I wondered if these webs had to be reconstructed each day. Having already had a taste of the muscular prairie winds, I couldn't imagine how such delicate orbs could hold. Indeed, how could anything hold in such sweeping openness? I felt myself barely holding as we rolled swiftly through the beckoning expanse of it. But I knew then I had an extra pair of eyes in David to help take it all in. And I was glad.

What I couldn't wait for David to see was something Don and I had first seen in the country between McIntosh and Crookston. It was a sight almost worth the journey entire—a field of sunflowers. No, the word "field" is much too small for what it was—it was more like a sea. Wild or tame, the prairie was all but oceanic. We had heard this, and yet the reality of it was just beginning to sink in. And soon David, too, was seeing it for himself.

Whatever flourished on the prairie, the wind moved—moved through it and over it, as over water. However soldier-like the crop of giant sunflowers was—all facing the same direction, sturdily upright, heads a bit bowed, marching south in orderly ranks clear to the horizon under a commanding blue sky—it was a sea of the brightest, yellowest gold, bobbing and swaying and begging to be plundered. And where there was wheat in tawny blond ripples and waves washing against the wayside, one wanted to wade into it. And where there was flax in bloom, it was the blue-green color of the sea itself quenching the mind's thirst, if not the body's. And all of it was on such an unexpectedly grand scale—especially the sunflowers— that again and again we were taken by surprise.

Chapter 21

You're Not Going to Outer Mongolia

By the time David and I caught up with the Walker, Don was more than ready for a break. I pulled over and climbed out of the front seat. David opened up the sliding door and, before Don walked up, quickly emptied Otto of the extra boxes so Don could get in and sit down if he wanted.

"Hi, David," Don said as the two shook hands, "Welcome to North Dakota. How was the trip out? You two have a good night?"

"Yes, thanks; flight was late, though, and we had to wait for another plane to get my luggage. But I've got those shoes you wanted, also some special insoles that I thought you might want to try."

"Is that what's in these boxes—shoes and insoles? Must be enough for a *dozen* round-the-country walks," Don said, eyeing the cargo.

"No, here, I'll show you what I brought."

Don got in Otto, sat down, and began taking off his shoes. I got Don something to drink and then stood by while David opened the boxes.

Out came three pairs of new shoes; a big packet of mail; a stack of sports and news magazines Don had requested; packages of different types of insoles; a pair of white, loose-fitting, lightweight cotton trousers for Don; also pairs of new socks; a couple of new baseball caps; heavy stacks of fresh paper for me; and two collapsible wood-

and-canvas deck chairs. All of it was what Don and I had ordered, except the chairs, which was the surprise David had mentioned.

"Let me try a pair of those new shoes," Don said. "These are in the nick of time. I had no idea how quickly I would pound out the cushioning in a pair," he continued as he slipped an achy foot into one.

"David, what are these chairs for?" I asked.

"It's so you and Don can sit outside on something comfortable."

"But then where'll I put them?" I sighed, more worried about storage than about sitting comfortably outside. Also, I knew at a glance we did not really want them. Don would want to get out of the sun on his breaks, and I knew I would not sit outside Otto advertising my aloneness. When I later explained this to David, he understood.

But just then it was clear to me, as I wearily surveyed the layout and innards of Otto, that a lot of work needed to be done. I somehow did not feel up to it. And while David caught Don up on news of home I had already heard, I stood there in a daze, staring at what was scattered about my feet.

The piles before me readily recalled the first frenzied packing last June; and I watched them change into the piles Don had lined up back then alongside Otto: at least a dozen boxed pairs of new shoes; stacks of clothing; a large trainer's kit brimming with foot powders, creams, ointments, jellies, and bandages; and a huge pile of miscellaneous items Don thought he would need. I had stacked up paper, typewriter, notebooks, field guides, field glasses, clothing, cooking equipment, and a huge pile of miscellaneous items I thought I would need. It seemed like all shoes and notebooks then, too.

Meanwhile, David was running back and forth between tool room, kitchen, bathroom, and various closets piling up things for both of us that he thought we would need—things Don and I hadn't thought of. David also was piling up things for Otto.

"Don, you'll never have room for all those shoes, if you leave them in boxes," I advised.

"Well, *I'll* figure out what I have room for. Tell me which cabinets and spaces are mine, Fran, so I can get this over with. I still have things to do in town."

I wanted to be in charge of organizing Otto, since I was going to have to spend the most time in him, so I told Don what spaces I had allotted to him, and then we both began the process of trying to fit everything in.

"You know, it's not as if you're going to Outer Mongolia," David said more than once. "You can surely purchase things along the way—anything you might have forgotten." But then, in contradiction to this statement, he continued to add things to the pile he thought were necessary. I was trying to talk him out of much of it, mostly to save some breathing space. I was also trying to talk Don into leaving some things behind using David's argument, which Don then used on me.

"Fran, you have enough paper there to write an encyclopedia. You can surely buy paper as we go."

"This is *special* paper and I have to have it. Why don't you leave some of those shoes at home, Don? Whenever you need more, David can mail them to you."

But the truth was that none of us really knew all we would need, and each of us feared being without some crucial item. The surprise was finding out that, in many respects, we did end up going to Outer Mongolia. Avoiding the big cities meant we really didn't come across places to replenish certain supplies. And in any city we couldn't avoid, the last thing I wanted to do was shop or try to chase down some particular thing. I had to do too much of that already, just getting the basics.

Somehow we got everything in, but I was not happy with how the space in Otto had shrunk. I hadn't realized it might continue to shrink once we were on the road.

So now David was with us, and I could not imagine, as I stood there in a stupor surveying the stuff strewn before me, how we were going to manage—plus, we were three bodies now instead of two.

"How in the world is this going to work?" I said, interrupting. I was feeling somehow as if Otto had been invaded—but most especially my space.

"Fran, we just have to do some rearranging," David said, losing patience.

Don took this as his cue to leave. "Hey, I'll find places for my stuff later. I'll just leave it in the back for now. Quit worrying, Fran. Don't spoil David's visit. Relax. I'm heading out. See you guys down the road in a couple of hours, okay?" He jumped out of Otto and stepped around a bit, looking at the new shoes on his feet. "These feel great." Then he grabbed a banana and left.

David and I dug in. And hours later…days later, David had made a difference in countless ways—miraculously making *more* room in Otto, even managing to free up the seat that had been occupied by an extra five-gallon water supply. David turned this seat around and somehow the water jug fit behind it, so, for a while, this seat became his. David also fixed Otto's broken window handle, so it could easily be cranked open without the pliers (which we could never find when needed anyway)—a blessing Don and I could not be more grateful for. David checked and tightened other loose bolts and screws, glued Otto's sagging roof-liner, and arranged for extra storage on Otto's roof. Having David along made all my regular chores easier, as well—even fun.

David was with us on the journey for eight days. Don's routine changed little. He kept up his thirty-mile hikes just the same. But we had all decided to splurge while David was with us—eat out more when we felt like it, get rooms in motels when showers and facilities weren't available otherwise, use the tent to expand our living space if we had to camp. David and I tried to scout motels with pools so Don could swim. Having David along was a boost to the Walker partly because I was a lot more cheerful, but also because if something went wrong, David was there to help. Later in the journey, when Don had someone join him on The Walk, I felt a similar boost, knowing Don was not dependent only on me to help cheer him on.

David's visit was a break in routine for me because I did not write anything but a few notes, which I would expand upon later when he was gone. We had plenty of time alone while Don was putting in his long hours on the road.

I could tell David was enjoying not only my own company but the company of the prairie. When I was making my notes, he would sit outside in one of the deck chairs on a patch of prairie out of the wind, reading a book or musing about the new land all around. Sometimes I serenaded him on my recorder. It was a peaceful interlude.

Chapter 22

The Heartbeat of the Journey

As Don walked from Grand Forks to Larimore to Lakota to Devil's Lake to Leeds to Rugby, we were all learning one thing: The North Dakota prairie is not *simply* flat. I began to be sorry I had ever used that word in my descriptions. The word "flat" does not convey the complex nature of the area, which was oddly rumpled and ridged and mussed in places, like a blanket on an unmade bed. And even where it seemed to stretch more smoothly to the horizon, if you got enough above it, you saw it variously pocked with irregularly shaped ponds and sloughs. We were all surprised at how often these small, wet, low habitats interrupted the planted fields. And on every weedy slough was a host of wild ducks.

David and I learned easily to identify ducks with the most distinctive silhouettes even from a considerable distance, such as the diving ruddy duck with its abruptly cocked tail and the dabbling pintail with its long and sharply pointed one. There were coots, too, and cranes and grebes and herons and bitterns, not to mention all manner of sandpipers.

At Rugby, North Dakota, there was a stone obelisk claiming to mark the geographical center of the North American continent—a milestone none of us knew we would be passing. I suppose we ought to have felt well grounded, safely in the continental middle, but I, for one, did not. It was too disquieting to learn what was beneath the peaceful face of the prairie. A postcard at Rugby boasted that if

North Dakota were a country all its own, it would rank fifth among the world's nuclear powers because of the Minuteman missiles buried beneath its surface.

At the heart of the continent, this sort of knowledge made the earth seem to quake a little beneath my feet. It was strangely and uncomfortably jarring that all of this fearsome weaponry was overlain by what otherwise seemed so idyllic. The very openness of the land made me think that of all places on earth, this was the most vulnerable. But the point is: no place is invulnerable and no missile makes it so.

From Rugby to Towner to Denbigh to Minot, David was with us long enough to see the prairie begin to show a few rough edges. The sunflower fields were behind us; there was more and more wheat and very few row crops anymore. Large tracts of a scrubby-looking rangeland sometimes interrupted the more-fertile areas. And here we noticed low-growing prickly pear and pin cushion cactus; also grazing cattle and horses. At the same time, I had to wonder if we weren't also beginning to glimpse—the West.

"Don, what do you think, have we gotten west yet? I mean, where does the West really begin?"

"I don't know," Don said as he climbed into Otto while David and I rearranged ourselves to make room. "I just can't believe the wind out there! It's like climbing a mountain to make any progress against it at all. And it's been blasting at me all day long—for days, really. It's awful."

David and I could imagine what he meant, just from our own short hikes. Even now, the wind was battering against Otto and rattling everything that was the least bit loose.

"It must be pretty dusty out there, too, with all that wind up," David said, handing the Walker a mug of ice water.

"Thanks. Dusty and miserable—but the headwind today is better than the wind yesterday that was always coming at me from the side. I was constantly being pushed off balance by it and having to take extra steps. I can't really believe it, even—is the wind ever *not* blowing around here?" Don grabbed a paper towel, dipped it in the melted ice water of the cooler, and wiped his face. Road grime blackened the towel. "Hey, did you guys notice those odd-looking blackbirds flocking in the fields back there?"

"Yeah, David and I were just taking a tally—what a mixture: red-wings, grackles, cowbirds, starlings; the yellow-headed, the tri-colored, and Brewer's blackbirds; also meadowlarks and bobolinks."

"Must be the yellow-headed and tri-colored that I was wondering about. Those aren't birds we have in the East, are they?" Don asked, taking another swipe across his brow with the wet paper towel.

"Neither is the Brewer's, but they look so much like grackles, they're hard to pick out," I said.

"So maybe we have gotten west," David offered.

"Hmmm," I took out the map. "Looking at the U.S. map here and heading straight south from Minot—you *almost* run into Colorado. That's west if you ask me, guys."

Don was not opposed to saying we'd gotten west; it gave him a boost to think he'd made that much progress. And when we all spotted a new highway sign not long after, designating Route 2 as "The Old West Trail," we were content that, for us, the West had indeed begun.

In Minot at day's end, David said farewell to the Walker for the time being. He would join up with us again somewhere else along the journey. I drove David to the airport at Bismarck while Don holed up in Minot; the following day I would catch the Walker again on Route 2.

Bismarck certainly did not have the same joy Fargo had bound up with it, but I was too grateful that David's visit had worked out as well as it had to lose heart. I felt stronger for his company, and the prairie itself was not less beautiful because of it.

The minute David was gone, I felt his absence keenly. He had taken full boxes of junk with him, including unusable cooking gear, Don's roadside finds, and the two deck chairs. With David's seat vacated besides—Otto suddenly seemed, ironically, terribly empty.

Also, I was freshly struck by how unlike home were my surroundings. Birds new to me filled the air with unfamiliar song. There was no hope of hearing the hermit thrush anymore—a bird of the dark wood. Even at home the time for it to sing was ending.

The last hermit's song I heard came from the depths of a Wisconsin forest. Loons, which had eerily called across Canada and the upper Midwest, had last been heard upon the Mississippi in Minnesota. Birds were flocking; the season was changing.

Wildflowers had been changing, too, not only with the season, but with our westerly progress. There were flowers I'd never known before, including new varieties of wild sunflowers, but also yellow gumweeds and bush clovers, wild blue lettuce, and the grey-headed cone flower—a sort of laid-back black-eyed Susan. I saw the shiny red hips of many a wild prairie rose gone by. Now and then, profuse patches of brilliant blossoms, such as the intensely magenta blazing star, gave hints of what the prairie must have once been like before it felt the plow.

I tried to learn some of the grasses and sedges. I made bouquets of the many kinds of bluestem, wheat grass, and grama. I marveled at needle-and-thread grass with its sharp, needle-like seeds around which the rest of the plant curled in random, thread-line tangles. Other low-growing plants also seemed to take on grassy characteristics, and added new color, texture, and tone to the land—the bright cranberry-red samphire and the silvery blue-green prairie sage.

But on August 13, near Stanley, North Dakota, I picked a shrubby wildflower that bowled me over with its heavy honeysuckle fragrance and deep rose-pink. I had seen a lot of it growing densely in the ravines and gullies, and I determined to learn its name.

I roamed about the little town of Stanley with a sprig of it, as I went about my errands, asking if anyone knew it. My eastern wildflower field guide was of little use any more. I inquired at gas station, post office, grocery, the extension service, and two flower shops—and though many admired the flower and a few recognized it as familiar, no one seemed to know its name.

I waited for the tiny town library to open and began combing the few stacks there for a book to help, with the librarian, Mrs. Ellis, at my side. She hadn't yet been able to get around to fully categorizing all the books, so it was a real search. And then, while we were hunting, a woman came in named June Kannianen, who did not know the flower either, but who did have a book at home in which she felt sure she could look it up, if I could spare her a leaf and a blossom. June wouldn't be home for a few hours, but if I could call her later, she might know by then. Mrs. Ellis offered the library phone if I wanted to come back just before the library closed.

And so I did, and June was home, and she and her husband had identified the now-bedraggled flower: western snowberry, sometimes called buckbrush. Hurrah—mystery solved! And I determined then to get my own copy of the field guide June had used.

But in the end, I think I was as glad to have met June and Mrs. Ellis and learn their names as I was the western snowberry. Something about David's absence on the prairie was an aching emptiness I'd have to fill somehow. It was back to hard rations and quiet so profound at times, it finally led me to a small discovery.

Alone, staring out of one of Otto's windows at some lonely ribbon of road reaching to a far-off vanishing point, I was often aware of only one sound—the ticking of Otto's clock. It counted out the half-seconds with dependable regularity, each individual tick a detectable mark of time. Sometimes I thought this tick incredibly loud (most especially after David left) and could imagine it echoing out over the open countryside, waking whatever slept in the afternoon heat. And then I discovered that this tick exactly matched one thing—Don's step.

Sometimes I would really have to listen carefully to tell the difference. *Is that the tick of the clock I hear, or Don's footsteps approaching Otto?* I would wonder. It could have been either. Sometimes, though, when it was the ticking of the clock, and I knew Don was due, I would listen closely until I could hear Don's gritty step coincide with the clock's own gritty tick. Sometimes, for a sense of company, I would purposely imagine I was hearing Don's step, however far away I knew him to be.

When the Walker told me he had done a step count—twice, for one mile each—and had come up with roughly 2,200 steps per mile (which made some 66,000 steps per thirty-mile day and 2,000,000 steps per month); and when the Walker said he had also figured out how many steps he took *by time*, counting two steps to the second, and that by this means he had also come up with the same exact number of steps per thirty-mile day, etc.—I explained to Don how I had already figured out that he was a walking clock.

The Walker's legs were swinging as consistently as pendulums, and the sound of his footsteps—or Otto's clock, either one—was the very heartbeat of the journey.

Chapter 23

This Is Not a Sightseeing Trip

"The land is going from rumpled to hilly in places. The hills seem to push against the cloud-burdened sky. I feel as if we are being lifted—or is the sky simply lowering? The sky was already seeming low, as if one could easily reach up and pull down a cloud for a pillow, yet now it comes closer still. This is the first time I have seen the prairie sky under a single cloud, though I have seen it entirely without cloud. More often it is as yesterday with something different happening in every quadrant. For a while there were some slightly pointed, treeless hills furred over with a crop of short, pale-green grasses. The hills closed in on both sides of the road at once, with the road running between them a long way ahead and a long way back. Don scared up some gray partridge on them. I love these barrenish hills—I wish I could run about on them like the partridge, but in places I can see a forbidding fence barring my way. Maybe there are missiles near. I don't know. I never know when the hills are going to appear. Now they're here, now they're gone."

Even as I was writing this in my journal, the North Dakota prairie was nearly all behind us. From Stanley, where I learned the western snowberry, to Ray, it was a thirty-two-mile hike for the Walker. From Ray to Williston it was a thirty-four-mile hike, and from Williston it was less than a day's hike to the Montana border. At the border Don would walk into another time zone. When he came to a halt at Williston at the end of the day, August 15, he had walked 1,772 miles in fifty-nine days, with only one day off.

"Don, we ought to be celebrating."

"We *are* celebrating," he said, taking a bite of his hamburger. "We're sitting in a restaurant, eating and celebrating."

"Somehow it doesn't feel like it," I said, trying not to sound as if I was complaining. Deep down I felt my recently gained sense of well-being sliding out from under me. David's visit was over; he had been gone four days. The next mail drop was still almost a week away. I didn't really feel like celebrating. I didn't know what I felt like, except I desperately wanted to stave off my homesickness.

"A woman I talked to back there in Ray, at the laundromat? She said we really ought not to miss seeing the North Dakota Badlands," I offered somewhat timidly.

"Fran, this is *not* a sightseeing trip."

How well I knew! How many times Don had said that! Most of the time, I even agreed. Neither of us really had the extra energy at day's end to go far afield. Still, I sat there staring at the map anyway. Mute and dejected. I meant to say, "But I've always wanted to see the Badlands, ever since I saw a picture of them in a sixth-grade geography book." But I didn't. I was too tired. The Walker looked beat, too.

"Here, let me see the map," Don said, pushing aside his empty plate. "Well, you know," he said after a long pause, "the northern part of the Theodore Roosevelt National Park isn't *that* far away. I wonder. We don't know where to camp around here, anyway. What time is it?"

"Going on eight," I said, wondering what Don was getting at.

"We could camp down there. It's sixty miles but, well, maybe we'd get a glimpse of some badlands before sunset. Also we could get up early and maybe drive around the park a little in the morning and not lose too much time. I don't really mind hiking a shorter day into Montana tomorrow. What do you say?"

"Let's do it," I agreed.

But after the first half-hour of the ride, Don felt his tiredness weighing more heavily on him. He yawned, looked at the map again, and began to talk half-heartedly about going only as far as Alexander, or Arnegaard, or Watford City. "If a campground pops up in one of those places, maybe we should stop," he sighed.

I was fading, too, and couldn't argue. The first few miles just south of Williston, as we crossed the Missouri River, the land had what we supposed was a badlandish cast to it, and we were encouraged. But then, after we crossed the Missouri, the land changed quickly back to prairie—wheat fields, corn fields, even a few oil fields mixed in. We kept on going, but the prairie had a level, monotonous, mesmerizing look to it. However far we were going, the distance began to *seem* great and tended to blur the land into a flat, featureless plain. But since we didn't spy any roadside campgrounds, we rolled helplessly on, the sun and my eyelids getting lower and lower as I drove.

And then, rather suddenly, we came to the edge of a rise. I pulled over; I wanted to be sure of what I was seeing. Was it a nightmare or a dream? There, far below and away, to the edge of all sight, something vast and strange had happened to the earth. Here, I understood the name "Badlands" for the first time. The faded picture I had gazed upon with curious interest in the sixth grade did not even come close.

Gouged out of the gently rolling prairie in erosive, multicolored, canyonesque strokes—the Badlands sprawled below and away, suggesting a hellish oblivion. I learned later that we were gazing upon the work of some sixty-million years' worth of erosion. Time, the elements, the meandering cuts of the Little Missouri, and an uplifting earth—had each made a contribution. It was beauty in destruction.

It was the excavation of the planet now set off by a westering sun, heightening the warm glow of earth-toned reds, golds, and oranges—sharpening and deepening the sculpted shadows. A horizontal layering of various materials was revealed in the rugged buttes and twisted declivities—sandstones, silts, clays, veins of coal, scorias. Badland scorias, I learned, were places where the lignite coal had caught fire and been baked a brick red. The reds often capped the peaks of many of the formations or spilled down from them like blood from a wound. It was easy to see that if you had been traveling across the gentler prairie grasslands by covered wagon, this sort of violent terrain abruptly interrupting one's crossing would make for a nightmarish vision. Thus, it was christened by the French explorers looking down upon it all for the first time—"mauvais terres a traverse"—bad lands to cross. But we did not have to cross them; we merely had to nestle among them for the night.

In the rising darkness as we entered the park, the place took on more mysterious aspects. We saw big-eared mule deer silhouetted against the twilight sky and heard the furtive scurryings of other wildlife, unidentified. What formations we once looked down upon now loomed darkly over us, impossible to comprehend. Otto stirred up a dusty and vaguely sulphurous odor as he carried us to our campsite.

Suddenly I was afraid of being unable to sleep. I am a frequent insomniac under the best of conditions, but here, besides the eerie atmosphere, just as we parked, a group of teenagers rowdily cut through our campsite.

"Oh, no, Don, it's Saturday night and I'll bet it's going to be noisy."

"Well, don't wake me up to tell me about it, okay?"

Nothing like the fear of not getting sleep to keep a body awake, I complained to myself. And when I closed my eyes to some distant rounds of hooting and hollering, I muttered, "Well, at least they went off to rabble-rouse at a campfire in the distance, where they wouldn't be so easily heard." Then, a while later, I added, "Or maybe they're trying to sound like a bunch of coyotes and spook us, Don?"

But Don did not answer. He had already dropped off. Anyway, I was strangely excited to be where I was, and as I pulled my sleeping bag up over my ears, I was determined not to be spooked or fooled or kept awake by anything.

Still, in the intervals of quiet, I was able to sleep only fitfully. Now and again I heard the carrying-on in chorus on the fringes of my consciousness. By some sweet grace, it was not really bothering me. When I would hear it, I would sigh and think to myself, *Ah, youth.* When the rowdiness did not always come from the same place, I figured there were rival groups of teenagers sitting round their campfires, trying to outdo each other with their lyric hoots and hollers and howls. Maybe they couldn't sleep in this strange place, either. Even half-awake I could recognize in their enthusiastic outbursts something of my own rebellious youth—and not far beneath that I also recognized something else—a kind of uncontained joy.

At last in the wee hours, Don was suddenly aroused by one of these wild choruses. He called up to me, asking me if I could hear it and wondering what I thought it was. Oddly enough, it was not until the moment Don asked that I suddenly *knew.*

"Don," I said, sitting bolt upright, "it's coyotes!"

"Really?" he asked.

"Really!" I answered, now listening as intently as I possibly could, but amazed that I continued to hear a human-like quality in the voices. Indeed, by no stretch of my imagination could I transform the sounds I was hearing into something more doglike—or into what I might have formerly imagined coyotes to sound like. I had never heard them before, but I knew what I heard. And how like a song it could be at times!—with all sorts of inadvertent, or maybe even intentional, harmonies—long, quivery tones, rising and falling and blending and holding. At their peak, the sounds were purely roisterous, like the jubilant cries of roosters trying to out-crow one another. But there were at other times more gentle sounds, riddled with tremulous wails something like the trilling of loons. And then there were short rounds of yipping and yaying that cannot be described as anything other than cheering. Once the choruses fairly surrounded us, so that I pictured on waking having to wade through coyotes to get to the camp outhouse.

Moments when it was most song-like, though, I heard in it strains of a creative, generative character. And then I felt as if I was sitting at the very spring of the earth, hearing the coyotes call all good things into existence—defying as they did any evil, downward, complex tendencies of the dark. Maybe I ought to have heard something bloodthirsty and cruel in it, but I didn't. Maybe I ought to have heard nothing in it at all—nothing, that is, to connect them with me. And yet I cannot deny it: what I heard at rock bottom, beneath it all, was…joy. A buoyant, confident, celebratory joy. The joy of camaraderie, it seemed, and all that comes of faith and love and truly sworn friendships.

Later—twice—after the sun was well up, Don and I heard the coyotes again, as if to let us know for certain we had not dreamed them. We were driving the park roads. We were silently marveling at all the fantastic scenes—near at hand and disappearing into forever down tortuous gulleys and gulches. The day before, I might have been awed by the place; now I wished only that Otto was a horse and I a roughrider. The combined effects of it all—sight, sound, and smell—were irresistibly inviting. I may have been seeing the backside of my own soul, something in me may have been nothing but wild dog or coyote, I may have been responding to something purely and primitively instinctual—but suddenly I wanted nothing better than to desert. Here—with wild turkeys gobbling, eagles circling, a marsh hawk hunting; with the company of mule deer, prairie dog, and flickertail squirrel; and with the park's herd of buffalo nursing their young, playing, butting, mounting, and rolling in the grass—I wanted to join in or join up. And I wanted to leave the journey behind. And I did my best to explain to the Walker just that.

"You can't, Fran."

"I know," I said, feeling the renewed ache of my homesickness rush in on me unchecked, but now, too, thoroughly mixed with something I didn't have any words for. "I know," I repeated softly, sadly. And finally, with defiance, "I know!"

We turned our backs on the badlands and drove out of them, back up and onto the plateau-like prairie. I bit my lip, tried to still my heart, and stared blankly ahead in the direction of Williston. I drove. The sky was ominous—a storm in every quadrant. Winds whipped at Otto, and now I had every sensation of riding a horse—Old Paint. I didn't want to leave the Badlands. I didn't even want to leave North Dakota.

North Dakota had been a friendly state—the friendliest so far, Don and I had agreed. People waved. People stopped to see if I had car trouble. People stopped to see if Don wanted a ride. People stopped to see if I wanted a ride on my walks to meet Don. Sometimes Don couldn't help getting impatient because it seemed as if he could spend all his time chatting beside the road if he wanted. Once, Thelma, a waitress at an American Legion Club where Don and I had eaten dinner, drove out two days later with her family, simply to see how far the Walker had gotten and to wave at him on the road. North Dakota had been a special place, and I didn't really expect Montana could be the same. For one thing, Montana wouldn't have David in it.

Chapter 24

Yippee Yi Yo Ki Yay

Up until the last inch of North Dakota, I felt somehow that we were being lifted. I thought it could have been the humid air drying out, or the cooler evenings coming on, or learning the meadowlark's song. It was not until we consulted the map concerning the elevations that we realized that from Grand Forks to Williston, Don had climbed over a thousand feet in elevation. We had been lifted.

At the border between Montana and North Dakota I waited for the Walker. Nearby stood a nightclub-bar sort of place, and across from it some dilapidated corrals and a few broken bleachers. Nothing else. Route 2 was roller-coaster hilly here, and I could watch the road undulating westward a long way into Montana like a rippled whip. Since there wasn't anything for miles in either direction, I thought finding this roadhouse was strange. I didn't want to park too near it. It looked busy, with an odd assortment of leather-jacketed motorcyclists and men in cowboy hats and boots coming and going—mostly coming. It was late in the day. I wondered if there wasn't a phone around, but I was afraid to go inside and ask.

And then finally I did. A rough-looking old woman sat at a kind of lectern, checking IDs in the vestibule. A lot of men's voices and loud music blared behind her in what seemed a great, smoky, cavernous, Christmas-tree-lighted darkness. I didn't want to look in. I could hear the racking of ceramic balls at pool tables and also the endlessly repetitive noises of video game machines. I asked about a phone, and the old woman pointed deeper in among the flashing glitter of the videos. I asked if it would be okay for me to use it, and when she responded with a soft note of concern and even kindliness, I was reassured and relieved. I had to plug an ear to screen out the noise in order to talk; I hoped my mom would not get wind of the barroom atmosphere when I got her on the phone.

I called my mother at least three times a week. She was closely following our adventure from a nursing home in St. Louis, Missouri. Growing up, it was an often-stated rule that we had better call home to report on our whereabouts and doings. "I don't care if you're in Hong Kong—don't forget to call home," Mom would say. The rule still applied, even if I was past the age of forty. But I also knew my mother's knowledge of our whereabouts on the journey, and the prayers she sent out daily were important to our efforts. It always did me some good to connect with her.

After I talked with my mom, I talked with David. For a while, in the interior darkness I completely lost track of where I was. And it did help to talk, however briefly, to that other world—the world in place. But afterward, I began feeling out of sorts with myself again.

When Don caught up, he also used the phone. Then I took his picture at the border—entering Big Sky Country.

Big sky? Who says? Miles and miles back at a rest area in the White Earth River Valley of North Dakota, I talked with a Native North Dakotan and asked him how the sky could possibly get any bigger in Montana than it was at that moment right over our heads open to every horizon in every direction as far as we both could see. The man's answer surprised me. He said that he didn't know how it could, but it did.

So now Don couldn't help posing at the border, stretching his arms wide and saying, "See, it does get bigger!" But I didn't see it yet. Wouldn't see it yet: I hadn't been born in the "show me" state of Missouri for nothing. Don just laughed at me.

Meanwhile, Don had walked into the Mountain Time Zone. I corrected the watch on my wrist but again left Otto on home time. We camped within moments of a following storm.

"Just in time," Don said, slamming Otto's sliding door. "Did you see what was coming?" A short while later lightning, thunder, and rain all struck at once. We'd had a couple of bad storms at night in North Dakota, but only a little rain by day. I wondered what sort of omen this weather might mean for Montana.

"Nine more days," Don announced.

"What do you mean, nine more days?"

"Countdown to vacation. Nine more days until we take a break from this road life. Wherever we are in nine days, we'll stop and drive the rest of the way to Hayden Lake for the reunion."

"Doesn't sound bad," I said, without much enthusiasm, knowing how much like a year each day could be.

"Hey, did you see the marker back there at the border?" Don asked.

"You mean the little green one that said 667?"

"Yeah," Don said, popping open a jar of spaghetti and rummaging in the drawer for a spoon. "That's 667 miles to cross Montana on Route 2. The second marker said 666."

"You're kidding. The miles are going to be counted down for you one by one by one? Won't it seem to take forever?"

"I hope not, but it might. Anyway, with the new time, tonight we get an extra hour of sleep. Do you think we'll hear coyotes?"

"I don't know." I couldn't really imagine hearing coyotes where we were now. I was still feeling disconnected, as if I had missed some golden, once-in-a-lifetime opportunity back there in the Badlands. I couldn't explain myself, but I felt as if I could have been in place in the Badlands, whereas now I was but a dog in prairie dog town, a mule among mule deer.

"Oh—here's some more stuff." And Don pulled out a five-eighths-inch wrench, a golf ball, and two dimes.

"Oh, boy," I said, reaching for a knife to butter a piece of bread. And then I laughed—a kind of crazy, wild coyote laugh. Maybe I'll sing with them yet, I thought—yippee yi yo ki yay!

Chapter 25

Home Cafe

From the very first, Montana was something rugged and unruly, something western, something big—a wild horse of a state. The land, revealing a cantankerous bent to it, did not want to be reined in. Thus, as we headed west, the prairie become the plains—the Great Plains. Farms became huge, sprawling ranches, and the words "neat" and "trim" no longer quite fit. The plow had been at work here, too, but more and more there were places that defied the plow. Even the road changed.

Across North Dakota Route 2 had been wide and mostly four-lane, though it was not an interstate nor heavily traveled. In Montana the road withered to two lanes with meager margins. Crossing Indian reservations in the state, the road shriveled further still, and in places had no margins for the Walker to hike at all. What did grace Montana highways were plantings of white crosses wherever a traffic accident had occurred and taken life—one little white cross for every fatality. Some places the crosses stood several deep in sobering testimony. We were glad the traffic was sparse, but when trucks did roar by the Walker, they seemed to take up the whole road, so that Don had to keep alert to the danger of them. Truckers would hardly be expecting to come upon a pedestrian along the long, lonesome stretches of the highway, and Don did not want to have a little white cross raised in his honor.

Sometimes the railroad, which had continued to accompany us, seemed busier than the road. Don took to counting railroad cars for a pastime. We both daydreamed about where the trains were headed, or, in moments of frustration, how to hop one and finally get somewhere. Who really cared where?

Along with the rougher road came a rougher road routine. The grubbiness factor set in. Long gone were the once-frequent swimming holes; long gone was the tidy prairie town offering swimming pool or campground shower. What we had for much of Montana was our own water supply and a bucket. And though the days could be hot, dry, and dusty—still climbing into the nineties—the evenings cooled down rapidly. Nights could be downright cold; mornings, too. It could easily happen that we lost our longing for a wash entirely when it meant ice-cold water out of a bucket in a chill wind.

What was good about all this was that it was different and surprising. The land was taking weird turns. In places it began to seem virtually uncontainable and exactly matched all those wordless yearnings of the human heart that never seem containable, either. Early in Montana I wrote, "So far the sky has not stretched to any bigger dimensions, I don't think—but I am keeping an eye on it anyway, just in case it begins to. The lands are rangier, the wheat harvest here mostly done—the wheat stubble a shining white-gold under bright sun, a ruddy gold under cloud. There are odd gangly hills in view off in the distance everywhere, rich with muted colors of the rainbow—reds, silvery greens, a smoky blue-purple, every hue of brown; there are occasional windrows; here and there a tree standing alone—and overall an ever-deepening quiet. I guess I really, really like the quiet. Even the great empty spaces seem good to me, as if there is plenty of room to dance and run and shout, even if I have nothing at the moment to dance and run and shout about."

But looking out over a scrubbier land where the ground often cracked from the dryness; where it sometimes sported prickly pear, yucca, and cactus buttons; and where a gust of wind or a herd of horses swept over the range, raising clouds of dust under a baking sun—we could not understand one thing: Why had we not left the mosquitoes behind? Where did they breed now? In the dust?

Don was so excited about the prospects of vacation that his first full day in Montana he put in a record thirty-eight miles. He was thinking that maybe the mosquitoes he'd met that day were but strays from North Dakota. But by the end of the third day's walk in Montana, Don complained with feeling about the near-constant company of these pests at times. "I'm afraid they must be full-fledged Montana natives by now," he said. "Damn!"

By week's end I was feeling my own discouragements. Some of the towns we'd been through looked exactly like they'd blown down over night and then hastily pasted up again that morning. Plains architecture, sturdy as it might have been, seemed all-too-often nothing but bad variations on the theme of "shack." Shacks themselves, abandoned here and there in the middle of some vast, windy expanse, endured. I was learning not to count on cafes, but cups of tea were spacing themselves days apart. I would have done better tracking down alcohol, since if a town had nothing else in these parts, it usually had a bar. Who knows, maybe some of the bars had tea. It's just that the bars were nearly always windowless and uninviting, looking more like garages or storage sheds. I preferred no tea at all to drinking it in a dark hole. And going on five days without a shower? Our only glimpse of water a distant view of the inaccessible Missouri River or an infrequent muddy tributary crossing our path? It could begin to get to a body.

We weren't sure about the people yet, either. We hadn't really seen many. What we saw was seemingly divided up between cowboys and Indians. More than once had we been warned against camping roadside on the reservations, though we never had any real trouble when we did. I suspected that the Indians themselves might have had their own warnings about traveling through cowboy territory. There just seemed to be a whiff of suspicion in the air, and whether it was hanging about us as Easterners or them as Westerners was hard to say, at first.

Outside Wolf Point on the Fort Peck Indian Reservation a roadside marker read, "A party of trappers poisoned several hundred wolves one winter, hauled the frozen carcasses in and stacked them up until spring for skinning. It taught the varmints a lesson. No one in Wolf

Point has been bothered by a wolf at the door since." I wasn't sure how to take this message. Was it a kind of joke? Or was it literally true? Somehow the specter of several hundred wolf carcasses stinking and thawing under the spring sun and getting skinned at once was so fierce that whatever else it did, it made me cautious. Wayside trash, broken bottles, abandoned vehicles—on the welcome mat of a town—did, too.

It was late in the day on August 19 when we rolled into Nashua, Montana. The day had been discouraging, with mosquitoes and heat. We were looking to cheer ourselves up with phone calls at the very least—maybe even get a sandwich someplace or a tip on where to camp. Things didn't look hopeful. Nashua showed so little sign of prosperity, we thought it might have shut down long ago. Only Route 2 was paved. When we happened upon a cafe, however, and when we realized we were just in time to get something before it closed, we easily forgave the town its shabby appearance.

Home Cafe. It had a nice ring. It had a rare convenience, too—a pay phone in a private anteroom between the bar and the cafe. Privacy was a luxury. Don ordered us some sandwiches, we took turns on the phone, and then we ate. I liked the cafe. It was clean, the food was wholesome and good, the decor a comfortably old-fashioned make-do, nothing false or pretentious.

We must have been the only strangers in the place (or so it seemed), because we weren't there long before we noticed that the entire restaurant was openly engaged in a single conversation from separated booths and tables. The lone waitress was part of it, too, as was the cook, who could not be seen but who chimed in loudly now and then from the back. For a while the subject was AIDS. But when this had gone on for some time, getting more and more cheerless, and when the discussion seemed on the verge of turning into argument, someone volunteered, "Well, hell, let's get on to something else now; guess we about talked that subject out."

I forget the next topic because Don and I started mumbling discreetly back and forth among ourselves about whether we might not ask someone in the cafe about where we could camp. People were so open and friendly to one another, we were sure to get help.

But feeling shy, neither one of us had the nerve to break into the *big* conversation.

Eventually I went up to the cash register in the back to pay the bill, feeling a mite conspicuous as I did. While I was counting out the money, I asked the waitress (in the lowest voice I could possibly muster and still be heard) whether she might know of a place close by where someone could camp. But what I'd been dreading and trying to avoid happened anyway.

"Anybody know of a place hereabouts where these folks can camp?" she bellowed out to the entire assembly.

After an awkward hush, Don, somewhat in shock, jumped in to explain. "You see, I'm on this walk about the country. I've walked all the way from Vermont so far, and we have this Volkswagen camper, and we were just wondering what the rules were about where you can park it and all? I mean, we wouldn't want to go breaking any laws."

To this, a man blurted out, "Why you could camp in the middle of the street out there and nobody'd bother about you or care!" This brought a burst of laughter, general agreement, and a round of joking side comments.

Meanwhile, Don got up and walked back to the cash register to see if I was taking care of the tip. Someone must have gotten a good whiff of him as he did, because the next thing we heard was, "Bet you could use a shower after all that walking!" And when the laughter over this comment died down, Don turned to face everyone and said, "Sure could." And laughter convulsed the place again.

And then to our rescue came Smokey and Vivian Stover, who announced before all present that we were mighty welcome to use their shower, and that they'd be pleased for us to camp in their side yard, too, if we wanted, 'cuz they were ready to be headin' out and we could just follow along right after. Which, after a few embarrassed thanks, was exactly what we did.

Chapter 26

This Featherbed of Civilization

The Stovers' place, a stone's throw from Home Cafe, turned out to be next to the railroad tracks. Their house looked to be in the midst of some repair, inside and out. Vivian apologized for the mess when we went inside, saying she'd been all out, what with canning and putting up vegetables. Smokey plopped down a huge, plastic garbage bag full of green beans that came up to the height of the kitchen table, saying they'd just come from a friend's where they had been picking beans before stopping at Home Cafe for a cup of coffee.

Vivian was a handsome, slim, fifty-ish woman, neat in her jeans and friendly, outgoing, and warm in her manner. Smokey, about the same age, was softer spoken, more reserved, but warm too and most interested in Don and his walk. Though begrimed with the day's dust from working road construction on Route 2, Smokey did not take to the shower ahead of us. He politely insisted we go first.

Don and I took our turns in the shower, which was about three feet from the kitchen table we all sat around. We used our hosts' soap, towels, and shampoo at their insistence. The conversation never flagged in the meantime. Smokey talked about being born across the street (which had never yet been paved), in a little house we could see from their side porch. He had traveled some, he said (Alaska, Texas), but most of his life he'd spent right there in Nashua. He'd been working road construction since he was seventeen.

Vivian showed us pictures of their grandchildren—one, a cute five- year-old who had recently been diagnosed as diabetic. Vivian also gave me some seeds of the angel trumpet vine I had admired in full and glorious bloom on their doorstep. These blossoms were the biggest version of a morning glory I had ever seen, and were distinctly fragrant. The seeds were taken fresh from the vine, and Vivian carefully explained how to dry them, when to plant, and what sort of conditions would be best for optimum growth.

And then, one of us, I can't recall whom, got up the nerve to ask about the mosquitoes. Smokey glanced at Vivian and they both smiled, looking a bit embarrassed. "Don't worry 'bout mosquitoes, Don," Smokey said, blowing a stream of cigarette smoke straight up into the air. "You ain't seen the worst of them things yet. There's a place you're still comin' to that's been named the mosquito capital of the world—Saco, Montana—and by none other than the National Geographic Society."

The night in the Stovers' yard was not a particularly restful one, and it wasn't just the thought of the mosquitoes getting worse that bothered us. What roared by in the night on the railroad tracks came a little too close for comfort. Smokey apologized for the noise when Don caught up to him later that day constructing on Route 2. "Never heard so many blasted trains in one night!" he said. "Guess I've gotten used to 'em, but thinkin' 'bout you all camped outside, you can bet I heard those damn trains all night long."

Hitting Home Cafe again for breakfast, we were surprised by more welcome Montana hospitality. Margaret Rees, who was cooking that morning and who owned the place, came out to say hello to us. She said she was about to offer us her yard as a campsite the night before when the Stovers beat her to it. To make up for this, she gave us a dozen homemade rolls for the road. She also chatted at length about her niece living in Vermont—at which mention my heart took a sudden leap. Margaret said she'd never been there herself, but she went on to give the place a fair description based on her niece's letters. Long after Margaret went back to the kitchen and us to the road, her words hung in the air about me with the good smell of home—1,898 miles from Nashua—and made me realize afresh how far away it really was.

If I closed my eyes, I could picture a covert of deep, bright greens; leafy shadows; a clear mountain stream dashing over boulders; a high, boggy meadow trimmed with ferns and dark, blue-purple gentians. At the same time, I knew, in my mental account of best-loved places at home, what the hidden hazards were—when the mosquitoes were the worst, where grew the poison ivy and the thorny thickets, what kind of snakes might surprise and what kind of weather. I knew what sort of rarer wildlife I might come upon, too, if I was lucky.

When I opened my eyes, the scene they fell upon might have made me guess "Montana" even if it had not been a living portrait. But I had never really thought what would compose the smaller details of such a picture, or ever guessed there was anything to disturb the peace in the great, wide-open emptiness carved out of the earth surrounding some barren, brown butte.

If one speeds through an area at seventy M.P.H., it might as well be a photograph a person's looking at out there, in terms of what can bite, sting, or harass. A photograph can tell something about what a place looks like, but it cannot tell what it *feels* like to be in that place. In *Coming into The Country*, John McPhee writes, "There is no substitute for being on the ground, for experiencing a landscape close at hand, for feeling the earth underfoot." Robert Louis Stevenson put it another way in *Travels with a Donkey*: "The great affair is to move; to feel the needs and hitches of our life more nearly; to come down off this featherbed of civilization and find the globe granite underfoot and strewn with cutting flints."

In many respects, this land was as new to us as to the first explorers. We did not live with the same uncertainties as Captains Meriwether Lewis and William Clark, who passed this way not even two hundred years before, and after whom Route 2 (as well as some other Montana highways) was designated a Lewis and Clark Trail. The hazards had surely changed since the early 1800s, yet to us the unknown of each day seemed as great. Don liked to fancy himself a latter-day Lewis and Clark and I his sometime scout and trusty bird woman, Sacagawea.

"Fran, Fran—get out quick! What in the world is crawling all over Otto? I could see it a hundred yards off!" Don yelled, when he caught up to me late one day west of Glasgow, Montana.

"I don't know, Don, what *is* all over Otto?" I yelled back, flinging down my notebooks, opening Otto's sliding door, and leaping out.

"Well, look!" Don pointed. And there I could see that, unbeknownst to me, Otto's white vinyl roof had been darkened several shades by being completely covered over and crawling with flying ants. The rest of Otto was, too, but where he was painted brown, it was much less obvious. When I saw some of these beasts fly inside, I slammed shut the door. I looked around. There wasn't a green plant or a drop of water visible for miles. Where did these creatures come from?

"We can't stay here. I'll skip my break. Get back in and try to blast them off. Drive like hell down the road a few miles. I'll catch up later. We can camp at the next stop, but get rid of the ants! Go, Fran, go!"

I jumped at the command and fairly flew into the driver's seat. I swatted ants crawling up the inside of Otto's windshield and across my forehead as I galloped down the trail at breakneck speed, praying all the while to leave the swarming horde behind. I itched all over just thinking about poor Otto crawling with ants. Then, too, I recalled the Lake Superior flies, and a bat that had come out of nowhere and had gotten into Otto back in Solway, Minnesota. Flies, bats, ants—what next? World-famous mosquitoes, apparently, if Smokey Stover knew what he was talking about. Well, at the moment anyway, I preferred those.

At supper, Don made a couple of inspections of Otto to be certain the ants were not with us, but he didn't stay out for long because of the mosquitoes. A short while later, our minds were blessedly relieved of such worries by spectacles far away but on both sides of us.

The hot, glaring clarity of the day was ending and the sky was growing big with cloud. To the west, the sun was sinking, painting all manner of reds and yellows about the atmosphere. When the sun dropped out of sight, it shot off crimson signal flares that were answered in the east by a march of black thunderstorms.

Don and I watched the strange phenomenon of ball lightning roll erratically about between the far-off storms and seem to explode in places, as if the fiery ball of electricity had gone tumbling down a precipitous butte and broken open. Following this was a long calm, and then in the wee hours a windstorm hit.

I was yet awake—bothered by allergies to the wind-born dust, wheat chaff, and pollen (from the giant ragweed commonly growing along the roads). I had been writing by flashlight and combing through field guides for hours. I was rather cheered, though, by something I came across in one of my bird books, which I couldn't wait to tell Don.

I had looked up nighthawks. Much of my life, I knew nighthawks to be at home in Midwestern and Eastern cities, happily nesting on the flat-topped buildings and hawking after the civilized insects of the realm. I was surprised to hear them at night on the plains. I somehow hadn't figured a bird could be at home in such drastically different habitats. What did my heart good was to read that a stomach analysis of two nighthawks showed that one had sucked up more than five hundred mosquitoes in a day, while the other had fattened on 2,175 flying ants!

I also read about Swainson's hawk, a bird that Don and I had both seen hunting on foot in the wheat stubble, or perched so low to the ground I often mistook it for the stump of a tree. According to the book, this large western hawk thrived mostly on grasshoppers— another insect we'd noticed in abundance. Along some stretches, every step Don took scattered grasshoppers like a foot-splash in a mud puddle. I often heard their hard-shelled bodies rebounding off of Otto as I drove.

Well, I was learning. The sometimes deceptively barren-looking sweep of the plains was plainly not so barren, however well swept. And I knew then that I would never again look at western vistas and imagine them empty.

Chapter 27

Ding, Ding, Ding, Ding, Ding!

For the first hundred miles west into Montana, Don followed alongside the Missouri River. Though we seldom had a view of it, we knew it was never more than a few miles off. At Nashua we left the wide Missouri to keep company with the Milk River. A roadside marker described this stream as being "crooked as a dog's hind leg." Only a few yards wide at most points, the Milk had its source far away in the Rocky Mountains, where we were headed, and had been given its name by Meriwether Lewis, who wrote in his journal, "the water has a peculiar whiteness, such as might be produced by a tablespoon full of milk in a dish of tea." Green tea, I would write in my own journal, since where I first came upon it, it was a lovely, limey shade of milky green. It was also bank full, icy cold, and had a strong current that I gauged by dangling a leg in it for a moment.

Near this watercourse, Lewis had written about seeing *vast* quantities of game—buffalo, elk, deer, antelope, beavers, geese, ducks, and swans—as well as their predators—fox, wolf, coyote, and bear. We were more likely to see vast quantities of cattle or even sheep, where the land wasn't taken up by wheat or immense hayfields of alfalfa and the native bluejoint grass.

But east of Hinsdale, I pulled over to spy on a shallow, weedy backwater of the Milk River. Something huge and white had caught my eye. Don had mentioned seeing some big, white birds soaring above him the day before, though he couldn't tell what they were. Now I had my field glasses trained on them. Pelicans? In Montana?

I recalled the spectacular diving abilities of the brown pelican and felt certain that if these white pelicans dove with the same force into this shallow slough, they would bury themselves in the muck. But as long as I watched, I never saw the white pelicans dive to get their prey. They fed as a group, somewhat in formation, driving and corralling the fish before them into the shallows. Cowboy pelicans. When they got tired of this, they took off together with supreme grace and sailed out of my sight with scarcely a wing beat.

After they were gone I turned my attention to some other large birds that I also associated with the sea—double-crested cormorants. A half dozen of these birds were perched on some low branches sticking above the water, while others swam about with their long bills angled haughtily upwards, showing off their bright-orange throat pouches, or sometimes disappearing underwater for a time to fish. When they wanted to join their fellows on the perch, they would clamber onto the branches and then stand there for a while with their great, dark wings held open like heavy capes to dry in the wind and sun. I also saw terns, mallards, pintails, coots, killdeer, miscellaneous flocking blackbirds, and a nesting yellow warbler. Montana was surprising. It had certainly not lost all its game.

In Hinsdale—a fine-looking Montana town—I got mail. Earlier in the week, I'd gotten mail in Glasgow, another fine-looking Montana town. Probably anywhere I was picking up mail was going to look the better for it. Still, on the surface anyway, Hinsdale and Glasgow had more to them besides the typical quota of gas station and bar—like school, church, bank, motel, restaurant, maybe even a park.

Mostly, though, Don walked through a town in such short order there was little more to get from it than a vague impression. If we camped near a town for the night, the impression was etched more deeply and sometimes indelibly. Saco, Montana, was destined to be one of the latter.

When I drove up to Saco at the end of the day on August 21, I thought it had a roguish appearance. The street front facing Route

2, opposite the railroad tracks, looked like the smile of an old man who'd lost half his teeth—with its, empty, falling-down, boarded-up storefronts.

I parked off Route 2 in an area set aside for travelers. I looked into the empty building next door to Otto and found evidence that Saco had seen better days. An out-of-date, mouse-nibbled brochure I picked up off the filthy floor boasted free use of showers and gas stoves to tourists passing through—in the very same ramshackle building I was standing in. All I found was a working toilet, at which I did not turn up my nose. The brochure also showed a picture of a one-room schoolhouse that had then recently been restored to commemorate the early schooling of news commentator Chet Huntley. (I later found this school on a drive about town, in need of restoration yet again.)

I also discovered among the overgrowth behind the tourist rest, where I had parked, a Charles M. Russell Memorial. On a stone was engraved a painting of this artist and the words, "Loop and Swift Horses are Surer than Lead."The scene depicted the killing of a grizzly in the Larb Hills south of Saco—by cowpokes wielding jackknife and lasso alone. It may well have been the last grizzly in the area, a bear once commonly at home on the plains, on which Meriwether Lewis reported extensively in his journal.

When Don ended his thirty-five-mile day, we decided to camp where we were for the night. Besides the convenience of a bathroom, this was *the* designated place for travelers. We thought camping anywhere else might be asking for trouble. We might have done better to ask for trouble.

Being sandwiched, by mere inches, between Route 2 and the railroad tracks proved to be even less fun than our night at the Stovers'. Trucks roared by at high speeds on one side of us, trains on the other. And since a road crossed the railroad tracks only a few feet away, every time a train came crashing down upon us, we had the ding-ding-ding-ding-ding in our ears warning of its approach, as well as the shrieking whistle of the train itself. Each time, I was sure we were going to be mowed down and obliterated. And each time, when we had been spared by a hair's breadth, Otto seemed to bounce and tremble in the train's wake well after the contraption had thundered off into the distance.

But the good thing about the trains and trucks was their ability to drown out other disturbances—the least of which was the incessant barking of dogs; the worst of which was Jake's Bar across from us on Route 2. Nothing like the cacophony of drunken patrons letting loose on a Friday night. It sounded no better than hell-raising at a rock concert interrupted by quieter brawls. When the bar closed down at five A.M., loud conversations and blustering arguments spilled out into the street. Only after that was it quiet enough to be bothered by the racket from someone's TV.

The next morning, Don, who had gotten little more sleep than I, set out to hike his two-thousandth mile. I braved the forbidding exterior of O'Brien's Bar-Cafe for a hot cup of tea. The word "cafe" gave me courage.

I ended up chatting with a young couple in the next booth who had a baby in tow. I was surprised to learn that these nice folks had recently moved back to Saco after living for a time in Oregon. They said Oregon was too crowded for their tastes and that they didn't like the hemmed-in feeling of the landscape there. They missed Saco and their families too.

For a moment, while listening to these intelligent, educated, and interesting people, who had chosen the mosquito capital of the world for their home, I was given a vision of the good life where I had snobbishly thought it could not exist.

What I saw most clearly of all was that the people in these parts had a magnificent share of the world's room. I could see it was a kind of luxury—one I, too, could acquire a taste for. Yet it was working its way into me far deeper than that and expanding my heart in a way I would not really appreciate until much later.

Chapter 28

How Can You Stand It?

Whenever the Walker took his breaks these days, he smeared himself liberally with sunscreen and insect repellent. But then, in spite of the heat, he began covering up more, as well. The repellent had a way of wearing thin in a good sweat. It was unpleasant to have to wear so much repellent—the sticky feel of it on the skin being as bad as the stink. I had been keeping to the confines of Otto more than usual, but to the eye alone, it was not always easy to tell that the bugs were bad. A few days' hike from Saco, I could stand being cooped up no longer.

It was my favorite time for a walk, late in the day, and the minute I got out I was exhilarated to be part of the landscape and out under the as-yet-to-be-acknowledged Big Sky. I tied my sweatshirt about my waist after determining there were no great swarms of mosquitoes. A light breeze blew against me as I set my pace for a good, long walk. I estimated the Walker to be about six miles off. Now and then I heard the whine of a lone attacker, but it was nothing to worry about—I thought.

An hour later, when Don saw me coming, he could not believe his eyes. I could tell he was greatly agitated about something, even before I got within shouting distance. Finally I heard.

"How can you stand it?" he yelled.

"Stand what?" I yelled back.

"The mosquitoes, you idiot!"

"What mosquitoes?" I laughed.

But that was my last laugh, because by then Don and I had met, and the second I had the breeze at my back and walked in the same direction as Don, I confronted the huge cloud of mosquitoes that had been following behind me. And now they were all over me, because the way the wind was blowing, they were protected from it once I had turned around. They were in my nose, my ears, my eyes, even my mouth when I tried to speak. I untied my sweatshirt and whipped it on, trying to walk as fast as I could as I did. I pulled a bandanna out of my pocket, knotted one end to give it weight, and began thrashing myself and the air about me to ward off the horde.

Don laughed and tossed me some bug repellent from his fanny pack.

"No wonder you're all covered up!" I yelled, wishing I had had more sense than to wear shorts.

Don laughed again. But that was *his* last laugh. He had mistakenly assumed he would be ending his day in another ten minutes. He was not happy to learn that Otto was probably a good hour's walk away.

The day cooled and the mosquito attack intensified as we hurried along. The stinging sensation of my knotted bandanna was somehow a comfort over the attacking mosquitoes. Unlike other mosquitoes we had met, these did not drift lazily about, exploring bodily opportunities, or land and then creep sneakily to a place vulnerable and unprotected. These creatures hurled themselves at a body, stingers ready, like speeding darts.

"See why I call them attack mosquitoes?" Don yelled to me.

"Yeah," I yelled back. "I guess I never really appreciated how bad it can be! They're driving me mad. If there was any traffic on this road, I think I'd offer myself up to it. Blagh!" I choked when a mosquito zinged itself down my throat. Better to keep the mouth shut.

Meanwhile, the sweat poured off me, effectively nullifying the power of the repellent, so that unless I came near to scoring a direct hit when swatting, the mosquitoes clung happily to my person. I wore hundreds on each leg, not to mention everywhere else. So did the Walker.

When I sighted Otto, I ran ahead so I could unlock the door, climb in the driver's side, and make way for Don. We dared not use the sliding door, for fear of sucking in the multitudes with us. We sat inside Otto, swatting mosquitoes a long time anyway. My legs were bloody with their squashed bodies.

And that wasn't the end of it. Neither one of us could think of eating or crawling into bed until we had washed the sticky repellent off. There was only one way to do that. If anyone had happened along while we took turns outside with bucket and flailing wash cloth, they could have had themselves a good laugh. I felt as if I might have been inventing a new dance when it was my turn to be out. Yet bathing was not as hazardous as going to the bathroom—where one had to hold still. Ah, misery!

I did not wish that night to end. With the beasts on the outside only, and a delicious breeze penetrating Otto without them, and the railroad tracks comfortably far off—I wanted to sleep forever and forget the journey. When I heard the coyotes calling in the wee hours, I was in no danger of joining up. I detected a complaining tone in their voices, and I was sure I knew what it was all about.

Chapter 29

So This Is the Big Sky

Some mornings in Montana broke without so much as a sigh of wind. Occasionally a mist hung in the air, as if to allow the mosquitoes a new medium in which to multiply. At such times Don dressed accordingly, adding mittens and a mosquito headnet to his rainsuit coverup. However hot and uncomfortable it was going to be in such an outfit, I knew how desperate Don had to be feeling to wear it.

"If this keeps up much longer," he said one muggy, mosquitoey morning, with a good deal of discouragement in his voice, "well, I don't know...I guess I never thought it was going to be like this." I watched the Walker disappear into the drizzly distance. He looked like an astronaut dressed for a moon landing.

By the time Don made Chinook, Montana, late in the day on August 24, the rain was coming down cold and hard. We drove around the outskirts, looking for a place to camp. We finally came upon a muddy, soggy, parklike area near a water-treatment plant beside the Milk River. Don wanted to knock at the plant and ask permission. I thought it hardly worth the trouble, since darkness was about to descend and Don was already soaked to the skin.

But Don's scouting paid off. Though no one answered his knock, he discovered two bathrooms with doors to the outside that were open—each with its own hot shower and room heater as well! God bless the Chinook Water Treatment Plant.

"Tomorrow's the day," Don called down over the drubbing of the falling rain later that night.

"I know," I said. "Gosh, this rain reminds me of home. I guess we've been pretty darn lucky as far as the weather goes. Checking my notes, I have to go all the way back to Michigan to find a cold, drenching rain by day."

"You know, I'm quitting at Havre tomorrow, Fran. That's only a twenty-two mile day. I want to have time to get a haircut so I'm not so scroungey-looking when we get to Hayden Lake. No more walking, after Havre, for six glorious days, anyway. It's been fifty-nine days since that break I took with Patty in Ottawa."

"That's amazing," I said. "I wonder if it's any sort of a record. I mean, sixty-eight days walking 2,082 miles!"

"Well, it's a record for me and that's enough. Could be a record number of miles through mosquitoes, more likely. Talked to a rancher today who stopped to say hello—he was *bragging* about the mosquitoes! This part of Montana has two seasons, he said, mosquitoes and winter. He said he had even been attacked in winter once, by a horde hiding out in his cellar. Said he'd heard tell of such things as sunbathing and picnics, but not in these parts."

"Yeah, I talked to a rancher today, too. He pulled alongside of me parked on his land and wondered if I had car trouble. I found out that the wheat harvest is poor due to lack of rain. He said that people have had to truck in drinking water since 1926, thanks to chronic water shortages. When I asked him how the mosquitoes managed, he said they had no trouble breeding in the gumbo hay flats watered by irrigation from the Milk River. Did you see those haystacks back there piled three or four stories high?"

"Yeah, but did you hear the *good* news, Fran? The other side of Havre, when we get out of the Milk River rut, we should start leaving the mosquitoes behind."

"It's about time. I thought you were pretty darn close to quitting The Walk forever this morning when you set out."

"I was," Don confessed. "I really was. The break is coming at a good time."

To get from Havre, Montana, to Hayden Lake, Idaho, we were going by way of Great Falls, Montana. In Great Falls we had signed Otto on for a thorough check-up and valve adjustment, something he needed since we had replaced his old jury-rigged engine with a rebuilt one before heading out on the journey. It was on the 110-mile ride from Havre to Great Falls that I finally made up my mind about Montana's Big Sky.

Just to be driving south after two months of driving west was a welcome change, not to mention going more than eight miles at a hop. But I was in no hurry; the drive was something from the very beginning—something disconcerting.

Our relation to the land seemed to change by the mile—now we were in the middle of something, now at the edge, now somehow above. The broad terrain had unexpected warpings to it. Small mountain ranges sat on pedestals in the distance; or unusual, gargantuan limbs of earth thrust themselves into the panorama as if struggling to get free of the planet.

The road skirted the Missouri River, and for a moment we had a glimpse of another world in another realm. I was taken aback by the rugged valley the river cut—the dramatic depth and distance of it. Then, near Fort Benton, we came upon another view of this river's cutting.

From the high, brown, wintry-looking plains on the horizontal, we could see to a shining river winding among soft folds of foliage— blue-green and misty, studded with the trappings of a toy town. But the drop between us was so abrupt—as if from table to floor—that I could not fathom a connecting road between. It seemed more appropriate, had we been going down into Fort Benton, to land Otto like a plane.

And, at times, Otto might as well have been a plane I was piloting, for the earth was not always palpably beneath us: Now the land swept round us broad, blonde, and grassy, dotted with antelope; now it fell away in striking stripes—long, ribboned swatches of planted wheat, alternating with equal ribbons of dark, fallow earth—until it ran into the strange eruption of some weirdly beautiful butte; now it slipped the very curve of the planet, careening into our path, rolling us helplessly off the edge of it and into the Big Sky. Even the bits of town we flew through seemed to have a tentative hold, as if another rise and rumpling of the earth would easily and quickly shake itself free of any mere house-riders hoping to hang on.

"So this is the Big Sky," I wrote in my journal later, "a place where the planet makes light of a body, tosses you up into it, tilts you over onto it, or slides out from under you to leave you hanging—searching wildly for an anchor somewhere to fix yourself to the earth once more. It's dizzying."

The runway we landed on, which brought us to earth again, rolled away before us from the high plains going down, down, down. I had to wonder as we came upon Great Falls whether the town got its name, not from the great falls on the Missouri River it sat below, but from the manner in which the earth itself seemed to fall away before us as we approached. And then, all at once, Otto was a van again and the city we drove about was as thickly treed and finely cultivated as cities anywhere. Night followed so closely behind us, we drove straight to the Volkswagen dealership and camped there. We would at least be first in line in the morning; and we were too tired to look elsewhere.

Part Four

SEPTEMBER

Montana, Idaho, Washington

Chapter 30

The Bet

"Now it is a strange thing," Tolkien wrote in *The Hobbit*, "but things that are good to have and days that are good to spend are soon told about, and not much to listen to, while things that are uncomfortable, palpitating, and even gruesome, may make a good tale, and take a deal of telling anyway." And so it was with us on our days away from The Walk, though the six-day vacation was a break in routine more than it was a rest.

For one thing, the Walker dove into all the activities offered at Hayden Lake like a fish released from the hook. He swam, water-skied, windsurfed, mountain-biked, played basketball, and rowed. Apparently Don didn't need a rest so much as a change of activity. For another thing, the better part of four of those days was taken up with traveling to and from Havre. Only two full days of the break were days spent entirely at Hayden Lake with friends. We might well have had an additional day but for some bad luck delaying our arrival there.

Something went wrong with Otto's check-up in Great Falls. Instead of becoming more fit for the road and the winding drive to Idaho through the Rockies, he began losing oil climbing the Continental Divide. We easily could have ended up driving Otto until he lost all his oil and his engine blew, if Don hadn't routinely checked his oil when we stopped for gas—a mere 150 miles beyond the VW place in Great Falls. At that stop, Otto proved to be a full two quarts low after hardly losing a single drop of oil the entire trip previous. It took two different mechanics at two different garages in Missoula to repair the leak, though it took a lot longer than that for me to regain confidence that Otto was fully himself again.

We returned to Havre and The Walk from Hayden Lake via a different, more northerly route. We saw more of Montana by doing this, and we saw more of the Rockies. Our appetite for these mountains had already been whetted by breathing the rarified air of them and by tasting the mystery of a cutting road working its way in among the long evergreen shadows and through the high, windy passes.

Yet this mountain preview did not prepare us for Glacier National Park. We came upon the park too suddenly, and it was almost too much. I think we were lucky to get through it at all. If ever the sirens sang for us both at once, it was here. We listened. We hardly spoke to one another. We stopped frequently along Going-To-The-Sun road and got out of Otto simply to catch our breath. The music of the park was everywhere deep, and, if I may be so paradoxical, silent. Breathing interfered with listening, with taking in the spell-binding harmonies of mountain, sky, and water so exquisitely combined.

In an odd way, it gave me a better sense of the role of the Great Plains: the long, slow gradual approach to this mighty beauty was like the many courtyards and chambers before the throne room of a king—a way of preparing, of humbling the petitioner, of letting him *see* that a great deal stands between the near-divine and the low.

And then suddenly, painfully, we were again east of the Continental Divide. Morning witnessed the Walker swatting mosquitoes as he hiked west out of Havre. No sign of the Rockies now, some one-hundred-seventy miles distant. But, like the newly addicted, our every glance west, to the furthest horizon, was an effort to recall them. Soon we began to think we had dreamed them: it was here that the Plains began to seem endless.

The first of September proved a hot and trying day for the Walker, soaring into the nineties. By now Don had had a taste of cooler weather with which to compare, and there was no comparison. All we could hope was that the heat would fry a few mosquitoes, or...

"Fran, you won't believe it." Don complained on one of his breaks near Kremlin, Montana. "There are gnats out there now in places, great horrible clouds of them. I'm sick of these torments. I was so hoping we were through with them. Also, I thought things would be cooler by this time."

Gnats? The plagues were unaccountable. Maybe we were doing something wrong. Or maybe we were caught up in someone else's contest with the Lord, like that of Moses with the Pharaoh. "And if ye walk contrary unto me, and will not hearken unto me, I will bring seven times more plagues upon you according to your sins" (Leviticus 26:21).

What were the gnats thriving on? The Big Sky was hard-looking like a stone, a solidified blue. The sun seared all beneath it, and yet when it fell from the sky these days, the temperature fell dramatically with it. When the fireball sun bedded down in a sudden sea of deep purple cirrus, and the afterglow of the sunset intensified, until it outdid in loudness the neon lights of the highway bar in Gilford that we camped behind, I felt maybe we'd been forgiven.

But the next day I wrote, "Today the wind is brutal—full of dirt, dust, grit, and chaff—from the wheat harvest still in progress here, also from the unplanted fields. It feels hotter because the humidity is up. As crazy as it sounds, I'd have to describe the sky as a brilliant gray—impossibly glaring. I have been snacking on wheat gum again. We are about 3,000 feet in elevation. I don't think the wind can get any worse!"

Don had learned the recipe for making wheat gum in North Dakota from some west-bound bikers who stopped to chat with him. "First" they said, "from a stalk of wheat you husk out fifteen to twenty of the kernels; pop them into your mouth, roll them around, and wet them down good with saliva; when the spirit moves you, you start mashing them with your molars until all congeals into a thick, pasty wad. Chew until heart's content or until all eventually dissolves." Wheat gum seemed a little like chewing gum—more pastime than nourishment.

Ever since North Dakota I had been learning about grain. In North Dakota we saw mostly durum wheat, a grain from which pasta is made. I learned to tell wheat from barley and oats—and bearded wheat from beardless. The higher we climbed in elevation, the further west we went, the later the wheat harvest.

The next day near Galata I wrote, "What started out to be a perfectly pleasant, bright, clear, cool, not-too-windy day has suddenly turned wild with wind—a blow-you-back wind that threatens to whip Don to death with his own clothes. Just when we think something cannot possibly get any worse—it does! Don's handkerchief is bloody from so much sneezing and blowing thanks to the air-born grit. I know Don is discouraged because he is napping!—something he almost never does."

When the Walker woke up, I said, "Guess what I learned back at Rudyard when I was at the post office, Don? Something to settle the dust and refrigerate the bugs."

"What?"

"It's supposed to snow."

"No, go on, I don't believe it."

"Well, that's what the postmaster said. And if it can snow here now, it may well snow in the Rockies up ahead of us. I bet you a dinner out that you get snowed on at some point on this walk."

"It's a bet," Don said, "with this qualification—I have to actually be out there walking when I get snowed on."

"No problem," I said. "It's going to be a very tasty, fancy, expensive, many-course dinner at the restaurant of the winner's choice—and if that postmaster knows anything about the weather around here, I might as well start salivating right now."

But if it snowed anywhere in the area that day or the next, we did not know it.

Chapter 31

The Rockies

Mountains in Montana were nearly always within our sight. Once it was the Little Rockies. For a while we traveled alongside a small range to the north of us called the Sweet Grass Hills, which were used not so very long ago by the Native Americans as watchtowers over the buffalo herds. We watched the Bear's Paw Mountains gradually disappear to the south of us. But what we strained hard to see each day were the big Rockies.

After four days of imagining in places that we *could* see them, we finally surely did, just east of Shelby. And from their familiar and distinctive silhouettes, we knew our earlier sightings had not all been wishful ones. Being able to keep the Rockies in view, however far ahead, was exactly the boost the Walker needed. It meant we had not dreamed them up, and it meant that there was, indeed, an end to the Plains.

My own heart thrilled at the thought—and yet at the same time, I was beginning to realize that these impossibly immense spaces had somehow worked their way into me. And how, if this was fully accomplished, could a person not be forever changed? How could one give it all up and go back to a world seemingly built on a different scale?

Not that everything we took note of in this part of the country impressed because of its grand scale. Sometimes the endearing aspect was but a tiny detail in comparison. The wayside embroidery of wildflowers against the dun-colored plains, such as the purple prairie clover; the densely flowered, snowy, prairie aster; the wind-blown, yellow sweet clover, tall and rank; the many kinds of sunflower—all—gave the eye a rest from the sheer broadness of Nature's strokes, inviting even closer scrutiny. Pollen grains of a brilliant orange crowned the purple prairie clover, while the dark-eyed discs of the sunflowers wore rings of beaded gold.

But best of all details, to me, was something heard and not seen—something to fill what otherwise could seem only achingly vacant—something that had not perhaps changed in the settling and taming of these lands. The song of the western meadowlark. Even a mere fragment of its song blown back from the ear by a rude wind could lift my heart. A full-throated caroling at daybreak or sundown could cut me to the quick. News of another world, it was, like that of the hermit thrush—tantalizing because it seemed to sing of what only had just fallen beyond reach.

The other detail of the land, easy to miss, if a body only responded to the great sweeping expanse under the big sky, was the people. I was surprised to write in my journal, "I've not met anyone that strikes me as hopelessly provincial, backwater, or hillbillyish. But why should it be any kind of a shock to find that people seem as good and as smart—and as familiar almost—as at home? I guess it's the strangeness of habitat and surroundings, so that you imagine it must take a different sort of person to live in every different sort of place—flat people for flat lands, mountainous people for mountainous lands. In truth, I guess it must take all kinds to make up the balance anywhere."

And yet, if there *was* a difference in the Westerner, it was one most noticeable on first impression before any ice had been broken by conversation. It was a lack of pretentiousness, I thought, contending with pride—a game of "how to keep down with the Joneses." Something in a Westerner's glance at an Easterner said, "Don't try to get fancy with us. Just look around you. What could you possibly make of anything that would not appear paltry in the face of such country as this?" And, I confess, more often than not, it was the Westerner who took a swing at the ice first: "Hello, over there! Now what in the world could you be writin' at so hard?" Some such greeting often came blaring across an uncrowded restaurant. I might have thought certain hardships would make a people crabby and bitter, but not here. If you showed so much as a spark of understanding or appreciation, the Montanan went you one better, blazing the way for more of both. I liked this. It kept my tendency toward shyness from making me into a total recluse.

But in spite of the encouragement of being able to see the Rockies, the last two days' walk to their feet, was rough going. It felt suddenly as if a cold shadow had fallen over us, making for uncomfortable presentiments. Partly, I told myself, it was the changing season. School had started. The Walker paused occasionally to watch the progress of a high school football practice or game going on. Darkness was finally, noticeably earlier. The sun rose late. The afternoon had that lonely, autumnal edge to it that comes with the diminishing light. Near Dunkirk, Montana, I heard the honking of wild geese and saw the first of many wedges flying south across the big sky.

When I took a walk late in the day, it seemed a little scarier now. Talk at Hayden Lake had been full of warnings, also news of the likes of the Green River Killer. I had to be careful, or such stories were liable to pop into my head unasked. For fear of the same kind of talk, I almost never listened to Otto's radio. I knew well enough that danger could be anywhere. I knew to be on my guard. But I also knew too well how I could scare myself witless, and I didn't see what good that would do me in a pinch.

The worst moment on my walk came when I was far out of Otto's sight and not yet in Don's. My heart would begin to beat like a drumming grouse, knowing how my aloneness was set off by miles and miles of emptiness on every side. I had my field glasses slung on a strap over my shoulder to give me confidence. I felt I could swing them pretty viciously if I had to. I could also use them to get an earlier sighting of the Walker. It was all too plain, though, that if someone had wanted to do any of us—the Walker, the Driver, or Otto—any harm, it would not have required much imagination to bring it about. We were vulnerable and we knew it—we felt it.

Maybe we had gotten used to the Plains and were simply fearful of the coming changes in the mountains, even as we longed for them.

Moving on so consistently as we were, it was difficult to say when or why something boded ill. The minute you felt you were home free for some reason, circumstances changed.

On the Blackfeet Indian Reservation, the road changed for the worse—no margin for Don to walk, none for me to safely park. When I scouted the town of Browning, Montana, for camping possibilities on Saturday night, I was dismayed. There were so many shacky bars, and what looked like gambling places, I turned away in disgust. We camped well east of town.

But the next morning, I found the Little Flower Church in Browning. It was beautiful—uniquely built of rounded stones in various shades of red and brown. And I was greeted more warmly here than anywhere else on the journey. Did they know my fears? The priest met me on the porch of the little church with a big, reassuring hug. A nun inside hugged me again. And then at the peace offering two elderly Black Feet women each took turns hugging me. When a young Indian playing guitar started singing, "Morning Has Broken," I could not hold back my tears.

After the service, when the Walker caught up with me at the church, we attended Sunday breakfast in the church basement. We sat next to Mike Little Dog and listened to his talk of a wolf pack on the reservation and of a recent grizzly mauling near Route 2 up ahead "in the timber."

And then this day, which had begun so brightly, turned mean on us. The temperature fell and brought down with it a cold, drizzly rain. I thought of my bet with the Walker, but it was already too cold in Otto. I did not want it to snow, no matter how great the restaurant or the meal.

We could no longer see the Rockies. They had been hung over with great rags of dark cloud. I shivered inside Otto, wearing layers of clothes beneath a heavy sweatshirt and a down vest, topped over all by a down sleeping bag, but I could not get warm. I would have gone for a walk to warm up, but I didn't want to get wet. There would be no place to get dry. I could not write, because I ached with the cold, and the ink in my pen was too sluggish. Don took only momentary breaks, bringing the wet and mud into Otto, but he couldn't sit long either without getting cold.

After several hours of this, not far from East Glacier, something inside me snapped. The next chance I got, I snapped at the Walker.

"I'm sick of this, Don."

A puddle of cold, brown rainwater was forming at his feet. He sat in Otto on a poncho and took off his wet shoes. Three pairs of wet, muddy shoes were now lined up next to the cooler. He reached for the fourth.

"I said I'm sick of this, Don."

"Well, what do you think, it's a picnic out there, walking in this kind of weather? I'm getting fresh blisters from all this wet, I can tell you."

"Well, at least you're warm."

"Right," he said, starting to make himself a sandwich with hands blue from the cold.

"And I'm sick of the Plains!" I said, more angrily.

"Well, the Plains are behind us now. We're about to head into the mountains," he said, raising his voice to match mine and trying to look out the fogged-up windows to see if it was really true.

"But what's the use—we can't *see* the mountains! And I'm sick of the fences, the mosquitoes, the heat, the cold, the wet, the ragweed, the lukewarm tea, the broken phones, going without showers, wondering where I am—(I'd been rehearsing this)—and most of all, I'm sick to death of this creeping pace and being cooped up in a metal box with no heat—pardon me, Otto!" And then, in spite of pinching myself to keep from crying, the tears came in a flood.

Don quit chewing his food and stared at me. For a long, cold, wet, shivery moment, the only sound was the dripping on Otto's roof.

"Look," Don finally said with a deep sigh, "I'm about done in myself anyway. So what if I only break twenty miles today. Maybe there's a motel we could get in East Glacier. A hot shower and some place warm and dry sounds good to me. Why don't you see what's ahead?"

When I drove off, I was only partly ashamed at having broken down so utterly. And when I came upon The Whistling Swan in East Glacier, I felt like Gretel in the fairy tale who, after days of wandering lost and hungry in the woods, suddenly comes upon a gingerbread house. This was the closest thing to a gingerbread house I ever saw. I really could have eaten it, and I didn't much mind if a witch ran the place. Candy-colored petunias and other bright flowers blossomed in the window boxes. The small inn was hewn out of the wood of the mountains, and did not have the shabby look of so many buildings on the Plains. It was rustic and loggy and real. And best of all, it had rooms available.

Well before the day ended, the clouds began to lift and the rains to cease. This only made us more sure that we had made the right decision. By then we were too comfortable to move on; we were under the swan's wings, snug as cygnets.

Chapter 32

The Plate for the Goblet

Walking the 166 miles from Havre to East Glacier, Montana, Don climbed over two-thousand feet in elevation without really noticing it. East Glacier was at 4,774 feet. From East Glacier to Marias Pass and the Continental Divide, the rise was a little over five hundred feet. At Marias Pass, Don was exactly one mile above sea level, and the climb to get there was an easy one—easy because this day the mountain air was clearer than the clearest water, virtually windless, and richly scented with mountain evergreen. Gone were the Plains. Gone the mosquito, the gnat, the flying ant. Gone the Big Sky. Here the sky was deeper than it was big. The world had closed in on us.

The long view ahead and behind was cut off by curves and rises, the Rockies hovered over. We had traded the look across the endless open for something near at hand—the plate for the goblet. It was intoxicating. Out on the Plains, one step was but the first of many. The emphasis was on the horizontal—on things out of reach and long suffering. The edge was missing. But here in the mountains, we skirted the brink; the emphasis was on the vertical, above and below. One step too near the edge—the close, keen, edge of life—could decide the difference, forever.

The day, September 7, could not have been more splendid. It dawned icily bright. Otto was furred over with a heavy frost, yet at the first touch of the sun's rays the white crystals dissolved and the sharp air softened. We were glad we had waited.

How late the season suddenly seemed. "There is gold in the air and scattered upon the ground," I wrote in my journal, "aspen and willow are turning. Snappy touches of scarlet fire up in the low foliage beneath the dark evergreens. And the flowers! Like so many letters from home strewn at my feet—purple aster, pearly everlasting, fire weed, red clover, and something like forget-me-nots. Where have they come from? Bouquets I might pick at home were I there this minute!" And I wrote to David, "In truth, I do not believe these really grow here at all. I think they have been but momentarily set in my path to lure me onward as if I could somehow come closer to home by leaving it ever further behind."

Once beyond Marias Pass, Don followed a path cut by Route 2 between Glacier Park and The Great Bear Wilderness. The Walker was within a few steps of either—each a mountain fastness rather protected from the ravages of man. I don't know how he kept to the road with so many trail heads beckoning. I certainly did not keep to Otto, though on both of our minds was the grizzly mauling we had heard about from Mike Little Dog, back at the church breakfast in Browning. At the same time, an unspoken contest had risen between Don and me. We each harbored a desire to spot a bear, if not go so far as to be mauled by one.

With this half in mind I hiked alone into the Great Bear Wilderness. I did not know that bears themselves were not perhaps the greatest danger this day, and I did not find out until later what was. I took two precautions. I slung my field glasses over my shoulder, though I didn't fool myself into thinking that swinging them would do much to daunt a grizzly. And I carried a big, juicy apple. The fruit was my insurance policy; I polished it to a fine ruby luster. I would offer it to whatever bear I might meet, in exchange for my life.

The trail was well trod by both horse and man; I did not have trouble walking softly. The strong incense of pine and other more subtle fragrances occasionally reminded me to breathe deeply and savor my new freedom. It was strangely exhilarating to think that no one, not even the Walker, knew where I was. For that matter, did I know where I was?

For a while, as I wound my way in among these great western pillars of red cedar, hemlock, tamarack, and Douglas-fir (any one of which two men together could not encompass with their arms), I fancied I did not have to turn around and go back. I recalled another perimeter walker I knew of, whose one-man support crew deserted him when he got to Oregon, and I had little trouble understanding why.

Deeper and deeper I went. How little light made it down to where I was on the forest floor! Standing still and looking up, I saw at least a hundred feet above my head, needle and branch idly scraping against the lofty blue. I felt diminished to elfin dimensions in the murky shadows beneath.

My ears were pricked. Once, I thought I could hear the soft pad of a bear coming up from behind. I turned so suddenly I scared an over-sized red squirrel up the nearest trunk. It angrily scolded me from an overhanging branch. My heart steadied. A little while later I caught a stunning flash of satiny blue disappearing into the forest ahead of me. A Steller's jay. Was it trying to lure me from the path? Not long after, I heard it raucously complaining in the forest depth, but about what? That was the last sound I heard for a long time.

I saw many dry mosses, no ferns, and few flowers—what looked like a western version of Indian poke and the blue bead lily. I came across huge, leathery-topped, golden boletes—gill-less mushrooms a person could almost sit upon. Yet the understory was so dry, for the most part, it didn't seem favorable for fruiting mushrooms much less ones built to a Western scale.

The swift, shadowy flight of a Cooper's hawk; the swooping dive of a red-shafted flicker; the darting, golden speck of a warbler—all were seen and not heard. The deeper I went, the more eerily quiet it became—the kind of quiet that cannot easily be explained. The longer it lasted, the more it began to seem that no one living thing dare break it.

And then I saw it. A good-sized pile of droppings a little to one side of the trail. Fresh, warm, practically steaming. Bear scat? It seemed all too likely. For some reason, I thought the bear had to be ahead of me, and I did not want to put my back to it. Somehow I forced myself to turn. When I did, a soft sort of galloping noise filled the forest. It took me a moment to recognize the tell-tale pounding of my own heart!

I didn't want to run, because I didn't want to sweat and become more attractive bait. I didn't want to make any noise. I felt suddenly that I had walked too long and too far, that only darkness or disaster could catch me now. I was trapped. I walked with the sureness of the condemned, my doom eventually confirmed when I suddenly saw bear tracks in some soft mud before me. But no, looking more closely, I managed to resolve them into something else—my own prints overlain by those of a deer.

And then, five minutes' walk before I knew with certainty that I would find my way out into the open and back to the civilized danger of the road, I stopped. I suddenly wished with all my heart I had met the bear. I waited. When it didn't come, I set my apple on a stump—in offering. Maybe the bear would find it. My life was intact.

I watched for the Walker from a wooden bridge over Bear Creek. When he caught up, he was all smiles.

"Guess what I just saw?" he shouted up to me.

"I don't even want to hear!" I shouted back.

Don made his way below me to the edge of the creek and took off his shoes. When he put his bare feet in, he breathed a deep sigh. Except for a faintly discernible line at his ankles, I could not tell his feet were submerged. So clear was the water they might have been dangling in air.

"Two miles back, Fran, I got my bear. Did you get yours?"

"No, I got a pile of…of…of bear droppings."

Don laughed. "Well, I didn't see a grizzly, if that makes you feel any better. I saw a black bear foraging in a patch of huckleberries—maybe five feet from me, across a small ditch. It scared me a little because I came upon it so suddenly as I rounded a bend. It turned to look at me but didn't seem a bit bothered—went back to attacking the berries. Just to be safe, I crossed the road and watched it from there. It was still happily munching berries when I moved on."

"Naturally," I said, "you see a bear inches from Route 2, and I risk my life alone in the woods and…well, I guess that's the scenario with the happiest ending, anyway."

Later that evening we saw a motley group of gun-toting, beer-drinking, camouflaged hunters gathered near a collection of highway dumpsters. One of the dumpsters had been messily ransacked. Bears. It was bear hunting season, we learned, though for black bears only. Grizzlies were protected. No hunting in Glacier Park, either. Was the bear Don saw so complacent because it knew it was on the safe side of the road? We also learned it was bow season for hunting elk and deer. Don was glad he was walking the safe side of the road. I was suddenly thankful I hadn't met any hunters on my hike. To both of us the hunters looked far more dangerous than the bears.

Chapter 33

Are We Being Followed?

West of the Divide, the midday air occasionally had something fresh in it, intimations of another clime, an unfamiliar balm. Here the season suddenly did not seem so late, and the same flowers going to seed on the eastern slopes of the Rockies were beside us now, still in full bloom. Gone, the red and gold homelike hints of autumn. The days' temperature swings matched the up-and-down terrain—plunging to cold, frosty nights and mornings, climbing to bright, warm, sometimes hot days. But however bright and hot the day, the mountain shadows and the mountain streams were sure and fast relief from any heat. Swallows, which I had noticed migrating south across the Plains, here seemed becalmed. Tortoise shell butterflies drifted lazily about the alpine meadows and lulled me into an unconscious assumption that somehow the hardships were behind us.

I realized how deeply this assumption had burrowed its way into me when, after a mere two days of this idyllic life, it was suddenly over. The awakening shock of getting so quickly through such ravishing country practically amounted to despair. Again, the fault was Don's pace. Though still in the Rockies, we had, in two days' time, come down in more than elevation; we had put the untampered-with wilds behind us. Suddenly, Don was making his way through the ugly outskirts of civilization comprising an asphalt jungle of fast-food joints, car dealerships, motels, shopping centers, etc., reeking with car exhaust. Don's route so far had rarely taken us through such strip development, and now, we thought, the miles and miles of it approaching Kalispell, Montana, were that much worse to confront because of what we had just come through.

The contrast was exemplified in our campsite that night when a state trooper actually advised us to camp in the parking lot of a Red Lion Inn Motel. He would be on duty there and thus would not report us. He claimed there were no other places to camp nearby. At that, we were lucky to find a parking place. Crowded, noisy, over-lit, full of comings and goings all night long—I thought the VW dealership in Great Falls a more peaceful abode.

It took another day to get beyond Kalispell to a more remote area of National Forest lands, but this was not pristine country and the walking was not always easy. Don hiked twenty-three miles one day through continuous road construction, with the dust constantly being raised by the road work and the traffic. Logging trucks reappeared in significantly bothersome numbers, and the dust raised by one of these could bury a bull elephant.

I don't know which was sadder to look upon: the devastation of clearcut logging, or the remains of a 12,000-acre forest fire—both of which Don found himself traversing. In my view it was worse to see the clearcut logging, since even less was left behind—the natural habitat being more thoroughly obliterated by man than by Nature. Then, on top of everything, presided a ruling drought which was no less terrible to see, as if Nature did not want to be outdone and was preparing the way for bigger blazes yet by piling up years' worth of dry tinder on the forest floor—knee deep in places.

At the Saddle Tramp Inn, September 11, near Lake McGregor, I learned the drought was going on into its seventh year. There hadn't been a really snowy winter in all that time, locals at the cafe said. One man had his theories about this, blaming the drought on too much land irrigation, clearcutting, forest fires, and hydro-projects. "Just too damned much tinkering with Nature," another man agreed. All present then expressed some resentment toward the major land holders in the area, the big logging companies.

Other talk was of the wildlife in the neighborhood, confirming our own previous days' sightings of loon, merganser, bald eagle, and osprey. One woman complained about pack rats. She had already caught fourteen trying to move in for the winter. The man with theories about the drought had caught eighteen. I thought about the deer mice I would catch at home this time of year—a creature probably less than a third the size of a woodland pack rat. The same woman reported on a deer kill a cougar had recently made on her property. The big cat ate the entrails and hindquarters of its prey, and the next night some coyotes came along to finish it off. Apparently the cat had made a big, splattery, bloody mess, while the coyotes virtually licked the place clean, leaving behind only a bit of hair and bone.

Wherever we were, the wildlife was welcome company, though never something to take for granted. To me, even a brief and distant glimpse was a blessing. Aldo Leopold said in *A Sand County Almanac,* "There are some who can live without wild things, and some who cannot." I am one who cannot. But you can't exactly pack Nature up and take it with you in a suitcase. Neither can you get someplace and demand that it appear. Indeed, the wild things themselves typically show little interest in man and his doings. And yet? Sometimes I had to wonder on our journey.

Many a morning the Walker had the company of mule deer, who would peek curiously at him from a short distance, as if they had never before in their life seen the like. If Don suddenly gave them a look straight on, they would bound away for cover like jackrabbits, only to quietly reappear further on to resume their observations of the Walker. Was Don being watched? Watched over?

One morning on the plains west of Saco, I noticed a red fox hunting its breakfast along a ditch near Otto, yet it seemed to begin doing so only *after* I had surprised it. It almost pretended, I half thought at the time, to go about its business.

West of East Glacier I made little friendly noises at a badger I came upon. It stopped, looked up, and seemed to listen intently. I thought I must have accidentally uttered something important in badger language. It went on. And then, for a time, we walked side by side like Socrates and Plato, conversing as we did. I was impressed with the badger's blunt claws, which alone seemed to extend in a curve the length of my foot. The poor creature looked bedraggled from the recent wet weather, and its mood somehow matched my own. Was that why we seemed to get along?

Next to the Fisher River in the Kootenai National Forest, I sat just wishing for some companionship, tired at day's end, trying to make do with what the murmuring stream had to say. In the middle of a yawn, I saw a mink coming straight toward me, as if he was sorry to have kept me waiting. And then a short while later, instead of sitting down for a visit he disappeared into the dark waters at my very feet, as if he hadn't seen me after all. I waited a long time. I was sure he would realize his mistake any minute and come back. But the Walker caught up, and the mink may have been shy, and I didn't see him again.

Odd moments? True. Coincidence only? I suppose. But about another creature my wondering had just about changed to something akin to belief. In the weekly newsletter I sent to friends and family, I wrote:

"Imagine, you've been away from home a long time, gone through a fair amount of country, lots of widely varied terrain—wet and dry, high and low; but every now and then, when you turn around at just the right moment, you see the same stately character, in the same natty blue-gray suit, the same mysterious look on his face, in the same serene pose. You have to begin to think you're being followed. So who's been following us? A great blue heron.

"I noticed him first along the shores of Lake Champlain before we left Vermont, but I saw him time and again in the still mountain ponds of the Adirondacks, along the placid river stretches of Ontario, beside the lakes and marshes of Michigan and Wisconsin, knee deep in the swamps of Minnesota, even consorting with the ducks in the sloughs of North Dakota. I was sure we'd lose him when we hit the Great Plains, but even there I caught him giving me the eye in unlikely places. Once, on a great, open, rolling sweep of brown, barren earth—erupting with buttes and dry as desert; where I could see a full hundred miles of emptiness in every direction; there was but one, shallow, weedy slough in a dip of the land—and there he stood, stalk-still, his knowing eye meeting mine straight on.

"'Hmph,' I said, 'I'll lose you yet!' And I dug my spurs into Otto and rode on to climb the Rockies. But even here he managed to surprise me at the very top of the Continental Divide. He started up not more than one, great, seven-foot-wing span away—out of the merest bit of puddle that could not decide which way to flow (whether to the Atlantic or the Pacific), as if to flap his message squarely in my eye: 'You'll never lose me.'

"And I haven't. I saw him this morning in Idaho, in a backwater pool of the Pond Oreille River—the same, self-assured, unconcerned, leisurely way about him. Just seems to want to make sure I notice him—appreciate the fact, that if he feels like it, he'll follow me all the round about way home. And I guess I'm not really going to mind. It's a kind of company, if at a distance; and in a reel of constantly changing faces, his is beginning to grow on me."

Chapter 34

Permission to Correspond
with the Living

September 13—"Not feeling good today, skipped dinner last night, froze in the night—took a long time for the sun I finally found this morning to warm Otto—and then to warm me. I am just generally feeling lost. It's true that all along I have not known where I was—but now and then it really gets to me. And I don't know that low points on this journey are any lower really than low points at home. Probably they aren't, for the most part, except for the underlying ache of homesickness itself that never seems to go away and that keeps any sense that all is well from establishing itself for long."

September 14—"I have felt good all day today—and I realize that my reasons for feeling good today are as inexplicable as my reasons for feeling bad yesterday. Do feelings even respond to reasons? I think not. Am I any less homesick today? Not really. Have things gone smoother? Well, yes, but who knows—I think I am simply feeling less put upon or else more up to being put upon. Nothing much about the journey has changed. We are merely one day closer to its end, yet as ignorant as ever as to what lies ahead."

Later: "I just get used to the land or something about the territory I'm traveling through and things change. All the moving on we're doing makes me feel that NOTHING stays the same—not even

177

love. And though in some sense I know this is true and always will be true—in another sense I know that at home I rarely have to put up with so many constant reminders. Living at home I am lulled by regular rhythms, and only every now and then am I jolted out of this lull and asked to cope with change."

September 15—"I have been searching for a metaphor—for a way of describing what this way of living is like to me. Then today I found myself writing to a friend that I felt as if I had died but somehow been given permission to correspond with the living. That is it—my metaphor. Life seems somehow only to happen back there whence the letters come. Here—things happen, but somehow, for whatever reasons and crazy as it sounds, it does not feel like life."

Maybe these kinds of thoughts, such as I wrote in my journal in Idaho, are the kind a person might have on a "here-we-go-round" (I was going to say *merry-go-round*, but the word "merry" isn't right. Yet the spinning is.) A person does have to have a sense of place, I think. We had to have this sense on the journey too, after a fashion. It came of anything that could connect one day with another, of what might repeat itself—such as our road routines, the larger land forms, or the train, the song of the meadowlark or coyotes, the great blue heron. Otto, too, was a physical anchor, a certain portion of the environment that did not change over time. Or did it?

That was one of our fears. In Idaho, and for no good reason, Otto's gas gauge suddenly quit working. When I checked into getting it fixed, the process was too elaborate and too expensive to pursue. It really wasn't awful to live without because I was already in the habit of keeping close track of the mileage. But what was hard was the principle of the thing, the capriciousness of it, the feeling of insecurity it encouraged. It made me want to say magic words over Otto to ward off other possible breakage. However important Otto was to us as shelter, he was even more important as beast of burden who could carry us home eventually. If he died on the way? Well, neither one of us liked to think about it.

And no, Otto did not seem mere machine. He had, like any living personality, his quirks. For example, at odd moments, on odd days, his windshield wipers would suddenly sweep back and forth—once or maybe twice. You could not predict the circumstances that would bring this about. Was he trying to tell us something?

His brakes squealed—but no, they did not squeal when I came to a sudden halt, pulling over in the middle of nowhere to catch a glimpse of some wildlife, but yes, they did squeal loud enough to raise the hair on the backs of people's necks two miles off and cause grimacing pain on the faces of people in the crosswalk before me at some busy intersection in a town. Otto undoubtedly knew where he would get the biggest reaction to his protests!

But the worst of his quirks was the way he set his alarm. With most cars, just taking the key out of the ignition means the alarm is off. Not necessarily so with Otto. You had to take Otto's key out exactly a certain way, which was not always achievable on the first or even fifth try. Not that his alarm would go off then—oh no, but after, in the calm of the night, when you got up to go to the bathroom, and you were camped where it wasn't strictly legal, and you were trying to be quiet so as not to wake the Walker, the dead, or anyone else—that's when it would suddenly blast off! We tried testing for this to make sure it was off before going to sleep, but it just didn't always work. Otto had his ways, and much of the time they were, like the peace of God, past all understanding.

When Don crossed the border into Idaho, he also crossed into the Pacific Time Zone. Now Otto's clock on home time showed three hours difference from where we were. A mere glance at his hands was a reminder of what was between us and home, not only time but distance. A quiet moment's loud ticking counted out Don's steps lengthening a trail that felt as if it was already stretched to the breaking point.

Don followed Route 2 in Idaho going south as much as west, and this area seemed to both of us a continuation of western Montana in terms of the mountain terrain. We weren't in Idaho long enough to describe it otherwise. There were plenty of logging trucks, warnings of "high" fire danger in the forests, and even smoke in the air at times. We had heard of forest fires burning in the western states; we hoped we would not be crossing paths with any.

Meanwhile, in Idaho we did cross paths with some other long-distance adventurers—a trio of young women bikers, all recent graduates of Dartmouth College in Hanover, New Hampshire. We had met up with a good many cross-country bikers before this, most of them heading west. A biker's progress was, to us, enviably swift, graceful, and carefree. These young co-eds were also headed west.

"Fran, I finally met those bikers who keep passing me," Don announced when he caught up to where I had pulled over in a restaurant parking lot. "They're Chris, Diana, and Maury. I see their bikes here. They must be in the restaurant. Are you almost finished typing that newsletter? I want to introduce you. But listen to this—they started heading west just about the *same time I did* and, well, they nearly fell off their bikes when I told them I had come practically the same distance in the same amount of time—*walking*. And they thought they had been making good time. I jokingly bet them I'd beat them to Seattle—that's where they're finishing up their journey."

"It sounds like a case of the tortoise and the hares to me. I'm almost through here; just want to be able to get this into the mail this morning. You go on in, I'll be right along. Probably, they're having some fun as they go and taking their time, Don."

"For sure, they went to that party we were invited to and passed up—the one at Little Bear's Tipi, the other side of Happy's Inn? Said it was really wild, that I ought to have been there. Went on all night long. Lots of crazy people."

"Yeah, if we weren't so tired and didn't have to backtrack and were only going to Seattle. Are you sorry you missed it?"

"Not really," Don said, and he headed into The Village Kitchen.

I could tell he was tickled to meet up with these bikers, happy to be able to report his progress to someone. It was at least another way of measuring his progress. Every now and then I would unfold our big map of the U.S.A. and trace the new distance gained with a bright-yellow marker. Don thought I was crazy, since I did this far more often than he would have. I found it strangely satisfying to extend the line even a half inch over new ground. And I liked to see the continuing connection with home.

"Just look at how far you've walked, Don," I'd say.

"Look at the long way yet to go, Fran." And that was one of the differences between us—Don went forward without a backward glance. I wanted to know whence I came.

Chapter 35

The Walker Meets the Runner

I was ahead of Don outside of Deep Creek, Washington, west of Spokane, when I pulled over to wait, tucking Otto into the only shade available under some towering, long-skirted evergreens. I was glad to get beyond the congestion of the city of Spokane, but sorry now, too, that we were well out of the Rockies.

Not long after I pulled over, a brand-new, luxury-liner RV that would have dwarfed a logging truck also pulled over. It bore an insignia with the words, "Run Around America." And now I recalled friends we met in Spokane saying we would be crossing paths with these people.

I leaped out to wave at the captain of this land-cruise ship when I could see he was trying to dock his unwieldy vessel. Otto, a mere mouse cowering in its shadow, was liable to get caught under the wheels of the thing. But the captain saw us, gave a friendly wave, and signaled for me to come on board. The next thing I knew, I was lounging on a soft couch, sipping a sweet drink, and being fanned by the imported, seaside cool of air conditioning.

Don was out there under a blistering sun, working on his 2,600[th] mile. A young woman named Sarah Fulcher was out there, too, coming from the opposite direction, working on her 1,900[th] mile. Sarah was the star of the "Run Around America" show. She left Laguna Hills, California, near the end of July and was *running* a thirty-mile-a-day pace and hoping to complete the U.S. perimeter, like Don, in a year's time. She was going for her second long-run record. (She first landed in the record books by running across the Australian outback—"from pub to pub," as she laughingly described it later.) This U.S. run was also supposed to raise money to help start a National Fitness Foundation.

Captain Mark was telling me all about Sarah and her efforts as I was telling him all about Don and his efforts. We were both waiting to minister to these athletes and their needs. We were somewhat differently equipped.

Twenty-five year old Sarah had a support crew averaging seven— including massage therapist, dietitian, professional trainers, and publicity people. In addition, *two* of these luxurious RVs (one was off somewhere getting a new insignia), as well as a car and some bicycles, were at Sarah's disposal. The RVs offered such conveniences as stoves, microwaves, dishwashers, TVs, VCRs, showers, toilets, and two-way radios if not phones. Forty-five year old Don had me, already-been- around-some Otto, a can opener, and a bucket.

"Of course, we haven't actually had to camp out yet much," Mark was saying. "So far, the publicity people have had little trouble getting the red carpet to roll out for us at hotels and inns. You guys should try it. It's great. We've even been put up at a governor's mansion. Still, just in case, we've got these RVs."

"Right," I said taking another sip of my soda and another look around me in disbelief.

"Oh, here comes Sarah now!" Mark announced proudly. "Ann, the massage therapist, is biking along with her for her safety's sake. See her? There she is."

I looked out the picture-window-sized windshield and saw a thin woman with bobbed hair the color of lightning bouncing alongside another woman riding a bicycle. And in the following hour, I hardly took my eyes off the ultra-marathoner. She seemed to me like a wind- up Barbie doll gone awry, though a Barbie doll might be even beefier than Sarah. Sarah's thighs looked the width of Don's forearms. During the course of our brief visit, she sat down, jumped up, disappeared for a moment, sat down, jumped up, opened up a cupboard, sat down, jumped up, grabbed a soda, looked out the window, stretched, ran a comb through her hair, sat down, jumped up, etc. I began to wonder if it was humanly possible for someone like Sarah to *not* run across and around vast continents. When Don finally came along and Sarah ran out to greet him, he looked like the rock of Gibraltar with a strobe light in orbit around him.

The Run-Around-America crew couldn't have been nicer to us. They were as interested in Don and his walk as we were in Sarah and her run. Ann, the massage therapist, grilled the Walker a sandwich, warmed him up some pasta in the microwave, gave him a foot massage, and offered some advice about keeping his feet in shape. David and Carla, the publicity people, talked about how they were making this venture pay for itself. Sarah cheered the Walker's efforts and told stories about her own adventures on the run. By the time we parted, we were all making plans to meet up again later on in the journey, where it seemed our paths might cross somewhere in the Southeast.

The questions in the back of our minds during this visit were impossible not to ask. *Weren't we envious? Wouldn't we rather be traveling with all those luxuries? Didn't it look like a lot more fun?* Well, yes, except for one telling observation—the Runner's life did not appear to be her own. For example, she had a small cold sore on her lip that was the topic of repeated discussions, few of which included the ultra-marathoner herself. Such comments as, "How can we keep her from bothering it?" seemed to show more concern for the wound than for the woman. Finally everyone agreed she should see a dermatologist in Spokane, but still it seemed that Sarah herself had not been consulted.

We thanked them heartily and wished them good luck, but as the Walker took up his simpler task, and as Otto and I galloped ahead to the next pull-off, neither of us looked back with envious eyes. On the other hand, I doubt the Run-Around-America crew did, either.

If we did look back now, as we headed west of Spokane, we could see the last range of the Rockies, the Selkirks, fading in the distance. Ahead of us it looked rather too much like a return to the Plains. At the border a sign had declared Washington "The evergreen state." And for a while, we feared that that was all that was ever going to be green—the tall firs standing about some lonesome farmhouse. For about a hundred miles into eastern Washington—from Reardan to Davenport to Creston to Wilbur to Hartline—Don walked through lands vaguely reminiscent of the Plains and through little towns rather like those on the prairie.

The Walker plastered himself heavily with sunscreen and pinned bandannas and dishtowels about him. The heat radiating off the jet-black asphalt road must have been 150 degrees. The sky was a blue desert; the sun a white-hot coal. In the thirteen days since the rain at East Glacier, we had seen clouds few enough to be counted on one hand. The blessings of deep shade and cold-running streams were but dreamlike memories here. The road stretched straight and shadeless.

"Fran, I thought that by this late in September, I'd be done with the scorching heat. I'm about to sizzle out there."

"How are those new boots that David sent?"

"Well, they're hot in this weather. And sometimes they're good and sometimes they're not. I guess if I have to walk pavement, they're not." Don quit drinking and began to unlace them. It was always a toss-up what Don would do first on a break—take his shoes off or grab something to quench his thirst.

"You'll be happy I passed up a real find back there on the road. Oh, here's another quarter—also a shiny penny I couldn't resist."

"What? You actually passed up a treasure?"

"Yeah, a perfectly good canoe paddle. If I wasn't going to have to walk so far with it, I might have brought it."

"You're doing fine, Don. We're rapidly filling up Otto again as is, and your road earnings now stand at, uh…eight dollars and forty-one cents."

Other recent treasures I had to find room for in Otto were: a quilted, navy-blue, nylon jacket; several shock cords, black rubber and multicolored nylon; an unexpired Montana dealer's license on a large magnet; one wire stripper-crimper-snipper; a hook-and-eye turnbuckle (which Don insisted was an extremely useful thing to have); an over-sized knee pad; a large, rubber hammer; a few small wrenches; another screwdriver; flotsam and jetsam such as marbles and plastic dinosaurs; and a letter from Harvey to Tura with enclosed *big* plans for the perfect car, house, job, and life—once, that is, Harvey got off his ship and out of the Navy.

Something about that letter Don and I understood completely. We could feel Harvey's longing for another life that did not involve the sea, even as we felt our own for one that did not involve the road. We had been on the journey a full three months now—a popular limit, I noticed, for some other writer-adventurers, like John Steinbeck in *Travels With Charley* and William Least-Heat Moon in *Blue Highways*. It was easy to see why. I wondered how long Harvey had been at sea.

"By the way, Fran, you would not believe how many hubcaps and license plates I've passed up. I wonder how long this is going to go on?"

"What about wrenches—don't forget wrenches. What do you mean, how long is what going to go on? The territory, the weather?"

"I don't know," Don sighed, putting his baseball cap back on his head and getting ready to go out again. "What day is it, anyway. I say it's Tuesday."

"Not even close," I said, "not even close."

But the plains of eastern Washington were not the Great Plains, and the differences were not only significant but entertaining. Though the wheat had all been cut so that there was no waving grain suggesting a sea in the usual sense, there was definitely something fluid about this terrain. The earth itself mounded and rolled and pitched as if halfway to storm swells—hills caught in some sort of undulant still-motion. And to contrast with the metallic sheen on acres and acres of sun-burnished, wheat-stubbled gold was the radiant new green of winter wheat just coming up. Both the old wheat stubble and the young shoots followed gracefully combed furrows over the horizon-ward rise and fall of the land. And with the late, long light of day reaching over and through it all, the land fairly thrummed—like chords of softly plucked strings.

Capping some of the rolling swells were what looked like dark teeth—black caps, volcanic outcroppings of rock. This detail gave a strange cast to the hills, making them look more like ancient burial mounds than accidents of geologic history.

It was the sudden openness, the lack of trees, the evidence of wheat that reminded the Walker of the Plains. What didn't was the lack of wind. But then the windless-ness gave rise to another phenomenon we hadn't met with elsewhere.

"Don, back there Otto crossed paths with one of those dust devils—what a jolt!"

"I'd like to meet up with one, myself," the Walker responded, dipping his bandanna into the melted ice water in the cooler and applying it to the back of his neck.

"I wouldn't mind getting a photograph of one," I said handing the Walker a drink. "A woman at the grocery back there told me that it's the small ones that pack a real punch. The bigger they are, the weaker they are—or anyway, that's what she claims. Otto doesn't want to meet a big one to find out, though. You wouldn't believe the force of that small one—I thought he'd been hit with a baseball bat!"

Dust devils were dust-laden whirlwinds produced by the sun's heat in dry and open farm country on near-windless days. They were most commonly the size of a man and could come striding toward you, or seem to dance a jig, or give chase and go tilting at one another. Generally these spinning updrafts were short-lived creatures, yet they peopled the landscape in a way that suggested they could have other purposes. After all, the Lord took Elijah into heaven by whirlwind, answered Job out of the whirlwind, and gave Ezekiel a strange vision in a whirlwind.

I was waiting my own chance. Perhaps if I had only waited long enough. In one place, that is. I certainly did plenty of waiting. Or maybe the one that crossed paths with Otto was meant for me! "Wake up!" it may have been saying—"Get ready for what's coming next!"

Chapter 36

Into the Coulee

"**I** heard the coyotes again last night," I wrote to David in eastern Washington. "I laughed in my sleep when I heard them. *They* were laughing, I swear. And telling stories! There was the wild joy in their songs again—that I first heard in North Dakota. So many songs and never the same song. I was still smiling when I woke this morning. I am, I know you'll be happy to hear, smiling even now, inside myself. Why am I so drawn to these wild creatures? Who says man only is creative? What is it about their songs—their utter abandon? And every morning I'm on the trail, like the coyotes, wondering in what dark hollow I might find a bit of breakfast, or be able to clean my chops, or be safe to do my work. But David, one of the things about their songs is how abruptly they seem to start up and end—coming out of nowhere, disappearing into nowhere—really, as if they must have a choral director! I do not retire at night without pricking my ears first for coyotes. I'm glad I can hear things in my sleep. Long may they sing!"

And while the nights occasionally rang out with the wildness of coyotes, the Walker pressed deeper into the state of Washington by day. The further in, the more he walked across coarsely interruptive lands sounding their own wild discord against the well-timed rhythmic roll of groomed and fertile fields. Now and again, stretches of a rough, arid scrubbiness would suddenly appear, scrabbling with black volcanic sores and lesions—areas known as the "channeled scablands." Well named, these natural but violent results wrought by the great Spokane flood some nineteen-thousand years ago. Yet "flood" seems too tame a word for some of the hugely savage effects we eventually saw ripped out of the earth's side.

And yet, I liked the channeled scablands just because they were wild—wildly interrupting, wildly forsaken, wildly themselves—lands without makeup. Their only adornment: straw-yellow blossoms of the big sagebrush just coming into bloom atop thick bunches of grey-green foliage. And here, instead of dust devils and wheat pheasants for company, we had killdeer, magpies, horned larks, and prairie falcons—mule deer and jack rabbits.

By late morning on September 21, Don had walked to Coulee City. At the edge of this small town in a desert-like setting suddenly appeared a lake. Banks Lake seemed more believable as a mirage. We learned it was formed by a dam on the Columbia River to the north. The lake partially filled what is called a coulee—a steep-walled, trench-like valley of varying dimensions. The day was hot, and there was a place on the lake for public swimming. Don and I both got in to cool off. Not another living soul was about.

"Did you see the sign back there, Fran?" Don asked as he waded out of the water, stirring up the mucky bottom as he did.

"You mean the one that says Coulee City is the friendliest town in the West? You want your picture taken in front of it?"

"We ought to have pictures of every Western town we've come to claiming to be the friendliest," Don said.

"I know," I said, "but we might not be able to afford the film. That was definitely one of the better signs. The thing that seems funny to me is that until now, I never really thought of Washington as "the West." And I never pictured it like this, either. The scablands are bizarre, aren't they?" I handed Don a towel to dry off.

"Well, where is everybody anyway, Fran? That sign's like a joke. Let me see the map." I spread it out on top of one of the picnic tables for the Walker. "Hmmm. Nothing for forty miles. Nothing here either, it seems."

But just west of Coulee City, the land got even more strange. For a while, because of a long, high rise, there were overlooks seeming to reveal unrelated worlds, in awkwardly close proximity. Far ahead we got our first sighting of the Cascades, and on either hand—sightings of odd, distant, out-of-scale formations in the channeled scablands. The Cascade Mountains seemed the more familiar face, though we'd never been in them. But the other, the hinder parts of earth, into which we got a long, deep view, were unsettling. Where were we?

When we hit some shorn wheat fields again, I was reassured. Wheat was comprehensible. It nearly always held a hopeful burst of meadowlark song. The world was not *too* strange. Maybe it never had been. But then, just toward day's end, the land changed again.

It happened when I drove ahead to scout the day's endpoint and to see if we might be able to camp there. All we needed was an out-of-the-way place where we could park safely off the road.

I soon saw *where* Don would walk the last mile of his day. It was out of the way all right. Even out of this world, I couldn't help thinking as I surveyed the area from a high vantage point. But I guided Otto down the dark asphalt road anyway—down, down, down into the darkening, day-ending depths of Moses Coulee. Somehow I was not really spooked by this place, yet I knew I ought to have been.

I pulled over to look at the map and confirm what the world had just done. All I could see was a certain odd twist in the red line designating Route 2. Incredible. I mean, to think that a map maker did not think it necessary to prepare a person for this. I drove deeper in.

I could see that the way out of this coulee was unobstructed, the road winding gracefully up and off to the west. But where I pulled over now there was a "Dead End" sign, and I found yet another way barricaded and labeled "Road Closed." *Of course, of course*, I thought, *these fit*. And, at the same time, I knew that I fit. I felt like a golf ball that had fallen neatly into its cup. I was in place.

Yet I might well have felt trapped, since both the way in and the way out were beyond easy reach. I did feel exposed. Anyone else traveling down, in, and through could see as far as I could—could see that there was no one but me in this wild, man-forsaken place. I wondered again why I wasn't afraid.

I left Otto and started back in the direction where I would, I hoped, eventually meet up with Don. I noticed a car far off, entering the coulee. I had thought I began my walk from the bottom of the coulee, but now I seemed to go even deeper for a while. I was being swallowed. The steep, sheer coulee walls were close-seeming, yet the flat-bottomed valley had to be a mile wide in places. The coulee walls were towering and dark. Some grotesque, lime-green lichen dribbled down their sides. And then I recalled, as I walked in that labyrinthine hollow, the forces that had once gouged out the place—forces unimaginably violent yet not evil. The flood.

I looked up occasionally for some sign of the Walker. I knew it would not be difficult to spot his light clothing against the dark coulee walls. I watched the car making its way down in. Several long, lonely minutes later, it whizzed past me. I was glad it hadn't slowed.

Now the sun reached the ragged edge of the western rim of Moses Coulee—dwarfed by the touch. The dimensions of the place were gargantuan. I tried to explain to myself why the subterranean feel. There was as much sky over my head as earth beneath my feet. But was it earth? It felt more alien—even Martian. And the effect remained: the place was as a tunnel over my soul.

And the quiet, I noticed, when the car had been gone a good while, was whispery—as if only whispers dared break the hush, or as if somehow the hush was made of whispers—whispers at the very edge of my hearing, warning me against my heightened exhilaration to walk soft, go slow, watch out.

That was it. That was all I could do. But when I was at the very pit of the coulee trench, I suddenly saw a great, dark eagle silhouetted against the furthest clear corner of northern sky. I watched it turn, seem to swivel on its still wings, and come swinging down into the coulee. But no, it was too big to be an eagle—must be a glider. But no, it was too big to be a glider, and it was flying far too low for one. What was it? I froze in study of this huge, low, steady thing coming silently toward me and seeming to fill the coulee trench. How so low and slow and silent? Why couldn't I hear it? It's aiming for me, I thought, watching it lower itself as it came. It looked as if it would simply glide to a halt on its belly where I stood. A tremendous urge came over me to run and hide, but where? I didn't move.

And then I saw another of these things swing eerily down out of the blue, following in the flight path of the first. At the same time, the sun deserted, slipping behind the coulee rim, sending a distinct chill into the deepening shadows. In response, the low-flying things suddenly cast forward beams of light, and for the first time, I could see the blurring spin of a row of huge propellers. But why no sound? And yet, even as I strained to hear, I caught the merest whisper of a muffled hum. Planes. Okay. Or maybe not okay—maybe Martian planes.

A few moments later, the first sailed over me—by so slim a margin I could have leaped up and grabbed the camouflage-painted wing it tilted toward me for a free ride. Instead, I looked into the cockpit and into the very human face of the pilot, just as he turned to look out at me. For one hovering moment we stared. He seemed as startled to find me walking Moses Coulee as I was to find him skimming the bottom of it. I waved after him, and then the next pilot tilted his wing like the first and followed down the long, empty airway of the coulee off to the south and out of my sight. I took a deep breath. I focused ahead on where the Walker would appear. He could not appear too soon.

When at long last I spied him, a faint sense of familiar reality stirred within me. I suddenly felt like celebrating. I walked a lot faster. I smiled. I felt like skipping. Finally, unable to contain my happy heart, at the top of my lungs I shouted a friendly "Hello-o-o-o" to the Walker. A full second later, an eerie cry stopped me cold. My own voice had come back to me, dressed up in a hollow, contorted twang. Disbelieving, I then let loose with a round of whoops the coyotes had taught me. And these, too, came echoing back in a haunting barrage. For a moment I wondered what I might have wakened in the place. And then, when I looked to the Walker, I saw him running for the first time of the entire journey. I figured he must have thought I was yelling for help, so I ran, shouting and waving to Don that everything was okay.

And everything was okay. Don had been running down the sloping road just for the heck of it.

"Fran," Don said, pausing to catch his breath, "maybe we shouldn't camp in this place. I'm not sure I like it or trust it."

"I know what you mean, Don," I agreed as I turned to match the Walker's stride. Far ahead I could just make out Otto huddled in a pool of darkness. "But I really want to stay. Just think, you'll be able to say you slept at the bottom of Moses Coulee—I bet there are golden eagles in their aeries here—and stranger things, too." And I proceeded to describe my encounter with the reconnaissance planes, yet Don had also seen them. He had been wondering what could have possibly happened to them when they literally dropped out of his sight.

That night the stars came out so bright above the black depths of the coulee, they fairly burned through the canvas sides of Otto's pop-up top. Don got up to go out more than once. So did I. I thought I might catch Jupiter rising. But when I looked up, the splendor was such that I forgot why I had. I suddenly felt, in that vast, stony darkness, like a child in some great palace ballroom—candlelit chandeliers far overhead, guests not yet arrived. And I wanted to dance. I listened, half expecting music, yet all I heard was the timid hooting of an owl who plainly knew better than to raise his own echo.

In the morning, with a flood of warm sunshine washing over the place, all was changed. Don walked out ahead of me. I hung back to get a picture of him climbing out of Moses Coulee. Yet I knew I wouldn't get it. Don flagged me down when I passed him.

"Fran, you just missed a round of songs from the coyotes!"

"Darn!" I said, but then I thought—probably just as well. "Lucky for you," I said, "I might have joined up."

Chapter 37

Skookum La Metsin

When Don walked out of the Rockies in eastern Washington, he came down to an average elevation of about two thousand feet. The last of Washington's plains-like plateau ended abruptly west of Waterville, a town at 2,600 feet, and the last of the scablands ended before that. Again, the map did not prepare us for any big change. A bit of a squiggle in the red line of Route 2 was all I found later. But in less than twenty miles, Don walked from Waterville, down 1,800 feet in elevation, following a winding, narrow way through a treeless series of dirt hills called Corbaley Canyon—hills yet alive with swooping hawks, black-billed magpies, and the whinnying of wild horses. Not even a trickling stream watered the gravelly hills or wet the fell bottom. The road was so twisted, our longest view was down the steeply flaring slopes.

In the hot, dry, parched canyon, the sky was its all-too-familiar desert blue. But then, suddenly and unexpectedly at the bottom, the humidity went from zero to a hundred percent and the temperature dropped precipitously. When Don rounded the last curve of the canyon, he came out to face the Columbia—wide, serene, and silvery-glassed. The great river was filling its own valley between more hovering peaks running north and south.

On the far side of the river were the foothills of the Cascades. The drop in temperature was due to the sun's disappearance behind the facing peaks. The sudden rise in humidity, entirely artificial, was due to an intense sprinkler system fed by the Columbia and watering the orchards that greened the gentler slopes and flats on either side of the river. Wherever the eye fell, heavy-laden apple boughs were propped up on sticks to keep the dark, red, pendulous fruit above the ground. The sprinklered water seemed to be pumping directly into the apples, like air into balloons. I wondered that they didn't burst.

The orchard greens with shoulder-high weeds between the rows contrasted sharply with the more barren, steep-sided hills, whose feet were soaking in the Columbia. The hills seemed dressed in a plush, brown velvet that had been roughly worn and pilled over time. Green-black evergreens were sparsely scattered about them like appliquéd afterthoughts. All the naked dryness accompanying the sprawl of lush orchards and the great river itself was uncommonly strange to us. We were used to seeing orchards in the Champlain Valley at home, but those seemed almost whimsical by comparison— rather more dependent on nature than man. Yet nature was having her way here, too.

The harvest was being held up by the unseasonably warm weather. The nights had not been cold enough to ripen the fruit. Thus, wherever we looked were groups of loitering men, who had come by the busload over long distances to "pick." Someone in Waterville had warned us about the town we would come to at the end of this day. "You won't find anything good in Orondo," he said as he spat. "It's a picker's town." And though the place didn't really seem too savory, we were stuck there for the night anyway.

We found a beach-like park and campground next to the river. "It's a good place to swim earlier in the season," the campground manager told us when he saw us inspecting the murky water, "before the algae sets in. You gonna camp here?"

Don said we were thinking about it.

"Bout as safe as you'll find for five dollars. I got a padlocked gate, see? And over there's the public shower you can use."

We thanked him, signed up for a campsite, and headed for the showers. Don waited on the men's side in a crowded line of migrant workers. It was a long, chilly wait for a brief cold shower.

It was cold water only on the women's side too, but I was the only one in there. A single door led into a huge and cavernous concrete room poorly lit with one shower head, no windows, and no ventilation. Cigarette butts littered the wet floor. I was acutely aware of all the men hanging about outside, and though glad to get clean, I was even gladder when Don finally came out and the showers closed down for the night.

Don crossed the deep, silvery stillness of the Columbia just north of Wenatchee, Washington, the next morning enjoying the dramatic views up and down its long trough cut through the misty, gray-brown hills. It was all orchards along Route 2 the first half of the day, sometimes opposite acres of sagebrush on land not irrigated. The sun made me thirst for these unwatered lands. Don's way into the Cascades was now all uphill.

Later in the day, Don followed alongside the Wenatchee River, the crisp cool of coniferous forests upon him—the parched brown hills and watered orchards now low to his sight. The air was as light and healing as the Wenatchee itself. I sat beside the falling, swift mountain waters much of the day, partaking of the "skookum la metsin" (Chinook Indian jargon for "good strong medicine") known to soothe and rest the weary wayfarer.

We camped that night beside the Wenatchee. Well after dark, Don swam in a deep, fast pool of the icy waters, trying to rinse off pesticide residue. He'd gotten sprayed by a low-flying helicopter covering one of the orchards he'd walked beside earlier in the day.

But the next day, we realized that Don had not been swimming in the river alone. Every deep pool we looked into had its king salmon or steelhead trout lying in wait, pointing upstream. They were waiting for rains to swell the stream so they could get further on up to their spawning grounds. Maybe the wait was "skookum la metsin" for them, too, since they had already swum hundreds and hundreds of miles in from the Pacific, following the Columbia a roundabout route to the Wenatchee. Huge and beautiful, these fish were clad in deep-blue mail with shining highlights of the rainbow. Often a beam of sunlight struck through the waters to show off their colors. And once, when one of these fish was startled out of its sleepy wait, it leaped sudden and clear of its rushing pool, taking my heart with it.

Don climbed from Orondo at 758 feet to Stevens Pass at 4,061 feet without complaint, though his legs ached with the two-day effort. But the grace of evergreen mountain lands—themselves seeming to cascade between the embrace of falling, rushing, jewel-like waters—was more invigorating than wearying. We camped near the pass.

At first light the next morning, we were startled awake at our campsite on a logging road—by helicopters. Helicopters logging! We got out of there as quickly as we could, yet not before we saw loads of whole tree trunks threateningly and precariously dangled above our heads.

West of the pass, a wild wind whipped up some chill, wet weather out of the low, scudding cloud wrack. When the day-long rain fell, I counted back eighteen days to the rain we had had east of the Rockies. But now the walking was all downhill, and the chilling way was eased somewhat by the occasional warmth of a mountain cafe.

This rain brought out the biggest, fattest, blackest slugs either of us had ever seen. If Don had inadvertently stepped on one, it would have been like slipping on a banana peel. Meanwhile, the busyness of the narrow road had increased to a constant and dangerous threat, so that the walker had to be alert in order to dodge both the traffic and the slugs.

There was a famous weekend fall festival attracting great numbers of visitors to the very Bavarian-looking hamlet of Leavenworth, among other places. Familiar signs of autumnal change were everywhere now—and almost everywhere threatened, it seemed. Don and I both noticed a great many two-legged leafcutters trimming the more colorful foliage back with saws, axes, clippers, and knives. We saw occasional truckloads of foliage headed up the mountains to decorate shops for the big festival, too.

Fortunately, there was some foliage well out of reach. High, high up in the small alpine meadows and ravines, where the taller evergreens could not follow, clustered and clinging round the rumpled and craggy peaks were intricate thickets of patchy color—

vibrant and intense. All the more vibrant because I knew I looked on at a distance, which wanted to diminish the brilliance. Somehow it was not diminished so much as deepened. I felt as if I was looking up to Eden-like gardens, perhaps tended by some shy and noble race of beings, perhaps even tended by the Sasquatch.

Chapter 38

In Ninety-Six Days

Coming down out of the mountains, approaching Seattle, a sense of celebration began to build. Don and I both felt a rare confidence, as if nothing could go wrong now. And people we met in the mountains who knew, better than either of us, how very close Don was to crossing the continent complete, began cheering the Walker's effort as if he had made it across already.

The Big-Y Cafe in Peshastin, Washington, gave Don a T-shirt sporting the cafe logo along with their congratulations. When Don caught up with Chris, Diana, and Maury (the women bikers from Dartmouth) for the last time in Leavenworth, he teased them about the race to Seattle. But since they were staying behind for the festival, they congratulated him and conceded his victory.

Just east of Seattle in Monroe, I stopped for a mail drop at a post office whose general delivery window was closed for the day. When I heard some noises in the back, I did a little frenzied pounding on a door, asking for help. A while later, the bottom of a Dutch door opened and a man handed out to me twenty-three pieces of mail! This was, I was to find out later, the first avalanche of birthday greetings for me from family and friends, orchestrated by David back home.

Even Otto seemed to revel in the happy atmosphere coinciding with reaching our western limit. Outside Monroe, the morning of Don's triumphant entry into Seattle, I stopped at a car wash. Suddenly Otto was afloat in the suds and giggles and glee of the Monroe Kickettes—

199

junior-high girls raising money for their soccer team's traveling fund. Otto loved it—all those petting hands on him. He purred on merrily for days afterward.

But no, there was no welcome committee nor bands playing, nor witnesses other than myself, in Seattle that Sunday, September 27— one-hundred and three days into the journey, ninety-six days' walk from Middlebury, Vermont—2,920 miles from home. Yet the sun did come out in a splendorous sky, the great blue heron flew over more than once, and a brightly colored flock of hot-air balloons following the valley of the Snohomish gave the day a festive air. And, too, because of all the sunlight on so many waters about the city, from the outskirts in, Don's way was about as spangly as he could get.

Meanwhile, we were both looking for Mount Rainier. We didn't know in which direction to look to find it. When I asked a woman passing by me at one point about the mountain, she said she'd never heard of it.

I was wanting to see Mount Rainier for more reasons than because it was *the* outstanding feature of the area—going from 14,410 feet to sea level in a mere forty miles. It was also a family memorial. Mount Rainier held a secret I would never learn—exactly how it took the life of my young cousin Julie, in a July snowstorm as she hiked alone from one outpost to another while working as a ranger one summer. For seven long years, Julie was just plain missing. All that time, not the least scrap of evidence as to what had happened to her could be found. Wild talks that she might have run off to join a religious cult or even been kidnapped gave us hope that one day she would still turn up. My uncle, her father, died without ever knowing what happened. It wasn't until some human bones were found by some hikers well off a trail—below a cliff, I think it was—along with a pencil bearing the name of her father's business that we knew for certain she died on the mountain.

When Don spotted the mountain first, I know why we hadn't seen it before. It was too big and too much there. Strangely enough, a person might not see it, but once seen it could *not* be mistaken. It seemed utterly unrelated to the puny, building-block city in its foreground. Don said that it seemed to be floating there. And so it did—in a ghostly, almost chilling sort of way—its feet severed from the earth by a thin, gauzy haze gathered below and around it. This was a mountain more of heaven than of earth, more of God than of man. It looked capable of taking any number of lives—and I knew it was not my cousin's memorial only.

"Well, you made it, Don! Congratulations!" I said when Don found me parked at the edge of Puget Sound, by the ferries.

"Partway, you mean, but thanks," Don said as I slapped the palm of his hand. I could tell he was happy, tired, and still looking ahead.

"Can you believe what all we've seen in a week's time? I mean, a mere six days ago we were at the bottom of Moses Coulee! It makes my head spin! So now what? Where do we go from here?" Since we'd left Route 2 behind at Monroe, our route had gotten more complex.

"I'm not sure," the Walker said. "Pass me the map."

While Don studied the map, I suddenly got a lonely sort of feeling—realizing, as Don must have already—that ahead of us were still endless more days on the road. How brief the feeling of success! I stared wistfully over the sound to the Olympic Mountains; the sun would soon be setting behind them.

"I don't know. I don't like the looks of the roads heading south of here, Fran. Too much congestion going through Tacoma and all. The roads on the Olympic Peninsula look smaller and better—but then, of course, we'd have to take a ferry."

I couldn't believe my ears. The Walker was considering a ferry? "Oh, Don, that sounds awfully good to me. And how 'bout a day off—I mean to celebrate. It would only be your eighth day off. We could camp over there tonight, maybe see something of the Olympic National Park tomorrow, maybe ferry over to Victoria, even—have a *real* cup of tea!"

"Now, Fran—"

"I know, I know," I interrupted. "This is not a sightseeing trip. Well, you decide."

Just then the foghorn hoots of the Kitsap Ferry sounded, and I could tell the Walker was mightily tempted. I didn't say anything. I hardly dared hope.

"Well, I don't know," Don said folding up the map with a frown on his face. "Maybe it will make The Walk seem less, but I'm not out there setting any records anyway—I'll do it. Let's take the ferry to Bremerton."

"Hurrah!" I cheered. "I only hope we're not too late to buy a ticket. Now, Don, about that day off, and maybe a little exploring—and, you know, the ferry to Victoria, and well, now that I've already mentioned it—that cup of tea in British Columbia, I almost wish I'd never thought of it."

"Fran, you win. You'll have your tea in Victoria—even though…"

And now we both said it together, "This is not a sightseeing trip!"

Chapter 39

The Attaché Case

For all the times I had pondered our progress on the map of Washington State, it never once registered, before we got there, that Seattle was not really our western limit. In my mind, The Walk roughly took the shape of a rectangle, with Seattle in the upper left-hand corner. But when I looked more closely at the map, it was obvious we would not hit our western limit until the southern coast of Oregon, thanks to the bulging of the continent out into the Pacific. Still, after Seattle, we no longer headed due west, and if we had not made a sharp left-hand turn to head purely south, we were at least now heading in a definite southerly direction. After months of heading west, this change felt good to us. Also, we were cutting off the upper-left-hand corner of that rectangle, and neither the Walker, the Driver, nor Otto was complaining.

But where had we gotten? It didn't take long to realize that the Olympic Peninsula was yet another world, like none we had seen anywhere else on the journey—barely like what we had seen previously in Washington. The western side of the peninsula had rain forests with rainfall averaging 170 inches or more per year; the other, inland side, in the rain shadow of the Olympic peaks, had seventeen inches or less per year. In addition, at the time we were passing through, the Seattle area was surviving its worst drought in seventy-five years. And yet, because of the way the westerly flow of weather might make it over or through the mountains, we saw pockets of tremendous lushness.

It was confusing. I kept thinking back to Moses Coulee. If a person rode east from Seattle in the back of a car and napped, in a mere five hours one could miss it all, Moses Coulee included. The land was surprising. The details of the land were surprising. Maybe when one is always in a hurry on the way to "somewhere," one cannot see "the way." But we were learning: the way itself is somewhere. But now which way?

"Don, I miss Route 2—the pure simplicity of it. I went wrong so many times just coming into Seattle," I complained in Bremerton as we both studied the map in a diner the morning of September 29.

"Well, nothing ahead looks anywhere near as congested or confusing as in Seattle. Anyway, don't worry, it won't be long before we get to the coast. And when we do, we'll just stick to the coastal route. Meanwhile…" Don said, pointing out the way he was going to walk with a tine of his fork, "it looks like Route 3 to 101 to 108 to 12, or is it Route 8?—well, anyway—to 107 to 101 again to 4 to 401 to…"

"Enough, already. One road at a time. I'll meet you eight miles ahead on Route 3. I hope I don't get lost. I guess I'll just have to get used to paying more attention."

The Walker had to pay attention, too. Walking the Olympic Peninsula was not as ideal as we had hoped. The overwhelming reason: the return of the logging truck. On Route 17 in Canada, Don's highest hourly truck count had been in the eighties, and not all of those were logging trucks. But now Don counted as many as 280 trucks in one hour, and most of these *were* logging trucks—loaded and unloaded, occasionally tripled up like short trains. More often than not, these monstrous vehicles barreled noisily along at ear-shocking speeds. On the skimpy secondary roads, Don had to look sharp. He had some narrow brushes even so, such as when a speeding car passing one of these trucks actually flicked Don's swinging hand.

And the weather? I wrote to David the second morning: "Well, it's too cold to be out there typing in Otto just yet. We're in oystering country, so I'm having a delicious bowl of oyster stew for breakfast at the Pine Tree Inn in Shelton. The sun is bright already so I expect it will warm up fast. Yesterday got amazingly warm. Don noticed forest signs warning of *extreme* fire danger, the highest rating we've seen yet. All I can think is, if a fire did get started, it would burn up a lot of roadside trash. The laundry is piling up again in this sweaty clime."

And later that day: "Phew! Another warm, warm day! I've just finished typing the weekly newsletter, but Don's gotten four hour's walk ahead of me. I hope he's not dying of thirst out there. Got to get ice, juice, this into the mail to you—and catch up quickly. Got to find a laundromat somewhere. Seems an unending summer—I best not complain."

Meanwhile, the landscape in this area, dedicated to the lumber industry, was something to see. Whole mountainsides were denuded by clearcut logging, instead of merely large sections, which we had seen in the Rockies. And whether it was true or not, as lumber people claimed it wasn't, this land looked rather badly abused. The scattered heaps of roadside trash did nothing to soften the ravaged look of the region, either.

We had noticed ugly quantities of litter in other places on the journey, too. Indeed, going in the manner we were, it was impossible *not* to notice it. But in this part of Washington especially, I was writing lengthy passages in my journal lamenting the widespread existence of it.

From Bremerton to Shelton to Montesano to Raymond to Naselle, my heart ached at the wholesale butchering of the land, at the acres and acres of waters clogged with floating logs, at what seemed a gluttonous rush to use it all up, and at the ever-present strewing of litter. In lumber centers like Shelton, Aberdeen, and Raymond we really could not see that logging was directly benefiting the people who broke their backs over it. Signs of recognizable prosperity were few.

But as far as the litter goes? "Don, I saw you back there! You know, where I honked when I passed you? What in the world were you doing—down on all fours in that ditch?"

Don blushed and laughed. "Fran, I just couldn't help myself. I guess I've inspected more ditches than that one. It's this fantasy I've had going on in my head for a while. You see, this old, brown suitcase caught my eye, and, well, I mean, it's possible, I keep thinking, that somebody might have somewhere, you know, in a big rush to escape the law, hastily discarded an attaché case full of—well, let's just say—hundred-dollar bills?"

"Don, I think you are going bonkers!" I laughed. "Well?"

"Nope, not this time—nothing in that suitcase but old magazines. But I'm not giving up yet."

"You mean to say there was nothing in that whole ditch-load of trash worth picking up?"

"Not really, but I did find this a little while later on the road— right in my path." Don handed me a trinket. It was a piece of cheap jewelry—a stainless-steel heart on a blue plastic background inscribed with the words: "I Love Don."

"It's a sign," I said, inspecting the thing, "A good omen. The road spirits are with you, Don."

Chapter 40

What's Wrong with Otto?

I only hoped the road spirits were with me, too. I mean, a little good luck could go a long way on this journey—and so could a little bad. It seemed my own luck was tested time and again. Later, something happened that I had been dreading and yet half expecting all along: Otto suddenly began making a peculiar noise.

It was a buzzing noise. I pulled over and listened. I'd never heard anything like it. I turned off the motor. I could still hear it. I checked to see that my lights were off. I took the key out of the ignition. I could still hear it. I started searching for it. I looked inside cabinets and under seats. I put my hands on things to see if anything was vibrating. I checked old switches, which had long ago quit working, but I flicked them anyway to see if I could stop the buzzing. It was maddening—the buzzing was right under my nose, so to speak, but I couldn't find it.

I went outside and inspected Otto. I could still hear the buzz, more muffled now, but seeming to come from nowhere in particular. I peered into the engine, but no, the buzz wasn't in there. I began to feel as if something might explode, that the buzz was a fuse, and I had only a short time to find the bomb. I panicked.

I leaped into the saddle and sped on to the next town. I spotted a firehouse, screeched to a halt, and ran inside to beg for help. A trio of firemen rushed outside, scrambled about Otto much as I had earlier, and ended up as perplexed as I. When they threw up their hands, they had troubled looks on their faces as if they shared my fears. They suggested I try a gas station. The buzzing continued. I was a nervous wreck.

I raced on and pulled into the first gas station I came to. I tried to calm myself. The buzzing continued. Maybe I still had time. A man pumping gas sent me in to get the garage mechanic, who was an expert on VWs. I found him wiping axle grease off his hands—he looked barely twenty. I began explaining the buzz and all the useless searches as I led him over to Otto. He listened carefully, tucked his rag into his back pocket, opened up Otto's sliding door, and climbed inside. I paced nervously without. The buzzing continued.

And then, after a brief search, the mechanic hopped out, carrying Don's ditty bag at arm's length—the buzz caught inside the small bag like a bee. In another moment, he pulled out Don's battery-powered electric shaver—and turned the thing off. The guy smiled and I laughed. I laughed with relief and I laughed because it was so silly. But once I got started, I could hardly stop. The garage mechanic looked at me as if I was nuts. I laughed so hard I nearly wet my pants. And I laughed again later when I told the Walker about it.

"Fran, I know it's funny, but is it that funny? You're getting punchy. Calm down. You're going to get a stomachache from all that. What you need is a good night's sleep. Or maybe a cold shower."

We'd driven down to camp—into a tiny, jungly sort of dell on a riverish sort of lake called Lake Sylvia State Park. It was a deep pocket of towering, lush vegetation.

"Oh, go jump in the lake," I giggled.

Which Don proceeded to do, and though he swam around for a while, he was fairly blue from the cold when he got out. The air was chilling down rapidly, and I began looking forward to a hot shower, not a cold one. Now Don was, too. All we needed were two quarters to operate the showers.

"Uh oh," Don said, "it looks like we have only *one* quarter left!"

"*One* quarter!" I moaned, suddenly sobering up, and then hating myself for realizing I would not have the heart to use that quarter on myself. "Oh, go ahead, Don!" I said, cursing my luck.

But when Don found another quarter in the men's shower room and brought it out to me, I cheered up again. Getting to bed clean, I knew, would go a long way toward helping me get a good night's sleep. It also occurred to me that if I had insisted on taking the shower, that quarter would probably never have been found.

As I snuggled into my sleeping bag and closed my eyes that night, I heard an interesting and unusual bird call. Sometimes it was a wail and sometimes more like a shriek. Sometimes it came from up high, sometimes down low. Every fifteen seconds or so, it cried out from somewhere. After a while I was so tired that I could *almost* fall asleep in one of those fifteen-second intervals—yet not quite. I kept thinking, this bird isn't going to keep this up all night long, is it? And no, it didn't.

Just before four in the morning, it quit. But after it quit, an owl started up. I was almost used to this, though, when at five I began to hear the distant roar of logging trucks on the move. Still, this drone was more peaceable and I finally began to drift off. Yet hardly a minute later, it seemed, came the dawn—at which a chorus of wakeup calls sprang forth like I'd never heard in my life. It was such a jumble of hoots, whistles, rasps, chitters, clucks, and shrieks, I really thought we *had* camped out in a jungle. The only familiar sound was the sprightly phrasing of an enthusiastic song sparrow. The rest was bedlam.

"What's all that racket?" Don complained as he started to perform his regular round of morning sit-ups on his bunk below.

"Don't ask me," I said crabbily. "Did you hear that jungle bird last night, screaming and whooping it up every fifteen seconds?"

"No, I was out like a light."

"Don," I said wearily, "you have all the luck."

OCTOBER

Washington, Oregon, California

Chapter 41

Too Much Reality

When the well-rested Walker hit the logging trail the morning of October 1, I drove into Montesano to do the laundry. This town had a neater appearance than some we had seen, but the laundromat I found was drear, and when I realized it did not even offer the convenience of baskets for its customers, I left. I had to drive out of my way to pick up mail in Aberdeen anyway, and since it was a bigger town, I thought it would have a better laundry.

Unfortunately, the laundromat I found in Aberdeen was even worse. And more unfortunately, I had all my wash going before I appreciated how *much* worse. I'd been in too much of a hurry—anxious to be done so I could fetch the mail. I looked around. Again, there were no clothes baskets for the convenience of the customer—but also no bathroom, no sinks, no change machines, no soap dispensers, and no tables for folding clothes. I noticed more washers and dryers labeled "broken" than working ones. One huge container overflowed with trash—with everything, that is, but what you might expect in a laundry—the whole of it stinking of vomit. The washers emptied into an open trough that looked and smelled no better than a sewer. Nothing savory about the two greasy-looking thugs in there, either, who, when I once dared look their way, leered at me with inexplicable smiles. What kind of hellhole was this?

I locked myself in Otto and waited for my wash to finish. I was afraid to go back in. I dreaded having to hang around to use the dryers, yet there seemed no way around it. When I did, I had to stand close by, since a quarter bought only three minutes of drying time—barely enough time for the dryer to heat up. While I stood there, I had plenty of time to notice the signs I hadn't before—signs posted on every vertical surface available: "These premises filmed on video camera for your protection."

I didn't even want to imagine what had prompted those signs! I was hardly reassured. Finally, after what seemed like eons, I ran out of quarters. I left with my half-dried laundry. I really and truly wanted to wash the stuff all over again immediately—some place far, far away in a cleaner, brighter setting.

When I picked up the mail in Aberdeen, I found I was showered again by a small avalanche of birthday greetings. I broke down and wept. It suddenly seemed to me that we have plenty of defenses to put up against the evil, the ugly, and the unjust of the world; but no defenses at all against the truly good, the truly true, and the truly beautiful. Of course, we think we don't want a defense against the latter. And yet, in truth, we are liable to be even more swept away—perhaps even destroyed, were we ever to feel the full brunt of it. In William Blake's words, "We are put on earth for a little space that we may learn to bear the beams of love." Herman Melville put it somewhat differently when he said, "In certain moods no man can weigh this world without throwing in a something somehow like Original Sin to strike the uneven balance." The letters were almost too much.

Besides the good wishes was a small package from a dear friend, full of funny little gifts—among which was a small kaleidoscope, "to guard against too much reality," she said. Indeed!

That was one of the troubles with this crazy journey—what *was* "reality"? One minute you were sipping a royal cup of tea in Victoria, the next you were in the snake pit of laundromats. I took a long, glittering look through the kaleidoscope, and then carefully laid the thing on Otto's dash, where I might always have it within reach.

That night we camped behind a small football stadium in the town of Raymond, within earshot of some sort of logging factory, which kept up its hissing, grinding, buzzing, and clattering round the clock as it sawed, stacked, chipped, shredded, and pulped its lumber.

"Don, now don't tell me you could sleep through all that ungodly racket *last* night!" I said to the Walker when he was eating his bowl of cold cereal the next morning in Otto.

"Hmph," he said with his mouth full, nodding his head in the affirmative.

"Well, I guess when I think about it, if I walked thirty miles every day, I probably could also."

The day I turned forty-two, it was chilly, gloomy, and drizzly. The Aberdeen laundromat still haunted me, and I was tired, as I wrote to David when I failed to get him on the phone that morning, "tired of this crazy trip, tired of being away from you, tired of being disappointed about dumb things—just tired, tired, tired."

I tried to call a couple of other people that morning, too, at the payphone outside the Willapa Inn—just in case someone wanted to wish me a happy birthday, but no one was home. I drank a long, solitary cup of tea at the inn, finished my letter to David, and drove on.

I could see a lot of water as I drove now, but it still wasn't the sea itself; it was Willapa Bay. The smells of salt and fish had been in the air for days.

"Where's the ocean, Don?" I said later, secretly hoping he would wish me a happy birthday.

"I don't know. What day is it anyway?"

"I don't know," I said, still hoping. "How far ahead do you want me to go this time?"

"Eight miles."

"Eight miles. Okay."

Disappointed, I drove on. When I finally found a place to pull over, I thought I might as well write up my recent laundromat experience, so I wouldn't have to think about it again. I looked for my little black notebook—one of the pocket-sized notebooks from which I could have reconstructed the entire journey, including the weather of each and every day. And though I turned Otto inside out, even popped his top and searched among my sheets and blankets, I could not find it.

I felt sick—sicker than at the Aberdeen laundromat. Could I have left it at the Willapa Inn? But I could not picture it on the white linen tablecloth where I'd been sitting. I searched Otto again. No luck. Maybe it's at the inn, I thought, but I didn't want to drive back the twenty or more miles if it wasn't.

Now, I recalled seeing, a good distance back, a sign to another place—The Blue Heron. If there was a phone there, I could try calling the Willapa Inn. The Blue Heron proved to be miles out of my way in another direction, but once I was committed I kept on going. At last I arrived, and from the phone in the cafe-bar-poolroom I got a Willapa Inn waitress on the line—who said she did remember seeing me scribbling away at my table when she came on her shift. She seemed very concerned about my loss. She went to look for the little black book. But no, it wasn't there. She was very sorry. I was very sorry. I thanked her and hung up.

I cried. And then stubbornly and furiously I turned Otto inside out again. And then I sat in Otto and out-gloomed the gloom, trying to accept the loss. If only it wasn't my birthday, I thought, surely I could.

I called the Willapa Inn again. Had they, by any strange chance, since I first called, possibly come across it? No, but the waitress said again how truly sorry she was, and how she understood how badly I wanted and needed that notebook. There was a long pause in which I struggled again just to accept this loss. But then the waitress suggested that maybe someone on the earlier shift might have found it. Could she call me back after she made a phone call to find out?

When I hung up this time, I was beginning to feel better—not because I had any real hope of getting my notebook back, but simply because the waitress seemed so blessedly sympathetic.

The phone rang. When I picked it up, the now-familiar voice said, "Fran, the Lord is with you. I have your notebook." I could barely believe my ears. For some reason, she had gone to make her phone call at the pay phone I had used that very morning, and there, on a shelf under the phone, was my little black notebook. I was on my way.

"Fran, have you been seeing the great blue heron like I have been seeing the great blue heron? It seems to be all over the place today," Don commented at day's end.

"I have—and thanks to another Blue Heron," I said, "I've had a better day than some." While mixing tuna and mayonnaise for supper sandwiches, I told Don the story about finding my little black book.

"Well, I know you think I forgot," Don said, when I was finished, "but I haven't. I know it's your birthday and here are some presents." He proceeded to pull things out of his bulging fanny pack. "A leather flash-attachment case, which I figure you can put your pens in; a fishing lure—to use in the ocean we're coming to, in case you have nothing better to do; a book to take your mind off your troubles, called *Sonny Goes to School*; and now, quit laughing, I know you'll like this next one—look!" Don dangled a fifty-dollar bill in front of my nose.

"Don, you didn't find the bank robber's attaché case, did you?" I asked, inspecting the bill to see if it looked counterfeit.

"No, but I searched the area where I found this for quite a while, thinking it might have flown loose from a bigger pile. This makes up a little for the laundromat, don't you think?"

I hadn't realized that my gloominess had gotten to Don. "Yeah," I agreed, "but it makes your other road earnings look kind of piddling now."

"Well, don't' report it in the newsletter. Let's keep it a secret—until the end. I still can't believe it; I just have this feeling I might have passed up other fifty-dollar bills out there."

"Don't worry, Don, there's a lot more road to inspect before you retire from this journey, and tomorrow a new state—Oregon."

Chapter 42

A Terrible Misnomer

The border between Washington and Oregon was marked by a four-mile bridge over the mouth of the Columbia River—an important milestone. On it, Don would walk his three-thousandth mile. I drove ahead to scout the bridge and retrieve mail in Astoria, Oregon, on the far side. After a cup of tea at The Brass Rail, I drove back a little troubled. I'd found a "no pedestrians allowed" sign on the bridge and a toll booth at the Oregon end. And then, while I waited for the Walker at a pull-off back on the Washington side, I got an idea.

"Fran, I don't like it. I'll feel silly. No, I'll just go ahead and walk the bridge. You said yourself there was room enough to walk in the bike lane." Don bent over to change his shoes and socks, which were damp from the morning's steady drizzle.

"Well, surely you agree it's a good idea to wear one of those fluorescent safety vests David sent in today's mail."

"Of course. I wish we'd had them earlier. I don't know why we didn't think of it, except that until recently I've had plenty of daylight for walking. Ever since that car nicked my hand, though—and this flood of logging trucks! But Fran, you'd better wear one too, you know, when you're taking your own walks."

"I guess, but I'm not on the road ten hours a day like you, so I'm not sure it's so important for me. Come on, Don, I'm worried about you on that bridge. A car passing you may report you to the tollbooth

218

at the far end. And if a state trooper should happen along? Anyway, what's wrong with my idea? There's lots of litter on the bridge and they must have to send people out to clean it up from time to time. All you have to do is take a garbage bag, pick up some of the litter on your way, and wear this pinned to your back." I held up a piece of paper on which I'd printed: "Official Litter Patrol." "Besides, if you do get arrested, surely your breaking the law will look a little better for having done this good deed."

"I don't want to argue, Fran," Don said with finality. "Any mail for me?"

While Don read his mail, I bit my tongue. I stared out the window and watched a cormorant being harassed by a gull. The cormorant was having trouble getting its fish juggled into position for swallowing, and the gull was trying to fluster the cormorant into dropping its catch. At last the cormorant won out. Somehow my idea did, too.

"Okay, Fran, maybe you're right. But I refuse to wear that sign. I think I'll look official enough with the vest and a big garbage bag."

And so he did. The plan worked. When Don came to the tollbooth on the Oregon side, he handed the woman taking tolls the bag of litter and said he'd been granted permission to walk the bridge to do some cleaning up (though he didn't say by whom).

"Well, they never think to tell me anything around here!" she responded with disgust, taking the bag from Don. "Now what am I supposed to do with this?"

It was all Don could do to keep from laughing. The woman frowned at him and waved him on.

The sky was as gray as the waters of the Columbia. Visibility was poor. Neither of us, looking west from the bridge, got any inkling the ocean was out there. Off and on a bit of light rain came down, yet not enough to bother.

We had heard there might be many such rains along the Oregon Coast. Indeed, we had heard a great deal about the Oregon Coast, but when people talked of it, they did not bother trying to describe it; they simply spoke in reverential tones and said we'd love it. We were eager to see it.

Don was walking Oregon's Route 101 now, and on the map, not too many miles from Astoria, this road looked as if it skirted the very edge of the sea. All day long, whenever we rounded a new bend in the road, we expected some vista would open up to us, presenting the Pacific. All day long we were disappointed, and by day's end we were downright skeptical. The litter was still rather unsightly. And if Don thought he'd seen the last of the logging truck, it was soon apparent he hadn't. We were surprised to learn that Oregon even claimed to lead the nation in logging. But it wasn't logging trucks so much as weekend traffic congestion that bothered us on our first day in the state.

"Fran, I think I may have *heard* the ocean a mile or so back there, but it's hard to tell with all these cars. Where's everybody going? And where's this wonderful coast everybody's been ooh-ing and aah-ing about?" Don asked when he found me at day's end, sitting with Otto's sliding door open as if I was on my front porch. I was parked illegally, unable to find any other place near the appointed mile. I had not been able to leave to do any exploring on my own.

"Don, don't tell me you don't think this is beautiful," I said sarcastically, handing Don the map. "So, where do you suppose the ocean is?"

"Well, obviously and according to the map, it's right next to us. But in this cloudy weather, maybe we wouldn't be seeing much of it anyway—even if we went out of our way. But are we going to have to go out of our way to see it? I thought I would be able to walk along and just have it be there."

"Frankly, Don, I'm *in favor* of going out of our way. What about finding a place to camp by the ocean? There's no place where we are now, here in Seaside. I couldn't even find a parking spot; it's all restaurants, hotels, and beach business—a far cry, I dare say, from what Lewis or Clark found when they ended their trek west here in 1805."

"Yep, well," Don said, looking to the map again, "there's a place called Ecola State Park not too far ahead. It's between the road and the ocean, anyway. It'll be tight, though—trying to get there before dark, I mean."

"Well, hop in," I said. "Let's go."

As we entered the park, a sign announced: "Four and a half miles—narrow, winding road." The sign makers might well have said more, for the way was not only narrow and winding, it was steeply pitched and enclosed like a tunnel. Otto had little clearance in our twisted, headlong descent beneath a dense shrub forest that reached out over the narrow road, effectively shutting out the sky. I rode Otto's brakes.

Meanwhile, as we went, a many-headed, snakelike mist wriggled out from beneath this woody understory. It was coming from the sea. I began to worry about getting caught in this maze, should the fog and the darkness congeal as one.

"Slow down!" Don called nervously from the back. "Watch out! Can't you read that sign?"

Otto was already barely creeping forward on all fours. "Danger! One lane road—Slide area ahead!" a sign warned. But I felt all we had done since we entered this park was slide—slide helplessly forward, toward some hidden edge. I had yet to take my foot off the brake. I downshifted to second.

"Fran, get over to the right! What if we meet another car!"

"For Pete's sake, Don, there is no getting over—it's one lane!"

This anxiety of the Walker's was one of the less well-known motivations for The Walk. Don, an incorrigible backseat driver, could hardly stand being on passenger status only. In every respect, he would rather walk than ride with me at the wheel. Not that I believe I gave him any real cause for concern. However, since I was *the* designated driver, I wasn't going to step aside, whatever the harassment. Besides, as I reminded the Walker from time to time, "It's two against one, Don. Give up. Otto's on *my* side. He knows who takes care of him— feeds him, washes him, checks his oil. And he doesn't like *his* driver being insulted—makes him nervous. I'm not sure Otto even likes *you*, Don—good thing you're the Walker!"

I downshifted to first. We crept on.

"Turn on your lights, Fran."

"They're on, Don. If ever I find that eject button—you're going to be back on your sore feet in no time. Just try to remember—you don't have a good perspective back there where you're sitting. Things look worse from back there." Better if Don took the seat next to me, but then that seat faced backward, and Don did not like to ride backward.

Soon, though, Otto came to a halt and we could go no further. The road had more or less ended. I rolled down my window. Something *big* roared without. It was a roar deep and deafening, as if some mad beast crouched below the foggy bluffs and was already in the process of devouring what was once known as the Oregon Coast. We had come too far not to have a look, but we both hesitated.

"This is the Pacific?" I asked. "A terrible misnomer."

"Sign over there says no camping," Don announced.

"Well, we better not stay long, then," I said, relieved to have an excuse *not* to stay.

We got out, went to the brink putting the dark forest behind us, and looked out and below. There it was—fifty feet down—a sea mocking its own name, frothing madly, waves upon waves wildly wrestling at cross purposes; luminous spume tossed, spat, flung high with every hideous lunge at the shore. The cloud curtain parted momentarily for a skull-like, gibbous moon to light the stage, as if we wanted a better look. But then a sudden chill snuffed out the moon, and the foggy vapors began to rise and take on dark, curious shapes of their own. Without a word we turned to leave, hardly knowing what it was we'd been looking at—hardly wanting to know.

That we had to camp later in a gravelly logging pullout within earshot of the noisy traffic did not really bother. There was even something comforting about cracking open a can of tuna and getting back in touch with the world as we knew it—a world a little less big, alive, and animated.

Chapter 43

Coasting the Coast

Not long after our first glimpse of the Pacific, I wrote in my journal: "Surely all the bragging about the Oregon Coast is justified—based on what we've seen so far! I'll be busy a long while yet with camera and pen if I expect to capture any of it. So far it's too big, too grand, and too new to do justice to. And I keep running out of film. High views of green mountains into sea; long views of undeveloped, uncluttered, unspoiled rugged coastline; stretches of beach here and there—isolated, secluded, protected—even in large part, deserted. To sober up I look away from the sea in places to the east and watch the unprotected lands being brutally logged off. Strange contrast."

And the next morning, I wrote to David: "I've been walking Rockaway Beach at first light—the only human among hundreds of gulls. Hundreds and hundreds of gulls standing like statues—silent—their unlikely silence as loud as the sea. Maybe they weren't awake yet. I'm finding it hard to imagine you with ten inches of snow beneath your feet and flaming October foliage above your head. It's supposed to be in the eighties here today—and warmer than normal all week. Not far south of here we heard it's in the hundreds. Picture me on fine wet sand, stirring up countless grasshopper-like fleas as I walk, skirting little slippery jellyfish, and trying to find an unbroken sand dollar."

Meanwhile, Don walked a shortened day October 5, from Rockaway Beach to Tillamook, Oregon, so we could drive east to

Portland and pick up Rick—a good friend from St. Louis who was taking a vacation to walk with Don for ten days along the Oregon Coast.

This rendezvous had been planned long before either Don or I were acquainted with the rigors of the journey. Now that we were well-versed in the hardships of the road, I found it difficult to imagine making room for anyone other than David. Yet somehow I was going to have to—I was even going to have to be a good sport about it! Do the support work for two walkers, put up with double the sweaty, stinky clothes and shoes, and make further sacrifices I couldn't foresee.

I wrote in my journal: "Not a good day—little rest last night— worried about not having the solitude or privacy I need when Rick comes. The ocean is overwhelming—waves just now coming in long rolling breakers—I have no words for it really. There is a light-scattering haze below me as I look out. My heart is heavy and I have no words for it either. I listen to the sea's din and feel a distance from this ocean I don't know how to bridge. It seems but a trivial thing to wade in it—as if to touch its hem can mean anything to the faithless. I hear no songs within it. I don't know which is heavier— my heart or the sea—perhaps the sea by a hair.

"And how can one get to know the sea? So much is hidden— the surface as uniform and un-revealing a country as any to be imagined. What can come of sailing about on it even—it is depth I cannot fathom, breadth I cannot span, volume I cannot hold. It seems a dangerous sort of company to keep—something you dare to walk in the presence of, turn your back on, walk away from, come back to. It is as dark as my heart; I can see no light in it."

Don and I were both rather belatedly realizing that while it's not hard to imagine having fun with almost anyone—it's not just anyone you want to share hardships with. Rick undoubtedly was having second thoughts of his own when he found himself nursing blisters on his feet after a day of matching strides with the Walker for twenty miles—perhaps contemplating as he did what could make a woman like me so temperamental. And yet before long we all made adjustments to one another and our spirits lightened.

For one thing, it was plain that the Oregon Coast (liberally studded with state parks, beaches, and waysides) was going to be a lot more accommodating than most stretches on the journey. Interspersed among the undeveloped areas were plenty of good cafes and restaurants. Since it was off-season, some parks and other places were closed, yet not enough to be inconvenient. When it was time to stock Otto's cupboard and cooler, it was easily done—and done to a fine turn, if desired, as when Don and Rick got a hankering for Dungeness crab. The pleasant camping facilities meant hot showers for everyone, and thus took some of the edge off living in close quarters. Rick had planned on sleeping out of doors—on top of picnic tables, actually (to escape the heavy dew). And while nearly everyone in the state was praying for rain, the drought gripping much of the West held on. Indeed, barely a drizzle could have been squeezed from skies so empty of clouds.

Rick brought with him the extra energy and good humor typical of someone on vacation from work in a beautiful part of the country. And though Don and I had been on the road too long to suddenly pretend it was vacation, Rick's jolly spirit did have a healthy effect on us both. Perhaps we got something of a vacation from each other by sharing Rick's company—definitely he broke the seal on our solitude. And somehow Rick's extra energy carried us all beyond the daily drudge and into the evenings to share some almost forgotten entertainments. The World Series was approaching, and we three baseball fans cheered the St. Louis Cardinals onto victory in several playoff games. We even attended a movie in Newport, and generally tried not to pass up any great restaurants.

And yet, the real entertainment for all of us, which made this stretch of The Walk so unforgettable, was the sea itself. It drew us irresistibly to it; it opened our eyes and ears; it woke each of us up in different ways.

"Don, I can't believe it, you haven't been in swimming yet—I mean, look, a whole ocean and it's all yours. I have to get at least one picture of you in the Pacific—you've swum in everything else."

We were on a deserted beach near Tierra Del Mar, and the day, with its sticky, seaside humidity and temperatures in the eighties, did seem a good day for it. Rick was not convinced, however, when he waded in to see how cold the water really was.

"I'm not sure, Franny, you want a picture of a blue walker?"

"I'll get you in it, too, Rick. You gonna let your old swim buddy and teammate be one up on you?"

"You bet your bippy I am. This stuff is liquid ice!"

"Don, you're probably not going to get a warmer day or better beach than this," I encouraged.

Don stared out toward the sea, without comment, considering for himself the attraction of a swim. But he did not go forward to test the waters as Rick had.

"All right!" Rick laughed when he saw the Walker toss his shirt and shoes and socks onto the sand.

Rick and I watched. I held my camera ready. Don ran into the surf and seemed to contract from the cold, yet he plowed forward through the rollers—and finally dove in. We watched him swim maybe ten yards before turning around and staggering out—dazed, breathless, clearly aching from the cold. We couldn't help laughing.

"So how was it?" we called.

"Like Lake Superior," Don said when he could catch his breath and stop his teeth from chattering.

But however bereft of humans, the ocean waters were hardly deprived of life. In protected bays and inlets we all looked on at wildlife making itself at home in the sea. At Boiler Bay I pointed out to the walkers what I took to be seals.

"Franny, they do look like seals, except why are they just bobbing up and down like that so lazily in the waves? They look like they're begging."

"Those aren't seals, Fran; they're something else," Don decided after studying them a while.

"I know," I said. "But I think we ought to call them 'seal weeds.' They had me fooled for a while before you guys got here. Anyway, I know there are seals around here somewhere."

And before long we did see seals—sea lions and harbor seals. And where the harbor seal fished, fishermen fished and crabbed, pelicans dove, skuas chased pelicans to steal their catch, gulls chased skuas or fished for themselves, and cormorants and sea ducks found the waters rich. Now and then we caught a great blue heron stalking the rocky shallows.

And all the while, the air was mild, hinting of nothing but summer. Tiny English daisies dotted the green lawns above the sea, yellow asters bloomed as profusely as goldenrod at home, and, in spite of the drought, perhaps living on dew and sea mist, there were other offerings—rampant, lush, overgrown, outlandish—that I could not name and cannot name still.

We were headed due south now. The Walk felt as if it was going downhill. We were no longer putting our backs toward home. I felt I could let up on Otto's gas pedal and simply coast—following the downward curve of the planet. No, from Tillamook to Oretown to Depoe Bay to Newport to Waldport Bay—we all coasted, eyes on the sea—two walkers, a driver, and Otto.

Chapter 44

The Pacific Beast

"Be careful! Look what the sign says!" Don yelled. "Don't worry about me; watch your own step, Don! It's amazing, isn't it? I just want to see if I can get a picture of the rainbow in the spray when the next big wave comes!" I shouted back above the roar.

"Where's Rick?" Don yelled.

"He's checking out picnic tables!"

"I thought we were going to eat out!"

"We are! He's checking them for sleeping—thinks we should camp here tonight!"

It was October 9. Don had just finished putting in thirty-one miles, ending his day at Cape Perpetua. I had taken him down a path called "Trail of the Restless Waters" to look at something called the Devil's Churn. We had all been noticing these names on the map—the devil's this, the devil's that—the Devil's Kitchen, Cauldron, Punch Bowl, Elbow. I'm not sure how the names fit the other places, but we were finding the name fit well enough here.

Following a walkway down, which had a railing to steady one's descent, one could at first only feel the presence of a terrible power below. But then, from a respectable distance, eventually a person could watch what was going on—how the ocean was thrusting a hard, driving limb into a deep, narrow passage edged with slippery, sea-sharpened rock. Again and again, thundering swells plowed into this vessel of volcanic gorge, spilling and crashing with a force impossible to be contained. Aligned with winds and an incoming tide, as it was when we were there, the earth quaked when the big waves hit, and the heart quaked with them.

When the walkway ran out and so did the restraining barrier, signs warned: "One slip could be fatal!" One slip and a body could be in the Devil's Churn, the devil's mashing machine. No, thanks. The trouble was, the sea tempted one closer. When a wave subsided, sucking in its liquid breath, drawing back its wet fist—in that long pause before it hammered in again—one wanted to follow it out. I watched Don and Rick both do this. They watched me. We all watched a young boy with his father—all of us daredevils, tempting the sea.

Each time a wave penetrated, it did so with greater or lesser force. But when all the energy of the sea, wind, and tide was coinciding to full effect, the resulting swell took everything with it—everything in one climactic, flooding frenzy. It swept the board clean, and one knew it would not have stopped at sweeping away a lifetime of human cells. Maybe we would see the big one coming, maybe we wouldn't. I finally turned away in fear—not for myself, but for the boy we saw clambering over the rocks. More horrifying than being swept away oneself would be to watch someone else taken; and more horrifying than that, a son taken while his father looked on.

Yet we could not completely pull ourselves away from this spectacle of the sea. After dining out, we returned to camp. We camped illegally. In the dark of night, the violent thud of wave slamming against rock only seemed to get louder, making the earth underneath us sound thin and hollow. I did not sleep well.

"So how was your night on the table, Rick?" Don asked over a breakfast of cold cereal the next morning.

"Super! Really great—loved it! Slept like a babe."

"Rick," I said in disbelief, "I can hardly imagine. I mean, how could you manage to keep from rolling off the table with all that quaking beneath you? You had to be able to feel every crack of those waves."

"Yeah, Franny, I felt 'em—but I didn't lose any sleep over 'em, and I've never rolled off the top of a picnic table yet."

"Well, if you ever were going to—last night would have been it."

After breakfast, the two walkers took to the road. I watched their happy-go-lucky figures disappear round a bend, and then I decided to go for a walk myself. Without really knowing where I was going, I walked away from the sea and the road and stumbled upon a trail leading up the steep side of a hill. A sign labeled the trail—St. Perpetua's Path.

I had read that Captain James Cook named Cape Perpetua for having found it on the day of the saint's martyrdom, March 6. I read much later that Perpetua died in Carthage in the year 203 with her fellow Christians, at the thrust of a gladiator's sword. She, a young mother with nursing child, left behind a written account of her persecutions while in prison, including the visions she had there before she was killed.

Perpetua had obviously never set foot on this narrow, steep, switchback trail, winding at first through dark, evergreen fern and rhododendron undergrowth, later coming into soft, grassy clearings open to a warming sun. I passed tall, magenta foxglove, the purple and the golden aster. I surprised a black-tailed mule deer with four-pointed antlers who did not take off until we had exchanged long, apprising looks at one another. I could hear his hooves drumming the path like a tympani for a long while after.

St. Perpetua's Path ended almost directly above the Devil's Churn— perhaps half a vertical mile high. I sat down upon an old stump and took in the wide panorama of Cape Perpetua and all that lay beyond. I was breathless from the climb and the view at once. Yet from this perch, I soon saw that the great ocean lying below me was a more pacific beast than I had yet understood it to be.

Looking down from this height on the powerfully roiled surf, crashing and seething inside the Devil's Churn, I could see it was only a bit of drink being playfully jostled in its rocky cup, now and then sloshing over the side and leaping into the air barely a millimeter above its dainty, dark, basaltic rim. Indeed, I saw lots of sea churned to a thick, frothy cream wherever the ocean met the land; but overall, taking into account the enormity of it now revealed (at least in part), the great beast was asleep. I could even discern its breathing rhythm— rippling patterns that gracefully came and went over its vast back.

How easy it lay in what must have been the widest, deepest hole it could find—hiding who-knows-what beneath it, within it, beyond it.

I now realized that what had impressed me before, such as the Devil's Churn, were but things for the beast to finger, to pick at, to toy with in its restless sleep. The great bulk of what I saw was in place—alive but deep in dream or contemplation. I understood Melville's words saying, "There is, one knows not what sweet mystery about this sea, whose gently awful stirrings seem to speak of some hidden soul beneath." But I was suddenly glad too that this thing had no real means to locomote itself, and that no bones nor skin would likely ever be designed to suit it, however much bone or skin it had and would devour. No, I said to myself; let sleeping oceans lie. And I got up to wander back down the zigzagging path.

Chapter 45

Exactly What I've Been Needing

"Franny, did you see back there where all the sea lions were? Not far back at all—maybe two football fields—tons of 'em," Rick said, when I pulled up to where the walkers had stopped to rest. I said I hadn't, that I'd been hiking St. Perpetua's Path.

"Well, you *have* to hike back and see them," Don insisted. "There's a great place to watch from the road. They look just like giant slugs."

We picnicked on a rock high above the ocean, and could hear the barking and yelping of sea lions as we did. Their carrying on echoed with resilient twangs coming out of unseen sea-cave hollows somewhere far below us. It made me eager to see them.

When the walkers took to the road again, I had no trouble finding the place with a good view, but I did not want to stand behind the highway railing. I climbed over this barrier and squatted among some low-clinging shrubs, knowing as I did how I would have hated to see anyone sitting where I was. One small, inadvertent scoot forward would have cast me more than a hundred feet down onto rocks padded with sea lions.

Looking through my field glasses and past my feet, I lost all sense of sitting on anything and felt myself effectively airborne. Yet so much was going on below, I soon forgot myself completely. If the sea lions had only been still, I might have seen them as slugs as Don had—but through field glasses, the creatures were so recognizably playful in all they did, I fancied I was watching a tribe of mer-people.

232

They sported, in groups and alone, in the cresting waves and out at sea, exactly like body-surfers. They reveled in the rough surf about the rocks like children on a beach. They surface-dived like snorkelers and frolicked like lovers. They played tag and gave chase and seemed, in whatever they did, to relish a physical closeness, making frequent body contacts and sliding silkily past one another whenever they got the chance. It looked like fun—and I saw no fear in them. They were, like the leaping orcas Don and I had watched on the ferry to Victoria, wild and free and at home in their element. "Yes," I wrote to David, "the more I watched them, the more I understood, and the more I understood, the more I looked on with a kind of longing. In another life I do not think I would mind at all being a sea lion—if, that is, I couldn't be a mermaid."

Only a few days in Oregon were not walked at the sea's edge, as when along Route 101 near the Oregon Dunes National Recreation Area, great, Sahara-like piles of sand hid any views of the sea from the walkers. Here we saw extensive areas of the spineless broom and its thorny, evergreen look-alike gorse. And to contrast with these butter-yellow blossoms was the showy, pink, wild bean—a flower I had scarcely seen since Ontario in July.

On another inland stretch near North Bend and Coos Bay, evidence of logging returned: logging trucks and lots of logging litter (miles of bark-strewn roadsides and driftwood timber). The train came back to us here, too—loaded with lumber, and singing its familiar songs. The weather had turned drear on this stretch, and though it did not really rain, without the ocean views the journey seemed to stall. The Walk was work again, even for Rick.

But by the time we came upon Bandon, Oregon, mid-morning October 13, the sun was shining and we were back at the sea's edge. I waited for the walkers where I had a pleasant view of ocean, rock, beach, and swirling surf. Yet I hardly saw what was before me. My mind was casting ahead to David's next visit.

"Some good finds on that last stretch of road, Franny," Rick announced, breaking in on my sea-daze. "Look at this." He handed me what looked like a small, weather-beaten packet of coupons, but which turned out to be a World War II ration book, complete with multicolored stamps.

I read the instructions on the back out loud, "Important: when you have used your ration, salvage the tin cans and waste fats. They are needed to make munitions for our fighting men." It had the year on it too—1943. "Gosh," I said, "what odd series of events do you suppose could have brought this to where you guys found it?"

"I don't know," Don said, "but I found something even better—here, look at this!" Don held out what he had been hiding behind his back when he and Rick had first come up. It was a handsomely made, leather-handled riding whip.

"Amazing," I said, admiring it. And then, in a flash of recognition I reached out for it. "Here, let me see that. Aha! It's mine now, Don. You have just handed it over. This is *exactly* what I've been needing." I leaped up and began brandishing the whip as if I was a driver of donkeys instead of a driver of Otto.

Don and Rick both jumped out of my way. "Don," Rick laughed, "I think you just made a *b-i-g* mistake!"

"No, you didn't, Don," I countered quickly. "I always knew I was the driver; it's just that now I can better live up to my title. It's like Robert Louis Stevenson said, 'We are all travelers in the wilderness of this world—all too travelers with a donkey.' He had Modestine, and I have you."

"You mean I have *you*," Don laughed. "Talk about a donkey—and stubborn!"

"Don's got a point there, Franny," Rick came to the walker's defense. "If we're talking 'stubborn,' I'd have to go along with you as the queen."

"Fine with me," I laughed, recognizing the truth, "but *I'm* the driver and I still claim the whip. Anyway, who isn't a donkey to someone trying to get their own way? *This*," I emphasized, wielding the whip with a flourish, "will make the difference for me. We may get home on time yet!"

Over lunch I briefly told the story of Stevenson's *Travels with a Donkey* and how much more smoothly Stevenson's rambles in the hills of the Cevennes in southern France began to go, once he acquired a goad to prod his donkey, Modestine, forward with better success.

I did not have the book with me then, but I know Don would have recognized as well as I the sentiments behind these words: "Of all conceivable journeys, this promised to be the most tedious. I tried to tell myself it was a lovely day; I tried to charm my foreboding spirit with tobacco; but I had a vision ever present to me of the long, long roads, up hill and down dale, and a pair of figures ever infinitesimally moving, foot by foot, a yard to the minute, and, like things enchanted in a nightmare, approaching no nearer the goal." It was that last phrase—"like things enchanted in a nightmare, approaching no nearer the goal"—that rang so true.

That night, we camped out at Cape Blanco, a more-remote and -forsaken setting than we had yet sampled on this coast. Here, sheep grazed a high and wind-blown grassy barren, while out to sea was a wonderful grouping of Waders.

The Waders—my name for the broad-skirted, giant stones weathered by wind and wave, bits and pieces of the coastal mountain range left standing in the surf, usually hugging the shoreline. They weren't everywhere, but they were common enough. Being common, they were yet rather singular—that is, there were never so many at one time that I was tempted to simply group them together and call them "rocks."

These huge, dark remnants of a former shore contributed a great deal to the picturesque qualities of the Oregon Coast. They peopled the shallows. They gave scale to the vast waters beyond. They did not even seem particularly inanimate—what with the waves kicking about their hidden feet, mists flung over them like robes or lifting in the sea winds like capes, and with the changing light glancing from their features so differently throughout the day. They were characters on the sea stage.

I even felt they should be named, given histories, or otherwise discovered for who they were. Some *were* named, things like Face Rock, Wash Rock, Table Rock, Five Foot Rock. But, to me, these rarely did them justice. *Maybe,* I mused, *if I didn't have anything better to do, I might return to Oregon in my old age and wander the coast as a bag lady writing a mythology of the Waders.* I would have little plaques made for the tourists to read, so that each stone giant could be called by its true name, known for its part in the story I would write, relating all the stone characters to one another—as indeed they are related, being of the same race of mountains.

Off Cape Blanco the Waders were rather far out—at least a mile, and to all of us they looked exactly like a pod of great whales. One entire whale was seemingly beached in the mists, but otherwise there were chiefly parts of whales showing, so that whales appeared to be sounding, breaching, waving a fluke, or surfacing to blow. And when, by some freaky coincidence, we learned that a group of paleontologists were gathering the next morning to dig remains of a prehistoric whale on the beach there, we felt we knew whence its bones had come.

Chapter 46

Dead or Alive?

Near the end of our trek down the Oregon Coast, I wrote in my journal: "It is a different journey with a third person in tow. The events of the day are different and we are more like tourists than we have ever been. This is partly the fault of being in a much toured area, but also Don and I have been less on our own. Rick is not all the time walking with Don; he is at times riding or sitting in Otto with me. This has taken a certain edge off our road life. I worry less about Don, about meeting the walker so punctually at the appointed mile (at least when Rick is with him), or about getting into trouble myself. But today, oh dear, today—today is a story all its own." It went like this:

I was ahead of the walkers when I came to a place called Natural Bridges Cove. With my field glasses and camera, I walked out along a fenced boardwalk to a safely corralled-in viewpoint. I leaned over the wooden railing, looking down and out upon a sea-churned cove dramatically bordered by two earthen ramparts—joined across their tops, like Siamese twins, by a narrow bridge of land. Waders in the making. While I was taking pictures of this rock formation, I suddenly imagined myself out there—sitting on that high, narrow, saddle-like bridge of land, well above the sea.

Without much thought, I climbed down out of the corral and found a path to follow. I was imagining it would be fun to be sitting out there on that natural bridge when Don and Rick came along, surprise them, take their picture.

And then I slipped and fell. When I slipped again a short while later, I paid more attention to what I was doing. Dry can be as slippery as wet, I cautioned myself. Where I was climbing down just then, there were plenty of shrubs, giant ferns, and even some trees to break a person's fall, but further down I knew there wouldn't be. I stepped more carefully.

A short while later I found myself out on a ridge, with lots of evergreen foliage overhead and with slim tree trunks, like fence posts, at my side to steady me. Here I noticed, though it did not make a bit of sense, a fat cat sitting upright on the horizontal branch of a nearby tree. The creature was just far enough away to bring into focus in my field glasses. Yet soon I saw plainly that I was looking at the backside of a great horned owl, with its tufted feathers sticking up like cat's ears.

Holding the glasses steady, I whistled a little, birdlike call, and watched the owl slowly turn its head round to face me. For as long as I looked, it was a staring contest, yet the owl easily won. When I finally let the glasses down, it turned its head back round to face forward, evidently not the least concerned. It wasn't until I moved past another tree, to look on from a more lighted area, that I saw it fall into the abyss below—wings opening at the last moment to silently catch itself when it found another perch somewhere down in.

I continued on, following a path that led me more and more into the open. The steepness was not only to the right and left of me now, but in front of me as well. And then, suddenly, clearly, the path was no longer safe. I needed no sign to tell me one slip could be fatal.

I don't know why I kept going—except I may well have sensed that it was just as dangerous to try to turn around where I was. The camera and field glasses slung about me made me feel awkward, top-heavy, encumbered. I knew I had slipped earlier because my shoes had little tread. I tried to focus on that narrow bridge still below and ahead of me; I felt that if I could just get to it, I might sit there, straddling it, and feel perfectly safe.

Then suddenly I was having to scoot and slide downward in a crouch, controlling my descent as best I could by grabbing onto roots as I went, even knowing it was a perilous thing to do. If a root had let go—that would have been it. Still, without the roots I knew my controlled slide would quickly turn into an uncontrolled fall. When I looked down, I could too easily imagine my fate flung to the sharp, tide-battered rocks beneath. I saw it was even possible I would only get half-killed by a fall, and that I might have several, cold, swirling moments of drowning before death could work its mercy.

When I saw I was going to run out of roots, I blurred my vision and somehow frantically slid the last of the way, until I was stopped by a narrow, level place, where I crawled on my sweaty hands and knees up a short rise and out onto my perch on the natural bridge. I did not feel as secure as I had imagined I would, but I tried to collect my wits and think why I wanted to be there in the first place. Oh yes, I wanted to take pictures of Don and Rick; but now, glancing at my watch, I realized I could have as much as a half hour's wait. Well, I thought, maybe it'll do me some good—steady my nerves.

And then I thought to look back and assess my retreat. My heart sank. The steep, dry, open, round-shouldered slope without roots and with vertical drop-offs on either side looked impossible to go up. I did not know how I would do it, and I was not ready to try. Somehow I had to calm myself.

But the longer I sat there, the less I could stay calm. Waves were battering in against the rocks below, and against the remnants of shore connected by the narrow saddle I sat upon. I could feel the shocking vibrations shudder through me. I suddenly recalled how very, very narrow this connecting piece of land looked from the corralled-in viewpoint. It struck me at once that *someday*—why not this very day?—the bridging land would collapse from all that battering. Perhaps I, myself, was going to be the straw that made the difference. *But if only I were straw*, I thought, as I felt my weight pressing against the vulnerable earth and listened to the slamming waves and surf seem to get louder and louder.

And the longer I sat there, the more frozen I became—not from any cold, but from fear alone. And then I began to get dizzy—my perch began to seem teetery; I might simply swoon and topple helplessly over. Again, I could not help staring down and seeing my body already cast upon the rocks below—lost in the crashing surf—unable, because of the treacherous nature of the place, to ever be retrieved. I saw my remains haunting the area. I saw the viewpoint barricaded from the curious. I saw how maybe even years hence, some bits of bright clothing would swirl conspicuously about with the seaweed, a grim reminder of a traveler's foolhardiness.

And then I thought of the owl. Ah yes, the place was safe for such. If only I could fly. The owl did not hesitate to fall. A simple flare of its wings was sufficient to catch itself. It was at home. And I thought of its soft, light body protected by feathery fluff—no tender skin exposed to flesh-tearing rock. And I thought of its feet able to lock onto a small twig and be fastened securely there, even while it slept. Whereas I? I ought not to have been where I was. I couldn't fly.

And then I thought of David. I remembered our reunion only days away—and suddenly it seemed the most unlikely thing in the world that I would ever see him again. I pictured Don phoning David to report "the accident." I pictured David wringing his hands and saying, "But how—how? How could she have done it?" I pictured Don going on with the walk anyway—alone—driverless—saying, "Fran would have wanted me to." Or "I'm doing it for Fran." Isn't that what they always say? Life goes on. At this thought I began praying—praying out loud—slowly, mechanically, as if in a trance.

If I hadn't glanced up a short while later to see the walkers waving down at me, I think my delirium might have won out. As it was, the sight of the walkers brought me to my senses. I took their picture—realizing as I did that it would not be much to look at later: they were as tiny as ants up there.

I took a deep breath, swallowed hard, and got onto my hands and knees. I crawled into the open. I told myself not to look down, not to look around, just look ahead, and just to the next handhold—when there were any handholds. Then I made a calculated dash up the slope to the first root and grabbed on. I did not hesitate. I wanted the whole thing to be over. I found another root. I did not slip. One by one, the roots held. I took more deep breaths; I told myself it was just like climbing a ladder—step by step. *Or a tree*, I thought, and I remembered all the tall trees I had climbed as a child and how impossible it always seemed, after scrambling up so easily, to climb down. *I got down safely then*, I thought; *I can get out of here now.*

When at last I was on my feet among the trees and ferns, I heard Don's whistle, and I knew what he meant by it: "Are you all right?"

"I'm coming, I'm okay," I shouted back each time I heard him whistle. But I was not yet shouting for joy.

As the sweat poured out of me from the release of fear, I had one last numbing vision of myself—which told me I was not really alive. I *had* fallen, only I was being spared the painful knowledge of it all—of having to face death on the rocks. Instead I was in that tunnel-like place people near death have often described—and the sunlight I saw ahead of me at the end of the forest was, in reality, some otherworldly light far, far removed from earth.

Still, I hurried on. I watched myself hurry. I watched myself climb back up and onto the corralled-in viewpoint to join Don and Rick. And even when I heard myself begin to speak—to tell my story to the walkers—another part of me was still wondering if hearing my own voice was absolute proof that I had survived. Perhaps I didn't really believe I was safe until I remembered to thank God for my rescue. And I prayed then, too—to know better next time.

Chapter 47

Smoke and Fog

Just a few miles from the border, in Brookings, Oregon, we said farewell to Rick. California lay ahead. It would be the last state for Don to walk at the western limit. We both looked on California as an important milestone and were thrilled to gain it, yet the place had its worrisome aspects, too.

"California's physiography is simple;" an encyclopedia says, "its main features are few and bold; a mountain fringe along the ocean, another mountain system along the east border, between them—closed at both ends by their junction—a splendid valley, and outside all this a great area of barren, arid lands, belonging partly to the great basin and partly to the open basin region." But what else about California can be described as simple?

Our *way* through California was not going to be simple. A good friend of Don's living near Los Angeles only half-jokingly warned the Walker to bring along a flak jacket if he planned to walk any of their freeways: that very summer, a rash of senseless shootings had occurred on them, supposedly by traffic-crazed and frustrated motorists. We knew, too, that it was illegal to walk the freeways, but Don figured, after studying the maps, that in certain places he would have little choice but to walk some freeway stretches.

The other factor complicating our way through California had to do with time that we would be taking off The Walk. California was going to be a bit of an obstacle course for us—with a conference

Don had to attend in Fresno, with relatives and friends in the state to visit (including my brother Joe), with David coming to visit twice, and with our sons coming to visit at Christmas. All this meant that commitments, logistical hurdles, and sidetracks lay in a jumbled, unsorted heap ahead of us. Neither Don nor I could see our way clear.

But mainly, at least for me, California just didn't seem to be a good place for living out of a camper by the side of the road. The state's reputation for "craziness" was too unsettling.

Nevertheless, there was nothing remarkable about the border crossing into California from Oregon; that is, no natural barrier such as a river marked it, and yet California immediately felt different. For one thing, Don put in his 3,420th mile, entering the state October 16, under a screen of smoke—or so I thought at first.

"Don, what is this stuff, anyway—smoke or fog?" I asked him, not long after I had taken his picture at the border.

"I thought it was smoke, at first, but it doesn't smell. I guess it's fog. Which reminds me—you'll never guess what happened to me when you were taking Rick to the bus station this morning. I was recruited to fight one of the big forest fires. The one they call the Silver Fire."

We had been seeing and smelling a lot of smoke in the air for the past few days, especially when the wind died down or blew from the east.

"Where did they say it was burning?" I asked.

"Somewhere in the rugged Oregon hills, where it's hard to put out. It's already burned ninety-thousand acres. It's been burning since August, they said, and was started by a lightning storm then. The same storm supposedly started fires in Montana, Idaho, Washington, and Northern California."

"Gosh," I said in disbelief. "It's so hard to imagine these fires just burning on and on and on."

"I guess that's why they're out there on the street, recruiting new firefighters all the time. I wanted to go help, Fran. I had a hard time saying no. People were saying they didn't expect the fire to really be put out until the rains came, in spite of all the fire fighting."

"Makes the drought seem doubly cruel, doesn't it," I answered, shaking my head. "But Don, have you forgotten you don't even like fighting fires! You quit the volunteer fire department back home not that long ago. And don't forget, you have that conference in Fresno soon."

"Oh yeah," Don said. And then as he set out again. "Still, Fran, it's true that I really wanted to help—but you're right, I'd hate the fire part."

But a few days in California dispelled some of my anxiety about the state. I began to look more into my surroundings and less past them. Breakfasting alone one morning, gazing out of a restaurant window, I watched a dozen California quail troop into a small garden enclosure between a rock wall and a birdbath to make themselves at home. Some snuggled into the grass near the rock wall out of the foggy wind; some flew up to peer at their images in the puddle of the bath. Their dress, with their bobbing tear-drop topknots, brown-and-white striping and scaling—and the male with his lovely bluish breast besides—was uniformly jaunty.

Later, on a walk, I found a bouquet—California poppies, a concentration of the famed California sun infused in their orange-gold cups. And, all through the day, there was the lofty company of the great redwoods themselves.

It was as if the state bird, the state flower, and the state tree were there in welcome. Why, exactly, Nature's presence tames my fears, I shall ever be pondering. However ruthless, cutthroat, and undermining Nature may be shown to be, there is something else about it that is equally the opposite; that is gentle, self-denying, even rescuing; whose presence reassures and whose absence condemns.

Don and I had both noticed an area where only the stumps of huge trees were prevalent. We assumed them to be redwoods. A nearby road summed up the spectacle best with its name: "Wonder Stump Road." We gawked at the occasional double-trailered logging truck carting one colossal log, where it would have typically carried two groups of ten to twenty. But when The Walk brought us into the protection of the first of a series of redwood parks, we felt awed and privileged to be among these living giants.

Coastal fog is part of what nourishes the redwoods, and there was definitely lots of it. Among the great trees, the fog seemed no worse than breezy curtains and veils, draped and lifting from the redwood pillars, slit and divided by chance sunbeams penetrating from above. It was dark below these titans, even when the fog briefly cleared, and difficult to take pictures. I hardly dreamed of shrinking a redwood into a frame, anyway. The fog only complicated the matter.

The fog had its enigmatic side. I never knew what would emerge from it. The minute we entered California, the traffic had escalated and so had the average speed of it—a great contrast to the stillness of the trees. We were still near the sea, and sometimes we could watch the fog boiling off of it, and sometimes we could only hear the sea's roar at the bottom of some wooded cliff. There were few safe places to pull over. Road margins for both walker and driver were dangerously slim. Don was thankful to have his fluorescent vest to wear; I wished Otto had one.

I was parked in a small pull-off one morning when, out of a billow of fog, a car suddenly zoomed in behind me. In another moment, a man with a sailor's rolling gait and a short, sturdy build came striding toward me; it was my older brother, Joe.

"No wonder I couldn't get you on the phone this morning!" I laughed and cried when I hugged him. "Great to see you! Don should be along any minute."

"I got your message," Joe said, "I thought I'd surprise you and come early, walk some miles with Don, and spend some time with you. What do you think of these redwoods—something pretty amazing, huh!"

And my brother Joe was something amazing, too. He graciously helped us work out our most pressing logistics problems, came laden with gifts, and later continued to go to great lengths to ease our passage through California.

Soon we'd made arrangements for Otto to stay behind for a six-day respite; Joe ferried us to San Francisco to meet David. David rented a car, then he and I drove Don to his conference in Fresno. The Walk was on hold.

Chapter 48

Among the Great

When I sat down later to try to figure it out—why this respite from The Walk seemed so demanding—I counted up four "all-day" drives in the six days off. There was only one day, a day with David in the sequoias, that I did not have to climb into a car and go somewhere. I did not have to do any of the driving, but I felt crazily "in motion" nearly all the time.

Partly it was the way time passed—so suddenly. We covered so much ground so quickly, I felt the world to be on "fast forward." This made me feel as if California was gyrating entirely on its own; that is, unconnected to the rest of the planet—subject to physical laws other than Euclid's or Newton's or Einstein's. There was an impetuous momentum about these days—roughly equivalent to the beginnings of a fall. In retrospect, I can see that I could feel "it" coming—though I had no real idea what form "it" would take or when "it" would happen.

"I'm about ready to head out," Don announced after breakfast at our campsite on October 27, his first day back on The Walk. "I should have no problem getting as far as The Avenue of the Giants today. It will be great to be under those trees again. And I'll be glad to get off the freeway, I'm sure. I wonder if I'll be able to catch Lisa. It probably depends on whether or not she got sidetracked anywhere."

"Who's Lisa?" David asked. He had one more day to spend with Don and me before flying home.

246

"Lisa is a biker we met on the road, just about the same time my brother Joe caught up with us—in fact, Joe met her, too," I said.

"She's been biking on her own around the country for two years—started out from lower New York State," Don added.

"In search of herself," I added. "She's rather good-looking, young—twenty-six, I think—in tip-top shape. And I don't know how she has been able to travel so adventurously without jeopardizing her health and safety. I know she was not giving out her plans to the two male bikers who stopped to meet her when we did. I guess she's learned to be cautious. I think my brother took to her, too. I saw him giving her his card."

"Well, I know I wouldn't mind meeting up with her again," Don chimed in. Makes me anxious to be off. I'll see you guys at lunch?"

"Right," I said. "Meanwhile, Don, we'll be packing up some of this stuff for home. Anything you don't want to go? We've got to try to find some extra room for all the supplies Joe gave us. I don't know where we're going to put it all. Otto looks like a delivery van!"

"Send home whatever you want. See you guys later!"

"Careful on that freeway section you have to hike," David cautioned before Don disappeared from sight.

It was getting to be a regular ritual, the reorganizing of Otto to make room for more road finds, among other things. I thought it was ridiculous what could accumulate. David and I worked as quickly as we could, eager to spend our last afternoon together out among the trees.

Soon enough, David and I were taking a long, quiet walk in what seemed a fairytale forest, each of us lost in our own thoughts. We might have been Hansel and Gretel beneath these standing ancients, trying to find our way through. The place was enchanted.

The varied and delicate plants of the understory were arranged so beautifully about the redwoods' feet—like embroidered borders trimming the hem of a gown—that it was difficult to think it had happened by accident. A bizarre fungus blossomed in our path, its bulbous, convoluted, tangerine growth dusted a powdery blue. Maybe we were in Wonderland? I was surprised not to find a note attached saying, "Eat me."

Forests of far-lesser dimensions have often been likened to cathedrals, but the redwood forest did not strike me so. Even the loftiest cathedral has columns one can see to the top of and a oneness overall, whereas the enclosure we found ourselves in was more complex—more like a castle than a cathedral—a castle of dreamlike dimensions, even.

The floor of the forest wasn't level. There were winding rises and falls, like spiraling staircases. The place was many-roomed on many levels, with balconies and lofts—with dungeons, too—and inside windows giving on outside windows giving on strange chambers giving on incomprehensible passageways. It was like wandering through an Escher drawing where the outside becomes the inside becomes the outside. *If only we wouldn't find our way out*, I dared to wish.

The sense of passageways, of nooks and crannies, was heightened by the many burned-out hollows at the base of the redwood trunks, known as "goose pens" (so named for having actually served as goose pens in pioneer days). The goose pen openings made the already towering trees appear to be standing on tiptoe—perhaps in an effort to see over their too-tall neighbors. Grotesque burls adorned the redwood's feet in places like huge warts, or gave them knobby knees, or higher up transformed themselves into gargoyles glaring down at us. But when the burls were festooned with wood ferns and ivies, they seemed more like planters and added to the indoor effect.

I left David's side twice. Once to follow a rather secretive bird, which turned out to be a varied thrush. And once to put my hand upon what looked like a trail blaze of finely beaten gold. Light penetrated the forest depths so unpredictably—filtering through layers of high foliage and shifting curtains of fog—that mostly we saw sunbeams suspended almost horizontally above our heads. But going after this medallion of gold so bright against the dark trunk of a redwood, I was surprised to find myself touching a stray splash of sunlight that had found its way down and through.

David laughed at me. "You'll never put that in your pocket."

"Gosh, David, what is it about being dwarfed by these giants that is so uplifting?" I said, returning to his side. "Do we think some sort of stature is conferred on us simply by association?"

David shook his head in wonder. "I don't know. I really don't know."

"Maybe it's more like this," I offered. "If you cannot *be* great or *do* great things—at least you can get out there and *be with* great things."

"I can't get over how different it is among the redwoods than among the sequoias," David observed. "The habitats, I mean—and how different the two species are themselves. The redwood needles are more like a fir or a hemlock. The sequoia's scaly needles are more like a cedar."

"Really," I agreed, "they don't actually resemble each other much— the sequoia is so bulky in its girth and less tapering. Doesn't really grow as tall as the redwood."

"But the sequoias grow to be older," David said.

"But which do you think is the wiser?" I asked.

"What do you mean?"

"Well, these trees are so old—some two-thousand years for an ancient redwood—some three-thousand for an ancient sequoia. I say they *have* to be wise. And shouldn't their wisdom somehow go to preserving their species?"

"Whatever are you getting at, Francesca?"

"Oh, I don't know—but don't you have to think that anything so long-lived must know a thing or two?"

"You and your imagination," David smiled.

I went on, undaunted. "The sequoia could be considered the wiser since it climbed into the high Sierras to make its home in a harsh climate—that is, a climate much less hospitable to man. The redwood is living here in a sort of Mediterranean balminess—look at all this luxuriant undergrowth. The understory about the sequoias seems bare by comparison. Of course, maybe the redwoods thought to hide from man in the fog."

"What about their wood?" David asked.

"Well, at least, the sequoias had the sense *not* to make their woody bodies commercially useful to man, although I guess a lot were cut down before this was realized."

"If the sequoia is the wiser," David asked, "then why do there seem to be fewer stands of them left?"

"Good question," I answered. "Hey, I wonder what this little plant is. Interesting, oaky-looking leaf. It's all over the place."

"Hmmm." David bent down and examined it closely, though without touching it or wading through it as I had. "I'm not sure, but it looks to me like it could be poison oak."

"Poison oak!" I gasped. "Poison oak—uh oh. I might have known. But I do hope you're wrong, David."

"I hope so too, but better scrub down good when we get back to the campground," David laughed.

"Poison oak! Ugh! Why didn't I stick to the path!" Already I had a sinking feeling, even before I could wash, that it was too late. "We'd better warn Don. I'm sure I have seen this stuff growing along the roadsides too."

It was raining when David took off in the pitch-dark forest to drive to the airport in San Francisco. The steady drizzle expressed my feelings perfectly. I wished him safe passage home. He wished us safe passage, too.

"It's not so very long until Christmas, you know," David said just before he drove off, while I stood beside the car in the rainy dark.

"Sure," I said, knowing in my heart that David's experience of time and my own would soon be light years apart.

Chapter 49

Imagination Kills

We had entered Northern California in a fog, and much of The Walk those first few weeks in the state (not including the six-day break) was shrouded in it. I had the feeling at times that we were purposely being kept from a more intimate knowledge of the area. Time slowed in the fog and made me feel claustrophobic. I wanted to wave it aside. Now and again I would think to get rid of it by wiping Otto's windshield or cleaning my glasses, as if the problem was an obscuring lens I peered through.

When the fog lifted in places, we couldn't help looking around with fresh wonder. The world was changing. Don's southward march was turning up new flora, native and otherwise, including many unfamiliar broadleaf evergreens—madrones, laurels, chinkapins, oaks. We began to see eucalyptus and even palms. Near towns, the brilliant purple or magenta blossoms of bougainvillea might suddenly climb out of the fog, or other exotic splashes of color cultivated by man in this hospitable climate.

On small lakes and lagoons, we observed various waterfowl. We often saw the great blue. But it was the pied-billed grebe that suggested the California world as I then knew it. When it discovered me watching, the bird sank out of sight like a submarine. Exactly so, the world sank out of sight again and again.

The day after David left, Don reluctantly hiked out of the last of the northern redwood forests, following the South Fork of the Eel

River. Near the town of Leggett, the Walker stepped onto Route 208 to head away from inland Route 101 and get back to Route 1 on the coast. Route 1 might be a longer route to San Francisco—at least an extra day's walk—but it promised to be more pleasant, and none of it was freeway.

By now, most of the U.S., including California, had gone off daylight saving time. This meant, of course, that the day was abruptly shortened on the evening end. It also meant that there was now four hours' difference between the time Otto showed and California time. Otto's clock did not so much exaggerate our distance from home as echo the truth of it.

Don tried to compensate for the early dark by starting out earlier in the morning, but this did not completely solve the problem: at this time of year, days were getting shorter anyway. To get all the walking done in daylight, Don had to pick up his pace and take fewer breaks. Evenings and mornings now had an uncomfortable, shadowy feel to them. From this a sense of foreboding arose that was hard to shake. Darkness, when it came, seemed to fall on us like a lead curtain.

Our first day in Mendocino County, Don was barely able to get in his thirty miles before the night clanged shut on us. We had no chance to go hunting for a campsite, so we simply stayed where Don ended his day.

We were in a densely forested area of steep terrain, and it felt as if we had fallen to the bottom of a deep well. We had a small pullout to ourselves and hoped for the best. Cafe talk earlier that day had been unusually coarse and unfriendly. I heard talk of a murder, but I thought it had occurred in a movie people were also mentioning. We were shouted at and honked at in the wee hours. And during the next twenty-four hours, I learned two things: how raw my nerves could wear, and that imagination kills.

We were gradually wending our way over to the coast on Route 208 via zigzags down and up a crazily pitched and narrow road, round frequent ten M.P.H. hairpin curves. It was hardly a populated area. Much of the land seemed owned by a big lumber company. Intimidating, hand-scrawled "No Trespassing" signs guarded the scruffy environs around infrequent, shacky dwellings—sometimes punctuated by a skull-and-crossbones painted in red. My brother Joe had warned us that in some parts of California, the inhabitants were known to shoot first and ask questions later. *Was this such a place?* I wondered.

The next morning, Halloween day, Don set out at 7:30. I recorded the time and mileage from Otto's odometer, as was my custom. I told Don I would drive ahead seven miles and wait. I was low on gas, and I was in the mood for a hot cup of tea, so I hoped I would come upon a gas station or cafe. I did not come upon anything, beyond a few houses and more "No Trespassing" signs.

I pulled over at the seven-mile point, near a hairpin curve, to wait the two hours for Don. I picked up my pen and the time passed.

And then an extra hour began to go by. I kept writing, but whenever a car slowed at the nearby curve, I would look up and check the time again. When a third hour was up, I got out of Otto to pace a bit and wonder where Don could be.

It was then I noticed a poster nearby with a young man's picture on it advertising a ten-thousand dollar reward for information about his recent murder. The poster also gave some known facts about the case.

Now I recollected the cafe talk about the murder. So it was true. This was the victim—a young geologist, a nice looking fellow, and not much older than my oldest son, Andy, who was studying to be a geologist. Andy might also go off one day on his own to do research in the field, as this young man had done. I suddenly felt sick; it was all so real and so close. Where was Don? Three hours to walk seven miles? This was not like him. There had been no phones, no stores, no restaurants to waylay him. Where could he be?

More time went by, then finally, in spite of being low on gas, I decided to drive the treacherous, snaky road back the seven miles to our campsite to search for Don—or some sign of him. There was no way he could have passed me without my knowing.

Slowly, carefully, I scoured the road. Nothing. I saw absolutely no sign of the Walker. I got out of Otto and looked all about our campsite, where we had been together only a few hours earlier. Then, after letting my mind consider all the possibilities, I could not help but think "foul play."

Then I figured the mileage again, tried to recall the details of our morning's conversation and exactly what Don had been wearing. I began to answer questions I thought the police might ask me. But how to find the police? And enough of this game—where was Don?

I turned to pull out of our campsite and scour the road again. A glimpse of a face drained of all color startled me in the rear view mirror; it was my own. I tried to get hold of myself as I drove the winding road, but I kept thinking I saw bits and pieces of Don's florescent vest in places. On closer inspection I found them to be markers of surveyor's ribbon. My head began to spin. Nothing. No Don. I didn't dare stop at the few doors I passed—not with such fiercely scrawled "No Trespassing" signs.

When I passed the seven-mile point where I had waited the morning, I saw the poster again, and soon more posters—only now my son's face appeared to be on them—or sometimes Don's. On I drove, my heart racing and my mind prey to wild imaginings.

And then, without warning, after miles of dark and cloistered woodlands, suddenly the road veered to face a cliff edge and the open sea. I felt as if I'd come to the end of the world. This sudden openness made my stomach turn and my heart sink. I could barely drive. When I came to a scenic lookout and saw that a couple had pulled over, having come from the opposite direction, I pulled over, too. Maybe they had seen the Walker.

I climbed out of Otto and nervously approached them. I told them my story as briefly and coherently as I could. But now, as I tried to explain what had happened, and at the hopeful thought of getting help, tears came flowing freely.

The couple looked at me suspiciously at the end of my speech. Or perhaps they simply stared in disbelief. There was an awkward silence. They looked at each other. Then the man looked at me without change of expression and asked, "Does he often do this?"

"Do what?" I asked.

"Wander off like that!" he answered.

It was now my turn to stare at them in disbelief. Obviously they had completely misunderstood me. I choked back my tears, but I could think of no better way to explain myself. I suddenly knew they hadn't seen Don anyway.

"If I were you," the man said coldly, "I'd seek the authorities at Fort Bragg."

Oh, great. Now I was convinced Don had been murdered. I drove on. Horrible scenes of what the Walker might have had to go through played in my head. I began composing the last newsletter, "Dear Friends…"

When I'd run through a dozen tragic scenarios, it suddenly struck me that Don might only have been kidnapped. Fresh hopes of seeing him alive made me bear down on Otto's gas pedal. Every moment was suddenly precious. But then I began worrying about the police. Maybe they wouldn't care or want to be helpful. Maybe they wouldn't be honest. Maybe they wouldn't believe me.

I lost all track of time and distance. I had no idea how far ahead was Fort Bragg. I felt I had been driving a tortuous lifetime of miles—when what do I spy down the road, a fair distance through my tear-blurred vision, but a fluorescent something on the move.

Could it be—could it possibly be? Indeed, it was! I pulled up short and the Walker came alongside.

"Fran, where have you been?" Don asked with some exasperation.

"Where have *I* been? Where have *you* been! How did you get past me without my knowing?"

"I was afraid of this," Don said, somewhat sheepishly. "I went into the woods to go to the bathroom, and when I saw I could take a shortcut back up to the road and cut off a curve, I did."

"Good grief—must have been the very curve where I was parked!" I wanted to kill him.

When I drove on to find gas in Fort Bragg, I wondered why I was so angry and why I didn't feel more relieved. Somehow I couldn't recover. I was still on edge. Don was on edge.

Later that day we found ourselves yelling and screaming at each other. It was the first time on the journey we had come to this. I was ready to drive off a convenient cliff into the sea.

Too late, we figured out our argument was all a big misunderstanding. It was stupid. We were both frazzled. We argued over whether or not I had scouted a campground with showers.

Near the end of the day, in the shadowy dusk, I hated to have to do all the scouting alone. By that time I was sick of scouting for things—gas stations, post offices, phones, stores—the Walker! I felt vulnerable in the early dark and did not like trying to explain to strangers that I was not really alone, that Don was out there walking, that he would be coming along. It somehow sounded phony. I got tired of trying to explain about The Walk, day in and day out.

For his part, Don liked knowing what there was to look forward to at the end of his day—whether there was a campground or showers, whether they would give us a deal, how near was a town or restaurant, etc.

We usually teased one another about our differences and laughed at them. We took turns giving in to one another. And most of the time, we scouted the campsites together. But even though we realized this argument was all a big misunderstanding, when it was over, an ungodly silence fell between us—a silence somehow worse than the argument itself.

When a man sneakily crept out of the bushes after me that same night, or rather in the wee hours of the morning—with God knows what on his mind—and I couldn't figure out what he could possibly have been doing hiding in some low shrubs behind the phone booth I'd been in—I cracked. It was the last straw.

I had gotten up at three in the morning (six in the morning Vermont time) to catch David at home before work. Beforehand I had wakened Don to tell him what I was doing.

I followed the labyrinthine paths of the jungly campground a good half mile before I came to the phone booth near the entrance. I lost all track of time while I was talking. There was no locked gate. No one was up. Impenetrable black night stood at the edge of the street light's circle about me. My flashlight was dim.

While I was talking to David, I watched a raccoon climb out of a tree not far from me. And then it disappeared. I thought I was hearing this raccoon climb out of the bushes behind me when I started to head back to our campsite. I almost didn't turn around. When I did, I saw a figure in a light-gray, hooded sweatshirt rising like a ghost out of the shrubs in back of the phone booth I'd been in. That's all I could see—the hulking sweatshirt.

My flashlight flickered before me. I held it up and pointed it at the man as if it were a gun. I was flustered. I said stupidly, "Need a light?"

He gave no answer. He was about twenty yards away but coming toward me. I shouted at him.

"I don't know what you are doing—coming out of those bushes at this hour of the night! If you know what's good for you—you—you'd better stay where you are!"

But he kept slowly advancing. I began walking backward at about the same pace. I was afraid to turn my back on him. I wondered how well he knew the campground. I wondered if I would remember the crazy route back to our campsite.

I shrieked at the man, "You're making me very nervous!"

And then I turned my back on him and ran. I prayed I would not get lost. I'd gotten lost in these maze-like campgrounds many times before.

Somehow I found my way. I don't know what that man was up to, but shortly after I slammed shut Otto's door and locked it, I saw him drift on by our campsite—a specter haunting the place.

I climbed to my upper bunk and lay like a dead woman. I felt no blood running through my veins. My heart did not beat. I did not cry.

Don was awake when I got back and tried to tell me that the man was not after me. I didn't care. I couldn't care. I was not even alive. I didn't speak. I had feared and flirted with death on the Oregon Coast, but now somehow I felt the darkness of it bearing down upon me and I did not resist.

My breathless silence must have worried Don. After a long while he started talking.

"Fran, I have an idea. I've been thinking. I know the journey's been hard on you."

"Don," I interrupted quietly, "I don't even want to talk about it."

"You don't have to talk—just listen. You're tired of this, I know.

Your nerves are shot. And I know you said once you wouldn't go home before the end because it would be too hard to leave again. But maybe you should. You could get away from things for a while. Rest up.

"And, I think—the way I've been figuring it—we're getting ahead of ourselves a little, if we want to be anywhere near Southern California for Christmas. You know, Vinny has been planning to meet us in San Francisco—well, maybe you could fly home then. I'll take some more time off—visit our friends, Max and Jan, stay at your brother Joe's, make some more school visits, maybe walk *some,* but not much."

Don kept on talking, gently elaborating on the idea that I could use a rest and he could manage without me for a while. And though at first I didn't want to hear what he had to say, the more I listened, the more it sounded like a good idea.

My heart began to beat again. I breathed deeply and thought of hiding out at home and being with David. In about a week Don could walk to San Francisco—in another day after that I could be home.

"Well?" Don was asking, "what do you think?"

"I think…I guess, I think you may be right," I agreed. "But if I do go home, it would have to be a secret. I mean, I always told people I wouldn't go home before the end—and, well, I don't know, I just want it to be kept secret—beyond telling my brother and Vinny, of course."

"That's fine with me," Don said. "We'll make arrangements with David tomorrow."

Part Six

NOVEMBER – DECEMBER

California, Arizona

Chapter 50

Rainbows

For six days then we followed Route 1 to San Francisco. The fog was no more upon us. We found ourselves in an area much less lush with vegetation than we had seen further north. The coastal road seemed to be treacherously narrow at times, and Don might have wished for a fog to hide the perilous route.

In places the dry hills were so eroded they were dangerously close to undermining Route 1. In places the skimpy road crumbled at the western edge and tumbled far below into the sea. In places there was no room for a guardrail. In places the guardrail had tumbled to the sea. In places we found telltale remnants of a former Route 1.

The Walker sorely missed the bike lane there had been along the Oregon coast, but here there was no room for one. Instead, occasional signs warned drivers to be on the alert for bikers. Pedestrians weren't mentioned.

Farther away than ever were the days when Don could walk merrily along, singing songs and telling stories to himself, as when he strode across the prairie. He had to look sharp and listen sharp. Fortunately, the logging trucks that still somehow managed to ply these roads made a great deal of noise gearing down for the crazy curves. Don couldn't help worrying about what he'd do if two trucks met when they were passing him. The land was often a towering cliff on one side of him and a precipitous drop-off on the other.

Once, he did have a close call. He heard the familiar, straining grind of a logging truck's approach, but he could hear something else, too. Without knowing exactly what it was, he jumped closer to the steep wall next to him and squatted in the ditch. While the truck passed, Don looked up to see a log, widely askew on it, batting against and scraping the rocky bank about where his head would have been.

This sort of incident encouraged the Walker to pick up his pace. He began routinely running around the worst curves to be sure not to be pinned there by speeding cars or trucks. He figured the less time he spent walking this route, the better his chances of reaching San Francisco alive.

I did not feel as vulnerable as the Walker, but I did have to skirt the scary sea cliffs as I drove south. I mostly had to be careful not to become enamored with the view or bird watch as I piloted Otto along the narrow, winding way. And if I wasn't nervous about being accidentally run off the road, or distractedly driving off a cliff edge into the sea, there was a peaceful side to some of the territory. Occasional sheep or cattle farms pried open the landscape and made for a welcome breathing space.

When the road wasn't dangerous, both of us kept one eye on the sea for migrating whales and one eye on the land for migrating birds and butterflies. Many western birds, as well as the western monarch butterfly, go south along the California coast for the winter. We saw so many migrants, it began to feel as if we were part of *their* journey.

Sometimes the company was grand—flocks of much-loved meadowlarks, all manner of hawk and migrating songbird—not to mention waterfowl, such as loons, grebes, cormorants, ducks, and geese that winter on these coastal waters. More than once, I thrilled to hear the plaintive whistle of a white-throated sparrow—a call that immediately could transport me to summery mountain meadows at home.

Our nights camping by the sea were sometimes restful, sometimes not. We might be serenaded by the barking, belching, mooing, and carousing of sea lions all night long, as when we camped out near Patrick's point or Anchor Bay. Or it might be bull sea elephants who bellowed and belched, as near Fort Ross. The latter did so at such a cavernously low octave, their rumpus rivaled that of an un-mufflered logging truck gearing down to take a hairpin turn.

But legitimate camping places were getting scarce. The closer we got to San Francisco, the more the land was spoken for. "No Trespassing" signs proliferated—and often a sign would have its message stated three ways: "Posted, No Trespassing, Keep Out!" It seemed each day closer to the Bay Area, the signs multiplied. We could see more and more estates, fancier homes, and lots of high walls, fences, and hedges to discourage wandering intruders.

The weather was mostly good to us, the climate a balm often filled with the fragrance of eucalyptus mixed with the sea. For me, the slightly medicinal and healing odor of eucalyptus had an old-fashioned, woody coziness bound up in it. Whenever I could, I would pause in a grove and inhale it deeply. The few storms we encountered did not last long.

Near Stewarts Point a westering sun fell out of a dark bank of clouds into the open sky and made a great rainbow to the northeast. I pulled over and got out to admire it, knowing how momentary these things can be. But it did not fade. It soon became a double, then a triple—and briefly even a quadruple rainbow. When the Walker came along, the main bow was still there, arcing above the California hills. I took Don's picture beneath it. It seemed a good omen and somehow meant to bless us all—the Walker, the Driver, and Otto.

The next rainbow Don walked under was painted on a tunnel overriding part of a four-mile stretch of freeway connecting Route 1 with the Golden Gate Bridge. It was November 5. Vinny had arrived earlier that day in San Francisco and had driven out to meet us. He joined Don for this four-mile stretch while I waited at the bridge.

Unfortunately, they were walking the freeway during rush hour. I thought I'd never see the two of them emerge from that tunnel. It somehow seemed unlikely that they would. It was the last hurdle. I hoped it would not be the last straw. Vinny had already hand-delivered my airline ticket, but I hardly yet dared to think I would ever be flying home.

I had plenty of time while I was waiting to imagine all kinds of gruesome things happening, when at long last I saw them coming. Hurrah! Time to start packing.

Chapter 51

The Music of The Walk

November 8, I wrote: "I have boarded a plane in San Francisco and am, at this moment, heading east toward home. Knowing I was going to have this trip home has been like an anchor to me. Yet now that the anchor has been pulled and the voyage is underway, I am upset. My feelings stir within like some strange witch's brew. I cannot seem to sort them all out. I cannot understand myself. Why am I not simply and plainly happy to be going home?

"I stare out the plane window and watch a continent passing beneath me—a continent Don has already crossed on foot—and yet he has not crossed any lands such as I see below. Reds, Yellows, browns in muted hues are shaded and splashed and dabbed and brushed over earth which has been ridged and rippled, heaped and gouged. Here and there blues and grays seep into certain features like pale ink stains.

"From this perspective—much removed—the country seems virtually scoured of all life. It looks hard and waterless down there— as empty of vegetation as people. We have crossed prairie, plain, and mountain—we have skirted an ocean, but this vast desert expanse? It looks forbidding. The only sign of man I can make out is—a path—must be a road—going unerringly straight for long distances, wiggling a bit here and there, occasionally sweeping in a graceful curve around some odd feature in the terrain. Overall, it looks no more than the thin scratch you might make dragging a sharp stick across the flat face of a rock. All this to come."

When clouds crept over to hide the earth, my thoughts turned in again and confronted my fears. Was I worried about having to leave home again? Maybe I was afraid I wouldn't be *able* to leave—that it would be too wrenching, now that I knew more what the journey was about. Still, I was anxious and eager, so why the confusion?

Something dark threatened from below—something I could not fathom. It was, in truth, very like what Robert Louis Stevenson wrote at one point in *An Inland Voyage*: "You may paddle all day long; but it is when you come back at nightfall, and look in at the familiar room, that you find Love or Death awaiting you beside the stove…"

As much as I wanted and needed to be home, I was also realizing that a good part of what was difficult about the journey was simply what was difficult about life. Home was not a place immune to life and all the complex realities. While on the journey, had I not made "home" stand for more than it ought? Perhaps my aching homesickness was really a sickness of some other sort?

However that may be, the instant my feet touched ground in Vermont and my eyes landed on David, my fears and ambivalence fled. Even sitting at home alone the next day at my own desk, while David was at work, I felt like one of those dry, compressed sponges suddenly tossed into water. I was gradually coming back to life, recovering an old resiliency, soaking up what I could no more describe than I could sort out my fears the previous day.

I looked out my desk windows in the long loft we call the observatory (because we stargaze through these high south windows) at the mountain chickadees coming and going from my high window feeder, and I felt as if they were stitching my soul back together with their scalloping flight. Home was real—unspeakably real. I felt myself to be suddenly *in place*—a jigsaw puzzle piece snapped into perfect, interlocking fit.

What did it matter that I broke out with poison oak on my shins and ankles almost the moment I arrived, or that the November world was stark and chill, or even that I was going to have to leave again before long? What mattered was that home was real—I had not made it up. And here I could rest—rest up *from* the road, rest up *for* the road. And I could think. I re-read the letters I had sent home and wrote:

"I keep seeing something like death at the heart of my puzzling—a kind of ultimate letting go—which I have alternately embraced and shunned. I have written more than once of feeling as if I had died on this journey and yet been given permission to correspond with the living. I see in my letters a great struggle—a battle with myself, I think. What is death but absence? What is life but presence? Am I struggling simply to make my presence felt because I am ultimately afraid of not being missed when I am gone? Am I really afraid my presence is somehow not only unworthy but insignificant?

"I am stretched thin by the truth. The journey is the concentrated acting out of this truth, that is, of what life really is. Home is but a place along the way. It does not negate the journey. Indeed, however temporary home may be, it is nonetheless a gift—it is a foretaste of where the journey itself is taking each of us by a myriad of differing routes. If only we can get there."

When I rejoined Don a week later at my brother Joe's place in Los Gatos, California, I was much renewed. I was under a good spell. I was even surprised at how eager I was to get back on the road. Don and I had talked on the phone while I was home, and I knew he was enjoying his break, but maybe he was being tested, too. I mean, why go back to The Walk when you're having so much fun?

Don had met up with Lisa again, the adventuresome biker from New York State. Lisa, Vin, and Don had walked the Golden Gate Bridge together and done some other fun things. Don had done two full thirty-mile walks on his own—to get himself from the Golden Gate to Los Gatos, but when Vin went home, Don had also met up with other friends in the area, so that he had plenty of distractions. He had plans to do some more things with Lisa, to help my brother with a project, and, well, I was beginning to wonder if maybe The Walk had shifted somewhat in the Walker's priorities.

"What? We're going to the symphony in downtown San Francisco, tonight? You, me, Lisa, and Joe?" I said in surprise. "Don, I thought you were going to start walking today?"

"Tomorrow, Fran," Don explained, "not today. What's the rush? Or maybe not tomorrow, now that I think about it—I'm pretty sure Joe has a dinner planned for tomorrow night at the Bella Vista Restaurant with your cousin, Mary Helen, and her husband. The next day. We'll go the next day."

"Gosh, Don, that means I'll have to write another weekly newsletter with precious little walking to report. I think I'll have to call this newsletter *The California Stall*."

Don laughed. "Don't worry, Fran, you'll be sick of the road again before you know it."

Of course, I knew he was right. Still, I hoped some rousing march at the symphony might stir the Walker and inspire him to get on with it before my fresh resolve disintegrated.

When the symphony program ended with Ravel's "Bolero," I knew my wish to be granted. Neither Don nor I had ever heard "Bolero" as we did that night. We both recognized it at once as the music of The Walk, the theme of the journey: perseverance.

The different voices of the orchestra each seemed to sing of the unique and changing features of the land, while the haunting theme itself, played again and again and again, sang of the connectedness of it all. The constant, underlying, and unchanging drum beat drove home the more relentless aspects of The Walk. As for the building of the music to its peak, it was like the piling up of the miles behind us, and, too, very like what I could imagine our hearts would be doing when the end of the journey was finally in sight—as yet a long way off.

Chapter 52

The Front Side of the World

When we finally took off from Los Gatos on November 19, we immediately began dealing again with an aspect of California we dreaded—the freeways. Route 17 at morning rush hour, twisting through the Santa Cruz Mountains, was a helter-skelter, high-speeding, crowded, multi-lane racecourse—the Indianapolis 500 on a steep tilt.

Don had gotten ahead of me while I did some stocking up for the road in downtown Los Gatos. When I caught up to him and then passed him on the opposite side of the highway, I thought I saw him signal me to stop. This was a risky thing to do on such a road, but I pulled over just long enough to look back at him and hear him scream to get off at the next exit, whatever it was.

By then I was realizing it was the only sensible thing to do. At that I barely made it. Otto had no power at all to climb the steep grade from a dead stop. He could hardly get up enough power to chug along at thirty. Changing lanes at such a rate, with traffic zinging past me on both sides at once going better than seventy, was pure nightmare. Otto was the road hazard and I knew it. Drivers angrily honked and cursed at me in frustration; I would not have been surprised to have gotten shot at. When the exit finally showed, I was only too glad to get out of everyone's way!

For Don to get off safely, he had to do some smart, fast running as well as leap over some barricades midstream. We met up again on Summit Road.

"Let me see the map," Don said wearily. "I don't want to get on anything like *that* again."

"Which map? My brother Joe gave us so many maps, we now have more maps of California that we had for all the states previous. Here, try this one."

"Thanks. You know, I would have gotten off that road sooner," Don said, puzzling out his future course, "but I knew you wouldn't have known where I was. I think we're both lucky to be alive. Lisa, too. Did you see her? No? She passed me on the road before you came along, but said she was getting off first chance she could. She's headed south, too, but I don't think she's much safer on a bike—anyway, not on roads like that.

"Hmmm," Don continued, "looks like once we get onto San Jose Road we can follow that to Route 1. But damn! Route 1 itself is mostly freeway until we get to Carmel. Hard to tell on this map if there's any alternative. Maybe we'll find some secondary roads when we get there."

And, whenever we did find a secondary road, over the next two days when we hit Route 1 again, we took it. There were a lot of places I could have gone wrong, so I tried to meet up with the Walker frequently to avoid losing him.

Since coming back to the road life, I found it harder than ever to believe that I was but two days earlier on the other side of the continent resting at home. Going from the already wintry clime of the northeast, where ice glazed the puddles and edges of ponds, where all the leaves were down, and where snow was more likely to fall than rain—to the coast of California, where I could hardly say what season it was—made me look around to try to figure it out.

The more I looked around, though, the more seasons I saw in progress at once. The only season I didn't seem to see was winter itself. I could stand in one place and admire autumnal colors in the leaves of certain trees (not native to the state), such as the sweet gum and ginkgo; I could see fall fruits, like the persimmon, hanging like tiny pumpkins amid scarlet foliage, and yellow and orange citrus fruits bulge on backyard plantings. At the same time, some trees and shrubs were just coming into flower, and the California hills themselves were every day visibly trading their golden hue for something more emerald—as if it were spring! Like summer was the California sun itself, when it was out, which could still manage to be bright and hot enough for shorts most days. *No wonder all kinds of creatures like to winter here*, I thought. *Imagine: winter means monarch butterflies in this place.*

The greening of the California hills meant rain, too, of course, and on November 20 Don saw lots of it. The day was filled with storms. Once, I found the Walker taking temporary refuge in a laundromat, having thrown his outer layer of clothes into a dryer.

A fickle wind kept whipping the hat off Don's head at odd moments, and every time he went to pick it up, he found it covered with tiny ants. Don concluded it must be raining ants.

There was plenty of mud, too. Sometimes the Walker was thickly coated with it from having it splattered all over him by constant traffic. It was good when the day ended on a drenching note to rinse the worst of it off.

We found a great place to camp in the pouring rain, but by the time it was dark, we'd gotten kicked out by a park ranger. No camping allowed—something we were aware of, but the place was so far off the beaten track, and it was such inclement weather, we couldn't believe anyone would bother to come enforce the rules. We ended up camping in a commuter parking lot wedged between heavily traveled Route 1 and a huge magnesium refractory. Meanwhile, it rained indoors that night, or so I first thought when I heard the telltale squish as I set foot on Otto's rug next morning. The cooler drain somehow let go again, as it had a few times before, and yes, we'd had another flood.

The next day we breakfasted at the Franco Hotel in Castroville, the "artichoke capital of the world." A local farm hand confirmed what Don and I thought we'd been seeing in the fields.

"Yep, brussel sprouts, cabbage, cauliflower, parsley—most anything you find in a salad—and artichokes, artichokes as far as you can see," the man said as he sipped his coffee.

"What about strawberries?" Don asked. "I thought I saw strawberries rolling about on the road back there."

"Oh yeah, sure, strawberries. Must have spilled off a truck."

"Strawberries?" I asked. "In late November?"

"Strawberries just about the year round—mostly go to preserves this season, though."

"Seems to me they pick off a crop one day and go right back to plant it the next—like lettuce," the waitress chimed in, refilling the farm hand's cup.

"Hmph," the man nodded emphatically, his mouth full of doughnut.

"But isn't it pretty dry here in the summer?" Don asked.

"Yep, not just the summer. We irrigate most the year—'cept right about now, really. Saltwater's gettin' into the water table, though, spoilin' more land each year. They've been goin' to put in a desalinization plant—soon—they keep sayin'. Settle some of the squabblin' over water rights to the Salinas River."

"Funny, I don't seem to see many farmhouses around," I ventured.

"Not many family farms left, if that's what you mean," the man said with a certain tone of resignation. "Taxes driven most of 'em off. Corporations runnin' 'em now. Manager flies in for a few days, then goes back to the city to live."

After Castroville, it was back to some more freeway walking for a while. When I lost track of the time, and Otto and I finally got tired of waiting for the Walker to show, I decided to do some freeway walking myself and see what it was all about. Anyway, I wanted to head back to a hill and see if I could see Don coming. But in the middle of my trek a state police car came up from behind and yelled from a loudspeaker, "Get off the freeway!" which just about made me jump out of my socks. I hadn't realized they might bellow at me with a bullhorn.

What seemed hours later, back with Otto, I heard a familiar whistle and saw Don the other side of the chainlink freeway fence. When we met up, I found out the Walker had been kicked off the freeway *three* times—the last, they'd put him in a squad car, drove him off to a bike trail, and threatened to put him in jail the next time they caught him on the freeway. It was nothing but luck we had found each other again. But now we were on the Monterey peninsula, and Don could walk some lesser roads. He had put on a lot of extra run-around miles and he didn't want to have to do that again.

After Monterey we hit Carmel. A sign warned, "No camping or parking on road margins or pull-offs next seventy-two miles." Good grief, I thought, they must have seen us coming. A friendly park ranger solved our problem that night by letting us camp out of sight of the road in a school parking lot. But before we got our campsite and while Don was finishing up the day's miles, I went to visit the old mission in Carmel, founded by Padre Junipero Serra in 1771.

Once I got over the disappointment of finding the mission in a well-settled residential area, I went in to find what turned out to be a very old-world atmosphere anyway—deserted of all visitors but me at day's end.

In the distance, I glimpsed the brilliant green of hills stepping gracefully into sea. The crystal air shimmered with all but the last light of day. I could hear the ocean if I listened for it, but strangely that was all I could hear. A hush hovered over. Little sunlight penetrated the stained glass of chapel and basilica. The candlelit indoor spaces were already dark as with evening. But the ceremony underway out of doors, within the mission walls, against the old, cobbled brownstone courtyard and into the translucent petals of flowers—was another matter.

Conducted by a westering sun, out of each waning moment of the day was created a separate vision. Somehow the steadily changing light cast everything into motion, however still.

And then I realized I was not alone in this sanctuary. As if they'd come to drink the last of the day's nectar with me, a dozen hummingbirds hummed and hovered over the gardens in radiant bloom (*Are California gardens always so?* I had to wonder). The long-reaching horizontal rays of the sun were a perfect foil for the headdress of the male—something crimson and purple gleaming— and for the cloak of the female—something greenly iridescent. Every flower lifted its cup to be drained as if it had waited out the long day of visitors for just this sort of attention. And my own overflowed. The next day, too.

It was Don's birthday, and he celebrated about as grandly as he could by breaking his four-thousandth mile while walking an area once named by the Spaniards: El Pais Grande del Sur—the Big Country of the South—now known simply as Big Sur. Route 1 reached dramatic heights here, climbing in places higher than a thousand feet above the sea. Opposing the blue Pacific rose the Ventana Wilderness, Los Padres National Forest, and the Santa Lucia Mountains. Redwoods towered again in places, and waving plumes of pampas grass caught the light like dry silver flames.

No logging trucks dogged Don's steps here, nor was there much traffic. What travelers there were seemed captured like us by "the views"—though the typical response after a car pulled over, the occupants scrambled out, and a few camera clicks were heard was: silence. The common click of the camera was the perfect emblem to register the insignificance and humility you felt before this splendor.

But it takes time to see. I was thankful we weren't going any faster than we were. True seeing requires recognition. I couldn't help wondering at times if I wasn't gazing at the front side of the world. G. K. Chesterton wrote in *The Man Who Was Thursday*, "Listen to me…shall I tell you the secret of the whole world? It is that we have only known the back of the world. We see everything from behind and it looks brutal. That is not a tree, but the back of a tree. That is not a cloud, but the back of a cloud. Cannot you see that everything is stooping and hiding a face? If we could only get round in front…" For a time I felt as if I had.

Still, being bombarded by so much beauty can be unsettling. What is one to do with it all? Mostly we have to turn away—as if we know perfectly well it is not meant merely for entertainment. Something is being shouted so loud we cannot hear—and painted so grand we cannot see. It is as Pascal says, "Our senses can grasp nothing that is extreme; too much noise deafens us; too much light blinds us; too far or too near prevents us from seeing." And perhaps, I might add, too much beauty pulls the rug out from under us.

"Fran, weren't the sea otters amazing today?" Don exclaimed that night as we pulled into Big Sur State Park to camp.

"Yes, they were—and what a life! Now I know where the idea for the waterbed came from. All those lazy critters lounging in the kelp—their snacks laid out on their tummies—oysters Rockefeller, it looked to me."

"Abalone," Don corrected.

"Well, whatever. Did you find anything today?"

"Nope, I don't think I looked down at my feet once."

"Too much to see, wasn't there," I agreed. "And I'll bet you never forget what you were doing this day. Happy Birthday, Don. Now, how 'bout some tuna Rockefeller—or maybe some vintage spaghetti out of the jar. It won't be quite like what we feasted on when we were celebrating your birthday with Joe and all at the Bella Vista, but…"

"Pass me a jar, Fran, and let's get on with it," Don said, laughing. "Who needs anything fancy after a day like today?"

Chapter 53

Where Is Your Cross?

Some people would divide California into two states—one northern, one southern. Clearly they are perceived to be rather different, perhaps especially by Californians who know the state well. I wondered where the border might be drawn and whether Don or I would notice some signifying jolt as we crossed from one into the other. But maybe there's a buffer zone between the two because we didn't feel the jolt.

Still, the last we saw of a more remote, protected, and less developed coast in the state was the stretch from Big Sur to San Simeon. Here too we met a memorable mix of Californians.

I was south of Big Sur watching the rather comical antics of a sea otter grooming itself. It bent itself about like a rubber toy bringing its back to its front, its bottom to its top, and every part of its body within reach of its face and short-armed forepaws. And what a face! An appealing puppy-like face that alone ought to have protected it from the threat of extinction.

But while I was observing the sea otters, a small sporty convertible with its top down swished into the pull-off beside Otto. So low and sleek was this silver bullet I thought it could have easily slid under Otto, supposing it wanted a little shade, that is. But clearly the rather glamorous looking couple that emerged was out for sun—sea otters too. When they had some trouble deciding whether they were watching sea otters or sea lions, I offered them my field glasses.

That was how I met Michael, a small-time Hollywood film producer, who surprisingly did not want to own up to any of his films by name. He said he was on his way back to L.A. from Lake Tahoe, where he had been filming on location. He said his girlfriend had not seen the best parts of California, so they were taking a long, scenic route back. Michael did all the talking and was interested to hear about Don and The Walk, and also that I might write a book about the journey.

"Who knows," he said, "maybe I'll be filming it one day. Here's my card. What will you call it?"

"I don't know," I said. "I haven't really begun writing it—just journals and notes, so far."

"I almost hate to say this," he said. "I mean, I don't really want to wish you bad luck or anything, but, you know, unless something on the disastrous side happens, I don't think you'll have much of a story to interest a publisher."

"I know what you mean," I answered.

As I watched the two drive off, their blonde and red hair gleaming in the sun and flying out behind them like two silken banners in the wind, I dreaded to think what catastrophes might yet be lurking up ahead that would interest Hollywood in my book.

But not many miles later, in the tiny town of Lucia perched picturesquely above the sea, I did meet a man Hollywood could make a film of—a self-confessed reformed drug smuggler and self-proclaimed founding minister of a now-defunct church he called "The Church of All Possibilities."

Pablo played a blues harmonica while pumping gas, and seemed as ready to talk and tell his life story as I was to listen. He told me his name and then, a short while later, he told me it wasn't his real name. And when he heard about what Don and I were up to, he proceeded to talk about a book he wanted to write about himself, including a long walk he took through the desert from Santa Fe to San Diego, and how he'd been bitten by copperheads and rattlesnakes, and how he found out he was immune to snake venom, and how he used to go to Beirut for his drugs. He also pointed out his tiny house on a rock above the sea, behind the gas station, and what rent he paid.

Then he began telling me how, if I wanted to, I could pick up jade along a fourteen-mile stretch of coast there.

But as I listened and watched this man's scarred and somewhat scary face, I found myself feeling uncomfortably mesmerized by his slow, overly calm, and yet sarcastic way of speaking. I was glad when Don came along in time to break the spell. I wasn't sure what to believe or not believe of what Pablo had to say, but I found out the next day he was right about the jade.

I had tea that morning at the Pacific Valley Cafe, and there I overheard a couple of surfers, who had obviously just met, bragging to one another about their wave prowess. When I noticed their cars later, parked where Willow Creek was falling out of the hills into the sea, I pulled over, too, to see if they were making good on their surfing boasts. But they weren't, really. The waves were big, rough, somewhat unpredictable, and did not roll up onto a beach but often headed for some dangerous-looking rocks, so that the surfers had to bail out early even if they did catch a ride. For a long while I stood watching the surfers. When I turned to go, I found myself facing a motley group of rather grizzly looking men.

"Thinkin' about joinin' them down there?" one of them asked, with a giddy sort of laugh. He had a can of beer in his hand that he used to gesture with between sips.

"I don't think so," I said.

"Would ya like a beer?" the same man asked again with another odd laugh.

"Not really," I said. "Thanks anyway." For a moment I didn't know if this man's giddy forwardness was friendly or menacing. I knew I should have just gone on, but instead I found myself addressing the group.

"So what are you all up to this morning?" I asked, immediately regretting my words, thinking I might have set myself up for something. These men had, it seemed to me, appeared as if out of nowhere. I hadn't even heard a car drive up, though now I noticed an old, orange VW van parked near Otto.

"Just havin' our mornin' usual," a skinny old codger with about three teeth answered with a broad grin.

"Usually find us here a nice mornin' like this," a young, chubby, dark-haired fellow said somewhat shyly—and then, almost as if to himself, "We live hereabouts."

And now I noticed some stumps placed in a circle, and that two of the men sat down, put their beers beside them, and began carving on stones they took from their pockets. But the one who first spoke seemed to want to distinguish himself from the rest.

"*I* don't live here," he said, pointing to the sky with his beer can. "I'm landed. You can call me Farmer Phil. I have a traveling home, and property, and a mining claim. And I'm not like these others here who're livin' like trolls under the bridges."

To which the others just laughed good-naturedly and said, "Sure, sure—*Farmer* Phil."

Farmer Phil did seem a little different. He had the most to say, anyway, and he began talking somewhat defensively about his mining claim—which few acres he said were all his just as long as he paid the assessment on them and could prove he was working them. Then he rambled on about being a professor at Cal Berkeley once, about his old lady who left him, about succumbing to dope in the sixties— and all the while breaking out here and there with the same nervous, giddy laugh.

He also seemed to want to speak for the others, saying that they all managed to eke out their living by selling jade, which they mostly found thrown up by the ocean in bits and pieces along this section of coast.

While Farmer Phil was talking and then showing me some of his mineral and jade collection, another man came up to join the group. He carried a somewhat wilted bunch of flowers, which he said he'd found discarded along the road, proceeded to trim off their stems with a pocket knife, then stuck them into a mayonnaise jar half-filled with water, and set them down before everyone on a small pedestal of rock.

When he, too, pulled out a stone to start carving on, I asked what they were all making. "Nothing in particular," they said, "it's soapstone—easy to carve, just somethin' to do."

And so for a while under a bright yellow sun with the blue sea roaring below us, tumbling the surfers and the jade, I heard tales of earthquakes, and forest fires, and rain for 120 days straight; and how a fairly recent mudslide had closed Route 1 for eighteen months, and how much money the bigger pieces of jade would bring them, and how the rangers had discovered a shack two of the men had built illegally and made them have a house burning—which they all turned into a kind of celebration.

In exchange, I told them a few tales of my own about the journey. The jade workers, as they called themselves, said they had wondered about Don walking by alone somewhat earlier in T-shirt and shorts, without a pack on his back, and they were interested in his story. Farmer Phil recalled that another walker had gone by earlier in the week heading south—a man dressed in a white robe carrying a large cross made of tree limbs. "Watch out for him," he said. "He's preachin' with a vengeance."

This was at least the fifth cross-bearer we had heard of. Somehow one was always being reported as just ahead of us on the road, but we had also received a news clipping from a friend telling of a man walking from Oregon to Maine with a cross. Seemed like every walker we heard of had a cross but Don.

I wondered about these cross-bearers. I wondered about myself. I, too, bore a cross—a small, silver cross on a chain about my neck. A few days into the journey, worried about a friend whose troubles at home seemed overwhelming, I sent my cross to her in the mail. And so for a while I was without one. But in Fargo, David surprised me by bringing me another one—this one a silver Celtic cross—and the moment I put it on, I knew I had been naked without it. I was meant to bear it. I had missed it.

Later, when I had a little time to think, I looked at my cross in my mind's eye. Many things in life bear down heavily upon a person like a cross. Perhaps most of these are thrust upon us and are not ones we shoulder willingly or always consciously—hence we feel the weight of them. Are these true crosses, I wondered? Or is the true cross the burden we take up voluntarily? "My yoke is easy and my burden light." Were these cross-bearers doing penance? Or were they up to something else? Was I doing penance? Was I making reparation to Don for past wrongs? I had thought I was paying a debt out of gratitude. Was it really guilt I was dealing with? Was I hoping to make amends and ease the burden of my conscience? Did I think the journey *had* to be a penance? I wasn't sure how to answer these questions.

Doing penance was a familiar concept to me. I had been raised on crime and punishment, so to speak. Once as a child, when I'd been caught vandalizing a new house up the street that nobody lived in yet, my dad let me set my own punishment. I found out much later that I more than doubled the punishment he had thought of giving me. He let my sentence stand, though he also let me off the hook early, I recall, for good behavior.

What had I done? I had found full paint cans and new brushes in an empty garage, while all around me the blank walls suggested a waiting canvas. But I must have had mixed emotions about what I was doing, because without thinking I proceeded to paint the walls with religious symbols—crosses with halos of light radiating from them. Did I think this gesture would protect me from discovery? I learned otherwise.

Before I said goodbye to the jade workers, Farmer Phil gave me a small piece of serpentine I had been admiring earlier. And, for whatever reason, the moments parting with these men were full of warm and generous emotion all round. They also wished the Walker well and told me to tell him to keep on truckin'.

Chapter 54

There's No Telling Everything

South of San Simeon, my brother Joe came and met us, and, leaving Otto behind, we went back to the San Francisco area to celebrate Thanksgiving with Joe and friends. Two days later Joe delivered us back to The Walk.

The next day, I lost the Walker. Recently built roads not shown on our maps confused us both. My watch went awry without my noticing it and further confused me. This made the time I spent cruising the roads seem very strange. Meanwhile, I began calling David to see if Don had called in. (This was a new emergency procedure.) I called home six different times before Don finally did. I put an extra hundred miles on Otto in a fruitless search. It wasn't until Don checked in with David that I realized how far gone the day was and that my watch had been slowing to a halt the entire time.

After Arroyo Grande we cut away from the sea for a while. Don walked by farms in the Santa Maria Valley, through the Casmalia Hills, beside a bone-dry Santa Ynez River, and along a winding road through Harris Canyon. We stayed in Lompoc, and I picked up mail on the road for us for the first time since I'd been home. One item: David sent me an arm support-splint for the tendinitis I had developed from writing long hours at night in the cold—something about pushing the pen with the ink half-congealed in it had ruined my arm, making it ache constantly and painfully, no matter what I did with it. It had been gradually getting worse for months, but the arm support David sent did bring some relief.

Meanwhile, even in Southern California we were beginning to notice the cold more and more. I was depending on the sun to warm Otto by day, which mostly it did, but nights came early and brought more hours of cold and dark than we knew what to do with.

The first day of December, Don followed Route 1 over the Gaviota Pass through the Santa Ynez Mountains back toward the sea. He got on the freeway again and got another warning from the highway patrol, just at the end as he was getting off anyway. We camped that night at Refugio State Beach and found half of the state park occupied by a company filming a soft-drink commercial.

Though the sun was almost gone, giant cranes armed with rows and rows of lights were doing their best to extend the day. Hundreds of "extras" shivered in the late, chill wind on the beach, skimpily clad in bikinis, trying their best to look as if they were enjoying a hot sun. Every now and then, when the shooting stopped, everyone grabbed frantically for the blankets and towels they had been lounging on and huddled beneath them.

We kept hearing about a big storm that was threatening—was supposedly heading down from the north and would hit any day now. A blustery, cold wind was already bringing sharp hints of it. We were just three days out of Los Angeles.

There was plenty of congestion around Santa Barbara the next day, more freeway too, but fortunately some bike trails Don could hike. By luck I didn't lose the Walker. All day I watched the darkening clouds pile up and the wind keep them herded like sheep grazing the hills east of us. Maybe the storm would move inland. I didn't know if it was the building of the storm itself or something less tangible in the atmosphere, but a kind of tension gained on us each day as we approached Los Angeles. Traffic sped up, there was more and more of it, and the chances of being able to pull over just anywhere, much less camp, all but vanished.

I was glad my youngest brother Kevin and his wife Heidi had offered their place as a way station back up in the hills above Malibu. On December 4, when we came to the turnoff to get to their home,

Don wanted to keep walking, since it was still early and he had done only twenty-four miles. But now some rain was beginning to fall and a battering wind to blow, and somehow I talked the Walker into quitting.

Each day, the atmosphere had thickened dramatically between deceptive lulls, and Don had walked clutching his hat and glancing over his shoulder at times to see what was following. We could both feel it coming.

It seemed like only minutes after we were inside my brother's place when the storm hit. Day darkened to night, the temperature plummeted, and something like a small ocean was suddenly dumped upside down on top of us, with accompanying rock falls and mudslides all over the area. We were both glad to be safely and cozily tucked indoors, sipping a hot drink and visiting with family.

But there's no telling everything. And how to keep from telling everything? Our own story is not unconnected to countless others, if not to everyone's. And the ways in which one story intertwines with another are not all known, but even what is known is enough to stop me in my tracks at times and make me wonder. If one has a home base and mostly stays put, then one is liable to feel somewhat at the center of things—a sun around which other events revolve. Our journey through life might not seem like a journey at all. Everyone else with whom we come into contact passes through *our* experience. Each of us is the constant. Maybe that's what makes us want to settle down in one place after all. But the truth is, none of us is a constant; and we are all passing through.

Long before we had begun journeying toward Los Angeles, I knew my closest childhood friend was nursing her dying mother. Her family had been a second family to me growing up. And now, when I called from my brother's, my friend told me her mother had died—the memorial service was the next day. All these many days on the road, and I was just in time to grieve with my friend. We took time to do so, but after a day we pressed on, knowing we would be back at Christmas.

Don walked the beaches of Los Angeles from Malibu to Topanga to Santa Monica to Ocean Park to Venice to Marina Del Ray to El

Segundo to Manhattan Beach. I couldn't always follow where Don walked the beaches and bike trails, so we tried to meet up frequently to keep track of one another. Even so, by the end of the day I had lost him.

I lost the Walker two more times on two different days during the stretch between Los Angeles and San Diego, and the last was the most harrowing for Don, since in order to flee from some harassment by the highway patrol, he escaped over some fence when he thought he saw the police coming after him. Suddenly Don found himself walking a tank trail in Camp Pendleton! The walker was immensely relieved to discover the marines were more understanding than the state troopers; they let him pass with their blessing.

But I find it almost impossible to describe the accompanying hectic pressure of these hit-and-run days in Southern California. It seemed as if we were running in and out of other people's lives, the lives of California friends and relatives, in a way that was dizzying and disorienting. It wasn't as if we were dropping in on others at their convenience or even our own, really—it was more as if we were all merging at once at busy intersections. How much this had to do with the rushing speed of life all about us, I don't know.

Everywhere I was, while Don was putting in the miles, I seemed to come up against some time limit. Every beach-side hamburger joint had a parking time limit. Even grocery store parking lots near the beaches Don walked had time limits. There was no leaving Otto for a moment, because I was always having to park illegally.

While Don was walking through certain areas on the west side of L.A., we heard of terrifying gang activities and of some citizens actually hoping to impose a *five-minute time limit* for anyone to be on the street!

Amazing as this news was, it also somehow fit. Here was a world that was obviously evolving toward some otherworldly limit of frantic, unceasing motion. Soon every body and every thing that was not "on the move" would be outlawed!

And not all the action in this area was on land. The ocean swells in the wake of the big storm carried all manner of brightly colored daredevils tethered at the ankle to their equally colorful boards.

Someone was always being tossed skyward, board lethally flying after, crashing waves subsequently burying both for long, breathless moments. And not all the action on the sea was surf boarders—windsurfers whipped over choppy inlets so fast they seemed to be jet-propelled, and sea-going motorcycles (called jet skis) jumped the waves and roared about louder than the sea.

But what surface *wasn't* surfed in Southern California? Skateboarders were everywhere, riding fixed waves of curb and concrete—and once, a young skateboarder took advantage of a green light and a steep hill, while I watched open-mouthed as he shot on through a dangerous intersection, just ahead of a stream of traffic about to charge after him.

I wrote in my journal: "I can see a sign from where I have been waiting in a fast food parking lot (ignoring the time limit), with non-stop traffic speeding by on every hand, saying: Mission San Juan Capistrano—four miles. But the Mission seems so entirely out of place compared to where I am now that I really cannot imagine it near at all. Here—though I feel the need for peaceful sanctuary to be overwhelmingly great, how can I believe it exists. Even such a thing as a swallow in all this crazy constancy of speed and rush is impossible to believe in. Every road in this area seems like a freeway—almost without exception—almost to each person's door, however off the designated freeway the person lives.

"And the very suddenness of things—where is anything that is old? Everything I can see looks brand new as if it all happened this morning. Can there really be an *old* mission somewhere about? It would be a very miracle, I think."

It probably did not help my disposition that I was viewing the motion picture of Southern California through Otto's windows while sitting on an itching field of fire. One day I was jubilantly writing home about my case of poison oak clearing up. A few days later I had to report the onset of another—a far worse case in a far worse place. I could guess how I got it, if not exactly when, since it broke out all over my back side. Now that the plant had entered its dormant period without leaves, it was impossible to tell where it grew; apparently the woody stems were just as virulent as the leaves.

"Fran, cheer up; tomorrow's the big day—I walk out of San Diego. I mean, I make that left-hand turn you've been longing for—we turn east!" Don said, ordering me a coke while we waited at a restaurant bar to say hello to Lisa, the biker, who had temporarily settled in the area. Lisa smiled when she spotted us and brought us our drinks.

"Congratulations!" she said to the Walker. "Aren't you about halfway home now?" But she didn't wait for an answer, as another table called her over.

"Well," I said, continuing our previous conversation, "Otto and I are definitely ready to get out of the fast lane. Seems every day you've walked since somewhere before L.A. has had a noisy, speed-demonish, squirrelly feel to it. Nothing in California manages to stay still for long, not even us, and nothing in Southern California even slows down. I've lost all track of the rhythm of The Walk—which I once knew like my own heartbeat."

"Yeah," Don said, "I know what you're talking about. There's so much going on everywhere—no space between events. You're in your corner with the clock ticking just waiting for the bell to ring telling you to get back out there and start battling again.

"Well," the Walker continued after a long sip of soda, "at least I had only one day walking in smog. I couldn't have taken much more of that. It helps to have decent air to breathe. Thank God for the wind. Really, though, Fran, I think we've been darn lucky. Now if only I can walk out of San Diego tomorrow without getting kicked off any more freeways. Another experience like Camp Pendleton and I'll be ready to hop into Otto and forget it."

"If I thought you really meant that Don—naw," I changed my mind, "at this point even I wouldn't want you to do that. Giving up now wouldn't really bring us home—it would only make us wish for the rest of our lives that we were back on the road, finishing the unfinished task."

"By the way, Don, is Lisa right? I mean, is this really the halfway point? You've walked 4,451 miles."

"It's not halfway if I'm going to walk ten thousand. But it's hard to tell—I'm not exactly sure how many miles it will take to get us home. It's got to be *close* to halfway."

We both sighed. It would have been nice to think it *was* halfway.

Chapter 55

What Time Is It, Anyway?

Don headed out the morning of December 14, from our southernmost point on the coast of California—the Mission Beach area of San Diego. (This was not the southernmost point of The Walk, which would come later in Texas.) We were 181 days into the journey. I let Don turn east before me. Staying with family and friends so many nights, I had let our supplies get low, and I needed to replenish them.

Also, I wanted another look at the Pacific, just to see if I might catch sight of one of the gray whales that migrate south along the California coast this time of year. Several people had mentioned them to us—even Farmer Phil and the jade workers reported that they thought they'd seen the first ones already. Ever since we'd heard of this migration, we'd been on the look out for it. But beyond Don's spying a submarine, periscope up, north of Bodega Bay, and both of us enjoying the company at times of pods of leaping, diving porpoises—we hadn't seen anything whale-like out there.

Anxious as I was to make progress east, I was surprised to discover that I had a noticeable twinge of regret thinking of turning my back on this ocean after so many days. I also regretted not having been able to come to a halt for certain natural retreats such as the tidal marsh at Morro Bay. Tidal marshes are rare on the West Coast. The day I might have been able to spend time in the marsh, I had lost the walker and had to spend time in search of him instead. Hundreds of monarchs beckoned at Morro Bay, not to mention countless birds and other wildlife. I was beginning to get to know the wintering shorebirds, and I delighted more than once in watching various combinations of sandpipers working sections of shallow surf together.

Once, I watched a long-billed curlew (whose extraordinarily long beak curves down), a marbled godwit (whose very long beak curves up), and a rather squat-looking, long-billed dowitcher (whose long beak doesn't curve at all)—all feeding together in and among each other's legs, which were of varying heights. I marveled that they didn't get their bills and legs all tangled up in one another. Pipers and plovers, gulls and terns, loons, geese, ducks, and more—I was about to turn my back on them all.

The very briefest glimpses of California's Nature, whether by waterside or roadside—or even the garish gardens now splendidly rampant with roses climbing about a house—I would miss. And it seemed to me that a great and precious responsibility lay upon this state, offering sanctuary to so much wildlife. When I heard the coyotes sing outside Arroyo Grande in several choruses, I rejoiced. I rejoiced that the wild could still manage to make a home so close to areas of such rapid growth, but I wondered how long it could be thus.

The San Diego Harbor proved to be better for sighting hulking ships and yachts than whales. I could hardly see beyond the forests of tall masts and branching spars. I looked for the telltale spouting of whales but saw none. After watching a harbor seal fishing among a circle of western grebes fishing among a circle of pleasure boats in place, I turned to catch up with the Walker and begin the journey east—the morning sun full in my face. I would miss all those various and glorious sunsets into the sea, but I felt the blessing of the rising sun and now gladly went to greet it.

I followed Friars Road and passed the Walker on Mission Gorge Road. Mission Gorge would take us to Route 67, and Route 67, though jogging due north for a bit, would take us into the mountains to Route 78, which would then take us more directly east. It was still morning rush hour, and when I passed Don, he frowned and made some meaningful gestures of frustration concerning the hazardous road; he also flashed the requisite number of fingers signifying how much further I should go to wait for him.

I fully shared his sentiments about the route. We were successfully avoiding the freeways, but not freeway-like roads. Dangerous speeding traffic, frequent congested intersections, artery-clogging strip development—all looked as if it would go on forever. I was thankful for the moments I'd taken to reflect a bit beside the sea, because there was little worth reflecting on now—including the huge billboards thrust up here and there, loudly advocating the use of condoms.

We were all day getting out of the densely settled suburbs surrounding San Diego. And for me, the day was nearly over before the most important sense of heading east sank in. I'd had to be too alert to the roads and the traffic to do much thinking. Indeed, I was beginning to wonder if we would ever leave the suburbs behind, when finally, north of Lakeside, I drove up into a new set of hills.

At first I saw the hills covered with thickly scattered patterns of brand-new housing developments with newly planted landscaping. I don't know how long this vision lasted, but when my head cleared I realized that I was looking at hills covered with rocks of pink stone, and low-growing shrubs, without a house among them. I breathed a great sigh of relief. It was the first houseless land I'd seen in a long time. The traffic was still heavy coming upon evening rush hour, but now I felt I had a little room to think.

That was the moment when I first really understood I was heading east. Suddenly I felt a very tangible tug at my heart, as if something or someone at the opposite end had drawn taut a connecting thread and gently pulled. It made me think of a sentence in one of G. K. Chesterton's Father Brown stories, about a thief being caught "with an unseen hook and an invisible line which is long enough to let him wander to the ends of the world and still bring him back with a twitch upon the thread." Thief or no, I certainly felt I'd been let go to wander, and now a gossamer thread was calling me back. Somewhere beyond those hills, home was not simply waiting but beginning to reel me in. Immediately an involuntary smile stole over my face. Our forward progress had new meaning.

At 4:00 the sun disappeared behind Goat Peak, the tallest of the nearby hills, and took the temperature down with it. The air instantly had a genuine bite to it. After a while of sitting and waiting in Otto, I literally began to freeze. To try to warm up I went for a walk to meet Don. I was surprised to find Don almost as chilled through as I was, in spite of walking uphill for the last several miles. By 4:30 it was as dark as the inside of Goat Peak.

"I guess we'll have to camp where I left Otto—I guess it's enough of a pull-off," I said to Don as we walked the last stretch together in the dark.

"I'm too tired and too cold to go on anyway," Don said wearily. "I should have taken an extra jacket at the last stop, but who would've thought it could get this cold this quick in this part of California. What's the mileage for today?"

"Twenty-four." I told him.

"Twenty-four! Geesh—that's not enough. If I don't get back up to thirty or above, I won't end up with a thirty-mile-a-day average. I've given up on some of my goals, but I'm not giving up on that one. Too many days off lately—I've gotten a little soft—and we still have the Christmas break coming up. I hope I don't lose my walking legs over it. Anyway, it's dark and I'm cold and we'd better quit for the day."

We ate a quick, cold dinner, shivering as we did in spite of bundling up. We had to retire to our sleeping bags to really get warm. After a while, Don called up to me.

"What time is it, anyway?"

"Quarter past five," I reported.

"A quarter past five?" There was a significant pause, and then Don said, "You mean we have nearly fifteen hours to lie here before the sun comes up? Guess I'm going to get some serious reading done. Hmmm. Good time to reread *One Hundred Year's of Solitude*. Glad I brought it with me. How 'bout you, Fran; you ready to break down yet and read something?"

"I don't know, Don. I'm tempted, especially with such a long night ahead, but…well, I guess I want to make good on one of my goals too."

When I left home I had sworn off reading. It may seem a funny thing to do for someone who typically is a voracious reader, but I had long been wondering whether or not it wasn't possible for a person to read *too* much. I sometimes wondered if I didn't have a tendency to hide out in books—from life, that is. I wondered whether I wasn't using books merely as a distraction—something to keep me from having to think. Would my brain deteriorate without books, or would I come to use it in new ways? Often too, I wondered if I wouldn't write more if I didn't read so much. Thus, I was working a kind of experiment upon myself. At least so far on this journey, I had all I could do to write up the day and keep my correspondence going in the nighttime hours. But now—it was too cold to write. Not only was the ink freezing in the pen, but my fingers were too stiff to push it. I was sorely tempted, but I did not reach for one of the books Don brought with him. I stewed. I prayed. I thought. I dreamt. I stewed. And sometimes I slept.

Now and then Don would wake up on these long, long nights and call up to me. "What time is it now?" he'd say.

"Would you believe it's only ten o'clock?" I'd say, or "just midnight." At which point we might talk a bit, but more often than not we'd try to sleep again or simply wait out the long night.

Chapter 56

How Changed the World!

When dawn finally broke, beneath Goat Peak, Otto was thoroughly frosted, and a mug of juice I'd left sitting on the dash was frozen solid—proof to both of us that the cold was real and not something we had imagined. Still, it was a little hard to believe—we were only twenty-four miles from the beaches of San Diego.

Don got going quickly, bundled as never before. I drove ahead to the next town, Ramona, with only one thing in mind—heat! It was plain that the sun wasn't going to do much to warm Otto. The sun wasn't even out. The lawns of Ramona were coated with frost, puddles were frozen solid, and it all seemed completely unaccountable. Wasn't this sort of cold an aberration in Southern California? We did not think it could last.

This was the coldest morning we had yet been through, but somehow the day was not proving any warmer. Clouds continued to hide the sun, and a blustery north wind came up. Slowly it began to dawn on us that we were steadily climbing higher and higher in elevation and that this was a least one factor contributing to the low temperatures.

Don picked up his pace, partly in response to the frigid air, partly in response to the early dark—and mostly he managed to keep warm. If he took a break, he did not sit down for more than ten minutes. He was determined to get back to his thirty-mile-a-day pace; he had barely nine hours of daylight to do it in.

I let Don pass me at Ramona so I could stay indoors in the warmth of a restaurant a while longer. But by the time I gained Santa Ysable, at nearly three thousand feet of elevation, later in the day, I was again frozen through. I had hoped for a cafe or restaurant at Santa Ysabel, but there was nothing open except a gas station.

There, for a while, I hovered near a bit of fire burning in a steel drum. Yet the atmosphere took most of the warmth out of the air. My questions and comments about the cold were answered with sarcasm; some of the men hanging about seemed to leer at me with barely hidden malice. I decided to wait for Don locked in Otto at a nearby bakery, which I wished with all my heart had been open.

"Don, you're looking a little blue," I said when he caught up.

"So are you, Fran. It's too cold to be just sitting in Otto with no heat. Drive on ahead to Julian—I hope there's more there than what's here. Find a warm place to wait and give me some of those chocolate bars before you go. It's only seven miles to Julian—maybe you could even find a motel. This cold is something else, again."

I drove on. But with the sun descending rapidly and the cold intensifying, I worried about Don. He had looked a little hypothermic to me and did not seem dressed warmly enough, so I drove only about four miles. I got out to walk back and meet him; it was my only hope of getting warm.

I stepped around old patches of crusty snow on the ground, and looked out over fields and hills sporting more snow than grass or rock. Threatening clouds hastened the dark. Only snow *could* fall at these temperatures, I thought. We were still going up in elevation. Julian—only three miles away now—was at 4,220 feet. Maybe I could talk Don into quitting early.

But no, cold or no cold, Don was determined to keep on. He was just able to make the hour's walk left. Thank goodness for the Julian Hotel, which was waiting at the end of the trail. Not since the Whistling Swan at East Glacier had a wayside inn looked so good. And of all the places we had come across in California, this was the closest thing in atmosphere we'd seen to a New England country inn. But I guess the most telling detail of all was a piping-hot wood stove, welcoming us not only with its warmth but with reminders of a hearth still a continent away—it was a stove exactly like the one we used at home.

But here we learned of a big snowstorm that was about to hit at any time. We may have had a lighthearted bet about the snow, but we were not really prepared to journey in it. Otto did not have snow tires or any heat to keep the windshield defrosted. I wasn't sure, if it got much colder, that Otto would even start. We would not come to a town in the next day's walk, but we would at least be going down in elevation rather rapidly. So, unless the storm hit overnight, Don still might be able to walk away from the brunt of it. Everyone assured us it would be considerably warmer at the lower elevations in the desert.

Early the next morning, the storm still had not hit. Don headed out down the mountain in hopes of leaving this threat behind. I stayed—only so as to be able to type the weekly newsletter indoors, where it was warm. It had gotten to twelve degrees in the night and was about twenty degrees when Don left. We were both thankful for some hot meals and a respite from the weather, but I, too, was hoping to get out before the storm.

I typed with as much concentration as I could muster and did not look up once to see what it was doing out of doors; but by the time I finished and was running to the post office, the snow was already falling thick and fast. I stopped to buy a pair of gloves at a general store, brushed inches of snow from Otto, and jumped into the saddle to take the twisty mountain curves as carefully as I could, slipping and sliding somewhat even so. The road was icy and treacherous. But soon, thank goodness, I was out of the forested mountain terrain with its thickening mantle of snow and into a transitional zone between mountain and desert, where it was only raining and not raining hard. The temperature had warmed to forty degrees, which I found tolerable (by comparison), if not exactly comfortable. Not many miles later I caught up with the Walker in the Anza-Borrego Desert. How changed the world! I could not take it all in at once.

"Don, I can't believe it—where have we gotten? And so quickly, too!" I said through the driver's window when the Walker came up. "Hey, by the way—and I want you to tell me the gospel truth—scout's honor, did you get snowed on?"

"Nope, not even a flake. Just rain spitting at me—no snow—none—el zippo!" Don said with noticeable triumph.

"Well, I did," I reported, "and you should have seen Julian when I left. I just got the newsletter typed in the nick of time! Any longer and Otto would not have been able to safely plow through the icy slush."

"Fran, I'm not going to take a break yet—go on ahead another three miles."

"But you've been at it for a good four hours already," I protested.

"I know, but this is a piece of cake compared to the last two days—and we're still going downhill. Don't worry, I'll be along."

I drove ahead, still stunned by the change of scene. When I pulled over, I got out to really look around.

The stillness—it seemed so sudden—was overwhelming. I loved it. How often had I said it can never be quiet enough for me. Now here was some kind of quiet. Not a single car came down out of the mountains that day behind Otto. (Later, from a San Diego newspaper Don bought, we learned why. A picture of the tiny mountain town of Julian had made the front page. For two full days everyone there had been snowed in—the roads impassable.)

The desert environment was entirely new to us. Besides speeding through it on trips cross country and picnicking briefly at some oasis, we had never spent any real time in one. The stillness struck me first and the fragrance of it second. The place was rich with a gently pungent odor I had never smelled before. Later I would learn this was primarily due to the scent of creosote bush brought out by the rain. And then, of course, s-p-a-c-e, a real sense of room, something similar to the great, wide-open stretches I'd come to love on the prairie and the plains. A peace I'd not really known before on the journey came over me here. It came over Don, too.

"You know, Fran, maybe it seems a little silly to say—but after all the visiting at other people's places off and on now for well over a month, Otto is beginning to really seem—well, you know, like home."

"I can't believe it, Don—I was thinking that same exact thing myself just now. Otto may not always be comfortable, but he's ours and we know how we fit, and we can be ourselves—especially in the privacy of this kind of space. Don't you love it already?"

"Well, the desert is different—I'll say that for it. And so far, maybe what I like best about it is that the road's all mine."

Chapter 57

A Dot Within a Dot

nd at least for the time we were in the Anza-Borrego, the road was all Don's. But Don followed Route 78 out of the Anza-Borrego to Ocotillo Wells (elevation 168 feet above sea level), and kept on it through the Imperial Valley towns of Westmorland and Brawley, below the Salton Sea. On the third day's walk in the desert we hit a place called Glamis, south of the Chocolate Mountains. I wrote to David:

"Last night over the phone, you said you could not find me on the map—and, it seemed, by your voice, that you almost desperately wanted to. You wanted to find the little dot wherein I was somehow magically contained. A dot in the desert—that's me. A dot within a dot. Well, but as soon as I hung up the phone—we had to drive back to camp. So I am a moving dot.

"Yesterday I started my third journal—exactly six months into the journey—and yesterday we made Glamis which I consider to be, even without any nightmarish events happening there, the worst place encountered on the journey so far. What is it? A hell-haven for all-terrain vehicles to go screaming and tearing over the nearby Sahara-like Sand Hills. The people I saw there were grim, unfriendly, and bent over their beers well before noon. The woman there running the dusty, dank, murky store (a solitary establishment somehow warranting a dot on the map) was horse-faced and cold. I see now that there are three designations of desert: protected, unprotected, and off-limits.

The unprotected parts are abused by people, such as might gather at Glamis; the off-limit parts are abused by the services—army, navy, marines, and air force, or by mining operations. The protected parts, like the Anza-Borrego, are pristine—God preserve them. I might have known such beauty and peace was bound to run out."

The quiet was perhaps the first to go, thanks to our getting onto a major truck route west of Westmorland. Not far from the Sand Hills, with all the ATVs scrawling their four-wheeled graffiti over the dunes, we came upon some sort of mining operation with enough threatening "No Trespassing" signs as to make the Walker nervous even to be strolling by. Not too many miles later, the beginnings of long stretches of barbed wire made Don even more nervous, thanks to the accompanying notice: "Danger—Live Bombing Area." *What if they miss their mark by a mile or two?* Don wondered.

Though I wanted to get out and explore some of the desert terrain, we had put the place behind us already where it might have been safe or pleasant. Now, too, east of Glamis, we cut south toward the U.S.-Mexican border from Route 78 by way of a road labeled S-34.

A strange road through the desert, S-34, and more than one carload of Mexicans was heading north from the border on it. For the first time on the journey, and far from the last, we became aware of the unpredictable, roaming presence of the gray-green border-patrol vehicles. We seemed miles and miles from any settled areas, yet there was plenty of trash—mostly in the form of bottles and cans strewn about.

The desert was dry, but because of the recent rains it did not have a parched look; indeed, a subtle wash of green was upon it in many places. But in the heavily irrigated Imperial Valley, the greens at times were as verdant and far-reaching as any I had ever seen. There was even a sense of spring to this checkered valley wherever the crops were young. And when the sun was out on a brilliant dawn, the western meadowlarks themselves, which I was only too glad to find wintering in these parts, could hardly hold back from hopeful bursts of song.

For two days after Glamis, Don had the company, at a distance, of another walker. I pointed him out to Don, during one of his breaks, once when the man was appearing just behind us on a near horizon.

This walker first passed me while I was sitting alone in Otto. The steady crunch of his footsteps coming up from behind on the sand-sprinkled road startled me, since they were so like Don's and I knew Don to have gone on ahead. This man was practically the only other walker I'd seen the entire journey, excluding hitchhikers. This man was not hitchhiking. I could not refrain from saying hello to him as he passed by. He did not turn his head, look up, or give any sign he was aware of me; yet somehow I knew perfectly well that he had heard me. He was blue, gray, and weathered—his clothing all in blue, his hair and countenance gray, his entire being weathered. He was old but not decrepit, and shouldered his few supplies or belongings tied up in a blue bundle hung from the end of a long stick. If Don hadn't seen him, too, I might have finally had to conclude that I made him up. He was too picturesque in that setting. I would have traded Otto, I think, for this man's story, but I never learned a word of it.

I watched him break camp one morning; he had slept in a discarded packing crate. When he passed me later, I said hello again, yet he would not speak. But perhaps he knew, too, the old blue codger, that his image would live on more surely—silent.

Don made Yuma, Arizona, after dark on December 20. He had had to get onto his last California freeway to do it—Interstate 8. Afterward we were both jubilant. We'd broken the tantalizing hold of California and gotten out; we gained a precious hour on the evening end by entering the Mountain Time Zone at the border; Otto's clock (still on Eastern Daylight Savings Time) was only three hours off now instead of four—representing a significant leap toward home! After sixty-six days—the longest we would spend in any one state— we had finally gained a new one—Arizona.

The next night, long after dark, three miles east of Mohawk, Arizona, Don had a bad bout of intestinal flu. We had camped well off the road in the desert, and at first Don thought he could probably throw off the offending germs by vomiting. And yet, after countless, helpless sieges, the nature of his suffering changed from one thing to another.

We raced back onto the interstate in desperate search of a rest area. At last we found one, and Don was sick there for another hour or so before we could drive on about 5:00 A.M. in search of another campsite. The rest area itself was too full of noise and fumes from dozens of parked trucks keeping their diesel engines running for heat; neither of us could stomach camping there. Even if we had wanted to turn around, we had to drive ahead to an exit; and when we did, we thought we saw a convenient place to camp. But no sooner had we nodded off than the border patrol awakened us, and, without giving us a chance to explain why we were there in the first place, demanded that we move on. We never got to sleep again that morning.

Over lukewarm tea at a place called Dateland an hour later, Don announced, "Really, Fran, I think I'm better now—a little weak is all—and tired."

"Good," I said, "I'm relieved to hear it. I guess it's a good reminder—I mean, a person's health can really throw a monkey wrench into the works."

"Yep, again, we've been pretty darn lucky that way. But I guess there's not much point in my walking today. We'll go back to Mohawk, where I quit yesterday, after Christmas break; I was only going to do one more day, anyway. We may as well hit Phoenix today," Don said, nibbling a saltine and sipping his tea.

"That's good," I said, "because Andy and Danny are supposed to arrive at Gram's tonight too. But then, guess what?"

"I know what you're going to say," Don said, reading my thoughts. "It kind of goes against the grain, somehow—backtracking to California, but it's vacation and that will make it different, and right now I feel like I need it."

"It's just so soon," I said, "only two walking days out of that state, and back we go. If David and Andy and Danny weren't going to be there, too, I don't know if I could bring myself to do it. It makes me think you're walking a treadmill."

"Oh, I almost forgot to show you what I found yesterday," Don said, reaching into his jacket pocket and unfurling a small banner before my eyes. Neon-lime-green slashes across a neon-pink field read—"Glamis, Glamis!"

"Oh boy, Don, sure glad to have that."

"Thought you'd be—Merry Christmas."

Chapter 58

Into the Desert Night

What was Christmas? In large part, relatives, friends, good cheer, celebration; in small part, disappointment and too much to do in too short of time with too much ground to cover. But it seemed useless to fight the pace of Southern California while caught in the rushing stream of it, so none of us even tried. We went with the flow. To me, the best gift and the finest moments had to do with getting to be a family again for a while--Don, Andy, Danny, David, and I. We had adventures together and some separate adventures too, but unlike the journey, it was all over in the blink of an eye.

January 5, Don and I were again at my grandmother's place in Phoenix; our sons, Andy and Dan, were headed back to school; David had flown home from L.A. the day before. Suddenly the rush was all behind us. For a day's quiet interlude I visited with Gram alone while Don went about Phoenix on errands.

In certain respects, the indoor setting of Gram's home—the pictures, furniture, mementos, etc.—were so little changed from where I first came to know my dad's mom when I was a child in St. Louis, that at least for the moments I was with her now, I was transported to a place seemingly safeguarded from time and its confusing flow. These were moments unlike any others on the journey.

Gram and I talked of many things, of old days and new. But, for the first time ever, I was able to tell her about David, whom she had never met. When she did not press me for explanations about how it all came to be, but generously and graciously accepted me at my word that it was somehow meant to be, I felt a festering wound within me heal another stitch. At the same time, the journey itself took on fresh significance. I could not help but wonder for a moment if I hadn't come all that long, crazy, roundabout way simply to receive her blessing. I had felt something similar meeting with old friends on the journey, but with my grandmother the healing naturally went far deeper.

We did not get back to Mohawk from Phoenix the next day on schedule. We underestimated the time needed to reorganize Otto. Otto had not gone back to California but had waited at Gram's. We had accumulated quite a lot over Christmas and now had to take a moment to decide what to send home, what to keep.

And yes, there was an accumulated assortment of road finds: two new American flags on sticks, one colonial; an aluminum dog tag inscribed with the ace of clubs; an old Judy Garland tape labeled "Fly Me to the Moon"; a large patch of nylon screening (saved for future mosquito wars); a lengthy and sarcastic memo from the San Diego Naval Air Station titled "So You Want the Day Off"; a large and voluminous weather-beaten paperback—*The Complete Guide to California*; a brass trinket with two Canadian pennies counterbalancing a crux ansate; Don's swelling collection of cumbersome California buckeyes: a huge and heavy Coulter's pine cone with scales as fierce as any dragon's claws...not to mention various other, less-notable paraphernalia along with more tools—wrenches, screwdrivers, pliers! These road finds could be mailed to oblivion for all I cared, but since we boxed them up with more important things to be saved, I knew they would be saved, too—though I didn't yet know what for.

Of new items we wanted to make room for: more shoes for Don (the ones to walk him on home, I hoped); an extra down sleeping bag for me on loan from our friends in Mission Viejo; and a whistling teakettle with small portable stove. Don bought these last items in Phoenix after hearing tales of travelers stranded by weather and fate far from easy rescue, and also after hearing descriptions of long empty stretches still to come in West Texas.

Although Don was mainly thinking of me in Otto, at first I did not like the idea of taking on anything new to clutter up the space I had to live in. In some ways, even the tiniest road find could look like the straw that would break the camel's back. But, as usual, with a little clever rearranging and some cleaning out, we found safe and convenient spaces for the teakettle, stove, and accompanying fuel. I could not argue the stove's value as an emergency source of heat, nor the solace it would bring in hot cups of tea.

Late as Don's start was by the time we drove back to Mohawk, the Walker still managed to put in his thirty miles. It just meant he had to walk on into the desert night. I walked the last miles with him, the stars strung out above our heads like low garlands of leftover Christmas lights.

"Doesn't the desert smell good?" I said, feeling refreshed by the air, the night, and the walk—if not by the frequent trucks.

"I'm too tired to smell," Don reported back. "My feet hurt worse than ever. I weighed myself again at Gram's, and I've put on a good ten pounds over Christmas. It's going to take me a little while to get back in shape. Still, I'm glad to be walking. I'm worried about the route, though; it seems to be this interstate or nothing, unless we want to add on a ton of extra miles, many of them not heading east."

"No, thanks," I said. "By the way, I found out when I called home that David doesn't know where the camera is, either. You've no idea where it could be, Don?"

"Not really. Like I said already, the last time I remember seeing it was at Kevin and Heidi's on Christmas Eve."

"But then I'm pretty sure I had it with me at Barb and Jim's on New Year's—and even later, when David and I went hiking in the Anza-Borrego, though I know I didn't take any pictures. I'm beginning to think that maybe it got left in the rental car," I said, with a sinking heart. I knew that even if I didn't feel like using the camera much just yet, I would miss it soon enough; and it was going to be expensive and somewhat troublesome to replace.

"You never know, though, Fran," Don interjected cheerfully. "Maybe I'll find one."

"Oh right, Don," I laughed, "be sure to keep an eye out."

Part Seven

JANUARY

Arizona, New Mexico, Texas

Chapter 59

The Ones Who Have Heads

Don walked to Gila Bend amid bomb blasts. He was skirting the Luke Air Force Bombing and Gunnery Range. It didn't do much to calm his nerves about walking Interstate 8. Signs at the highway entrance ramps clearly reminded us both that pedestrians were prohibited. Still, even if it wasn't a pleasant route to be walking, it seemed safe enough: the road margins were more than ample and the flat terrain allowed Don a long view ahead and behind. Finally, though, late afternoon on our second day back, the Arizona State Patrol broke the suspense. Just before the Walker was about to catch up, I saw a state trooper zero in on him.

"What's the verdict?" I asked Don a short while later.

"I can't believe it, Fran! He said it would be okay! Real nice guy too—wanted my card to show his wife. Said he would spread the word."

And I guess the trooper did spread the word, because from then on, Don never got stopped again in Arizona; and we both got the friendliest flashing of headlights, honks, and waves whenever a state trooper passed.

The next day was not much quieter, until we began leaving the bombing and gunnery range behind. The following day, we traded Interstate 8 for Interstate 10 at Casa Grande. No other route seemed to be going our way, so neither of us complained. I wrote to David:

"I am having a hot cup of tea brewed on the new stove and it does taste mighty fine. The stove does not have to be on terribly long to boil the water, and then the hot tea kettle, which holds quite a bit, radiates a good deal of heat afterwards. Also, if I want, I can sponge off with the leftover warm water which is nice. Now I am wondering how I ever lived without this luxury.

"But I am beginning to miss the camera—most especially for the Saguaros. But also for the terrain. Though it's flat where Don's walking—flat as a table top—always somewhere in the distance are mountains or mesas or some unique feature of the earth thrusting above the horizon. But the flatness itself seems the perfect setting for the Saguaros. And if I do not have a camera, before Don walks out of them (people say there are none of these cactuses in New Mexico or Texas), I'll absolutely have to come back some day to photograph them.

"The Saguaros are riddled with personality and are sometimes almost comically contorted. When I'm driving along on one of my short hops, they even seem animated—as in a flip-book of cartoon drawings. But otherwise, when I get to staring at one, I cannot help thinking it's trying to communicate something with its single hieroglyphic gesture. And yet, if I turn my back on one of these headless giants, and then take a second look, it's almost as if it might have done something other than simply stand there while I was looking the other way. It's spooky.

"Don loves keeping company with them, and we both think there's something human about them. When we learned today that the Papago Indians have *always* thought so, describing them as 'that which is human and habitually stands on earth…' well, all I can say is—it's easy to believe, David. And the more limbs one of these cactus creatures has to gesture with, the older it is—even hundreds of years old, some of them! Who can believe they do not have something to say? Sometimes I think they're mocking *us*—the ones who have heads. But, as I mentioned earlier, it is the flat landscape that sets the Saguaros off against the desert sky so magnificently. It almost seems that any other background could only detract."

The more I saw of the desert, the more I liked it—but also the more I worried about it. After five days I wrote in my journal, "A good bit of the time we've been here—perhaps every single day to some extent—we have noticed varying thicknesses of dirty haze obscuring the horizon—and, of course, obscuring the near and far mountains standing so bold in the desert you think you could touch them, yet walking all day you never seem to come any closer?—well, it doesn't seem to hold true anymore, sad as it is to have to report such a thing."

I didn't much appreciate the litter I saw, either, nor at times the areas extensively farmed or ranched. It often struck me as completely bizarre to suddenly come upon some fenced-in acreage with hundreds of grazing sheep jammed into it, or some type of orchard. Whether they were or not, commercial interests looked far-fetched and out of place to me. On the other hand, an irrigation ditch here and there did nurture some wildlife that might not have been there otherwise. I found it oddly reassuring to watch a marsh hawk working these alleys of water—birds I had seen now and again the entire journey.

And when I discovered the Great Blue Heron himself stalking its prey in one of these desert ditches near Piedra, Arizona, our second day back on the walk—and Don had discovered it, too—well, I wasn't sure what was more amazing, the desert or the heron! *Why had we not left this remarkable bird behind by now?* I wondered. But the moment I became aware of it—whether by its graceful flight or silent presence— wherever we were, I felt as if some special blessing had been conferred on us—on our journey. If things weren't going well, or I was nervous about the unknown, or weary of certain repetitious trials—such a blessing seemed to bring down a wave of peace and confidence at once, out of nowhere. And because this great bird somehow always managed to take us by surprise, I never once took it for granted.

Near Picacho Peak, I began to seriously mourn the camera's absence, though I knew David was already working on replacing it. Here, I again saw the desert in its more pristine loveliness. I hiked and explored alone off the beaten track.

With the help of field guides, I was becoming familiar with desert plants and birds by name, yet there were moods and colors and effects impossible to name—perhaps impossible to photograph, though I surely would have tried. I wrote to David:

"Today I saw something I have never seen before. It may have been caused by the low angle of the sun at two in the afternoon, though the sun seemed high enough even so. Anyway, I saw the sunlight seem to fall—just as water might have (had there been any) over or through or across a craggy opening in some rock. And it fell straight and high and far, as if it had weight, and as surely as water would have—as beautifully too, but, of course—soundlessly. I could not take my eyes from this streaming light-fall for a long while. There were shadows to either side but not black shadows—dusky blue ones which seemed delicately sprayed as with a mist from the cascading light."

One evening near Red Rock, as we were deciding which patch of desert to camp in, we came across some falconers. We had first thought they must have pulled over to camp, too, but it wasn't long before I realized they were up to something else. I got out to investigate while Don was doctoring his tired and somewhat freshly blistered feet.

There were three of them—two young women and a young man, but they had four birds: two buteos (a red-tailed hawk and a Harris' hawk) and two falcons (a prairie falcon and a kestrel). I was only familiar with the red-tailed and the kestrel, which are common in the East. I listened to the falconers describe their hobby (or obsession as they referred to it) and admired at close range the birds they held. But tethered or not, it was rather terrifying to behold the larger hawks— all beak and talon and cold eye, ready to strike at anything if not fed. The falconers had brought their birds out this evening more for exercise than for training, though the woman who held the prairie falcon had brought a pigeon or two along in case she thought her hawk was up for a hunting session.

But I was most taken with the beauty of the kestrel, the smallest of these birds. Icarus, as he was called, was a blend of creamy whites, shady desert blues, and rust oranges with striking black accents. The smaller size, exquisite coloring, and overall downy look to this bird softened its fiercer aspects, making it more attractive to me, less intimidating to confront eye to eye. I stood a long while in the sharp cold gazing upon it, occasionally feeding it tidbits of raw beef heart before I turned away. The bird might well have been feeding on my own heart at the same time, I was so smitten.

The Sonoran Desert was proving to be a rather comfortable and fascinating environment—camping places were easy to come by; the nights (already less long than they once were), though cold, were tolerable; while the days usually had enough sun in them not to worry. I didn't worry. I wasn't worried. Yet I might have guessed there would be things to worry me soon enough.

Chapter 60

Only Halfway Home?

"Geesh, Fran, don't you know how to drive Otto yet?" Don said with a combination of disgust and impatience early one morning.

"Don," I yelled angrily, "I'm just not fully awake yet. I don't know what's wrong. I can't seem to get him into reverse."

Otto made an ugly grinding noise at that—as if I had injured him internally.

"Maybe I'll just *hike* the extra miles back out to the highway. This is ridiculous."

"*You're* ridiculous," I fumed. "I'm doing the best I can, Don." I wanted to scream at him, but I knew he would be accusing me of screaming at him soon anyway.

"Fran, you just don't understand how to drive Otto! Here, let me show you. You're not moving the gears right."

Now I was literally screaming inside myself. The nerve, I thought, I mean, after two hundred or more days on the road—to accuse me of not understanding Otto—as if I didn't know how to drive? I wanted to hit Don, but I was so furious I couldn't do anything. I opened the door, jumped out, and slammed it. I felt like running off into the desert sunrise and exploding like one of the bombs we'd seen go off.

Don climbed into the driver's seat from the back of Otto. I knew something was wrong, but I knew we were in a bad spot to break down, and I truly hoped Don would have more success getting Otto into reverse than I did. He didn't.

"Well, I'm sorry, Fran—I guess it really isn't you," Don said sheepishly. "Here, get back in. I'll roll you backwards in neutral and then you can get him into first and drive out."

I did. And while Don hiked toward Tucson, the end point of that day, I spent time later at a payphone, calling garages to see if I could make an appointment for Otto to get checked the next day. I was glad Don wasn't around, because I stupidly forgot I couldn't get reverse and then proceeded to park where I would need to. I hated myself for this idiocy and cried. Thank goodness the place I'd parked was level enough so I could roll Otto myself. But then I suddenly had trouble getting him into first! I was so upset I couldn't tell if the problem was all Otto or all me—or some of each. My confidence was badly shaken. Maybe I really didn't know how to drive him.

When I couldn't get first gear again at lunch, Don and I both thought I should drive on ahead to Wagenhaus in Tucson, where I had made an appointment for Otto. Don could catch up later. We thought we could probably camp out in the parking lot at the garage and be first in line in the morning.

By the time I got to Tucson, I was praying to be able to make all of the traffic lights. I made a lot of them. When I didn't, I had to start Otto up from third gear. It was the only gear I could still get! Thus crippled, we finally arrived. I figured the whole transmission was going. I figured we might have to trade Otto in for another vehicle or fork out money we could ill afford. But I figured all wrong.

By some good luck the place was still open and not busy when I arrived. Up Otto went immediately onto the lift, and a crew of mechanics looked him over. Aha! All he really needed was a new shift-coupler, a relatively inexpensive part that was easy enough to replace. The manager proceeded to go fetch the part himself at another garage, a few minutes' drive away. In an hour—before Don could even catch up, Otto was virtually better than ever. The mechanic had done some other helpful things for him, too. But reverse, which had always been a tricky gear to get, was now a cinch.

Don arrived in time to hear the mechanic discuss the problem and say the shift-coupler had probably been "letting go" for a long time.

Don celebrated our good luck by getting his head shaved the next morning. He had been threatening to do this for some time, but it wasn't until he took off his hat and the glare just about blinded me that I believed he really had. Over the next weeks I think he might have secretly wished for his hair to be back on his head, or for a comfortable fur rug in its place.

Something unexpected was happening. Without climbing any detectable hills whatsoever, we were nevertheless climbing in elevation. The tabletop must have been tilted. In the desert in California we had gotten down to sea level. At Tucson we were already back up to two-thousand feet. The next night at Vail we were above three-thousand. By Benson it was three-thousand five-hundred. We were, I learned somewhat belatedly, gradually leaving the Saguaros and the Sonoran Desert behind and getting into the Chihuahuan Desert, whose average elevation was more like five-thousand feet. The Chihuahuan was not going to be so cozy; it boasted a colder, harsher, less predictable climate. Reading about it in my field guides, I knew suddenly and certainly that winter was finally going to be overtaking us.

Don and I were discussing this turn of events at a truck stop outside Benson, Arizona, over tamales and tacos, when an old filling and a good portion of one of my lower molars fell out.

"Agh!" I groaned.

"Don't worry, don't panic," Don reassured, "we'll get through this desert okay, too."

"Agh—mmmmph—groan," I grimaced, with tears in my eyes, trying to examine the pieces that had fallen out.

"Fran, what's the matter with you—calm down—what? Are you going to be sick or something?"

But it felt as if the whole nerve of my tooth had suddenly been laid bare. It throbbed unmercifully. And by the looks of the very small town we were in, I did not have much hope of finding a dentist, or a good one, at any rate. In addition, I had that irrational and irreconcilable fear of dentists that some people have. I figured I would be laid up for days; that I would have to have a tedious root canal; or that what was left of my poor tooth was unsalvageable; that the time, expense, and trouble of getting it all taken care of would jeopardize The Walk. But though I had a long, restless, painful night of it, I learned in the morning that I had again figured it all wrong.

Don set out on foot the next day on his regular schedule, leaving me in the hands of Doctor Preston. This man not only rebuilt and refilled my tooth (which looked as if it *might* need a root canal, which I didn't have time for—but I can say now, years later, whatever he did—did save my tooth) and fixed me up for about the same cost as Otto—well within our budget—but he gave me a couple of entertaining hours at the same time. He knew the local Arizona history well and described it colorfully, with little-known anecdotes and tales of the old Butterfield Stage, Geronimo, Cochise, the U.S. Calvary, and exactly where in the area certain memorable events occurred. I felt, reclining there with my eyes closed, and with the kindly voice of this talented and imaginative man in my ears, as if I had gone to the movies instead of the dentist. I think if I had died the following week and had anything valuable to will to someone, I would have willed it all to him. His warmth and expertise made up for the bitter frost that night, and the night after, and the night after...

But one morning when Don was ready to leave, I felt it was too cold to get up. I decided to wait until the sun was a little higher. Maybe it would melt the frost. Meanwhile, I would try to write a letter while still bundled in the two sleeping bags where I was relatively warm. We were now above four-thousand feet—about the same elevation Julian had been where it had snowed so heavily; though now, of course, we were far from any moderating influence of the sea. Don took off. We agreed to meet at the first restaurant nearest to the exit to Willcox, which was the next town. But if I felt some of the chill lessen as the sun rose, I felt another chill descend later when Otto wouldn't start.

He turned over okay once, but then—nothing. I did all I could think of to do—read his troubleshooting manual, which was no help; looked at the engine, said incantations over it; rocked and pushed Otto back and forth (don't ask me why—I mean, maybe he wasn't awake); and every few minutes tried to start him again. Nothing.

Okay, I'll hike to that house I saw not too horribly far away, off that little side road, and ask to use their phone—but no, when I got within range of this shack and the gate at the end of its long drive—a sign quickly turned me back—"Beware of Dogs." All I could think of were pit bulls—which were all over the news just then for taking a child's life.

No, I'll go out to the highway ramp and hitch for some help, or maybe get a ride to someone's house to use the phone. But though dozens of cars had stopped from time to time at many different places in the country to ask me if I was having car trouble and needed any help—now, when I needed it, when I wore a face of desperation—people would slow, take a good look, and then pretend somehow they hadn't seen me and speed on.

I hiked back to Otto with a heavy heart, knowing Don was now hours ahead. Maybe I would just have to follow in his footsteps on the interstate. But then I tried one more time, and, as if Otto had only been fooling with me all along—he suddenly started! I wondered, but I didn't question. I drove on.

Now, if there weren't three exits to Willcox (instead of one), and I hadn't found a half-dozen restaurants to search at each one, and I hadn't had to put another hundred miles on Otto circling fruitlessly, or I had only guessed right as to where Don had decided to walk— maybe I would have been in a better mood when I finally found him.

"Any more days like some of the ones we've had this week," I said after describing the morning's rounds, "and I'm going to join up with the next band of coyotes I hear rabble-rousing under the bright desert moon."

"Well anyway, Fran, tomorrow's a new state—and, as of yesterday, we're past the five-thousand-mile mark. That's halfway home, for sure, now."

I know Don meant to be cheering, but somehow, with most of the Chihuahuan Dessert and a state like Texas still to cross, not to mention all the others—well, it just didn't sound all that good to me. If I thought back to the beginning of the journey and all that had transpired since, it felt as if I was looking back centuries in time—or across a couple of world wars. And it's *only* halfway home? "I don't know, Don," I sighed. "It's still a big country."

Chapter 61

Catching the Cross-Bearers

Before we left the subtropical Sonoran Desert completely behind, I felt it had begun to teach me a few things. One afternoon I wrote: "The ocotillo plant, which blooms whenever conditions are ripe and not only in spring—is blooming now in many places because of the recent rains. Its bright flowers wave like small crimson streamers, or licking tongues of flame, from the top of its tall crooked stems. It is a good idea, I think, to put forth a few blooms like the ocotillo whenever the time is ripe.

"But how like a sea this place is—that is, the underwater world of a sea freshly drained! The flat sandy bottom I walk upon is, at times, wind-rippled much like the coastal waters, in which I have waded on this journey, have been wave-rippled. All the plants about me are strangely sea-like. The ocotillo itself, though stiff to the touch, seems flexible to the eye and appears to sway its many arms about at the whim of invisible currents like some gigantic underwater anemone. The various cholla cactuses are like varieties of coral. Spiky yuccas and agaves cling to the gravelly sand like great spiny sea urchins. The yellow palo verde and the Mormon tea are like graceful sea fans, and the ever present creosote bush at a distance, a cross between a sea fan and a mounded coral. Here and there I bend to study a colorful annual, like the orange globe mallow, or stoop to pick up some bizarre or oddly colored rock—just as I might bend to plant or place the same when decorating an aquarium to make it more like the sea. And then, when I discover shells strewn about my feet? Well, I begin to realize the analogy is not in my head only."

This desert had begun to teach the Walker something, too. At lunch one day when I was raving about its beauty, Don interrupted me.

"But there's one thing, Fran, some of these prickly cactuses—well, they're not exactly harmless. I was just standing back there, doing some business with nature, you know, and I swear—one of them attacked me! I deliberately did *not* brush up against it or anything. Still, a clump of this cactus with spiny little daggers on it suddenly grabbed onto my shirt. I'm not kidding!" Don complained, showing me the rips in his T-shirt where he had beaten the segment of cactus off with a stick.

"Must be what they call the 'jumping cholla', Don. You're lucky you didn't get one of its barbed spines in your flesh. I've read they're as bad as porcupine quills to try to get out."

The Chihuahuan Desert also had a certain sense of the underwater world about it, but Don and I both noticed it did not support as wide a variety of plant life as the Sonoran. Even so, I found it a fascinating environment, and I felt oddly at home in it from the first. It might have been the great, wide-open spaces that had gotten into me from our traverse of the plains, or it might have been something else again. Yet why should it seem at all homelike? In terms of the surroundings, in terms of flora and fauna, it was perhaps the environment least like home of any we would cross—with one stunning exception.

When I looked up at night in the desert, the winter stars sent me suddenly spinning home like a good dream. Not that it's quite the same—the desert night sky and a wintry clear night at home. The first is broader than it is deep; the second, deeper than it is broad. But I know the winter stars—many by name, and in the long, cold night—especially in the Chihuahuan Desert, the stars flared forth like flaming watch fires in a way that summer nights, or any mild night, will never know—and in a way I was familiar with.

It was so easy to orient myself at night in the desert that, more often than I ever had previously, I could understand for a while where I was. We had two brilliant planets in the evening to set us right— Jupiter on high, Venus rising in the west. But we had in the desert, too, because of the low horizon, the sun and moon rising and setting with so little to obscure or obstruct at times that the close and constant company of these sky wanderers was befriending.

When the elements—that is, all the vagaries of winter weather—turned against us, a break of clear calm, whether by night or day, renewed hope for us both that the worst could not endure. And because of the lowness of the eastern horizon, which was quite unlike home, I found hope where I could never have looked for it there. I saw the earliest seasonal rising ever of what I call the spring star—Arcturus. Promise of an early spring, which is what I thought it heralded, would help us both to keep from losing heart.

There was, however, one disorienting effect of our steady progress heading east, exactly opposite to what we noticed heading west during the summer. Though the days were supposedly lengthening now that we were past the winter solstice, as we tended east in the time zone, we gradually lost daylight at the evening end. Once, early in Arizona, the sun was setting as late as 5:45; further into New Mexico, it set closer to 5:30; and further on, it set even earlier—until, that is, we crossed into the next time zone. This odd and contrary effect was a confuser, a subtle damper on hopes that otherwise might range too high.

The cold itself was a not-so-subtle damper. As tame as Arizona and the Sonoran Desert were in mid-January, New Mexico and the Chihuahuan Desert were fierce. We learned first hand the climatic difference between the low desert and the high. Strong winds, clouds of blowing dust (if not an actual dust storm), and bitter nighttime temperatures laced with snow and ice ushered us across the border into New Mexico. Our first dot on the map was Steins, a ghost town. Our second dot was Road Forks, not really a town but a kind of way station specifically founded for truckers in the 1930s by a man named John R. Graham. It boasted a truckers hall of fame, among other things.

We camped that night outside Road Forks. And we had a brief supper there in the restaurant so choking with cigarette smoke, I could smell the stuff in my sweatshirt (which I slept in for warmth) all night long. I realized that night how critical our timing had been when things were going wrong. I was filled with fresh gratitude that Otto had managed to break down in Tucson rather than Steins; and that I had had to have dental work done in Benson rather than Road Forks.

When we heard the truckers complaining nonchalantly over breakfast the next morning that worse storms and a worse cold would yet descend, and when a brief appearance of the sun managed to melt the glazing of ice on Otto, I went scouting ahead for shelter. That night's cold outside Road Forks had forced Don to use the space blanket (which we had along for emergencies), and because of the condensation of moisture from his warm body, his sleeping bag was now wet.

We had two simple hopes contradicting all the evidence: that the bad weather might blow over quickly, and that it might be a fluke never to be repeated. With this in mind, Don decided to quit early after doing twenty miles in five hours. This brought him in the early afternoon of January 17 to Lordsburg, New Mexico, where I had found inexpensive lodging. Besides the cold penetrating the Walker's resolve, a television in the motel room was a further temptation. The Super Bowl was but a couple of weeks away and Don decided he wanted to see at least a few of the playoffs.

With some sun providing a little solar heat, I could sometimes manage to keep warm in Otto even when the outside temperatures were rather low. But without the sun it was impossible, and under storm-threatening skies, there was no sun. Any warmth from either stove or teakettle dissipated far too quickly to counteract the cold.

Between visits out to the road to check on the Walker that morning, I squeezed in a warm mass at St. Joseph's Church in Lordsburg—a service beautifully sung partly in Spanish, partly in English. At another time, I scouted out our lodging for the night and walked about the town, which I found to be in large part a truckers haven like Road Forks. I was surprised at how little besides the lengthy string of cheap motels there was. Nevertheless, over the next few weeks, we would often find ourselves wishing for a place with even a tenth of what Lordsburg had.

In the late afternoon, having little interest in watching football, and with my road duties completed for the day, I decided to take up the priest on his invitation to the public to come to the parish hall to hear some convicts from the prison in Roswell, New Mexico, speak about their lives. It was mainly for the benefit of the Lordsburg youth about to be confirmed in the church, and when I arrived that's mainly who was there—with standing room only.

I didn't know what to expect. I was somehow surprised by it all. The prisoners were not from New Mexico but many other parts of the U.S. They were not of any one ethnic group nor race nor economic background. The crimes committed, which were at times briefly alluded to or described, ranged from the violent to the nonviolent, from murder to embezzlement. The convicts were as young as twenty and as old as sixty. I think six had a chance to speak—none in a manner that suggested they had done this very often before. They took turns, talked informally off the tops of their heads, and were simply cut off by one of the persons in charge when a certain amount of time had elapsed. Except for the big-time embezzler, once a straight-A student on scholarship at an ivy league school, all the crimes were complicated by involvement with drugs and alcohol. Yet the prisoners were there because they had one thing in common, and I thought the first man to speak put it best.

This man began almost angrily, in somewhat broken English, seemingly frustrated both by the language and by what he wanted so badly to convey. Because of this, he was more eloquent than he could know. He said in effect, that he did not understand God's love at all; that its power was too much for him, too much beyond him; that it was so big he was completely lost in it; that it baffled and confused him. He could not comprehend, he said, how God's love could include someone like him, after all he had done; and when he himself could hardly do more than hate himself for who and what he was. He then proceeded to illustrate these words with descriptions of his life—what he had destroyed, what he had lost, and finally, what he had found. From the blackest abyss he had been rescued by the merest thread of a tattered and unraveled faith.

I could not help being deeply moved by this man's story. He told how he had tried to end his life at one point, driven by despair and self-loathing, by stabbing himself with a screwdriver. To me, it did not seem less than a miracle that this man—as well as the others—had been healed after all each had been through. But their remorse, their sense of responsibility for what they'd done, their resolve to make amends in some fashion—in these, I recognized something of myself. I felt as if I had at last caught up with the cross-bearers, and I could see, even without words, what we had in common.

Chapter 62

A Barren and Comfortless Condition

After seven full months and 5,115 miles walking, Don crossed the Continental Divide, heading east. He had last crossed it at Marias Pass, heading into the Montana Rockies. It was going on our fourth day in New Mexico. We had yet to descend significantly in elevation. We had yet to wake up to weather that didn't contain ice or snow. Indeed, by now we had all been snowed upon—the Walker, the Driver, and Otto. But Don had not been snowed upon (technically speaking) while he put in miles on The Walk. I had not yet won the bet, but I was not much interested in winning it, either. In the vicinity of the Continental Divide, Don slogged on through a bitter sleet.

January 18, I wrote in my journal: "It has been cold! Still too cold to continue as before. After I left Don on the road this morning, I had to drive ahead a long way to Deming, find another motel, try to make headway on the newsletter, and go back and forth checking on Don. So much snow on the ground this morning I could not get on the roads safely in Otto, at least not for a long while. Don will not get his thirty miles in again because of his late start. He hates this.

"Deming is the first real town in New Mexico we've come to that is more than a strip of motels, though it is that too. It claims to be the home of 'pure water and fast ducks' or is it 'pure ducks and fast water'?

"It's hard—these motels—but the cold has been frighteningly cold, and we don't have much choice. And the rhythm of the journey is changed, and I don't know—it's hard. I guess, I like to feel I have found a way to survive by at least having a certain routine. It's dumb of me. The road is always changing, and thus the requirements of the road. I ought to let go of any pretense of being in control and simply try to accept being a vagabond at the mercy of fate."

January 19: "The weather did not break as expected. The tail of a much bigger storm is what this part of New Mexico has been whipped by these few days—and just to the north it is, of course, much worse. Don hitched a ride out to his starting place today, since we thought the road in the early morning too icy and treacherous for Otto. Tomorrow we are hoping to get back to our regular routine.

"I will feel so thankful at the return of warmer weather. Don too. It's bleak driving back and forth with no heat in Otto to meet up with Don. It freezes me thoroughly before I am done. Otto's little comfort to the walker on his breaks either. It helps to know there is a warm room waiting in Deming, but after a while we won't be able to use Deming as a base. I noticed that in Vermont, oddly enough, it was warmer yesterday than where we are. Winter is everywhere!"

January 20: "Another cold night. We're still at the same motel in Deming. I am still ferrying Otto back and forth to Don. The cold is not supposed to go away as soon as we hoped. It's worse today than yesterday. The melt water in the cooler has frozen solid."

January 21: "The sun is shining today in Deming. We are giving up this motel room finally. I've been hanging around here so long the Deming Headlight (local paper) finally got wind of the Walker and is going to interview him on the road. But, I should, thanks to solar possibilities, be able to stay warm in Otto today, even though the temperature is not supposed to rise much. It's been going down to zero at night—and not very far north of here below zero. Also, more talk of another storm system coming through. And now, trouble starting Otto again this morning. A mechanic says he thinks it's a sticking choke. Frankly, I think it's less complicated than that. Otto obviously *hates* the cold. He probably would have come into the motel room to get warm if he could. In his own inimitable way, Otto is reminding us that he was promised a winter-free year when he blithely romped out of Vermont one bright warm day late last spring. Was it only last spring? And speaking of spring—Don and I saw a flock of robins on a frosty lawn in Deming today looking a little lost.

"But hurrah! The new camera arrived in this week's mail drop, and that's cheering. But what about the camera batteries in the cold? The manual says something about protecting the camera body from the low temperatures. In Otto? Oh, dear, it's always something."

Thoreau, not known for being a great traveler, said somewhere in one of his journals, "The traveler's is but a barren and comfortless condition." He said also, "Only that traveling is good which reveals to me the value of home and enables me to enjoy it better." And further, "We only need travel enough to give our intellects an airing." I ran across these quotes in one of my notebooks, and when I tried them out on Don just west of Las Cruces, New Mexico, he answered enigmatically.

"How far is New York?"

He then proceeded to whip out a huge, three-foot-long, black and lurid-green, like-new, rubber snake—tongue intact.

"I'm not riding with that thing, Don. Otto's allergic to snakes— dead, alive, or pretend. Throw it back, please. What next?"

"I'll show you," Don said after he flung the snake back out into the cold with a flourish. And he dangled a ten-dollar-bill before my face.

"That's a little more like it," I said. "You've been picking up so much Mexican money lately, I've been wondering whether to start a separate count of it. Hmmm. That makes twenty-four dollars and two cents (not including the Oregon fifty)."

"Well, I guess Thoreau's right," Don said, taking off his shoes and checking for blisters. "It has been pretty barren and comfortless at times. I think of home too, Fran—and there's no doubt about it, my intellect's been aired. Still, it's the cold that gets to me the worst. It wears me down.

"We may get a change in elevation by the time I make El Paso, I don't know," he added. "After Las Cruces tomorrow we'll be heading south for a good bit. Maybe that will help it warm up. I'll be walking a parallel route to Interstate 10 along the Rio Grande, which should be an improvement—fewer trucks. Things will get better."

But things did not exactly get better—they changed. The cold held. Yet, for a while anyway, we thought we were getting hardened to it, so that it lost some of its sting. We were at least able to camp again, because the storms abated. Just before we entered El Paso, Texas, I wrote to David:

"The snow is *off* the mountains. A very good sign, I should think. We have to get through El Paso today; we more or less skirted Las Cruces. I hope I don't lose Don—that's always the challenge of a city. There is nothing green around here. The mountains without the snow are brown and barren. They dominate the landscape and surely give these southwestern towns their identity. Over Las Cruces loomed the beautifully jagged and rugged Organ Mountains. Over El Paso, the San Andres, among others.

"I did not see much in nature yesterday and because of the dogs and unfamiliar territory, I did not walk much. Farms usurp the wild—and though trees do not appear to be a natural feature of the land, there are endless pecan orchards (all leafless this time of year) watered by the Rio Grande. This river is about as low as it can get and still be called a river. Evidence of other crops too—cotton, which sometimes litters the roadside, looking like dirty snow—and dried red chilies, looking like dented and discarded Christmas ornaments. But the wintry-ness of the land combined with natural dryness scrapes the vistas bare.

"I am happier camping in Otto despite the cold than stuck in the grim setting of a concrete block motel despite having both heat and hot showers. I wish I spoke Spanish. It's hard sometimes to tell if people are friendly or not. Otto gets some peculiar looks. Is it his license? Two hours in one spot isn't long enough to find out what people think. Lots of iron bars over windows and doors of even shack-like houses—lots of fences and hedges too in this area. Every shanty seems to have a nasty pack of dogs in attendance. I don't know, David, we're heading south again, and I can feel the thread go slack between us as we do. Yet if it would only mean some warmer weather, I guess, I'd feel better about it."

But on the other side of El Paso, two days later, I wrote to David: "Otto's odometer and speedometer began working again about noon. I guess, they just froze. I felt heaps better when they started working somewhere in Montana. The cold is taking its toll on each of us. I could not start Otto again this morning, and with Don yelling at me that I don't know how to start a car right, and me yelling at him that I'm ready to join up with the coyotes—and then me giving up a couple of wild, fruitless screams of frustration to the desert solitude— and all this *before* we found out Otto's odometer and speedometer weren't working???? Well, the rest of the day I think we were both spent—witless, tired, only able to keep on going by the sheer force of inertia. We're both worried about Otto slowly succumbing to the cold—so that finally we'll arrive in Middlebury—*us* carrying *him*—or maybe not arrive at all. And now we have been harassed by the Border Patrol besides, which doesn't help one's nerves. They've searched Otto more than once—maybe they don't believe Don's story—some people don't, you know.

"But we are back into the high, cold, Chihuahuan Desert, and have left the commercial farms and Rio Grande behind. We are still above 4,000 feet. I prefer the desert. I feel safer here. And, just by accident, at the day's end point—which is nowhere in particular not even a dot on the map (so don't bother to look for it)—I came upon a no-name, nondescript, highway cafe. It's nothing much—food's very poor fare, but it means we can sit up a little later before turning in—and it means I can write to you for a while in the warm—and it also means a breakfast in the warm. So things are looking up in spite of all. And yes (three cheers), we're well into the lone star state—and yes (three more cheers), we are heading east again! Reel me on in."

Chapter 63

The Unquiet Grave

Texas: we had heard much about this state ahead of time. Indeed, as much as we had heard the coast of Oregon praised before we ever got there, we heard the lands of West Texas maligned. "It's a bear," a man and his wife from Houston told Don at one point when they stopped to see what the Walker was up to in New Mexico. "We hate it—there's nothing there. You'll hate it." They shook their heads with pity at the whole idea of crossing it on foot. And they weren't the only ones, but most of the other people speaking ill of this part of Texas weren't Texans.

This worried us a little, but not much. Texas was in our way and we were going to be crossing it. I really could not imagine that there wouldn't be *something* to see, and I felt that it was the hurry to get somewhere—to get from here to there *as quickly as possible*—that blurred the lands into the dull and featureless. For many people, speed is the antidote for dullness, which, in the long run, might make things even more dull. Still, I wasn't going to make up my mind ahead of time.

Yet so far, the first four days or so in Texas, I was intrigued. Some of the birds I had gotten to know in the Sonoran Desert were still with us—huge cactus wrens, which now and again would inspect Otto's roof load of cargo, commenting loudly as they did; the black-throated desert sparrow with its high, sweet voice; the gilded flickers; not to mention wintering flocks mixed with sparrows, finches, juncos, buntings, and larks. We saw stranger birds, too—at small oases and along the Rio Grande—a black, silky, fly-catching, cardinal-shaped bird called a phainopepla; a pretty, red and gray pyrrhuloxia, which is a closer cousin to the cardinal; the brilliant vermillion fly catcher; and the rare, rosy-throated becard.

I also continued to spot wintering western meadowlarks, about which I wrote: "The daily sight of a meadowlark, or a mere snippet of its song, is better than a daily dose of vitamins, I do believe, as far as ensuring my physical health. It does something to lift my spirits I can't explain."

But the two birds I wrote home about were none of the above, and I was in Texas when I got to know both quite well. January 24, I wrote in my journal: "I am within three yards of a burrowing owl. I discovered this bird while looking for a place to park Otto in the sun. It's reading thirty degrees on the thermometer in Otto, my feet are frozen, my pen is sluggish; but I have such a prime view of this little, long-legged, sandy-colored, diurnal owl that I have not moved Otto to take warmer advantage of the sun. Now there are two! Their eyes are bright, the color of butter, and menacing. They are giving Otto dirty looks—as if they can make Otto go away by staring him down. They carry themselves like pompous little judges. Now one's giving up and going back into the burrow. I can't believe it—I mean, I am actually watching an owl crawl into a hole in the ground!"

The other bird was less reclusive and often even impressed the Walker, who was far less of a bird watcher than I.

"Fran, I saw another roadrunner—this one with a huge lizard or snake hanging out of its beak," Don called with some excitement as he approached Otto for lunch east of Sierra Blanca. "Right back there a ways, and it went along that pile of rocks with its catch. If you hurry, you might still be able to see it there."

"That's okay, Don—I've discovered something else about them— something I just confirmed this morning, though I dare say it doesn't say much for my recorder playing. I was working on that Appalachian folk tune, you know, the one called 'The Unquiet Grave' that has a certain mournful cooing quality to it? Well, I hadn't been long at it when I heard some rustling in a clump of bushes behind Otto. When

I stopped playing and peeked out, I finally saw a roadrunner emerge. It hopped up onto a snaggy piece of wood and looked this way and that. I put the recorder to my lips and began playing again. And it seemed to get all flustered, raised its crest, and really acted as if it was being called. No kidding, Don, don't laugh—this is like the third time it's happened! This morning I was just confirming it. And aren't they pretty even, up close, when you see that green-black iridescent shine on their tail feathers?"

"Not to the lizards," Don said, untying his shoes. "How far is New York?"

Chapter 64

The Peace of the Road

It would have been considerably shorter crossing Texas sticking to Interstate 10; except for the trucks, it wasn't a bad road. But at Van Horn, we decided to take two-lane Route 90, which headed south as it tended east. We thought we might get lucky and escape the next onslaught of cold.

Meanwhile, just before Van Horn on January 26, Don walked into the Central Time Zone. Suddenly, we gained an hour on the evening end. And even if it meant losing some daylight in the morning, we had the day lengthened where we could use it the most. Better still, though Otto's clock showed two hours' difference from home time (having stayed on Eastern Daylight Savings), in reality our time was only *one* hour different from home. In terms of making phone calls and tuning in to home in other ways, this was encouraging. Every such milestone was a significant leap forward now, going far to compensate for hardships and the long, long miles. When the weather moderated unexpectedly as well, we could look about and take renewed joy in all we saw.

The Chihuahuan Desert terrain continued to fascinate. We had been following a route designated the Texas Mountain Trail, and so far there were mountains always about, if not always close at hand—some making up small ranges, some standing alone—none alike, none without some beguiling feature. The vegetation was largely creosote bush; tarbush; occasional yuccas and chollas; a huge, Texas tumbleweed; a low-growing, rosy-skinned prickly pear; little clumpy annuals; and dried blonde bunches of grass—but with the long light in it all at day's end, the place fairly glowed. And in the early light of a crimson desert dawn, the lands might as well have been blooming with roses.

Perhaps because we were half expecting a general dullness to descend at any moment, we were delighted with all we saw. The desert held our attention, its face etched with living details never once monotonous or quite predictable, even when we felt we were getting to know it well. And where I did look out upon a certain uniformity in the landscape, I did not wish it away.

I wrote in my journal: "I really do love it here. Somehow, even an endless vista of creosote brush appeals to me. It does not bore me at all, but rather I feel embraced by it and even befriended. I like the wide open spaces. I like to see a wild expanse. I like the big sky around and about—and Texas does have a big sky. It is as Emerson wrote: 'In every landscape the point of astonishment is the meeting of the sky and the earth…' How good it is somehow to see these two touch!"

As for the way we had chosen, I wrote to David: "Route 90 so far seems almost too good to be true. For one thing it is much less traveled. Well, *that* even is an understatement. I mean, you can count the number of trucks that pass in a twenty-four hour period on one hand! The quiet is intoxicating. I can *hear* the desert now, and it is something to listen to. This desert quiet is not empty but full somehow—Don notices it too. And today, for the first time in ever so long, there was no sharp edge to the air.

"But we are still high—just now perhaps 4500 feet and surrounded by all that is ruggedly picturesque. The shape and contour of the horizon—different on every hand. None of the mountains, I am happy to report, have snow on them. The other side of Van Horn, we passed some hillish mesas with soaptree yuccas growing along the crest. Don commented later how they looked like Indians in formal headdress silhouetted against the sky. And so they did. The mountains closed in on us in places there too, and we climbed to nearly 5,000 feet from 4,300 or so. Somehow, it was all very dramatic—the closing in, the rise, the opening out again—as if the land is more alive than we know, more capable of response.

"Well, I don't think, David, I am being too clear—but it is somehow what I am feeling. There is great movement in what I see, a varied rearranging of effects—and even at our slow pace, I feel it speed us on our way toward home."

This part of Texas with its clean lines also struck us as blessedly clean of litter. It was a relief to the eye not to have human trash fraying the edges of nature, as if the road had made its necessary cut through the countryside taking as much care as possible. Don had a lot of room on the road, considering the nonexistent traffic, and yet he was sometimes not on the road at all. Railroad tracks closely paralleled Route 90 at times, and paralleling these was often a dirt track in the desert that was easier on the Walker's feet than the pavement or the gravelly road margin.

Trains did not seem quite as frequent here as they had been on the Plains. Indeed, they were so frequent on the Plains that Don and I both felt we knew the friendly engineers who waved and smiled when they passed. In the desert quiet, we could hear the trains coming a long way off, and because of the flatter surfaces between the mountains, we could see them laid out at great distances, too—mere toys, or ornaments, like boxcar beads on a pull-toy string.

Abandoned homesteads were not an unusual sight on the Great Plains. Here in the desert it was more common to come upon whole towns left behind. Between Van Horn and a town called Marfa, a stretch of seventy-three miles, the map showed two dots: Lobo and Valentine. At the former we came upon a hodgepodge of boarded-up ruins—brick, wood, and adobe with a large, hand-painted, hastily done sign: "This was Lobo."

Valentine still existed, but there was plenty of evidence it, too, was vulnerable and had seen better days. There was a tiny grocery-general store still open, a post office, and even a school; yet in material terms there were no clearly recognizable signs of prosperity. But the couple who ran the general store was friendly, and the woman at the post office offered to hold some of my mail a few more days, until Monday, when the special Valentine postmark for February could be used.

I used to wonder, when I was younger, and before I had ever lived in a rural setting myself, what people did when they didn't have the trappings of a city all about them for entertainment. I never wondered that now, because I had long since learned how much of life is not concerned with entertainment—that is, the problems of living, such as raising a family, or being a part of one, getting an education and one's livelihood, keeping a roof over one's head, and, yes, chasing a few rainbows. These concerns happen anywhere and everywhere and take up the bulk of one's hours. One might have to go further afield for one thing or another in the great wide open; one might have to do without a few things from time to time; but the good thing is that the good things in life are not necessarily more scarce here than elsewhere—perhaps even the contrary is likely.

Much of city life is a mirage—a glitter of things to do and to have that seem to be closer at hand than they really are. More things *seem* possible in the city, yet I am not at all sure more things *are* possible. Except because people often prefer to be distracted at all costs from having to confront life in its simpler, more universal terms, a busy, hustling city is often the chosen place to settle. It's a good place to hide—from many things—even from life. For the sake of something called "convenience," having countless things within easy reach, we sometimes box ourselves in to the point we cannot move to respond to anyone's need but our own, without falling over obstacles and practically killing ourselves.

I knew that as passers-through, Don and I could not in a true sense understand how vital was the life of a town or an area merely by the look of it. Impressions can be wrong and yet, for all that, somehow worth recording.

"I can't believe it, Don," I complained over breakfast the morning of January 29, east of Valentine. "I mean, you'd think we'd know better by now—camping right on top of the railroad tracks, for Pete's sake. That first train last night was the worst. I could hear it coming from so far off, and as it got louder and louder, well, I kept thinking it couldn't possibly come any closer, it was so loud. And then, when it kept on coming, I had to think it was somehow aiming exactly for Otto and was just going to wipe us out!"

"There were eight trains in the night—I counted them," Don said matter-of-factly, putting away the cereal.

"Well, that's eight too many, if you ask me. Even if otherwise I love the train and its sounds. I just don't like camping on top of them—or them on top of us."

"I'm not arguing with that, but I really don't see we had much choice last night. Pass me the map. I wonder if there's such a thing as a motel anywhere ahead. I was hoping maybe to take Sunday off and watch the Super Bowl.

"Hmmm. We'd be about to Alpine, which is in fairly big print and in red. That's hopeful."

"Uh huh," I agreed, looking over Don's shoulder. "But look down here a ways—any chance of a little side trip to Big Bend National Park? It's not too much further out of our way than the Badlands were, really. I mean, the Super Bowl isn't on all day, is it? Or, what if we quit a bit early the day before and drive down to camp there at night, and drive back to Alpine the next day for a motel?"

"I guess I could pick up my pace some," Don said, "long as I could be sure of a place to watch the game. But we'll have to see what we find in Alpine. By the way, I finally got around to reading that little booklet last night that that man gave you at that grocery store parking lot back in Tucson—you know, *Fly With the Snowbirds in Retirement,* all about life on the move, escaping winter in a big RV?"

"Kind of makes you think about the future, huh?" I said. "He was a nice man—his wife, too. Seems like Otto's license attracts other travelers in these parts more than anywhere—especially in grocery store parking lots. Former Vermonters, or people that know people back home, or maybe it's just an excuse to say hello."

"Seems like everybody we've met on *this* road is saying hello," Don said, preparing to start the day's walk. "Notice how everyone waves?"

"Yeah, I like that. Reminds me of North Dakota. People stop to ask if I need help more often, too. Guess everyone knows this is no place to break down. Yet for some reason, I don't feel so scared about that here. There's so much room to think, and it's so peaceful on this road."

"It sure helps to have some milder weather," Don said, smearing some sunscreen on and peering out the window at a flawless blue sky.

"Now, if I can stay off the pavement some more today, maybe I can save a little on my feet."

"Do they still hurt the same as ever the last five miles or so?" I asked, more or less knowing the answer.

"Pretty much. I just hope I'm not doing some sort of permanent damage to them. Though, if a doctor came along and said I was," Don paused, adjusting his hat and straightening out the bandanna attached to the back of it. "Well, I guess I'd still keep on—no matter what."

"Well, no matter what happens now, Don, you've walked darn far. It really doesn't even seem possible—even though I know you're not the first. It's amazing to see someone do it, that's all—no matter what!"

I watched the Walker take off and grow smaller in the distance. His walk had changed some, I suddenly noticed. He was coming closer to putting his heels down; the old bounce was rather diminished—and yet, it also was clear that the determination in each step was as strong as ever.

Chapter 65

Some People Would Not Take to It at All

Don made thirty miles and the town of Marfa—hardly pausing except to climb a fence at one point to get a better view of the old movie set of "Giant" which, though it was in a rather dilapidated state, somehow gave Don a sense of where he was.

Marfa was a surprise, a little town beautifully laid out with lovely churches, a substantial town hall, a bank, a library, some motels; and without any accompanying strip-development to detract. We were still well above four thousand feet in elevation. Marfa claimed to have the highest golf course in Texas, and it also claimed to be as Texas used to be—uncrowded, unpolluted, planted in the midst of territory where the deer and the antelope still play. It was also famous for having a weird phenomenon—"ghost lights."

"Don, look, I see some! They *are* weird. What could they be, I wonder?" I exclaimed late that night, camped on the far side of town. A brochure said that these predictably present, hovering, and sideways-moving lights were thought to be everything from UFOs to car lights on a distant section of highway. Don sided with the latter opinion.

"I'm sure they're just car lights," the Walker finally pronounced, after staring long at what I had been staring at. "But since the road has been straight as an arrow for miles, you just don't expect to look

340

back and see them like this. But look, remember how you descended those curves—coming down in elevation as you approached Marfa? That could explain it."

"Maybe," I said. "But I'll tell you, if we hadn't read about these things in a pamphlet, and if we were anywhere else on the road and not so close to such a cozy little town. I mean, if this were going on near Lobo—I think I would really be spooked."

The next day, Don set out in the dark before dawn, walking a brisk pace to make the twenty-seven miles to Alpine as early as he could, his heart set on a motel, a day off, and a big football game. He was in high spirits.

The Walker's spirits were boosted even higher while coming through Paisano Pass, when he met up with a lively and enthusiastic couple from Dallas (who had earlier stopped to talk with me, noticing Otto's license and exclaiming, "Ma'am, you're a mighty far piece from home!"). The Tuggles, Lila and Jim, were impressed with the Walker's efforts. Jim awarded Don a new hat and calendar with Jim's business logo on them, and Lila offered him a beer out of their cooler. Don turned down the beer, but enjoyed talking with Lila and Jim, and got a kick out of them wanting to film him heading back out on The Walk, rounding the next bend of the pass.

Alpine turned out to be all Don had hoped for, so he quickly arranged for a motel room with TV for the next day, and climbed into Otto a happy man. He grabbed a magazine, leaned back, and put his feet up, saying, "Drive on, Fran—I don't care where." I did. I thought I knew where I was headed.

But after a while on Route 118, aiming due south from Alpine, an eerie feeling began to rise up inside of me that I was driving to the end of something. Or even that I was being driven. Out there, somewhere ahead of us, was a limit of some sort. I could feel this as sure as I could feel the road humming beneath Otto's wheels. At first I told myself that maybe it was because there was a political boundary ahead, and yet at the same time, I knew that that wasn't it at all. No, out there was some sort of irresistible edge drawing us on, a brink, some terminal extremity—or something else I couldn't quite define, but the longer I drove, the stronger I could feel it.

I knew from looking at the map that there would be nothing, not even a crossroad, for eighty miles. I was familiar with this situation from Route 90, and yet somehow it felt as if we had turned aside from the last human habitation to go where no one had ever been. But sure there was a road. Someone had been there. Maybe it was just that *we* had never been there. And yet it was more than that, because the feeling continued to nag and grow that something was urging us forward, sucking us down—momentum somehow not our own. It wasn't as if Otto needed any gas, or a foot on the gas pedal, or someone to steer. We were on a track, and the track had been greased to roll us on in, or down, or out to that limit I could feel but not envision. The more it pulled, the more my heart raced to meet it.

I wondered if Don had looked up at all from his magazine. "Don," I called back, "do you see where we are?"

The land passing by was all surprise. A range of rocky peaks here, a softer mesa over there, a sudden jutting butte, a warped and barren declivity—all weirdly colored and arranged, drawn to a variety of scales, and put into unexpected relations to one another—and to us. I wondered if it wasn't purposely meant to confuse or even to mock? I got the sense that some primary earthly order was being toyed with, or thoughtlessly cast aside, or even violated with abandon. And though at times we did climb in elevation, the overwhelming sensation was nonetheless one of always and everywhere heading down and in— deeper and deeper in.

We never passed another vehicle. We were alone in this world.

"Don," I called again, "do you see where we are?" And I turned round to look for a moment. And when I did, I knew that he saw, but he just shook his head, not bothering to try to find words.

I was startled when I turned back a second later to see a sign seem to jump out in front of us saying simply, "No center line." *No center line*, I repeated to myself, puzzling it out. Why, of course; here only are extremes—no golden mean. And I let myself look closely enough to see that here the desert was wearing a harsher face than what I had seen before. And this was true without a burning heat or icy freeze descending, but instead with a shudder of both at once. Fire and ice. Dazed, I drove on.

Eventually another sign appeared warning, "Pavement ends." *Pavement ends*, I said to myself, this time astonished. And then I began anticipating what the *next* sign would say—"End of earth" or "Planet ends here." But when the pavement ended, I slowed and drove on, following the rugged track—now unsure of what was beneath us in spite of the rough ride.

For the first time, my heart began to draw back from what pulled us, though I did not think for a moment of actually turning around. And then it came to me—maybe there wouldn't be any *next* sign—no final warning, just a black and gaping abyss conveniently opening out for us to silently plunge down into.

Again and again the land took unexpected turns—now there would be sheer walls beside us, and then without apologies, falling off from this, a sudden open plain, tilting toward infinity. At last, to take the edge off my feelings, I pulled over.

"What are you doing, Fran?"

"I don't know, Don, I've got to get out." And then, to appear more sane I quickly added, "I want to take a picture."

And that helped. How easily the camera cuts away the true dimensions of a thing. I felt some satisfaction, knowing I was shrinking all I saw into a very small frame. Yet it was a false and momentary triumph, because the minute I was driving, I realized the place was taking hold of me again on the inside—expanding without regard to the limits of my poor heart or brain.

I stopped again.

"Now what, Fran?"

"Another picture—why don't you get into it, Don? Otherwise, maybe it will seem we weren't really here—wherever 'here' is."

And then, I can't even say why—maybe simply to defy the stony silence of the place, I suddenly shouted at the top of my lungs, "We are here!" And while I was raising the camera to my face and gesturing to Don where I wanted him to stand—the voices began to come back to us—surrounding us in what seemed a complete circle: "We are here, we are here, we are here, we…"

That was enough. No more stops. *Let's just get there*, Don and I wordlessly agreed. Wherever "there" was.

Looking back on it now—the eighty-mile drive to our campsite that night was exactly like falling—but falling, somehow, despite all the sense of foreboding—comfortably into place, like a cat onto its feet. And just as after a terrifying roller-coaster ride, one suddenly has the urge to do it all again, I can wish myself back there to those same earthly ends—about which the Chiso Apaches said, "When the Great Creator made the earth and had finished placing the stars in the sky, the birds in the air, and the fish in the sea, there was a large pile of unused stony material left over. Finished with His job, He threw this material into one heap and made the Big Bend Country."

I spent most of the Super Bowl ransacking my brain for some way to describe Big Bend to David. I wrote: "I may not get back to some places, but I think I shall have to get back to this one and bring you with me. It's a place that is somehow maybe a bizarre mix of the Badlands and Moses Coulee—or perhaps if you put Glacier Park somewhere down closer to the equator, drained it, and hacked indiscriminately at the peaks—you could come up with a place not unlike it. One thing for sure—you could easily get lost in it—lost, forgotten, baked, eaten by vultures—or Chihuahuan ravens. Some people would not take to it at all.

"I think the coyotes love it. They sang last night in another new way. Every time I hear them I try to describe how their song is different, if it is, as it was last night. We have heard them most consistently in the desert. And I wonder if it isn't the desert night that works on their souls—or is it just working on mine? But I suppose it is the different kinds or shapes of space that color their voices as they carry on. I don't know. Once, when I heard them a few days back, I swear, it was like they were whooping it up under water. And in Big Bend? Well, somehow their song equaled the place, that's all.

"What is it, David—why does anyone want to gaze upon the face of nature wild and untouched? Do we think it is Eden we're looking at—before Adam, that is? Someone said—I think it was John Burroughs—that 'we run to nature because we are afraid of man.' If that is true, well, I guess, it could explain a lot about myself.

I think Burroughs means too that we run to nature at times because we are afraid of ourselves. I don't know, I suppose I'm not making any sense. But I think it is a good thought—having a place to run to—and well, Big Bend is a place like that."

Part Eight

FEBRUARY

Texas, Louisiana

Chapter 66

Towns That Are Not Towns

The first day of February in Texas, in the eighty-four-mile stretch between Alpine and Sanderson, we came upon one town—Marathon. It was as tiny as any we'd seen and rather on the shabby side, with one handsome exception: a two-story brick building called The Gage Hotel.

It was fun to learn that the place had been built in 1928 by a Vermonter, Alfred S. Gage, who left the northeast to become a successful Texas rancher in the Trans-Pecos. He had it built to house himself when he was out surveying the far-flung reaches of his land. The structure had history enough to have fallen into disuse and later be restored as a hotel. I had tea there and admired the eclectic décor of Mexican, Indian, and cowboy artifacts of the region.

The fifty-four-mile stretch of road from Marathon to Sanderson, without a town to pass through, was wonderfully uneventful. I might have guessed it was a lull before a storm. The weather had warmed considerably, reaching ninety degrees. The milder air led us both to thinking maybe we had left winter behind. Groundhog Day had passed and I was ready to think about spring—even to begin anticipating it.

Something was helplessly stirring inside of me in Texas by this time, yet I wondered if I would even recognize a sign of spring in such a different habitat? West of Sanderson I saw a pair of kestrels mating, and realized then and there that the signs were too universal not to be recognized.

I wrote to David: "I am waiting with Venus for the moon to rise—a bit of a butte is in the way. The afterglow of the sunset is clear and delicate. The sun went down early behind a ridge of buttes. We are encircled by them—set as they are atop a whole series of conical hills.

"Aha! There—the very first glow—I see where the full snow moon will come up. Now a kind of spark…now a single thin ray…now like a star…now like a headlight…and now like the moon. Hmmm. Sometimes so near the horizon the moon looks huge. Not tonight— it seems brilliantly small, a marble of cold white fire.

"I hear the very soft and quiet hooting of a burrowing owl, the ticking of Otto's clock—yet these do not break the desert silence so much as enter into it. I think the moon made more noise than these rising. There are the gentlest sweeps and wisps of cloud about, the brightest stars—which are yet undiminished by the moon. But there's something new in the air—I can feel it, as if a weight of cold is about to drop."

That was the last clear sky we saw for a week. The cold that came on was indeed sudden. The next morning, Don and I both thought it was only a matter of putting on extra clothes and gritting our teeth. Yet soon enough, after a morning cup of tea, I realized I was not maintaining even my body heat sitting in Otto, so after catching the Walker I told him I was driving ahead to find shelter.

When I came to a bit of town named Dryden, I found the empty and boarded-up shells of a few buildings—and a post office. Disappointed, I tried bundling up more and throwing a sleeping bag over my lap while I wrote, but when my hands began shaking from the cold, I decided to try the post office door. It opened and I breathed a sigh of relief.

But the postmistress inside was almost as cold as Otto. She looked at me suspiciously, then suggested I might be warmer sitting in my car than standing in her lobby. Later, after I had been standing there for a half hour or so quietly writing, she softened. We talked.

Alma Littleton was her name; she was seventy-two and had lived on a ranch outside Dryden all her forty years of married life. Not so long ago, she told me, the town had a school, a couple of cafes, motels, grocery stores, gas stations, and other such. Alma warmed as she talked, and soon she was inviting me round the other side of the counter to the inner sanctum of the post office, saying, "Well, seein' as you're gonna be around a while, might as well set down by the heater here. There's a stool for ya. Pull it up right close there."

I did as Alma instructed and was thankful to be near the tiny butane stove trying to warm the place. All sorts of buckets and pans were spread about on the floor around us, catching the steady drips from the light, cold rain making its way down through the rickety roof.

According to Alma, if I had only come through a few months earlier, there would have been a gas station in Dryden for my convenience, and just weeks before that a grocery store too. "I'll tell ya plain," Alma said, "it's a fact, I've been wanting to retire for some time now, but sure as shootin' the minute I do, they'll shut down this post office. And then what'll there be to Dryden?" Right about then a big chunk of soggy ceiling let go and landed with a loud splat beside me.

"Of course, it's not just Dryden, that's been disappearing in these parts. If you lumped the workin' contents of all the places in the hundred-and-twenty-mile stretch between Sanderson and Del Rio, why I don't know that the accumulated total would live up to the word 'town.' Shelter'll be hard to come by, I'd say."

Alma was interested to learn about Don's walk, and then quickly recalled that not many years earlier, another walker had stopped in at her post office to pick up a pair of overalls being mailed to him. She was sure it was Peter Jenkins, of *A Walk Across America* fame, who was on his trek west at that point. Meanwhile, the hour-and-a-half we talked, the place did not have a single customer. When Don was about two miles out, by my calculations, I walked to meet him. Later I introduced him to Alma, who came out from behind the counter to shake his hand and wish him well.

Chapter 67

Amazing Grace

The cold rain continued, although it looked like it could change to snow at any minute. We skirted Pumpville, which was just off Route 90. Alma had said I wouldn't find any shelter there unless it was Sunday morning, because all that was left of it was a tiny Baptist church. Don told me to drive on to Langtry and come back to check on him later.

I found a fancy, brand-new visitors center at Langtry. Another traveler, a woman who once lived in Vermont, found me. I had just finished surveying the center and its contents commemorating the "Law West of the Pecos," as upheld by self-appointed Justice of the Peace, Judge Roy Bean. I learned that the judge was notorious for fining a dead man, among other things. But I was disappointed that the visitors center offered no place for a visitor to sit down. So I was standing in the cold considering my next move when this woman came up and asked me if I belonged to the Vermont license plate.

We had a friendly chat acknowledging places in common back home, if not people. And then she gave me a little Biblical tract and wished me luck on my journey, and I wished her luck on hers. She drove off in a comfortable-looking RV headed for some tropical part of Texas we had missed.

I wrote to David from a place I found open across the street: "Except for the visitor center built like Fort Knox which matches nothing we have seen on the road in all the wild West, I think Judge

Roy Bean would still recognize Langtry. The place is tumbledown and ramshackle, and I have a feeling it always was, though it must have been busier once. If the dingy place where I am writing now was a saloon instead of a dairy bar, I'd say almost nothing had changed. So don't picture me in civilization 'cause I'm not."

I put down my pen. I then picked up the tract the woman had given me, titled "God of All Comfort." It ended with the words, "His triumph in the midst of testing; His joy in the midst of sorrow; His peace in the midst of trouble." I realized I ought to feel more grateful. And when I picked up my pen again, somehow I did.

Don made thirty-one miles that February 5, in a numbing drizzle of sleet. He rushed his last miles to make the Jersey Lily before it closed at five, in order to dry out and warm up before we had to camp. We found a campsite on the banks of the Rio Grande, the same river we had last seen near Fort Hancock, south of El Paso.

Here, too, we noticed the Rio was not so "grand" as it once must have been; the huge bed it had cut and once filled was now choking with salt cedar, the water itself no more than a thin, winding ribbon of jade. We watched a small motorboat plying the river below us and knew that nothing much bigger could have. The bluffs opposite us standing on Mexican soil were gouged with caves and blackened by some sort of growth that made them look as if they'd been dribbled with tar.

"The border patrol stopped me again today," Don said as we nibbled some popcorn I had popped to make a little heat in the camper, so we could put off climbing into our sleeping bags a little while longer.

"Well, we're back at the border again," I said, "so that's to be expected. But what about this cold? I did hear that there is a motel up ahead in Comstock, but that's at least thirty miles from here, and I guess it'll mean more driving back and forth. The 'forth' I don't mind, but every time I have to go 'back' on our trail, well, it's like the journey has stalled. It's a lot of extra miles on Otto, too."

"I know," Don agreed. "I hope he starts okay in the morning."

"Well, yeah," I said. "One of the worst things about the cold is the worry about Otto starting or something breaking. But at least we have come down another twelve-hundred feet in elevation."

"I don't think it's as cold as it was back in New Mexico or earlier in Texas, but it sure *feels* as cold—it's so damp," Don said. "Pass me the map."

I gave Don the map of Texas, and to cheer myself up, I took out the big map of the U.S. to color in our recent inch or so of progress.

"Gosh, Don, I think they're right. I read in some pamphlet today that the 'real West' is said to begin when you cross the Pecos River. That means when we get east of the Pecos tomorrow, well, we'll be out of the West. And look—straight up from where we are now, we hit the panhandle of Oklahoma; then above that, Kansas, Nebraska, South and North Dakota. That's *mid*-west!"

"Except we're still in Texas," Don countered. "I have trouble thinking of Texas as anything but the West or Southwest. Though it does seem, since Sanderson, as if the land has begun to change, so maybe they're right."

And I had noticed this, too. The land *was* changing. It was somehow as if the earth was struggling to stretch itself out, or as if it had somehow been drawn tauter, or someone had unsuccessfully tried to iron down the mountains only to make more wrinkles— shallow canyons, washes and gulches, barrancas and arroyos. The vegetation changed, too, and along with this the use of the land. We were gradually leaving the High Chihuahuan desert behind. When we saw any ranches now, there were fewer with cattle, more with sheep and goats. Sotol, lechugilla, various yuccas, and creosote bush were giving way to a scrubbier deck, thickly dominated by mesquite and prickly pear.

Another plant we hadn't seen before cropped up about this time. I wrote in my journal: "Thank goodness for the purple sage—or Texas silverleaf, which does much to soften the thorny look of this land. A good-sized shrub, though not in flower now, it has a flowery effect upon the landscape. Even up close the foliage is petal-like to me— tiny silver-grey rosettes of leaves. Against the darker scrub in the distance, the plants appear to be full of small snowy blossoms. Would that I could linger to see it flowering purple later this spring."

I didn't mean that the way it sounds. There was not the slightest temptation to linger in the bleak cold. But I did realize that I would miss, and probably not by much, many of the first flowers of spring in the area. I could almost feel parts of the earth ready to burst forth, at a gentle coaxing of the first warm rain.

Meanwhile, we awoke that morning beside the Rio Grande to find Otto weirdly plastered with ice, as if it had been blasted on by a mad artist. Then Otto surprised both of us by readily starting, though the weather continued grim. The cold air had the smell, taste, and feel of wet metal and was about as much comfort.

Don doggedly pressed on to Comstock without complaint, but he could not hide his disappointment at day's end when he found that the motel there (and practically the only building in sight), where I had taken shelter at intervals during the day, was without phones or TV.

The next morning, we breakfasted at a no-name cafe across the way that was without a menu or choice of fare (one took what the owners were eating at the only other table in the place). No tea, milk, butter, or other such; but if the body was going to have to do without extras, Jackie and Lou Ann, the owners, were ready to make up for this by generously nourishing the soul.

While Don nibbled at his eggs, Jackie got out his guitar and asked if we minded a little music. He then began strumming and singing a gospel hymn, "One Day at a Time."

Neither Don nor I had mentioned The Walk. We had both been silent and glum. I was feeling about as stony and cold as the weather and had refused even to eat. But when the words of this gospel hymn began sinking in, it was as if a fire was suddenly kindled among the four of us. The warm glow of it expelled not only the cold but any cold, ungrateful thoughts. If we had been in danger of forgetting exactly how the journey made itself bearable, Jackie's enthusiastic singing of "One Day at a Time" brought it all back.

Don was visibly moved, and I struggled to hold back my tears. Music of any sort undid me. But when Jackie went on to sing "Amazing Grace" and came to this verse—"Through many dangers, toils, and snares, I have already come; 'Tis grace that brought me safe thus far, And grace will lead me home"…well, I gave up and let the tears come.

A while later Don surprised me by suggesting I play my recorder in exchange. I had coaxed roadrunners out of hiding, I had once gotten a dog to howl along, but I was nervous about playing for people—yet I somehow managed to do it. The small room was so spare and hollow—bare floor, bare windows, bare tables, bare walls—the wooden recorder sounded clear and full. We left feeling blessed and encouraged. We were being watched over—who could deny it?

Chapter 68

Long Way to Go

Crossing the Pecos, we left the "real West" behind. The weather continued cold and wet. For two mornings and three nights the journey felt stalled, since I had to hole up in Del Rio, Texas, hovering, between road visits to the Walker, in a motel room for warmth. It snowed twice, but both times in the night.

We were at the Mexican border, and Don decided it was only fair, since he had walked in Canada, that he should cross the Rio Grande here and walk a few miles into Mexico, even if they were extra and out of his way. I walked across the border with him into the Mexican town of Ciudad Acuna.

I hadn't observed that Del Rio was particularly prosperous, though it was the biggest town we'd seen since Van Horn. But after our walk in Ciudad Acuna, Del Rio seemed like the Palm Beach of Texas. Walking the Mexican town in a down vest, I felt as if I was wearing a mink coat. The streets were wet and muddy and the smell, at times, was of open sewers. The town's merchants were so hungry for the American dollar, they did everything to get a person into their shops except physically drag a body in. But we hadn't thought of shopping, so neither of us had any money on us.

Relieving the weighty sense of poverty, however, was an almost raucous gaiety—Mexican music was piped into the streets, and boat-tailed grackles whistled and called like raunchy road workers. One memorable sight stays with me.

We passed a young girl—ten yours old, maybe, standing alone, thumbing through a magazine, beside an open fire in an oil drum, at the corner of a junky courtyard. She wore a bright skirt and blouse, sandals on her feet—and appeared as strikingly fresh and immaculate as the courtyard was not. Such a contrast to her surroundings was the glowing sight of her, cutting swiftly and surely through all the grimy dark, it made my heart suddenly soar. She seemed nothing less than a vision of hope.

At Bracketville, Texas, we were surprised to cross a creek with running water—so many had been dry. Gradually, trees began to appear along our trail through the countryside, and not just in towns where people planted them. The mule deer and antelope herds disappeared, and in their place we spotted occasional Texas white-tailed deer. The commonest roadkill changed from black-tailed jack rabbits to armadillos.

In Uvalde, we learned of a threatening "blue norther." I had heard from Texans on the journey, long before Texas, about blue northers—hard dry winds under a clear sky, with the sting of arctic ice in them. We noticed several flights of sandhill cranes heading south that day, as if fleeing in the face of it.

The nightly temperature did drop to the low teens, but at least the sky had blown clear. The winds were hard on the Walker, but the sun made Otto a lot cozier and more comfortable for him to be in on a break, and for me to be in most of the day.

In Sabinal, at the Pepper Patch Cafe, we met Lewis Cole, a local rancher. We were interested to hear him speak of the land and the continuing drought. He said the Edwards Aquifer was responsible for the green fields of oats we'd been seeing. But he and another rancher complained of the expense of having to pump water, and that they'd all be goin' broke if a good rain didn't come soon.

Lewis was interested and pleased to hear our impressions of Texas—what we thought of the land and the people. When we told him we thought Texas and North Dakota were running neck and neck for being the friendliest state, he kindly picked up our tab for dinner—perhaps hoping as he did to cast the tie-breaking vote.

A big sign greeted us in the next town: "Welcome to Hondo—This is God's country, Please, Don't drive through it like Hell." I didn't. Don counted his longest train of the journey here—ten engines and 147 cars.

At Castroville, claiming to be the Alsace-Lorraine of Texas, we were a day's walk from San Antonio. The temperature got down to fifteen degrees that night, and the next morning Otto started okay, but neither his speedometer nor his odometer were working.

"Gosh, Don, I don't like this at all. I feel like I'm flying blind with no instruments."

"Maybe we shouldn't have camped last night in a cemetery," Don answered lightly, as he took off his shoes and socks and put his feet up for lunch. "It might have been bad luck."

"Don, this is nothing to joke about. How am I going to keep track of the gas in Otto?"

"Well," Don sensibly counseled, "if his gauges don't start working— we'll get him fixed up in San Antonio, okay?"

"Okay," I said, "there ought to be some good garages there. I guess we are just plain lucky that when things go wrong, we're near a place where we can get them fixed. Anyway, I hope it's not like the gas gauge—more trouble and expense than we can afford, in terms of time and money. It's weird driving along with all the dials dead. And they can't be frozen still, it's too warm out."

"Yeah, must be at least sixty degrees out there now—and it feels good. Pass me the map."

"Hmph," Don continued between bites of his sandwich, "after San Antonio we have a lot more choices of roads, lots more towns, also." Don paused, considering while he chewed, "Lots more Texas, Fran. How far have I walked in Texas to this point?"

"Just a second—let's see now...well over six-hundred miles, anyway."

"Six-hundred miles," Don sighed, staring long at the map.

We were both silent. The atmosphere grew suddenly heavy, as if in each of our mind's eyes, we could see the miles until home multiplying ahead of us. We had come *far*, there was no doubt about it, but we were about as far past the halfway point in Texas as we were past the halfway point in our journey. *Long* way yet to go, that's all there was to it.

"Oh," Don said, physically shaking off the silence by rummaging around for a fresher pair of shoes, "I forgot to tell you, I saw one of those herons yesterday on a backwater of the Nueces River."

"You mean, the great blue?" I asked.

"Yeah, the one that keeps following us," Don smiled.

"Well, that's a good sign." And after marveling to myself about our seeing this bird in the most unlikely places and in every state we'd been in, I added, "What do you think, Don, maybe the great blue is just checking to see if you can really do what you set out to do."

"Well, he better keep on checking, then," Don said, grabbing another banana as he set out, "because I'm not done yet."

Chapter 69

When All Is Said and Done

February 13, I wrote in my journal: "I feel exactly as I did sitting in the dentist's chair under the drill—only it's not me this time, it's Otto. The odometer and speedometer did not come back to life in spite of warming weather yesterday. I am at International Auto Services of San Antonio, and it looks like Otto needs a new cable, except that Reynaldo, who barely speaks English, can't find one long enough, so he is drilling some holes in Otto to make a shorter one do. I hope he knows what he is up to. I worry that while fixing one thing—another gets broken.

"Now Reynaldo is on his back under the front of Otto (who is only partially jacked up) with countless screws, bolts, parts, tools scattered like jigsaw puzzle pieces all around. If a single bolt or screw is left over after Otto's put back together—well, I hope I don't notice. I wouldn't know where it went. I've been here for hours already because the cable—even this one which is too short—had to be sent for. Don is going to wait for me at The Alamo if he gets there before I do."

San Antonio was the biggest city Don had walked since San Diego. It somehow simplified things for me to be out of the way while he walked the bulk of it. But I was surprised, when I finally did meet up with him at The Alamo, that he wanted to walk some of it again—particularly a winding way called the Riverwalk, which cut below the level of the city streets and followed alongside the enclosed flow of the San Antonio River. He wanted me to see how strikingly pleasant it was to walk these four miles or so out of the traffic stream yet still in the midst of downtown. When I drove on again, we decided to meet at day's end at the San Antonio Coliseum.

It turned out to be both a good idea and a bad idea to meet at the Coliseum. We could each get directions readily enough to find the place, but what we hadn't realized was how many other people were on their way there too: the rodeo was in town. By the time I found the Coliseum and a place to park, it was well after dark. I wasn't really sure how to locate the Walker in the teeming crowds, but instinct led me to the ticket counter.

"Thank God you're here," I said when I found him. "I got carried away reading some literature at the Alamo. Been here long?"

"A while—I was just starting to worry," Don said as we moved away from the crowd to stand under some rodeo posters. He went on, "It's a little crazy, isn't it? I had no idea what it was going to be like here. I noticed the rodeo signs, but I didn't realize what a zoo it would be with the carnival and livestock show going on at the same time. I'm glad you thought of the ticket counter. Everything still seem good with Otto?"

"Yeah, so far, anyway. I forgot to mention that the bill was only forty-seven dollars, though they made me pay in cash. It sure is nice to see those dials spinning. But what about today's mileage?"

"I guess we have no choice but to estimate. I did walk extra miles downtown, so I think it's darn close to thirty. Going by hours on the road, I'd say even more. Hmmm, well, let's just count it as twenty-nine. That's close. But I do know I've walked more miles than ever get counted in that notebook of yours, Fran. Still, I don't want anyone to think I'm rounding the miles upward."

"Hey, Don, now that we're here—what do you say? Let's get tickets and see what it's all about?"

"I don't know, Fran. I'm hungry and I'm really beat," Don said, looking up at the poster I was staring at.

"We can get something to eat inside. It just seems so perfect somehow—ending up here," I pleaded, "after all the days we've spent in the West?"

"You're right," Don said wearily but still unconvinced. "Anyway, it definitely makes me think we're still in the West."

"Well, just think again, Don; there's a seat inside for you a lot closer than Otto is—and I bet with all the animals in there, no one would notice if you took your shoes off, either."

"Well, okay," Don laughed, "but if I fall asleep, you may just have to carry me out."

There was little danger of Don falling asleep. Thirty miles a day for thousands of miles undoubtedly takes its toll on the human body, but a few minutes on a bucking Brahma bull looked like it might just surpass it. All those bone-jangling, rag-doll-tossing, body-whipping events kept us both rattled and awake.

We'd been so long steeped in the stew of cowboy culture, I was not going to be sorry if this was the last to be savored. Not that I didn't enjoy the West, but I knew it would definitely be a significant milestone gained to have left it behind at last.

East of San Antonio I wrote to David: "I'm having a great breakfast in a little cafe—three flour tortillas wrapped around potatoes, cheese, and eggs. Occasionally, when I stretch and look up, a very near and very large photograph of the Pope confronts me. And, as if that weren't enough, over the cash-register counter, hanging upon the varnished particle-board wall, is a tapestry-rug depicting the Last Supper. Counteracting these two influences though is a large portable radio on top of the soft drink cooler blasting away the contents of a rock and roll station in English—though at the moment everyone in here but me is speaking Spanish. Well, if I'm not absolutely sure we are still in the West—I do know we are still in Texas."

We entered Texas on something called the Texas Mountain Trail; later it turned into the Texas-Pecos Trail; later still the Texas Hill Country Trail; and now, since we had left Route 90 and were making our way on Route 87 east of San Antonio, we found ourselves upon something called the Texas Independence Trail. But where was the Texas Exit, we couldn't help wondering. As good as the state had been to us, we were beginning to look ahead on the map a little longingly at smaller states squeezed into areas less expansive than Texas. Shorter-term goals might give us a better sense of our progress.

Meanwhile, the lands about us continued to change, and yet still did not look like any lands we had previously crossed. The barren and rugged openness gradually began giving way to something much less sweeping to look at, something more tangly and confined, something harder to sum up because we couldn't get a view of much of it at once. Mesquite and other thorny shrubs still tied up the land, but evergreen oaks began studding the roadside, along with other deciduous trees, which were not yet in leaf but often were festooned with great, green bouquets of thriving mistletoe.

After San Antonio, near the little town of Westhoff, I wrote to David: "The trees are so numerous in some places now, they might even be considered to constitute a forest, though a scraggly one at that. Still a ton of prickly pear about—it likes to grow along the fences. The land continues to be divided up into huge sprawling ranches, but the ranches do not look like any we have seen before, and the boundaries are fairly invisible since the trees and taller shrubs cut off a wider view. I saw Spanish moss hanging in some trees today for the first time.

"I feel the austere and majestic beauty of desert country bounded by distant mountains, mesas, and buttes to be receding ever further behind. Yet I do not dislike what we have come upon either—it *is* interesting land. But what will I do if it ever is *un*interesting? How will I keep my mind off of you and home?"

And yet, much as I worked to keep it from my own consciousness, a certain impatience had surely begun to rise in me—in the Walker, too. We didn't dare speak of it, because already our progress could seem incredibly slow at times—however steady Don's walking pace held. The worst fear, unspoken between us, was that the closer we got to home, the slower The Walk would seem to go.

About his own travels Steinbeck said: "A journey is a person in itself; no two are alike. And all plans, safeguards, policing, and coercion are fruitless. We find after years of struggle that we do not take a trip; a trip takes us." Don and I were both learning what he meant. The journey had its own sense of time—its own momentum. It had made of the months and moments a new calendar and clock. It was trying us and testing us according to its own philosophy. And if I had learned anything yet, I knew that it was not done teaching us.

Chapter 70

Cross Check Ranch

"Fran, let me see the map," Don said after breakfast outside Victoria, Texas. "I am already sick of Route 87. Too many people driving along in that breakdown lane—some of them old farmers who can hardly see—I know, because I almost got hit by a couple of them yesterday outside Cuero, the so-called turkey capital of the world. I had to jump into the muddy ditch twice to save myself."

"I know what you mean," I said, digging out the map from under a pile of notebooks, "I don't like it, either. The faster traffic expects me to pull over into that narrow lane, and Otto almost got pushed into the ditch himself yesterday. There's no looking ahead the long lonesome road now, is there? I wouldn't go doing those push-ups along the road-edge anymore, either, Don."

"Don't worry, I haven't even been tempted. Hmmm. I wish I knew if those people were going to be home tonight. I called twice yesterday but always got a busy signal. We could take this farm road 616—I doubt it would have much traffic. Their place is supposedly somewhere on the way. I wonder if it's going to rain all day again," Don added, looking out into the wet gloom.

"Well, at least it's not snow. Pass me the map. Hmmm. We can call the people again when we get close. Anyway, it's sort of hard—we don't know that they wouldn't be happier if we didn't call, and we might be too tired by day's end to be decent company ourselves."

"Yeah, let's wait and see," Don agreed. "Now, didn't you say yesterday that you were going to head back to the Victoria Post Office again this morning?"

"Yes. That letter I got from David yesterday didn't make any sense. It's like we didn't get all of the mail he referred to—and since I practically had to break down the post office door to get that one measly letter—I'm going back. There may well be more back there.

"It's discouraging, though—that new post office ruling saying post offices can close down so many hours a week. Apparently in one town they could be closed on a Thursday, the next on a Wednesday, and the next on a Saturday. This is going to make it hard to plan a mail drop. A priest was with me yesterday as anxious to break down the door as I was. And I think the post office people were frustrated, too, because they did look for our mail and give us some, in spite of the locked door and the "closed" sign over the service window. What can you take for granted on this trip, I'd like to know?"

"Not much," Don said as he opened Otto's sliding door and stepped out into the steady drizzle. "Aha, Fran, here's something else," Don said, bending down to give whatever it was a closer inspection.

"What did you find now?" I asked, a little exasperated, thinking it was a new piece of litter I wouldn't really want to add to our collection.

"Otto's gone flat. His right rear tire seems to have picked up a nail."

"Oh, great!" I said, now wishing it *had* been a piece of litter. And then I muttered to myself, "I thought it might be fun to change a tire in the rain this morning."

But thank goodness Don had a better idea. We pumped more air into Otto's tire at a nearby gas station, and then drove to another station the Walker had noticed the day before that specialized in tire repairs. Don did not want to use our spare if we didn't have to, and he thought the bad tire could probably be saved.

When we drove into Stan Heinhold's Station, what happened next seemed rather like a fairytale. A whole crew of uniformed men, who were just standing about when we arrived, immediately, at a signal from Stan, the owner, went to work on Otto.

Meanwhile, Don chatted about The Walk with Stan while I listened and watched Otto undergo repairs for the second time in a week. I thought I heard Don mentioning again at one point that Texas and North Dakota were the two friendliest states we'd been in so far, and that it was hard to decide which was the friendlier—but I'm not sure now. Anyway, when I pulled out our charge card to pay the bill, Stan suddenly waved it aside, saying, "Hey, no problem—it's on the house. Best of luck to you both. Just send me a postcard when you get home!" And that was that. But the kind and generous spirit of this man didn't stop there; it seemed to set the tone for the entire day.

Not only did I collect a lot more mail at the Victoria Post Office, but the sun came out, and by day's end we were making new friends with the Marlows (relatives of friends back home)—and enjoying the first home-cooked meal since Gram made her famous mostaccioli for us in Phoenix in early January.

We finally called the Marlows when we were only a mile or so from their place. Don had walked his thirtieth mile and ended up at a combination grocery-post-office-gas-station, which constituted the tiny town of La Salle. When we couldn't get the payphone outside the store to work, we almost changed our minds. But then the two elderly women who ran the place encouraged us to call and let us use their phone. When, ten minutes after we arrived at the Marlows, one of these kindly old women called up to check on us and to see if we had had any problems following their directions, we knew we had been looked after.

Something about being made to feel at home on so little notice at Cross Check Ranch was as fairytale-like an ending to the day as Otto's repair had been to the day's beginning. It was as if Diann had waved a magic wand over a jar of cold spaghetti, transforming it into chicken-fried steak, milk gravy, mashed potatoes, and avocado salad. There seemed so much to talk about with Dave and Diann, and talk came so easily, it was as if we'd known them all our lives. Adding to the happy atmosphere were the Marlows' children—Jennifer, an eighteen-month-old toddler, and Robert, in first grade.

Don made friends of Robert and Jennifer in no time at all by parting with some toy treasures he had collected as road finds. Don also promised Robert, since he would be walking by his school the next day, that he would stop in and say hello to his class. The only thing

367

I felt bad about was Don and me looking like the married couple we weren't, but there seemed no easy way or appropriate opportunity for clearing the matter up.

Diann was a robust, energetic, low-voiced, Texas-born blonde and seemed as happy-go-lucky, outgoing, and straightforward as darker-haired, Massachusetts-born Dave was soft-spoken and reserved. Both were equally warm and responsive to us.

It wasn't until the feast was set before us, and the day well behind us, that Don announced that we were really lucky to be with the Marlows, because it was a perfect way to celebrate some important milestones.

"Fran, I wonder if you realize that today we've been eight full months on The Walk. Also, I'm pretty certain that today we passed our southernmost point."

"Well, I *am* surprised it's eight months," I said. "I thought it was eight years."

Everyone laughed.

"You mean you're not going to walk all the way down to the tip of Florida, Don?" Diann teased in her rich, Texas drawl.

"Well, he obviously cut off the deepest part of Texas, so he might as well cut off Florida," Dave observed. "I would."

"Well, I would, too—since you did say you were walking the *approximate* perimeter," Diann responded. "It's going to be far enough already. But where'd you think you hit the southernmost point—back at Placedo?"

"Right," Don said, "because if you go from there to where I'm thinking of turning due north in Florida at Daytona Beach—well, the path winds around a bit, but I'll definitely be angling north from here on out."

"Also, Don," I said, "today you walked your six-thousandth mile, so we might as well celebrate that, too. If it's ten thousand miles you're aiming for, then we're three-fifths done. Cheers!" And I lifted my glass.

At which point everybody else held up their glasses and we toasted the Walker's accomplishment. And then talk went on to other things.

Dave filled us in on the history of 15,000-acre Cross Check Ranch, owned by his grandfather, General Bennet (one of the two original ranchers in the area). Diann talked about being able to garden year-round, what the rest of the winter might have in store for us, and where to get a good meal up the road in Blessing.

After dinner, Don and Dave traded trophies. Don hauled out our favorite road finds gleaned from the Chihuahuan Desert: the tail of a black-tailed jackrabbit and the bleached skull of an unidentified animal Dave immediately recognized as belonging to a native wild pig called a javelina—an animal we had glimpsed more than once in all its bristly flesh in the desert.

Dave brought out a shoe box loaded with rattlesnake rattles—which had been cut from rattlers he had killed on the ranch. Holding one up, he said he had just killed the first rattler of the season earlier that week. Don and I both heeded this warning—along with other tales of hurricanes, water moccasins, and alligators. The road ahead was not going to be without its hazards.

But it was Diann who proved to have the most helpful warning of all, which she gave us the next morning after cooking a wonderful breakfast. Dave had taken off on an errand when Diann led Don and me out to inspect a rather innocent-looking mound of dry earth in their side yard. It turned out to be the home of myriad, tiny, mostly red, stinging ants—fire ants. Indeed, we had heard of these, but if it hadn't been for Diann we would not have known so easily how to avoid them and their homes. We did not know then that this was but the first of countless fire ant mounds Don would come upon directly in his path as he walked through the South.

Diann first took a stick and gently poked into the mound, from which the tiny beasts suddenly burst forth in a flood. She jumped back out of the way, then described how vicious the ants can be—blistering up a person's skin, killing newborn calves who did not readily get to their feet, and famous for swiftly swarming over a victim (without the victim's knowledge) and then, upon some secret signal between them, all stinging at once! Their name comes from the feeling the victim has of having been set on fire!

Dave arrived back at the ranch just as Don and I were saying thank you and goodbye—with a bushel basket piled high with oysters! We could have all we wanted, Dave offered. Don and I stood there a while, contemplating the unexpected sight, mouths ajar and watering. Yet our cooler was full, the day was warming, and I was afraid the oysters wouldn't keep, so we reluctantly turned them down. Still, the sight was a further testimony both to the Marlows' generous hospitality and to our changing environment. We were closing in on the Gulf.

Chapter 71

Did You Hear What I Heard?

Slowly but surely, again the world was being transformed about us—the land, the culture, the climate, the season. It was hard to keep track of it all. In retrospect, I see that many of these changes were announced as early as Victoria, Texas. In Victoria we got a sudden glimpse of flowering trees and blooming tulips, but it was short-lived because back in the countryside the progress of spring retreated. I almost felt as if I had dreamed those splashes of bright color.

The architecture also seemed to change in Victoria, though it was hard to say exactly how—more churches, more wooden buildings, more porches on houses. I wrote: "I love particularly the older two-storied wooden houses losing their paint which sport unscreened porches upstairs and down. These are the quaintest and most graceful structures I have seen in ages."

Near Sugar Valley, Texas, on Route 35, I wrote to David: "It's a scroungy, littery stretch of road. Lots of dead animals by the way, enough armadillo parts to pave a sidewalk from here to Florida, a bloated dead horse in a green sluggish creek not far back. Where are the vultures? There are lots of vultures—I've seen them, but I suppose there are even a few things vultures won't eat.

"I have not seen a prickly pear for some time now. Lots more Spanish moss, lots more big, old, gnarly oaks both evergreen and deciduous. I've begun noticing some kind of low growing fan palm here and there. And now that I know about fire ants, I see their dirt mounds everywhere—small fields with nothing but fire ant mounds polka-dotting the area—every ten feet. Lots on the roadside for the walker to dodge too.

"But to make up for some of the scruffiness and all the fire ants, there are bluebirds. Near Francitas yesterday I saw a flock of eight or more—mostly males. If only I were going home with the bluebirds, David, how soon I might arrive! Instead, I can only think the world is too strange and I am tired of wandering."

I was envious of other migrants to the northeast, too—we were now on the wintering grounds of many an eastern bird. The eastern phoebe was another I spotted in Texas—one I knew might even be flying to our very house to build a nest over our porch light, as it had done for years previous.

The Walker also had begun to notice familiars. One morning he counted ten male cardinals singing up the sun on a fence behind Otto. But to Don, the really unmistakable sound of spring was the musical jingle he heard plying the streets and neighborhoods of Bay City, Texas—emanating from an ice-cream truck.

After the sparsity of life on the desert, it was almost a shock to come upon such sights as those I saw while parked near Blessing, Texas. Thousands upon thousands of grazing snow geese were raising a din that was almost deafening. There, too, unlikely as it seems, every now and then a meadowlark's song cut through the squawking discord as neatly as a flute in a clamor of untuned cellos. The Walker counted a dozen flights of snow geese heading north at another point. And flocks of sandhill cranes, early each day, went this way and that, drawing attention to themselves with their low musical rattlings. We had rarely seen life so abundant. Something was afoot besides the Walker. The coyotes, for one thing.

February 14, I wrote: "Really and truly David, when I heard the coyotes last night, and though I couldn't see them, I swear, I know they were *dancing*. There was such a breathless rhythm to their song that when I suddenly envisioned them dancing and leaping, it made perfect sense. It was like a celebration. A rite of spring! Why not? The warm night air might have stirred their blood."

February 15: "I heard the coyotes again, but now their songs in the much colder night air—seemed like blazes of song—somehow like flash fires—their voices shooting up like flames and then dying out."

February 16: "Coyotes! Coyotes! Coyotes! *All* through the night—well beyond sunrise—close—but not so as to be seen. I did not get a wink of sleep, though I did not mind the coyotes either. A coyote convention! I don't know what they are up to, but if it isn't something to do with spring, what is it?"

And they sang for us the next four nights, too, as Don marched closer and closer to the Gulf. Were they coming with us? Would they follow us home? I liked the idea of them joining up. But what I didn't know then was how soon and how much the world was going to change *again*. If there was a signal to this change, it might have been the last night we were to hear the coyotes in Texas.

"Don, did you hear what I heard last night?" I yelled down crabbily to the Walker, who was exercising on his bunk below me the morning of February 21.

"What? Coyotes again?" Don said breathlessly between rapid sit-ups. "I didn't hear coyotes…so much as other things…last night."

"Right! The coyotes, when they struck up, sounded like a church choir in comparison. Never again! You know, we really ought to find out if there are rooster and hen yards about *before* we camp."

"And trains," Don added, puffing.

"Well, trains haven't been a problem in a long time—but those roosters! I thought roosters only crowed at dawn, but if so, the sun must have been rising on the hour all night long."

"And those hens," Don grunted, egging me on.

"Right—those hens clucked up like a crowded field of geese every time the roosters carried on. But I also heard a barred owl hooting, and *something* that roared."

"A lion," Don laughed, as he started putting away his bed.

"Well, hey, Don—really, something *did* roar, and maybe it was a cow or a bull or something explainable, but I never heard the like before this. I can't imagine what it was."

"Fran, your ears! What about those earplugs your brother Kevin gave you?"

"Well, believe it or not, they actually seem to sharpen my hearing. It's like—when I put them on, my brain says—'listen up, ears, you're going to have to hear through thick wads of foam now'—and then they do!"

"I wonder if we'll get close enough to see the Gulf today," Don said, changing the subject as he poured out his cereal.

"Well, by tomorrow you'll be walking beside it. Mountains, prairies, plains, deserts, and ocean—what's your favorite kind of country to walk?"

"It's more the conditions I care about—something easy on my feet, wind at my back, no trucks to worry about, no fire ant mounds in the way," Don said, digging into his breakfast with characteristic relish.

And, for a moment, I saw before me a man whose mind was as present to the task at hand as mine was distant. If Don thought ahead, it was to plan more adventures; he did not look back. Me? I could almost sympathize with Lot's wife. I felt I had to keep looking behind in order to correct a course I could see always tending to veer out of bounds.

Chapter 72

A Long Trail of Footprints

"The big news today," I wrote to David on February 22, "is—we are at the Gulf of Mexico in Texas. Hurrah! We first met up with it at Surfside Beach looking more lake than sea, barely ruffled as it was by frothy, inch-high breakers. The unclouded sky lent some of its deep, late-winter blue to the waters below; though for clarity, the sky surpassed the Gulf by many magnitudes. Yet locals say the gulf is seldom so calm and bright—and thus it has proved. But how the world has changed! We are seeing yet another face of Texas."

To get to Surfside, Don walked eight miles along Route 332 from Lake Jackson, where he had spent part of the morning speaking at Beutel Elementary School to a hundred second-graders.

(A chance meeting led to this invitation to speak, but throughout The Walk, Don made time for such school visits whenever he could; he drew energy from these impromptu talks. And though a speaking engagement might give him a late start on the day, it did not mean he would not reach his thirty-mile goal. Indeed, he pushed himself beyond the thirty miles consistently in order to make up for any days he had fallen short.)

Those last eight miles to the Gulf, we passed the biggest conglomeration of oil refineries, storage tanks, derricks, and associated factories we had yet seen. Oil rigs out at sea greeted us at the beach, but seemed blessedly distant in the haze. It was the first time we had actually seen the oil industry dominating the Texas landscape, but not the last. I thought the oil rigs intrusive and did not mind when they faded from sight. When we found the beach at Surfside strewn with what looked like the strings of countless dirty mop heads; which on closer inspection proved to be some sort of worms, we wondered about the effects of the oil industry upon the waters.

In general, it seemed a clue to the health of any body of water to notice what it cast up. When the beach detritus looked foul, it was difficult to feel good about the water.

The beach at Surfside on Follets Island was broad and flat; the sand, hard-packed and fine-grained. We were amazed to find it a thoroughfare for cars with speed-limit signs and even occasional stop signs. But since it was not yet the season for frequenting the beach, perhaps because the Gulf waters were still a wintry fifty-five degrees, we did not see many vehicles. I tried driving Otto on the beach, but he did not like the feel of it. Besides, it did not seem right to be defacing the sand with tire tracks, so I decided to stick to the paved road.

But to the Walker, the flat, sandy beach-way was a welcome change, and, at least for a while, agreeable to his feet. Surfside marked the beginning of a long trail of footprints Don left on Texas beaches. This beach walk was also the beginning of the end of Texas. I am surprised to realize, when I look back on it now, that we kept company with the Texas Gulf for only four days. It felt much longer.

February 24, I wrote to David: "Old! This trip is so old it's growing a long, grey beard. We are camped on the beach near a shipwreck—a rusty, iron fishing trawler which is yet less rusty than I feel. Waiting, waiting, waiting, waiting, waiting! The livelong day! I tell you this trip is getting old. It is well beyond retirement age—it is, it is, it is! If you detect an incessant underlying roar to these words, it's either the Gulf or me—neither of us knows when to quit.

"David, I don't believe there is enough interesting wildlife, land, or people left to carry me on home. I am running down. I *am* down. I am flatter than this pancake sea prairie. If I am able to go on at all, it is only because of pure inertia and because nothing has stood in my path for miles—not a tree, not a shrub, not even a rock. All are unheard of in this place. Rumor has it, though, that an obstacle is coming up—a place called High Island. They say it's the highest point of land on the Gulf Coast from the Yucatan Peninsula to Mobile, Alabama. It's on a salt dome looming thirty-eight feet above sea level. I'll probably get altitude sickness."

Never had I seen such flat and open country—so open and flat that it was impossible to see out of. Often there was nothing to mark the horizons to help one realize the distance one was looking across. Any houses or buildings near the Gulf were perched on stilts—sometimes with cattle grazing under them, but many had enough clearance for giraffes. At first I thought the height of these structures was mainly as a protection against times of high water, which I do not doubt it was. Simply crossing such vulnerable land made one feel daringly exposed; a hurricane blowing in off the sea would meet little resistance here.

But at San Luis Pass, where I climbed two stories up to a store on stilts, I realized a lofty vantage point also gave an impressive view over miles of marsh as well as out over sea, relieving the claustrophobic feel of the land. The bridge at the pass, connecting Follets Island to Galveston Island, did, too. But walking the beach, or even the road next to the beach, the Gulf waters actually seemed higher than the land opposite. They bulged, and I couldn't help wondering what was holding them back.

Something else drew our attention at San Luis Pass.

"Fran, guess what?" Don sprang into Otto, slammed shut the sliding door, and went rummaging in a drawer.

"I think I know, Don, I noticed them too."

"But that teacher at the school I spoke at yesterday said we had three weeks until mosquito season," Don complained, trying to stuff a small plastic bottle of repellent into his fanny pack after quickly smearing some on. "I haven't had to carry this in a while. Hmmm, I guess I don't have any more room in here."

"Maybe it's not the season yet, maybe these are just a fluke, Don. Anyway, there don't seem to be that many."

"Yeah, but they're big. I thought they were flies at first. And then I got bit. You know, we could…"

"I know," I interrupted, "we could have mosquitoes all the way home if we're so lucky. What's all that in your pack?"

"Shells, and—I don't know what this is—looks like some sort of a tusk. Also," Don went on, as he continued taking things out, "a roll of duct tape, three golf balls, a Super Ball, and these." He pulled out six broad buttons with slogans written across the face of them. "Actually, I found these buttons a few days ago—forgot I had them."

I picked one up. It was red, green, and white and said, "Ay Chihuahua," in black cursive. "Six of these, Don?" I questioned in disbelief. "Did you find them all in one place?"

"No, strung out along the road between Bay City and Van Vleck. Look at this." The Walker handed me a small stuffed animal attached to a wrist band labeled "watch-dog."

"And these," Don added. "At first I thought they would fit the watch-dog." He handed me a tiny suit of crumpled clothes made of pink and white flannel with blue pom-pom buttons.

"They're pajamas," I laughed, "and I'll bet they'll fit Bubba." Bubba was a little monkey-mascot from home who had come along for the ride. When Don gave a talk at a school, usually the highlight for the kids was marching out of school afterward to view Otto with his top popped, all of Don's shoes lined up alongside, and little Bubba sitting there looking like he was in charge. Don always told the kids Bubba was our protector.

"Look, Don, they fit Bubba perfectly. Only they'll have to be washed; he thinks they're a little grubby feeling."

Ever since we got out of the Chihuahuan Desert and into more-populated areas, the road finds had increased accordingly. Since San Antonio, among the more interesting artifacts we had acquired, thanks to the Walker's discriminating eye, were: one decorative air-freshener in original packaging; a very new-looking, red, white, and blue toy truck; an adjustable steel wrench made in China (which was so shiny Don couldn't pass it up, in spite of his resolve not to collect more tools); a "Charley the Tuna Anniversary Watch" keeping good time, but whose watch band disintegrated when Don went to pick it up; a large umbrella in good condition with bright orange and brown panels; a tape of popular classics and movie themes; a black and gold ribbon invoking the Tigers to smoke the Eagles; various interesting rocks; more small change bringing our road earnings in that category up to $26.60; and, now, of course, shells.

I hoped the multitude of shells—mostly angel wing, murex, prickly cockle, cat's eye, and lightning whelk—were a testimony to healthy waters. Otherwise, the brown, turbid, and amorphous surf did not reassure, especially when, more than once, Don came upon a beached bottle-nosed porpoise. We were not tempted to swim. The murky waters writhed with uncertain currents, and, once a person was in, there was no way to know what was in there with one. Still, on a bright day, the Gulf could be lovely company—the salt haze intensifying the glare, giving the ocean waters a metallic sheen, as if in places it was really only so much rumpled foil.

"One more thing here, while I'm at it," Don said, reaching into a corner of his pack. "I've been meaning to show you this."

"Good grief, Don, it looks like a rattlesnake rattle. How did you come by that?"

"Pulled it off a dead rattler," he answered, trying to hide a smirk.

This was a little too hard to imagine. "I'll bet it came from Dave Marlow's shoe box collection," I said, glad I had suddenly thought of it. I did not prize this treasure. "Why don't you just keep it in your pack there—you know, for good luck."

Chapter 73

Now Here

Don crossed the bridge at San Luis Pass to Galveston Island and walked three more miles before ending his day. The next day, he walked more Galveston beaches, enjoying the occasional presence of the great blue heron and the near-constant company of sanderlings skittering in the wave edges beside him. He hiked the length of the Galveston Sea Wall, where the main entertainment, toward the end of it, was wet-suited surfers.

I left the beach area only long enough to get lost in the city of Galveston's maze of streets, searching for a post office. I was startled to find that most of the streets were without names, which led me to imagine the town springing up rather too rapidly. North and south, the streets were numbered; east and west, they were lettered—sometimes with a fraction added. For example, I finally found a post office at forty-seventh and Q½. By day's end, Don had walked to the Port Bolivar ferry landing.

The ferry to the Bolivar Peninsula seemed a sweet luxury. Not only did it mean we did not have to go out of our way to skirt Houston in order to get around Galveston Bay, a savings of many miles; but it meant, for a brief while, I had the feeling Otto was a cruise ship and Don and I merely passengers. Something about being carried across water, even for a short time, was as soothing to me as being gently rocked in a hammock. As we went, the sun sank into a cloud of purple and crimson glory, trimming the bay. We watched a long flight of gleaming, white pelicans gracefully glide through it. I had last seen white pelicans on a backwater slough of the Milk River in Montana.

I also couldn't help thinking back to the ferry ride from Seattle to Bremerton, and then Don and I both recalled a ferry ride further back still—but one the Walker had declined. Don had ended his first day's walk at the ferry landing on Lake Champlain at Larrabee's Point in Vermont. But because the ferry did not start running until eight the next morning, Don borrowed a boat and insisted on rowing across before the ferry left. It wasn't his eagerness to be walking so much as his desire to beat the other Team Ross members to Long Lake, New York.

How long ago that reunion seemed. How long ago it seemed in Minnesota when Luke caught up with us on his motorcycle and brought photographs of the party at Long Lake. Much had happened since then—not only to us.

Letters and phone calls were always bringing news of changes back home. The tall, old locust by the library, which used to shower its fragrant blossoms all over downtown Middlebury in June, had been cut down to make way for a new addition. Quite a few friends had moved, though most were still in the area. Vinny had bought a house. Patty had rented a house from the college. A close friend of mine had designed, built, and moved into her dream house; another was trying to sell hers and was contemplating divorce. David had been making some changes on our own house, which he would only allude to.

Andy and Dan, our sons, were looking past their college graduations in May: Dan, to a program that would send him to China to teach English; Andy, to doing geology field work in Alaska and on the Juneau ice fields. Family and friends had gotten ill and gotten well, but some were fighting new and life-threatening battles with cancer and heart disease. In short, life had gone on without us. Had I thought about it, I might have seen that we were still a part of all these changes because we were certainly not forgotten; but it didn't really feel that way. Our almost hourly change of scene kept us in the "now here"—another way of spelling "nowhere."

The next morning, at Johnette's Triple H Dairy Bar in Port Bolivar, we met E. J. Stephenson, who took pride in claiming to be the oldest living man born and raised on the Bolivar Peninsula. He even gave us a book (he said he had lots more at home) on the history of the peninsula, in which he was a featured character. He was eighty-six years old and bragged to the Walker, as he leaned upon his cane, "Why, the mosquitoes around here will pick you up and drop you into the bay, if you're not careful—any month of the year!" Fortunately, a fierce wind off the Gulf that day blew all the mosquitoes to Houston or beyond.

That day, too, the broad beach narrowed and sometimes threatened to bury Route 87, so that the beach at times became the road and then again became the beach. Someone must have had to regularly plow sand and tidal debris off the road. A high tide would easily have made parts of it impassable. By days end, Don had made it beyond High Island, which was swarming with birdwatchers hoping for stormy weather. When a storm hits this time of year, apparently all kinds of migrating birds swoop down out of the skies and head for shelter on High Island.

I wrote to David: "I think the birders may be jumping the gun— the deciduous trees here do not yet have any leaves. Nothing is in flower here either. I haven't seen a burst of spring to equal what I saw in Victoria since. I guess, we are somewhat further north, but I'm still surprised at the wintry aspect of things. Or maybe it is the winter in me that I can't escape—all my creative energies are dormant. I wait for the spring light to put on fresh leaves."

The last day on the Gulf, Don walked the beach off and on for thirty-four miles to Sabine Pass. We camped at Sea Rim State Park. I wrote in my journal: "I have endless miles of open, brown salt marsh sea prairie on my left, and endless miles of open, brown saltwater sea on my right. Above is a great vault of blue spanning them both. Between is a ribbon of road stretching on—and now, at long last, pointing the way out of Texas. Flat and nearly without features as it is, I can appreciate this sea-rimmed land. It has texture and simplicity— water, grass, road. The water and the grasses are in motion; the wind beautifully at work on them both."

But the last memorable sight in Texas was watching the Walker make his way across a high bridge over the Intercoastal Waterway into Port Arthur. He looked to be entering the industrial equivalent of a redwood forest. What seemed a thousand towering smokestacks, some blow-torching the smoky atmosphere with visible flames, protruded from thickets of trawlers, and oil tankers—all of it creating a noise and stench it felt good to put quickly behind.

From here, in 1901, one year before the oldest living native of the Bolivar Peninsula was born, the first barrel of crude oil was shipped—having spewed from a gusher at Spindletop in nearby Beaumont. Apparently, many doubted then that oil could ever be a worthy fuel.

On February 27, the 256th day of The Walk, Don trekked out of Texas in a drizzly rain, just east of Orange, trailing a loyal following of mosquitoes. He had put some forty miles between him and the Gulf of Mexico and wouldn't be keeping company with it again until Mississippi. The drear weather, punctuated with the whine of insects, did not dampen either of our spirits that day. We had put a big milestone behind us.

My own excitement only increased when I called home that day to learn that David had been able to arrange his work schedule so as to meet us at the end of March somewhere in Florida. It was still a month away, and would mean the longest stretch of The Walk without a rendezvous, but my heart was suddenly pounds lighter. It was as if I had been laboring under the unconscious fear that there wouldn't be another visit.

"Well, that's the last of Texas," I said to myself as I took the Walker's picture climbing the stone monument that welcomed us to Louisiana. Afterward, Don decided to change his wet shoes.

"Fran, did you figure out those statistics yet?"

"Yep, you were right, Don," I said, consulting my notes. "You actually did walk more miles in California. I'm surprised. You did 1,070 miles' worth of Texas in thirty-five walking days. But you did 1,259 miles in California in forty-five walking days. I also figured out Montana—which I remember thinking at the time was a mighty big state—a mere 682 miles in twenty-two walking days. But in terms of miles per day, your best average was in Montana and your worst in California—thirty-one miles per day in Montana, compared to not quite twenty-eight miles per day in California. You've been pushing thirty-one miles per day again in Texas."

"I'll have to keep that up, or maybe even do better, to end up with the average I want," Don sighed. As if in answer, the drizzle suddenly freshened to rain. Immediately Don took the baseball cap off his head and reached for his rain hat.

"Well, if you can do it," I said, trying to sound cheerful, "we'll get home that much sooner. Texas was so good to us, I wonder what Louisiana will be like?"

"Only one way to find out," the Walker said. "See you on down the road." Don left Otto and me behind, whistling a tune I had often heard him play on his trumpet, though I didn't know its name. The rain quickly changed back to drizzle as I watched the Walker disappear in the gloom. The unknown of a land—I didn't know whether to call it the new south, the old south, or the deep south—loomed ahead. Perhaps it was all of these. But we were northerners, and I had to wonder if we would feel at home—if anyone would want us to feel at home.

Chapter 74

Red on Red

The uneasy feeling I had as we entered Louisiana recalled the early months of the journey, when every state's border was a reminder of lands leading us further and further from home. Now we were no longer heading away, yet every new state had to be met on its own terms. Typically, it did not take more than a few encounters with people for Don and me to feel at ease, if not exactly at home. But the initial impressions of Louisiana were not particularly promising.

I wrote in my journal February 28, west of Holmwood: "For the first time on this journey I am tempted to sit on the floor of Otto—simply to keep out of sight. I don't feel safe and I don't really know why. The laundromat I finally found in Lake Charles yesterday was close to the worst I've seen; the road today has been noisy with hot-rodders and badly littered with trash; the day is as drear as they come.

"But worse, a short while ago, when I tried to nap in this spot—which admittedly is not nearly far enough off the road to be safe because of the swampy ditches—a Louisiana state trooper pulled up, got out, and banged so hard on the side of Otto with his night stick, I was surprised not to find a huge dent when I looked later. It startled me so that my insides are still on fire. I explained about Don's walk as best I could, but this trooper must have had something else on his mind. He didn't seem to hear anything I said. And when I asked if he might have a suggestion as to a better place for me to wait, he muttered something under his breath, turned back to his cruiser, and sped off. I hope he wasn't simply reacting to the "foreign" license plate. I'm tired of people staring at Otto's license as if it said 'Mars' instead of Vermont. And yes, you guessed it, I'm tired period."

Don was not happy to hear about the unfriendly trooper, and he was not happy with the road margins of Route 14, which gave him little room between the watery ditches and the road edge and were built of sharp little bits of oyster and clam shells that easily flipped into his shoes. We thought to cheer ourselves up by making some phone calls, so I drove on ahead to scout a phone.

Since Lake Charles, the area was gradually becoming more rural. I came to a little town winding about a sharp bend in the road, parallel to a set of railroad tracks. I did not see a phone, but I got out to inquire at an old gas station-garage. I walked around the few deserted buildings and then around the bend in the road, where I could see an ice-cream stand that appeared to be open about a quarter mile away. When I walked back to Otto, I discovered a payphone I had overlooked near the open bay of the garage, where it seemed as if the owner had just stepped out for a minute. And though I almost felt as if I was trespassing, I picked up the phone to call David.

We had a long, lazy, Sunday afternoon talk about nothing in particular. We seldom did this. Usually, we were too conscious of the expense, or else circumstances simply did not allow it. The talk was reassuring—something else was, too.

A group of teenagers ambled by while I chatted. A long while later they came by again, heading the other way. When they saw me still hanging on the phone, they smiled. I smiled back. And suddenly I felt entirely at ease. It was such a simple thing, but I was no longer so worried about Louisiana.

"Fran, did you find a phone?" Don asked, as he stopped to scrape some mud from his shoes before he climbed into Otto.

"Yeah, right behind you—over by that garage. Also an ice-cream stand round the bend and a little ways up the road. Did you see a sign for this town anywhere? Maybe I missed it."

"Nope, pass me the map. Hmmm. I don't know," Don considered, figuring the number of miles he walked from the last town." I guess it's just not on here. Maybe it's not a town. That's a switch—finding places not marked on the map—instead of *not* finding places that *are* marked on the map.

"Hey, you know, I think that trooper who scared you was, well, maybe he was just having a bad day. Two pickup trucks full of teenagers have since stopped to ask me what I'm doing—and they have been the nicest kids, really friendly. And just a short while ago a woman pulled alongside who saw me walking yesterday—way the other side of Lake Charles—and she wanted to know what I was up to also. She just seemed amazed when I told her—the kids did, too."

"Actually, Don, I am feeling better," I said. "It's funny how you can somehow expect that people the other side of a border will be different—like suddenly they're not going to want you to trespass in their state or something."

After a short stint on the phone, Don set off again; we were both in a lighter mood. "You know, we haven't really celebrated getting out of Texas yet, Fran," the Walker called back after he had walked about ten yards. "Maybe tonight. Keep an eye out for a restaurant, okay? I could use a hot meal."

That sounded good to me, too, on a damp, gray day that was promising to turn into a damp, gray evening. But by the time Don's endpoint came up making for a thirty-three mile day, I hadn't spotted anything in the way of a restaurant.

Back in Lake Charles I'd seen all kinds of places—a great many with the adjective "Cajun" attached. At the laundromat, strange but pleasant cooking odors kept drifting in from a cafe next door. When I walked out with my laundry, I caught sight of mounds of colorful food I did not recognize. Somehow the scent had not completely faded; it was as if the clouds hanging heavily about were mixed with the steam coming off some exotic cooking pot. Something was in the air, but it sure looked like it was going to be familiar road fare for us that night.

"Fran, why didn't you stop back there a couple of miles at that restaurant?" Don asked in angry disbelief that I would pass up what he'd been counting on—not to mention lengthen his day.

"What restaurant?" I asked. "What? Are you beginning to see things that aren't there, Don? You're just hungry, that's all."

"No, I saw a restaurant. Really. Come on, get Otto going and I'll show you where."

And so he did. But I found out later that the inconspicuous sign, sitting at the edge of a tiny parking lot, was not out when I went by. There was nothing about the nondescript building to give it away as a restaurant, either. Harris Seafood Restaurant was on the outskirts of a little town called Hayes that barely had any in-skirts—a backwater, rural, farm town in Acadiana (a word the tourist pamphlets used for Cajun country). We didn't know what it meant to be in Cajun country yet, but we were about to find out.

Don and I had first heard of Acadia, and the mass exile of French Catholics fleeing religious persecution and searching for a new home (many of whom finally settled in southwestern Louisiana), when we went camping with our sons many years earlier in Nova Scotia—the place from which the Acadians fled. I remembered it, too, from Longfellow's famous poem, "Evangeline"—"Fair was she and young, when in hope began the long journey; Faded was she and old, when in disappointment it ended."

Anyway, exactly what Evangeline might have been looking for in Louisiana was not what was on our minds as we entered the Harris Restaurant—which made no overt claims at all to being Cajun any more than a place on the Champs-Elysees would claim to be French. But if the exterior of this place did not suggest anything promising, the interior was more sobering still—the decor strongly hinted that a monastic bowl of gruel would not be out of place.

Immaculately clean, no table cloths, a bare cement floor, rolls of paper towels standing in for napkins on the cluster of small tables— the place had just opened its doors for the evening and we were the first customers to arrive, which did not soften the austere atmosphere one bit. However, as we entered, a wonderful aroma transfixed us, suggesting a culinary magic that could possibly transform the surroundings into something worth staying for. I wanted to order whatever was responsible for that smell emanating from the kitchen, but the menu was long and varied, and I wasn't sure. We went for the specials—seafood gumbo and fresh, boiled crawfish.

As it turned out, everyone who came in that night (while we were there, and we were there a long time) ordered the boiled crawfish. Many ordered it to take out. We didn't know, but the season just getting underway was the long-awaited crawfish harvest. Crawfish—creatures I had never once dreamed of eating, though I could easily do so now.

When we were informed we would have a bit of a wait, Don asked if he could use their phone. It was attached to a post in the middle of the room and was not a payphone. They didn't mind a bit, they said, speaking in a buoyant cadence and accent we later learned to identify as Cajun. The owners didn't seem the least worried that Don might run up a bill calling long distance, either.

The gumbo was delicious, but when the orders of crawfish arrived—well, I don't know what impressed me more—the sight, the smell, the taste, or the experience of getting at the succulent morsel of meat caught inside each miniature lobster's shell. I'll never forget those heaping trays—each mounded high with four pounds of crawfish the color of red-hot coals, steam billowing off the top, and crowned with two boiled, red potatoes. Red on red—apples on embers. I laughed when I saw such huge portions, but the bouquet of it all was too intriguing to laugh at.

Our waitress got a kick out of us asking exactly how we were supposed to eat the little creatures, and, after demonstrating the technique of beheading, de-veining, and extracting the meat; she waited for us both to try our fingers at it and to see what we thought of the reward. When she was satisfied that we appreciated what had been set before us, pointing out how extraordinarily large the individual crawfish were, she left us alone with the feast.

The pile of shell discards we heaped up was as generous as the servings. No wonder the bare tables and floor and rolls of paper towels. What a mess we made—especially the Walker, who liked to dip his meat alternately in hot butter and cocktail sauce. And this was not food to be quickly done with, though I noticed we got much more adept at what we were doing further down in the piles. Still, it was a long meal that not even the impatient Walker would have wanted shortened by a single crawfish.

That night I was a little worried that going to bed on a full stomach would keep me awake. Many times I had skipped dinner, thinking I would sleep better. And this night, camped in some shrubby thickets next to a frog pond, which connected up with a knobby-kneed swamp of bald cypress, proved to be as wakeful as I feared; yet, disturbed as I was, I'm not at all sorry now I was kept awake. Neither was it the work of the crawfish quietly resting in peace.

The swamp symphony started out innocently enough with a friendly whirring of spring crickets. Indeed, the musical ringing of these insects in the bell of the wet hollow was easy to take. And maybe I dozed a little at first, because I did not mark the change from this major innocence to what followed. Later, even when I recognized some of what I was listening to—like the hooting of a barred owl, I couldn't help being spooked by the watery twang it took on over the dark, unmoving pond waters. But the familiar sounds were relegated to the background, and not even the owl seemed to be proclaiming that all was well.

Sudden shrieks and moans made me shiver; not to mention singular, drawn-out wails and whines; furtive little whimperings and gurglings bubbled up from low registers to high; some were repeaters and some one-timers. It was the one-timers that worried me. I was surprised to hear the coyotes in the wee hours, but their chorus, too, became a weird harmony of comments carried across the resonant swamp from some distant hillock. I didn't know it then, but it was the last time we would hear from the coyotes until long after we were home again in Vermont.

I lay there awake until the dawn, when I was relieved to note the change from minor key to major as the morning carols of familiar songbirds gradually triumphed over the ghastlier sounds of the night. Don's comment at breakfast let me know that he too had had to ponder what had been going on in the dark.

"Fran, before you start saying anything about what you heard last night—I want to say *one* thing: I know that it can all be rationally explained, so don't go making it into something haunted."

"Haunted, huh? Good, Don, that's just the word I was trying to think of. Thanks."

"Haunted, huh? Good, Don, that's just the word I was trying to think of. Thanks."

Part Nine

MARCH

Louisiana, Mississippi, Alabama, Florida

Chapter 75

The Wandering Maiden

Our turn inland from the Gulf, winding its way through the swamps and beside the bayous of Louisiana, before slowly working its way back to the Gulf again, made for a sudden leap toward spring. Here the weary browns of winter gave way before pale, soft, blushes of green and a freshening spectrum of colors long absent from the countryside. Sunny jonquils overcame the gray days as early as Toomey, Louisiana, soon followed by the wine-red haze of flowering swamp maples and the blooming of red bud trees, whose intense color wavered somewhere between a warm pink and a cool lavender. All manner of shrubs I couldn't name were everywhere leafing out. About the Walker's feet, in places, blossomed clover, the blue-white Chinese forget-me-not, and the white, six-pointed star-of-Bethlehem. Something, resembling what I knew as ground ivy at home, and appearing as early as Castroville, Texas, hiding in the grass, was now rampant, forming brilliant carpets of rose.

I began thinking again of picking wildflower bouquets to draw from. Something I hadn't thought of doing for months, something I could turn to when the hours seemed extra-long. It was a welcome change to be distracted by the pageant of spring, well before I could have expected anything like it at home. I was not ungrateful, but if I wasn't careful, I would begin to think it was April or even May.

"Don, why do we have to be on the road when the year is actually a whole day longer?" I jokingly complained from my bunk on the night of leap day, February 29.

"Just our good luck—think of it as an extra day of spring."

"Don't tell me you don't think it's been a long February, Don?" But just as I said this, there was a small explosion that temporarily silenced the sounds coming from a nearby marsh—especially the incessant piping of a killdeer. After a while, the night chorus resumed, along with the killdeer.

"What was that?" Don asked.

But before I could say, "I don't know," there was another explosion and then another.

"Hey, I'll bet it's one of those carbide guns—you know, Don, like Dave Marlow described. That marsh out there must be a rice field; the intermittent noise of the exploding gas in the guns is supposed to disturb the geese and cranes—keep them on the move."

"Well, I'm glad it's not any closer. I think I can sleep through it. What about you, Fran?"

But just then, as if to reassure me, Westminster chimes tolled somberly in low, dark tones from another direction—from an unseen church tower. "Oh well," I said, "it's all just part of the fun—a whole extra night of it. I won't even have to open my eyes to count the hours passing."

The next morning at breakfast, Don studied the map of Louisiana and projected how many more days it would take to walk out of it. When it looked like a week would do it, we were both kind of surprised. Apparently the map of Louisiana was on a different scale than the map of Texas. For half a moment it suddenly seemed as if we would be zooming along.

Yet that week I wrote in the newsletter: "I don't know, it might take the walker a longer time to get out of Louisiana than Texas if he keeps following his nose. Late yesterday morning a place in Kaplan waylaid him well past the lunch hour. It was The Bill Suire Restaurant, and since crawfish wasn't on the menu till evening, Don signed up for the buffet.

"But the chef, Bill Suire himself, must have spied some budding crawfish connoisseurs because when he found out that neither the walker or the driver had ever tasted crawfish etouffe, he insisted on bringing out some he'd been cooking up in the back. The tall, greying chef explained that etouffe was French for 'smothered'— and in this case it was the tender, peeled crawfish tails which were getting smothered by a Cajun gravy in the pot he set between the walker and driver. This rich treat was 'on the house' and went down as smoothly as a hot fudge sundae for dessert.

"Later, Juanita, Bill's wife, wandered over from the bank down the road where she worked and wanted to know who had come all the way from Vermont—and then proceeded to welcome the walker and driver with warm hugs and hearty congratulations."

This part of Louisiana had something of home in it, too. The spring green I saw in the farm fields about me was not unlike that of the Champlain Valley, much later in the year. The pastoral setting itself was similar, if not the field crops. Here were acres of rice, soybeans, and sugarcane; yet the crops were not far enough along to be recognized and might as well have been the corn and hay fields of the north. It's true there were no mountains or even hills on the horizon, but there were French names, and that was certainly like home where the French Canadian influence from Quebec penetrates deep into Vermont.

But, I guess the homeyness had as much to do with the people as with the setting. Hardly a day went by without some new experience of Cajun hospitality. It was going to be hard to part with this territory. Thank God for the trouble of wet weather and mosquitoes or we might have lingered longer than we did. But even the rains conspired to bring out the Cajun warmth.

March 2, Don and I were soaked to the skin walking Route 90, coming into Jeanerette, Louisiana. Don had been successfully dodging showers all day, but we both got caught in a heavy downpour when I decided to walk to meet him at day's end.

When we came upon Le Beau Petit Musee, in Jeanerette, where I had left Otto, we hoped to go inside just long enough to take the chill off of us before we went to scout a place to camp. The museum—

displaying local art, historical artifacts, and wildlife specimens of the area—was just preparing to close. And once we saw the formal decor, we were embarrassed to have come in dripping wet anyway, so we quickly decided to go.

But as we were leaving, Don suddenly thought to ask the friendly and motherly museum director, Kay Fortier, (who also just happened to be the director of the chamber of commerce)—if she knew of a place we could camp. This led to her asking what had brought us to Jeanerette, which then led to her calling Karma Champagne over from the Jeanerette Enterprise to photograph and interview Don about The Walk, and finally led to our staying long after dark and well after our clothes had dried.

In the meantime, while Don was being interviewed, Kay was on the phone several times and even left the museum once on errands—all on our behalf. For one thing, she squared it away with the local police and the park director for us to be able to camp and use the hot showers at the recreation park.

And when she came back from her errands, she was loaded down with Cajun treats she insisted we just *had* to try with our supper. From the local meat market (Robichaux's) and bakery (Le Jeune's) she had brought: hot boudin, a kind of stuffing made of cooked pork, rice, and seasonings packed into a casing; gratins or hog cracklings, which was deep-fried pig skin; warm French bread; and ginger cakes for dessert. We thoroughly enjoyed the unlooked-for bounty, but none of it was any finer or warmer than Kay herself.

From Jeanerette, Don followed alongside the slow waters of the Bayou Teche, past old plantations, lovely antebellum mansions, more rice and sugarcane fields, and into the swampy backwaters of the lower Atchafalaya basin, the second-largest swamp wilderness in the U.S. and the last undrained river-basin swamp in the Mississippi Valley.

Outside Franklin, we found a place for rent: Frances Plantation; and beautiful home though it was, I liked it because it was the smallest of these bayou-side mansions we had come upon with no chain-link fence to separate it from its neighbors, and because it had a huge, old oak draped in Spanish moss and bursting with air ferns. And yet, if there was a place I would have wanted to set down roots for a while, it wasn't Frances Plantation—it was the swamp.

I couldn't help thinking I was seeing the Atchafalayan swamp at its best—golden ragwort gilded the shallows; the palest green veil of leaves invited a penetrating look deep within; great, white, yellow-billed, black-legged egrets prowled about, exquisitely mirrored in the dark, still waters. Indeed, everything was reflected in the black mirror—mystery, most of all. I longed for a dugout canoe called a pirogue—and maybe a guide, maybe not. But I was not satisfied with merely seeing, and I knew as I looked on that I had to return someday—that is, if I didn't spy out a boat and a pole anywhere tempting me, before I left this swamp wilderness behind.

"Hey, Fran," Don called, catching up to where I was parked east of Chacahoula on Route 20 (which we had taken because it looked on the map as if it cut off a longer loop of Route 90). "You'll never guess what I could have picked up out of the ditch back there. And if you don't believe me, you can just drive back and see for yourself." Don climbed into Otto and shut out a few disappointed mosquitoes.

"I don't even feel like guessing," I said. But by this time I didn't think I could be surprised, either.

"A computer still connected to its keyboard," Don announced. "It's the first thing I've seen, besides maybe some tools, that I would guess was heaved out of pure frustration. It's a sign of the times, Fran, I'm sure of it. Soon they'll be choking the landfills."

I laughed. "One thing I know, Don, it wouldn't be any fun to pick up trash around here. Everything's wet, or floating, or three feet under."

"Yeah, and you don't know what might grab onto you, either—you should see the size of the frogs and turtles and snakes scrambling out of my way. Sometimes all I hear is a splash as I go by—and maybe I glimpse a long tail slithering out of sight. I've spotted a few small alligators, too, and a lot of those big, muskrat-looking things."

"You mean—nutria," I said. "I've been noticing them, too, and in some places fish jumping in yard-long leaps. But the last place I was parked, I heard a splash and turned just in time to see a kingfisher come up with a minnow out of a small ditch. It flew to its perch, whacked the fish against the branch it landed on until it didn't wiggle, then juggled the thing about, finally swallowing it whole—head first."

"One-hundred days, Fran," Don said, changing the subject as he opened the cooler and surveyed its contents for a snack.

"What do you mean?"

"Well, we've been gone now a full 260 days—so it's a good chance we have only a hundred or so left. I can't figure it exactly just yet, but *I'm* ready to call it a hundred. It's countdown time!" And with that, Don popped open a juice and lifted it high.

I thought so, too. I grabbed another juice and clinked bottles with the Walker, toasting the last hundred days. But I thought of Evangeline again as I did. "Thus did the long sad years glide on, and in seasons and places—Diverse and distant far was seen the wandering maiden." I only hoped that by the finish I would not be as old and faded as Evangeline.

Chapter 76

What's Your Cause?

Much of our way through Louisiana was punctuated by heavy clouds and erratic storms. The sun did not make an appearance between downpours, even when the lull managed to last a full day. Somehow the air was wringing-wet, whether it was raining or not. Everything in Otto was moist to the touch—all of Don's shoes, all of our clothes, even our bedding. We had met the hot, the cold, the dry— and now the damp. Constantly breathing the musty odor of mildew made me wonder if my lungs weren't growing moldy. I was bound to begin harvesting a bumper crop of fungus in Otto if conditions kept up; there was little reason to believe they wouldn't.

A glance out the window revealed a green world whether trees had begun to leaf out or not. Luxuriant mosses climbed over everything in sight—living or dead—trees, logs, stones, houses, old crowded cemeteries of above-ground tombs. Sometimes, in the interior gloom of an older town, I was tempted to think I was seeing glimpses of the Emerald City, yet the city of Oz was closer than I suspected.

Two days' walk west of New Orleans, the air ever so gradually began to lift and lighten. Our spirits followed suit. We could sense the promise of blue and gold long before it arrived, and we anticipated something else that quickened Don's pace and my heart—the Mississippi River.

East of this great, wet, muddy, milestone, we knew we would be *east.* We were nearing its mouth; seven months earlier Don had swum across it near its source; before that, outside St. Louis, we had once lived within an easy walking mile of it. An old friend—the Mississippi. As a child looking at a map of the U.S., I thought of the big river as dividing the country into a big half and a small half. The country left to traverse, after we crossed the great river-way, was the smaller half. The bulk of our journey in the West, we would leave behind. And though the celebration of Mardi Gras was already two weeks past, to Don and me, it might have been still to come.

As far as sixty miles out of New Orleans, Don began picking up discarded Mardi Gras beads. By the time he reached Gretna on the west bank of the Mississippi, directly across from the city, he had collected at least forty unbroken strands of colorful plastic beads. He would collect another dozen before we would leave the Mardi Gras capital behind, and he might have easily collected more, except for my pleading that enough was enough.

The night before Don made New Orleans, we camped on Bayou Des Allemands. When a pretty green frog with delicate gold markings leaped up at me out of the drain where I was brushing my teeth, I felt instinctively as if I was supposed to kiss it. Magic was in the air, and I might have enjoyed the prince who was bound to appear. Instead, I watched the little frog creep away on sticky pads up the vertical surface of the slippery bathroom wall until it was well out of reach.

Meanwhile, when I walked back to our campsite, I found Don in animated conversation with a couple of bikers. It was almost dark, so I could not get a good look at them, but it was not hard to detect an English and Irish accent. The bikers were apparently heading on in the morning—going the direction from which we had just come, after having been in the area a few months for the purpose of organizing a rock concert to raise money for Operation Mexico. The six-thousand dollars they raised in New Orleans would go to help build a hospital to aid earthquake victims in Mexico City.

Though Alan O'Donnell was from Ireland and Adam Bates from England, the two had begun their money-raising bike trek in New Brunswick, Canada, and would not finish until they had biked all the way to Mexico City—organizing fundraising rock concerts in cities along their route. Interested to learn about Don's perimeter walk, they nevertheless seemed rather surprised to learn that Don had no "cause" spurring him on.

This was not the first time the topic had come up. Indeed, in some places—particularly throughout California—the commonest question put to the Walker was not "Why are you doing this?" but "What is your cause?"

I arrived on the scene just as the two bikers were registering their disbelief that Don would go to so much trouble simply on his own behalf. I guess to them it seemed an effort without purpose. I didn't know what to say to them. Don wasn't disturbed in the least by their reaction, but after we said good night to the altruistic bikers, I brought the subject up again.

"Don," I said, as I climbed up to my bunk in Otto, "do you think we should have had a cause? I mean, don't you feel unforgivably selfish after talking with those guys?"

"Not really," Don said, pulling out his bunk and unrolling his sleeping bag. "Anyway, what sort of cause should I have had?"

"Oh, I don't know. You could have collected money and sponsors for cancer or heart disease or any number of things, I suppose."

"Well, remember how late it was when I finally found out that I even got the sabbatical? I really didn't have much time for organizing any fundraising effort. Some people did suggest it to me, though, but I think I would have felt like a phony because no 'cause' was really what was motivating me, beyond the idea of the adventure itself. I thought about it, but Fran, if you don't have a cause, you don't have a cause. You think there's something wrong with adventure for the sake of adventure?"

I did not answer right away. I'd been thinking about this question since it had first come up. I thought about it again whenever I heard the cross-bearers mentioned, who, for a while, were always reported as just ahead of us on the road. I even wondered at times if people weren't really saying to Don, "Hey, where's *your* cross?"

In truth, or deep down, I respected Don for his honest approach. I might have been the sort who would have liked to have had a cause, mainly to camouflage my more selfish motives. But I think what the question was also bringing up for me was any number of the hidden "whys" of the adventure.

Somehow I could sense more reasons for this journey than what we told ourselves or what we might say to others. It was good to have a pat answer because nearly everyone wanted to know *why*. But having a pat answer could keep one from thinking about it further. So often in my life I have learned the true "why" of an episode long after it was past. I guess I am a slow learner, but I can't help thinking we are meant to learn about ourselves somewhat *after* the fact, and that we only fool ourselves if we think we can know all of our motives beforehand.

"Well?" Don asked, still waiting for my answer.

"No, Don," I finally spoke up, "I don't think there's anything wrong with an adventure just for the heck of it."

"Anyway, Fran—I'm sure you know I'm really doing this for you."

"For me!" I said, ready to let out a big guffaw. "I thought I was doing this for *you*!"

"No," Don teased, "get this straight—I'm doing this so you can have a worthy subject for a book."

"Oh," I laughed. "I get it. Well, as far as that goes, I doubt I'll have a book when this is over. Remember what that Hollywood producer said, Don? If nothing big and ugly happens, who's going to publish it?"

"That doesn't mean the big ugly thing has to happen to both of us," Don said, chuckling to himself.

"No, Don—just to you—the *worthy* subject of my book." And then we both laughed, after which I said a silent prayer that the big ugly thing would not happen to either of us.

Chapter 77

Fear of the Big Ugly Thing

Not long before we made New Orleans, late in the afternoon of March 6, the sky finally cleared and we felt the sun as we had not felt it since Texas. It added some glory to a day that did not really need it. I was so excited, I could have leaped across the Mississippi in a single bound. And I was even rather thrilled when Don got turned back by police as he attempted to illegally walk a bridge connecting Gretna to New Orleans. Better to cross the waters by ferry, better to feel the river beneath us, better to ride the swell of this milestone, if only for a while.

I wrote in my journal later: "I saw something of home reflected in that big muddy brew of a river. I felt the connection with my past in St. Louis, and yet, I sensed us being urged onward to our Vermont home too. How could I not love New Orleans uncritically from the start?"

Further downstream I could see a more modern skyscraper section of the city and, more directly across, the intriguing outlines of older buildings on a much smaller scale. Fishing trawlers and shrimp boats, barges, a fireboat hosing a fountainesque spray out over the river, a big paddle-wheeler loaded with tourists—were headed upstream and down, as we plied across the teeming currents. Don was excited, too. And though he had already walked thirty miles, he agreed to spend the last hour of the day meandering about New Orleans on his aching feet.

I was astonished again and again at the inexplicable joy I felt in this city. I couldn't seem to look at it with the suspicious eye I usually reserved for such places. Where we walked were mainly other walkers, the streets largely unmolested by vehicle traffic. And everywhere was music—every sort of music spilling out of every sort of urban watering hole—all of which seemed to be without doors, so that the spirits, the music, and the people could overflow and mingle in the streets, which they did. On some street corners we could stand at the crossroads and hear various rhythms and melodies—Dixieland, rock and roll, jazz, folk—overlapping, and in the process seeming to create something altogether new for the eager ear.

We saw a lot going on, all color and manner of people, the atmosphere of Mardi Gras itself refusing to let go. An old wizard, or a new Oz, with glittery blue robe and star-studded dunce cap told fortunes on the street; a group of energetic Black youths were break (-neck) dancing for a crowd, on nothing more than a slick piece of paper, a boombox blaring in the background; fat, old, patchy drivers drove seedy, horse-drawn cabs. And from the beautiful iron grillwork of the French quarter to the flower-bedecked balconies overhanging various curious back alleys to the smallest, dingiest street-side cafe—a dilapidated sweetness permeated the old-world character of the streets we walked. Perhaps an hour is nothing in such a place, yet it seemed a fine way to walk the sun down.

Once it was dark, we drove Otto uptown to the corner of Napoleon and Tchoupitoulas. We knew we had come to the right neighborhood when many of the parked cars began to sport bumper stickers saying, "I'd rather be Cajun dancing." The bikers for Operation Mexico had mentioned to Don that if we were at all inclined to hear some good Cajun music, we had to go to Tipitina's, where every Sunday night Bruce Daigrepont's Cajun Band played from five to nine.

And the minute we heard the happy rhythms of the noisy, Frenchy, upbeat Cajun song pumped out into the night air from accordion, fiddle, guitar, voice, and drums—well, even the foot-sore Walker had to squeeze onto the crowded dance floor at least once before the night was over. Not that either Don or I could do much more than approximate "Cajun dancing," which looked to me like some wonderful, quirky cross between the polka and the jitterbug.

At seven, when the band took a break, red beans and rice were served "on the house" to all comers as long as the supply lasted. And considering it cost us only three dollars apiece to get in, I thought this was a rather generous tradition to keep up.

Tipitina's was jammed and jammin' the whole time we stayed—old people, young people, babies in tow. And, as long as the music played, everyone, whether seated at tables, crowded at the bar, or vertical on the dance floor, was rocking, and swaying, and jumping, and bouncing to the beat. When I went outside more than once for a breath of fresh air, I was surprised each time not to see the rickety building itself dancing on its foundation.

It was a clear night and, city lights or no, I easily found what I went out to look for—the conjunction of Venus and Jupiter in the southwestern sky. These brilliant planets seemed to hang like jewels just inches beyond my reach. On many clear nights in the desert I had been watching while they approached one another, traversing the fixed fence posts of stars—Venus more recently rising out of the west, Jupiter coming long months from the east. I had seen their conjunction once before, many years earlier on a sojourn in the Caribbean, and I wondered how many years it would be till I saw them again, and where I would be then.

But we did not get out of the area of greater New Orleans the next day with our charmed visions of this city undisturbed. Even while we were at Tipitina's, when we happened to mention that we were camping, we were warned by means of some grim stories to be careful.

The next day, while Don was walking the city, I went on an errand that took me in another direction. Besides swallowing the day completely, I found my trusting confidence devoured in the process. I met a young woman who was about eight months pregnant at the Triple A Office, where I was replenishing our travelers checks. We had a long wait in line together and she began telling me of a recent episode in her life.

It seems, in broad daylight, boxed in by cars on all sides at a busy intersection, when she was temporarily held up by a red light, some juvenile delinquents threw a brick through her car window (brick and broken glass hitting her in the stomach) in order to snatch her purse off the passenger seat next to her. And though she was lucky enough to find a policeman right away, while still keeping in sight the gang of delinquents who apparently had not run far, the policeman refused to go after her purse. He said he wouldn't go up against so many for such a trifle. When the woman yelled at the policeman in her frustration, he threatened to arrest *her*. When she got her car window fixed, the place that fixed it told her they get dozens of broken windows like that a week—broken for the same reason. When she tried to get a newspaper to print her story as a warning to others, they refused, not wanting to hurt the tourist trade.

I was as much moved by this woman's righteous indignation as I was shaken by her account. Her story hovered over me like a phantom. Suddenly I could see the dark underside of the dilapidation and decay, which I had thought so charming only the day before. Well, but it was charming—yet obviously there was more to it.

I was thankful I did not have to park and wait in much of the area I drove through that afternoon to get out of the city, but I still had a rather nervous time, finally, getting to the section of Route 90 where I was to meet Don. Not long before I pulled over to wait for the Walker, I had driven through a trashy stretch of rundown businesses and massage parlors that revolted me. Visions of thieves and drug-maddened criminals, of lackadaisical police and helpless victims—played in my head. I kept hearing the young pregnant woman's voice expressing sadness, anger, and frustration. I hoped Don was okay. It felt strange and unsettling not to have seen him all day.

While I waited, I pondered where I was. By the map and various signs, I was still within the city limits of New Orleans, but it really didn't look like city anymore. That was the thing I had to keep learning about this journey: we were never long enough in one place to be sure what really went on in a particular area, or what was its most recent history, or what it was liable to become. Were places *always* what they seemed? Of course not, but whatever I told myself, I just couldn't shake the bad feeling I had.

I felt as if I had been warned to keep up my guard, without really understanding how I could. Every car that passed me seemed to be going a little too slowly—looked suspicious, and now that the sun was getting lower in the sky, there weren't enough cars. It troubled me that we would have to camp somewhere in the vicinity. How quickly the mood of the journey could change—from seeming triumph to seeming disaster. All my instincts said, "Move on"—and when the Walker appeared at long last, without any more bad news to report, we did move on—at least as far as finding a safe place to camp, which turned out to be in the back yard of a small marina, with permission of the kindly owners.

Chapter 78

Ninety-Three Days

Don walked out of Louisiana in the rain. He hiked a fairly narrow spit of land between Lake Ponchartrain on the one hand and Lake Catharine and Lake Borgne on the other, passing between dozens of little cottages perched high on stilts with names like "Mom's Dream," "Here 'Tis," and "Blisters 'n Corns." Sometime after noon, the Walker crossed the Pearl River into a new state—Mississippi. I waited at the border and took Don's picture—in the rain.

Don had planned on walking Mississippi in three days. He stuck to his plan. It rained with little let up the entire first day. Early in the state, a sign greeted Otto and me: "Unlawful to track mud onto highway." Somehow that struck me as ridiculous, or at least difficult to keep from doing, as there was a lot more mud around than pavement, and I was in the habit of pulling off the road to wait for the Walker. I could only hope the rain would quickly wash the evidence of Otto's misdeeds away.

When it rained nonstop again on our second day in Mississippi and the postmaster at Bay St. Louis called it "monsoon season," I didn't expect we'd see the sun again before we got out. What I could see of the state through the heavy, gray curtains of rain made me wish for clearer weather.

From the border much had changed. It seemed to me that the composition of the swamps was different. I didn't notice the bald cypress trees so much, and some of the trees to replace them I didn't

410

know. But suddenly, too, pines appeared—tall, skinny, telephone-pole-type pines. We began to see logging trucks for a while, yet not so many as we once had. Don could count a day's worth on one hand, which was fine with him.

And then rather suddenly, too, we were back at the Gulf. The beach sands had changed. Gone was the stone-gray, fine, hard-packed sand—now the color was that of French-vanilla ice cream, or possibly a pale mocha—and the sand had a softer, moundier look. The color of the seawater still seemed mostly brown, but it was hard to tell under such glowering skies.

In one area, Don walked past a series of long, long piers with thatched-roofed fishing cabanas at their misty ends. The rain made it seem as if the earth's horizon ended abruptly at the far-off cabanas. Sometimes the rains would seem to let up, but only perversely, that is, when the Walker was taking a break. Don walked beach walls, occasionally the beach itself where it was firm and flat enough, and sloshed through mud puddles for most of Mississippi.

And though we both looked out over the Gulf of Mexico, we wondered why there were no waves to speak of—especially on such stormy days. We only realized later that we were skirting the Mississippi Sound, protected by a string of outlying barrier islands forming Gulf Islands National Seashore, which stretched across Mississippi, the tip of Alabama, and into Florida waters. No wonder huge mansions and stately antebellum homes dared go without stilts and roll out their lawns studded with bright gushes of azaleas nearly to the water's edge—separated only by a boulevard and a beach.

Don hiked through Biloxi gawking at these palatial homes, "Beauvoir," the last home of Jefferson Davis, and still a shrine to southern independence, prominent among them. The Mississippi coast was a well-toured area, and neither Don nor I made any out-of-the-way discoveries or saw anything a tourist guide would not point out—until the last day.

I wrote to David: "Guess what? Later today we make Alabama! I love these smaller states—really makes me feel we are getting somewhere. And yes, we are finally breathing some dry air, the sun has come out. Not a wisp of cloud, not even a smudge of haze to murk up the blue. I have discovered a new clover—crimson clover—so deeply, vibrantly, ruby-like in color, this clover, that clumps of it look like soft beds of plush velvet. Also new—a wild, pale yellow flax; pink flea bane; and a magenta vetch—but wonder of wonders—flitting gently and leisurely about these blooms, as they work their way north—monarch butterflies! I would have never expected to see them in early March come all the way across the Gulf from their winter in Mexico! Of course, their return has nothing whatsoever to do with me, yet I feel personally blessed by each one—as if somehow I had suddenly done something right and merited this great reward."

The last night in Mississippi also brought on something not mentioned in tourist brochures. We were camped near the Singing River, though it seemed more ocean inlet than river.

"This is horribly stuffy, Don," I complained, throwing off my sleeping bag in frustration.

"I know, but what's the alternative?"

"Gosh, I don't know, but I'm so used to having a little breeze and the fresh night air that I think it might be better to brave the gnats."

"No way, Fran. Those gnats are killers. They come right through the screens and bite all night long and are about to drive me crazy. There are some in here right now, and if I don't kill them, they are going to make me kill something. We have to keep the windows closed."

"Do you think it's the time of year, or where we are camped, or—"

"I don't know," Don cut me off. "The mosquitoes are bad enough when the wind dies around here, but I think I prefer mosquitoes to gnats. At least the mosquitoes give you a clear target to swat at. Also if you don't see 'em, you're bound to hear 'em. And anyway, the screens keep them out. These gnats are so tiny they are practically invisible. I don't know what they have to bite with, but it feels like the point of a dagger."

"Well, I guess it's better to have gnats than some things," I said, philosophically.

"Like what?" Don wanted to know.

"Well," I mused, wondering what Don would think worse than gnats, "better gnats than, say, canebrake rattlesnakes. Remember that stuffed specimen they had at the museum in Jeanerette? Why, it was three times the length of my leg and as wide as my thigh at its mid-section. Someone said it could swallow a fawn whole—maybe a small deer, maybe a small person!"

"I think I would choose death by rattler over death by gnats," Don insisted. "It would be quicker and cleaner and you'd know you were dead. These gnats—only make you wish you were dead."

"I wish I was home," I countered. "David wrote today saying the snow on our deck looked like a layer of pearls, and that a cardinal has been visiting our feeder, and that—well, uh, the other news I'm not supposed to tell just yet. (For a second I'd almost forgotten that Don did not know that Patty, head coach of Team Ross, was planning to surprise the Walker with a visit in less than a week. I was dying to tell Don this news, because I knew how he would be cheered by it.)

"Ninety-three days," Don said.

"Ninety-three days," I echoed. It was a new way of saying, "Good night." But when I closed my eyes, I pictured something else David had mentioned in his letter. He said that the gossamer-silk thread he was reeling me home by was beginning to form quite a sizable ball. He said he was going to have to store it outside, it was getting so big—what with thirty or more miles' worth of it to wind up each day, and more than a couple thousand miles of it since California. I smiled. I felt the connection as if he was just drawing it taut. And, for the moment, that was all that mattered.

Chapter 79

Sanctuary

"Yes, this is Alabama," I wrote in my journal on March 12, east of Fort Morgan. "And somehow from the very first moment it has had its own flavor. We had only a taste of Mississippi and will have only a taste of Alabama, but at least the taste has varied.

"Now suddenly we see the red earth on the dirt back roads and where the pavement is ripped up for repairs. But the pines we saw in Mississippi are still about. I have noticed a few pecan orchards, which I last saw in the desert—these look more in place. The golden ragwort so prevalent in Louisiana has disappeared, and now the wild flowers come in various shades of purple—violets in the grass, spiderwort, the lyre-leaved sage.

"The magnificent evergreen magnolias and flowering redbuds, we have seen elsewhere, but not camellias—the state flower of Alabama. From a deep, rich carmine to a pale, pink peach to ivory white—these open, rose-like blossoms ornament good-sized, often tree-like shrubs, of dark, shiny evergreen leaves. Various types of camellias, someone told me, are in flower from September through April around here.

"It didn't register at first, but I think I actually drove some hills back there where we cut inland from Route 90 near Grand Bay. But now that we have returned to the Gulf where it is flat again, I could almost believe I imagined that beautifully uneven terrain—the sloping, tilting earth. Alas, the progress of spring has retreated again near the sea."

It was our second day in Alabama, and so far the main thing it had in common with Mississippi (besides mosquitoes, which we had learned to tolerate) was gnats. We had camped our first night in the state beside the Fowl River, not far from Heron Bay, south of Bayou La Batre, and suffered another airless sleep in Otto with all the windows shut tight. For all the stuffiness of it, it did not keep out the noises in the night. I could hear what sounded to me like knuckle-cracking frogs—the knuckle cracking somehow ascending a musical scale.

But by now, even if it meant a sleepless bout, I had mostly come to appreciate nature's nocturnal entertainments, as well as the dawn chorus of spring that followed on its heels. By now, too, Don and I were experts at finding out-of-the-way places to tuck Otto into, so that we could avoid, more often than not, the trouble and expense of having to hunt down or stay at official campgrounds.

After the town of Heron Bay, Don walked a long series of exposed bridges and causeways surrounded by saltwater and sea life—gulls, terns, and red-billed black skimmers—from Cedar Point to Dauphin Island, where we then ferried across Mobile Bay to Mobile Point, near Fort Morgan.

While waiting for the Walker on Dauphin Island, I found a sanctuary—not "bird" or "wildlife" sanctuary, but simply "sanctuary," which I loved the better for its inclusiveness.

It would have been pleasant to have the whole day, instead of a mere hour, to wander the enclosed and forested sanctuary paths. The moment I set foot inside, I knew it had been far too long since I had had the thrill of being away from the road on a walk. No matter where I was or what the weather, an hour's walk was an hour well spent; but to wander away from the road, or even from the path, to a place where one was beckoned by that mysterious, undefinable something, never fully understood—was to step out of time for a while and have the soul restored.

On the half-hour ferry ride from Dauphin Island to Fort Morgan, after skirting more oil rigs, we noticed the water color of the Gulf gradually changing from brown to green. The beaches leading from Alabama into Florida were changing, too—the sand getting whiter and whiter, the waters clearer and clearer. Cars and dune buggies were not allowed on the beach here, and small, sheltering dunes were fringed with sea oats and other salt- and sand-tolerant plant life.

State parks protected the Fort Morgan beaches from abuse and development, and later the Bon Secour National Wildlife Refuge did—where I suddenly had my feet upon a path again for the second time in one day; and where the chief thrill, besides the wild solitude, was the purported presence of alligators and an impending thunderstorm. I missed seeing any alligators and got soaked instead. When I got back to Otto, the Walker was just finishing his lunch—dry and smug.

"Fran, I met an armadillo and I heard an alligator roar," Don announced excitedly, making room for me as I climbed into Otto dripping with the recent shower. I sat down on the cooler, wanting to avoid getting the seat wet.

"It was back there—I saw this big alligator—at least four feet long, and the next thing I knew, it roared, then splashed down into a swampy pool, and disappeared with about four little ones going after it. But the armadillo was just poking along, when I was cutting back from the beach to the road, and it didn't notice me at all—and I swear, I had to step out of *its* way. I don't think they see too well—very strange looking, those things."

"Don," I said, taking a towel to my head, "you see all the alligators. I haven't seen any. And I have only seen dead armadillos—acres of them." I felt sure I had missed my last chance for alligators, since ahead of us the shore areas were more dedicated to people than wildlife. "You heard an alligator roar? I didn't know they roared. They always look so spookily silent, lying there in the zoos. I didn't know they made any noises."

"I've heard them hiss, too." Don bragged.

"Well, next time don't scare them all off and come get me, Don. I would love to see an alligator in the wild. Or even, for that matter, a live armadillo."

That would have been all we saw of Alabama, except Don decided to take off Sunday, March 13, to meet up with his old friend and swim buddy Rich Mazey, from Washington University (in St. Louis) days.

We drove back to Mobile via Route 98, through pretty little Alabama towns like Point Clear, Fair Hope, and Magnolia Springs. This was after Don had walked a morning's leisurely stroll along the beach at Gulf Shores, not far from our campsite, where the college students were beginning to swarm on their spring breaks. Don enjoyed the endless parade of these kids up and down the beach as much as he did the sea.

But when we got to the Mazey household in Mobile, I thought it was even more playfully congested than the beach. Rich and his wife Susan had plenty to do on a Sunday afternoon, with five children under five years of age—the youngest three of them triplets, eighteen months old. I don't know how they fit us into their busy schedules, but we not only went out on the town, Dr. Mazey also arranged a physical for Don at the Pro-fitness Center early the next day.

"Quite a family, huh, Fran," Don commented on our rushed drive to get back to The Walk again at Gulf Shores.

Amazing—all those little personalities—so much going on at any one time—so many needs to be met. Remember diapers, Don?"

"What do you mean—wearing them?"

"Right. Hey, what's the verdict as far as your physical?"

"Mostly the test results won't be in for a while. They'll be sent home to be compared with tests done before The Walk and after. But my weight's holding at 144 pounds, and I have 11.2% body fat, and nothing seems to be malfunctioning."

"I guess not," I said. "Hey, the radio said it got down into the twenties last night and is going to plunge again tonight."

"And I thought we would have seen the last of winter by the time we got to Florida," Don said.

"You haven't gotten to Florida yet," I corrected.

"Well, I will have by the time we're camping tonight, Fran. Do you think there's enough flesh on a gnat to freeze?"

"That's a hope, isn't it. Maybe their daggers will get brittle and fall off."

Chapter 80

Like a Stroll About Town

That night, we camped at Big Lagoon State Park in Florida, after Don had walked beaches and beach roads off and on for twenty-five miles, a cold north wind keeping all flying insects at bay. While the sun was out, there was plenty of warmth in Otto, but the minute it set, it wasn't gnats I was worrying about freezing. I decided to warm myself up for the sleeping bag by taking a hot shower, but when I got back, Don said we were invited over to our camp neighbor's RV for tea and toast. Now this sounded like a real treat before bed, and it was.

John and Helen Kallis were snowbirds from Maine who were about to head north again. Spring was clearly signaled, not so much by the weather as by the influx of the college crowd, apparently. John and Helen reminded Don and me of his late Pinel grandparents from Boston. And then it turned out the Kallises once lived in Boston and even knew of the Pinel family. These petite, elderly people in their late seventies looked like a couple of snug hobbits in their cozy winter home on wheels. I gazed a little longingly at their thermostat when Helen got up once to adjust it for more heat.

John and Helen talked about their travels as snowbirds, the jobs they once held, and how John had been ill with a terminal form of cancer many years before. John laughed and said that he had fooled the doctors by outliving each one of them. Helen had been a nurse on the floor, and they hadn't been married long at the time. When she took the liberty of reading John's chart at the foot of his bed, she discovered it said, "Prognosis: death."

"We changed the way we lived after his operation then," Helen said in her homey-sounding Boston accent. "We didn't take life so seriously. We slowed down. We lived each day as it came—one day at a time, that is, as if each day were a gift."

"You know, that's just what makes my walk possible," Don agreed.

The theme of The Walk was the theme of the week, it seemed, even when I thought back to conversations with the Mazey family, but it came up again the following day. I had driven ahead of Don to scout out some morning heat; I finally found a little place called the Time-Saver Deli.

The atmosphere inside was more grocery than cafe, but there were a few tables, the tea was good and hot, and I decided to stay where it was warm and catch up a bit in my journal. A couple of men having coffee smiled at me and politely wanted to know what I was working on. I briefly told them about The Walk, but it didn't seem to lead anywhere until the Walker himself came along.

I introduced Don to the two men, Ron and Herman. Don exchanged a few comments about the weather, but did not sit down, simply grabbed a couple of doughnuts, said goodbye, and marched on.

After Don was gone, suddenly the two men seemed to come to life with curiosity. They both shook their heads in disbelief, wanting to know how in the world Don could keep up that pace, day in and day out. I told them the one-day-at-a-time story. And at that, the men laughed and nodded their heads enthusiastically.

"Why, that's exactly *our* philosophy," Ron said. "We're both members of AA—Alcoholics Anonymous. That's what we believe—just try to stay dry one day at a time."

"It's a pretty good philosophy," Herman agreed. "Guess it'll work for a lot of things."

"Hey, you're a writer," Ron said. "Any chance you could stick around for a while? I think you should meet a friend of ours. He usually comes in, long about now."

"Sure," I said, a little hesitant and curious. "I can stay for a while, anyway."

"You see, Fran, he has a remarkable story—you might be interested in it." And then Ron and Herman proceeded, by turns, to tell me about their buddy, Bob.

Bob was a Blue Angel fighter pilot shot down in Vietnam—but was apparently the only American to be taken and held captive by the *Chinese* during that war. He spent five-and-a-half years in solitary confinement—five-and-a-half years without any human companionship or even conversation. I think they said that the only book he was allowed to have was a dictionary. He suffered a broken back from his plane crash, which was never properly taken care of, and had other permanent disabilities thanks to the tortures and cruel treatment of his inhumane incarceration.

Ron and Herman were both amazed that Bob did not seem even a little bitter over his experience, and they both thought that someone should write his story. And there was an ironic twist. It seems that one of Bob's main Chinese interrogators, and exactly how they knew this I don't know, was now working at the Chinese Embassy in Washington, D.C. Moreover, Bob had expressed a desire to meet this man again, his Chinese interrogator, though he had no vengeful feelings toward him and felt the man had only been doing his job.

I sat there musing for a while, trying to imagine what this reunion might be like. And then I was reminded of the woman Don had met a few months earlier at the conference in Fresno, California, who was looking for someone to write *her* story—about being shipwrecked and stranded at sea for months with a friend and two men, who ended up being at odds with the two women, and who threatened their lives in various ways the entire time.

Well, I was beginning to wonder who didn't have amazing stories to tell. A perimeter walk could seem like a stroll about town by comparison.

Bob never showed that morning, and though Ron hoped I could maybe drop in again the next morning, I really didn't think I could. That was the day Patty was to arrive. But I left the Time-Saver Deli immensely touched by the encounter with these men. They were rugged-looking, not un-handsome men in their fifties, I was guessing, who had seen a lot in life but who, in spite of all, still had enthusiasm for it and hopes for the future. I didn't really know if I was their writer or not. First I would have to sit down one day and try to tell my own story. Yet I would not forget these men, nor the fighter pilot I hadn't met.

Chapter 81

Someone from Home

Florida—we were actually in Florida—the state that would bring the Walker to the East Coast, the state that would complete the third side of the roughly rectangular walk, the state in which we would at long last make that left-hand turn north to head more directly home. True, it was not going to be a quick walk to cross it, but Patty was going to be visiting, and not many days after she left, David would be visiting; and though the wind blew rough and chill out of the north those first few days, it served to check my overheating sense of anticipation. Neither was the Walker tempted to linger on the breezy beach in the sun.

On March 15, Don walked from Big Lagoon State Park in and around Pensacola, and did not make it back out to the beach until late in the day. He spent his last five miles walking the bright white sands on Santa Rosa Island. He did not know Patty was coming the next day, but he was so cheerful it was hard for me to imagine he didn't know. I was sorely tempted to tell him anyway, and if I hadn't been distracted later by a beach walk myself, where we had driven back to camp at Fort Pickens, I might have blurted out the secret simply to relieve my own mounting excitement.

Instead, I suddenly lost all track of where I was, or even that my feet were connected to the earth. Indeed, Don also seemed to forget himself while climbing over the dunes and strolling lengths of beach to see the sun go down. But it wasn't so much the sunset that was diverting as it was some indescribable harmony of dune, and sandbar, and sea life caught between water and sky—caught but not fixed—moving, changing, shifting, seeming—as the sun fell.

Water that seemed not water, but depending on whether I turned toward the light or away—was now millions and millions of yards of silken sheets spread wrinkling to the horizon, somehow lit from below; or now, looking into the sun, became a beaten gold glazing the crumpled surface. Closer at hand, the water seemed only one great liquid jewel, yet with such optical clarity one could read a book looking down through five feet of it. The colors of turquoise, sapphire, and aquamarine saturated the jewel with every subtle shading possible.

Yet there were details fitting none of this, as where a troop of sanderlings and larger pipers hunched over and probed the lacy wave-washed sands for hidden creatures that nevertheless sent bubbles to the surface—bubbles that the long-reaching beams of light then transformed into individual, flaring star-fires, or so many dozens of diamonds twirling on edge, dazzling the eye. And all the while, the bubbles burst one by one or the diamonds fell or the stars went out—whichever—only to come again.

Later, though I saw the folly of trying to describe any of this, I couldn't help myself. I wrote and ended thus: "The goodness of something unspoiled is as far beyond words as heaven itself. Perhaps one ought to be reduced to silence, and undoubtedly at the deepest level I am. What, of all that ineffable beauty, can be contained in a mere matter of sentences anyway. And yet, with all my heart and soul and mind engaged, I am driven to respond, striking out upon the white page, as if a glimmer might yet rub off."

At day's end on March 6, while Don was making his way through a throng of pedestrians near Fort Walton Beach—suddenly a familiar face appeared among them, coming toward him. Patty bobbed along nonchalantly, carrying a red rose, and deliberately trying not to see Don or smile. But when the Walker recognized Patty, he managed to catch her eye, and, even before they met, the two of them started laughing. And though Don admitted later that he knew nothing of this beforehand, he was not all that surprised that Patty had come, since the two of them had long ago formed a mutual admiration society founded partly on cheering each other on in just such athletic endeavors. Patty had been at the Long Lake reunion too, and as head coach of Team Ross, wanted to report back to all the other members how the Walker was "really" doing.

Patty had also come recovering from a bout of bronchitis and needed to rest and relax, and so planned to put in a fair amount of time on the beach in the sun. And though she joined the Walker for some walks, she mainly kept him company on breaks, and, like Rick who had visited in Oregon, lent to both of us the enthusiasm of her holiday frame of mind.

I knew Patty and Don had many things to talk about that did not concern me, so I took advantage of some of my time alone to do some wandering from the beaten path and to relax in a way that simply wasn't possible when Don and I had only each other to depend upon. It felt good to be able to let down my guard somewhat. Also, Patty had a car, which was an advantage—whether for helping me do errands during the day, or scouting out campgrounds, or using it when she and Don wanted to take in a movie or go out on the town after the day's long trek.

As long as Patty was with us, from Fort Walton Beach to Apalachicola, the mood of The Walk, whatever the typical daily grind of miles, was more carefree than it had been for months. Indeed, we were a lot closer to participating in the general party atmosphere then invading the Florida Gulf beach towns than we would have been without Patty's good humor tempering both Don's and my own.

She couldn't have come at a better time. The unseasonable cold quickly moderated, the sun could suddenly almost be depended on, and our campsites were miraculously free of gnats. That week we had plenty to celebrate—nine full months on The Walk, the seven-thousandth mile, crossing into the Eastern Time Zone (Otto's clock now only waiting for Daylight Saving to finally be synchronized with home time), and the vernal equinox, the first official day of spring—not to mention the first and last swim in the Gulf.

Patty's last day with us, Don took the day off—only his second day off in over two-thousand miles. We spent much of the day on the beach behind the high dunes in St. Joseph Peninsula State Park.

"Pew! I thought I would never get past that paper mill in Port St. Joe yesterday," Don commented, as the three of us read or simply relaxed on the sand. "It stunk up the atmosphere so bad, I almost did not want to come out here for fear it wasn't far enough away. I guess the wind is blowing in the right direction. You guys were lucky you weren't walking through."

I looked up to see a father-and-son fishing team suddenly land a stingray on the shore. They took it off the hook and left it flopping on the beach and did not add it to their bucket of fish.

"Must be eighty degrees today or higher," Patty said, closing her magazine and unscrewing a bottle of sunscreen. "It's almost hot. I wonder what it is back in Vermont."

"I talked to David already this morning, but I don't think you really want to know, Patty," I said. "Boy, you've really managed to get some sun." And I thought to myself how healthy and aglow Patty was—just as if she *had* been on vacation. I hoped she felt as good as she looked.

"No, come on, Fran, tell me—what did David say?"

"Well, it was ten degrees below zero on the mountain this morning, and all of five degrees in Middlebury."

"No," Don said, incredulous. "Below zero this late in March?"

"That's right."

"It's a good time to be on The Walk, then," Don said.

"Well, anyone up for a jog? I might as well overheat myself while I can. Tomorrow I'll be back in the arctic cold," Patty said, stretching and getting to her feet. "And hey, anyone want to go rescue that stingray with me?"

"Yeah, let's," I said, jumping up, "but I pass on the jog."

"I'll jog with you," Don volunteered. "But I won't try to keep up. Still, if I don't move my legs back and forth a little today, they might start to get the idea that this is a permanent halt."

Patty and I approached the fisherman and his son. I asked if they were planning on keeping the stingray they caught. When they shook their heads no, Patty and I each grabbed a winglike fin and dragged it to the sea's edge. I breathed a sigh of relief when it seemed to come to life again at the touch of the water. We stood there watching until finally it sailed through the shallows, out of sight. Don and Patty then took themselves down the beach—two athletes on a run, a skier and a walker, perhaps the prime of youth and the prime of middle age. It would have been hard to say who looked more fit.

March 21, I wrote in my journal: "Patty is gone. I feel the painful absence of a good companion. I know Don does too. I saw it coming and I prepared for it to no avail. I cried anyway. I had forgotten how much richer is the company of someone you know, and who knows you, than that of strangers—most especially someone from home. All those laughs—she did us much good, and I can only hope we did her some too.

"Now what to do until David comes? Four more days? I might as well start counting the seconds and get it over with. What's that about living one day at a time? Fat chance. And yes, I begin to comprehend eternity in an hour, William Blake."

East of Apalachicola, we camped one night on a dirt clearing at an oysterman's put-in. At dawn a few oystermen began arriving in the heavy fog, so that I waked to see these men standing up and poling their old wooden oyster boats slowly out into the mists. A woman had told Patty and me the day before what hard work "oystering" is and how heavy are the tongs that the men use to pluck the oysters from their beds—more than ten-thousand acres' worth of them in the territory.

Later that day I wrote: "I have just walked Carrabelle Beach. I must assume the water is polluted because of the disgusting flotsam and jetsam the sea throws up. We are no longer on the open Gulf, but St. George sound, and though this beach looked pretty from a distance, walking it was not a savory experience. I do not even want to report what I saw. Don's walking it now, otherwise it's been Route 98 ever since somewhere before Fort Walton Beach. I'd say the last we saw of really pristine beach and be-jeweled water was back around Destin. The paper company at St. Joe surely has murked things up that once were clear—I don't know what else has, too many cities too near the beach, I suppose.

"I have been playing my recorder without relish. I have written one letter. I am not productive. I am hardly interested in my surroundings.

I am becalmed and not good for much of anything. Time feels like a leaden tomb."

East of Lanark Village and south of Sopchoppy, after more than two-hundred miles on the Florida Gulf, the Walker hiked inland. The next ocean water we would see would be the Atlantic. Inland Florida somehow seemed a surprise. It suddenly had a rural, almost deserted feel after the congestion along the coast. Rivers, springs, swamps, forest land, and a dearth of people meant more wildlife. It was just the distraction I needed. We had encounters with anhingas, armadillos, and alligators—black vultures, snowy egrets, and yes, the hated gnats.

"I can't stand it any longer," Don suddenly yelled in the dark of early night. We were camped beside the Econfina River, miles from any town. But it was too warm of a night even for Don to sleep with the windows shut, and the gnats had not given him a moment's peace.

"Okay, Don, I'm ready to do whatever you want me to do—but first, have you tried insect repellent?"

"Yes, and it's not working, and I don't care how far we have to drive or where we have to go—let's get Otto moving. We've got to get a motel—whatever the expense—that's the only answer."

And so we drove ahead fifteen miles or so to Perry, Florida, and took refuge indoors at a motel. At least we were safe from gnats. The noisy cool of air conditioning was a pleasant drone to sleep by. The Walker slept. Me? I lay awake in the cave-like dark, hoping the ten days David was going to visit lasted as long as the three I had just spent. A jumble of Lewis Carroll verses played in my head—

"The time has come," the Walrus said,

"To talk of many things:

Of shoes—and ships—and sealing wax—

Of cabbages and kings—

And why the sea is boiling hot—

And whether pigs have wings…"

"All mimsy were the borogoves

And the mome raths outgrabe."

Chapter 82

Hills and Bears?

March 26, I went to pick up David at the airport at Daytona Beach. I left the Walker somewhere on Route 98, west of Cross City, put over two-hundred-fifty miles on Otto going and coming, and got a blurred preview of Don's planned route across the Florida peninsula.

Don had long since decided that he would not extend The Walk very far south in Florida. He was beginning to think more closely of the timing that would bring him home again on, or just before, the last day of the school year. He couldn't be absolutely certain yet how much time he would need to walk the East Coast, but it made more sense to add some extra miles to the coast of Maine rather than to the coast of Florida, since Don would be closer to home at that point and could better time his arrival.

The drive to the Daytona Airport to get David seemed at least twice as long as the drive back to The Walk, once I had David at my side. But on the way I did have to drive through a bad thunderstorm, and was also held up by a terrible traffic accident—an accident I knew had suddenly and tragically either ended or dramatically changed the lives of its victims. Not many days later would be the thirty-first anniversary of just such an event in my own life, and I was rather badly shaken by this vivid and timely reminder.

But once David was with me in Otto, I have little memory at all of the return drive. We had a lot of catching up to do, and it was such a pleasure to talk at our leisure, I'm not sure how I did manage to drive. I think Otto must have been on automatic pilot.

"So, Francesca, what were you going to tell me about alligators and armadillos?" David asked, after I had devoured his news from home and there had been a lull. "You said when you called yesterday that you weren't going to bother writing it in a letter or tell me over the phone. You don't look to have been attacked—I haven't noticed any fingers missing. Got all your toes?"

I laughed. "No, well, I mean, yes, but it wasn't me—it was Don, but then he wasn't attacked, either. He could have been, though. It was a few nights ago. We got permission to camp in the parking lot of a lodge at Wakulla Springs State Park. We went way out of our way to get to the place, only to find there was no camping allowed in the park. Thank goodness the manager of the lodge took pity on us—not that the lodge parking lot was anything great. Anyway, Don decided to swim in the springs there, just at dusk. And I was thinking about getting in, myself. It wasn't until *after* Don got out, and I was exploring the bank, still half-wondering whether to take the plunge, when I noticed a sign—'Alligators—swim at your own risk.'"

David laughed. "You didn't go in, did you?"

"No, but then the next morning, while Don was doing his exercises in Otto, I had tea in the lodge. And that's when I found out about a big, old alligator that used to hang out there. And I mean *big*, David, and I mean *old*! Supposedly alligators can live for as long as two-hundred years and grow to be as much as twenty feet long. And this one was one like that!"

"But did you actually see any alligators there?" David asked.

"No," I admitted, "but I saw some just a day or so later—basking in the sun on a sandbar in the Fenholloway River. There were three of them—one about four feet long. Don saw them first, and then I drove back with him to get a look. Don dropped a stick near one—just as I was taking its picture from the bridge above it. I probably only got the tail because the gator fairly leaped into the water at the drop of that little twig. I was surprised at how fast it moved. But ugly? I mean, David—those creatures are ugly. The thought of swimming in the same water with one—well, it gives me the creeps. A two-hundred-year-old alligator must be pretty good at getting his meals, don't you think?"

"I prefer not to think about it," David smiled. "What about armadillos?"

"Well, they're not very cute, either. Yesterday I tried to take a picture of one nosing about an anthill, but before I could focus the camera, it noticed me and scurried into a flooded culvert nearby, which was covered with a steel grate. Still, I could stand directly above this armadillo and really get a close look. It floated in the water, just inches below the grate, blowing bubbles with its long, pink snout. I whistled quietly and talked to it, but I got no response. Yet when I picked up a small pebble and let it gently fall into the water next to it, suddenly it swam back, crawled out, and made a mad dash into a nearby swamp, every now and then leaping up as if someone had goosed it. I couldn't believe the noise that creature made—still in a crazy hurry a long while after. If anyone had come along just then, they would have thought an elephant was crashing through the swamp.

"Oh, David, I think I must be dreaming."

"Armadillos, or alligators?"

"Neither—but really, I can't believe here we are—in Florida again—I mean, exactly nine months ago, to the day, we were here. The year is almost over."

"The year is almost over," David repeated reaching over to give my hand a squeeze.

"Oh, I hope it's a good visit for you, and that we can escape the gnats somehow. I don't know what we'll meet up with in the middle of Florida of any interest, but in four days Don thinks he can make it to the coast, which should be fun. So then, gosh—this time I won't be combing the beaches of St. Augustine with Captain Kangaroo."

"Hey," David said with mock seriousness, "any more wisecracks and I'll shave it off again."

"Well, at least we don't have a crazy schedule ahead of us like California," I said. "It's just the routine of The Walk. Maybe it will be kind of relaxing, like North Dakota. And the next reunion—"

"The next reunion will be a lot closer to home," David interrupted, finishing my sentence. "But now let's concentrate on this one. We have *nine* whole days until I fly back from Jacksonville."

"But let's not count the days," I said. "Nine days really doesn't sound like much, to me. I think I prefer to lose all track of time for a while, if possible."

But I guess it wasn't entirely possible, though my sense of the passage of time did change. Except for jotting down a few daily notes, I wasn't writing—no letters, no journal, no newsletter. I would catch up with them later. Undoubtedly, that alone made the time David was with us pass differently. I had to realize, though, that slowing the journey itself was not all that desirable. Don's weary feet were ever and always counting out the miles—a continuing bit of harsh reality to work against other, more selfish considerations. Still, if only because I didn't have to be quite so alert, there was something rather dreamlike about those days.

The inland route following Alternate 27 to Ocala, and Route 40 afterward, did not have the best road conditions for the Walker. We had learned by now that wet areas meant almost no road margins, and rural routes too rarely had adequate breakdown lanes. Don was forced at times to walk more cautiously in the lush grass of spring, which often hid fire ant mounds, or holes and dips that could easily turn an ankle. The now bright, hot Florida sun was not necessarily a blessing to him, either. Heat meant more opportunities for blisters. The Walker complained about these things, but he also, it seemed to me, recovered his good cheer even more quickly than he normally did—as if a complaint to a sympathetic audience of two, rather than one, had more satisfaction in it.

But the Florida interior did have its blessings. We were all astonished to come upon a series of lovely hills—especially Don, whose legs had almost forgotten what it was to climb up, or down, for any extended period of time. Every now and then, at the peak of one of these hills, we could even catch a distant view—which filled Don and me both with a certain nostalgia, however fleeting.

West of Ocala, the green and rolling hills constituted "horse country"—the heartland of the Florida thoroughbred industry. East of Ocala was the only subtropical national forest in the continental United States, punctuated by bear crossings, no less. All of us had been to Florida many times, but hills and bears had never formed part of the picture of Florida with which any of us was familiar. The bubbling springs in the Ocala National Forest were also a surprise.

"What do you think, Don?" I asked the Walker, who was pulling himself up out of a clear, freshwater pool after an end-of-the-day swim at Juniper Springs. "Pretty nice, huh?"

"Great," Don said. "No warnings about alligators, either. I'm glad you guys discovered this place. Hey, how did Otto's big tuneup go in Ocala?"

"Expensive, but anyway it's done, and I hope he's fit for the final push home," I said.

"What do you say to camping here, Don?" David asked.

"Sounds good—I wouldn't mind taking a morning swim, too," Don replied, wrapping the towel he had used to dry off about his waist.

"We found a great nature trail too, Don. You should hike it, though I don't suppose you could stand any more walking, but I almost think it would be worth it. You should see the way the springs bubble up through the white sands in the slow, limpid streams—looks like they're boiling almost, sort of like cream of wheat would."

"No way, Fran. The swim felt great, though—anything to get off these aching feet. But I'm ready to head back to Otto—that's enough walking for me."

"Don, what *is* your secret? People following The Walk at home often come into the store and make some comment about how hard it must be mentally to face the road each day," David observed.

"That's the secret right there—mentally it's not hard at all," Don tried to explain, sitting down again. "There is plenty to see and think about out there on the road; there really is. One has to stay alert. It's the physical aspect of The Walk that I have never really gotten used to. Every day seems like some new challenge to my feet. I thought I could get used to walking thirty miles—but all along my legs have wanted to quit at twenty-five or even twenty."

"It's amazing, though, however one looks at it—that you can keep on keeping on," David responded, shaking his head.

"I'm afraid it'll have to be tuna sandwiches for dinner if we camp here," I said, changing the subject and beginning to pack up to go.

"That's okay with me, if it's okay with you guys. Oh, but hand me my fanny pack, Fran. I forgot to show you what I picked up today. We could even hit a restaurant if there were any around," Don said. He pulled out a five-dollar bill, two ones, and a blue-and-green plastic egg.

"Not exactly enough for a feast, Don," I said, "but that will raise the road kitty some."

"What's in the egg?" David asked.

Don tossed it to him.

"Oh boy," I said, when I saw David take out the steel-blue rubber robot inside. "Someone might miss the money, but Don, you can never pass up a toy, can you?"

"But Fran, this is unique," David teased. "Don't forget the collection—this will be another historical artifact." David tossed the egg back to Don.

"Anyway, Don, it's time to do another clearing out and send this stuff home. Whatever are we going to do with it all, anyway?"

"I don't know," Don said. "Let's eat."

That night we were surprised by fireflies and the first of many evening serenades to come of the chuck will's widow—whose loud, repetitious rounds of declaring its name I could never quite get used to.

The next day, while Don pounded out more miles on the road, David and I swam and hiked at Alexander Springs. Here the main clear water spring formed a small lake and was so deep that scuba divers far below us were almost the size of the little blue robot in the plastic egg. To float above these underwater explorers was to feel as if one was flying.

Our hike later on the Timucuan Indian trail turned up all sorts of familiar flora, including jack-in-the-pulpits surrounded by lush bowers of poison ivy—common enough later in spring much further north, but strange to see in the company of cabbage palms and other exotic, subtropical plants. Were we closer to home than I realized?

Chapter 83

In Less than Twenty-Four Hours

March 31, after nearly seven-thousand three-hundred miles, the Walker turned due north. From Ormond Beach, just above Daytona, until Don hiked out of Florida, he kept to the shore as much as possible. The sand beaches, especially at low tide, were just wide, flat, and firm enough to be good walking, and there was little if any vehicle traffic to be concerned about. It was also entertaining.

"I don't know," the Walker said to David and me at one point, "with all these college kids around on Easter break, sometimes I can almost think I'm one of them. Except for one thing."

"What's that, Don?" I asked. "Your age? No homework hanging over your head?"

"No—it's like this. There they are—practically naked at times, trying to get as much sun as possible—whatever they happen to be doing. And then I come along—completely covered up, looking like Lawrence of Arabia. Someone sees me and points a finger, and they all laugh, which usually makes me laugh, too. Sometimes they ask what I'm doing, sometimes they don't."

On April 1 Don made St. Augustine Beach. David and I had looked forward to revisiting St. Augustine, but The Walk brought it within easy range for only two days. Indeed, it was the continuing lesson of the journey that Don's pace, slow as it was, seemed incredibly swift whenever the terrain was particularly appealing or I was tempted to linger.

By Saturday of Easter weekend, April 2, Don was already setting foot on the beaches of Jacksonville. David and I, in charge of scouting campsites or hotel accommodations, realized a little too late in the day that we had a problem on our hands.

Of the camp sites in the area, we found that not a single one was available. And though there were literally skyscrapers-full of hotel rooms and hundreds of motels and beach bungalows, apparently none had a vacancy. We had trouble driving from one hotel to another, even to inquire about rooms, because the traffic at the beach was as slow and thick as crystallized honey—it took forever to move. Jacksonville was crazy. I imagined from a certain perspective, above, it must look like a swarming anthill. I felt panicky. The next day was Easter— David's last full day with us. I didn't want our final moments together spoiled by having to camp illegally or otherwise put up with road hardships that were going to be returning soon enough anyway.

And then, just as dark was about to descend, David came back from the last big hotel we had any hopes of getting a room in—with an interesting grin on his face.

"Do they have room for us there?" I asked hopefully.

"No—but don't worry, I think I found something that will do. The people in there were very helpful and let me call a place they knew about. Here, I'll drive—let's go rescue Don from the beach before it's too dark to find him."

And that's all David would say. But the next thing I knew, he was driving Otto up to a resort, far away from the busy beach scene, that sported a guard at the entrance gate, valet parking, and a class of cars in its parking lot that made Otto look like an abused mule. Instead of having to crowd into some shabby room of a fourth-rate motel— suddenly we had a suite in a rather palatial setting.

Don and I both wondered about the cost, but we were assured by David that we were getting once-only bargain rates, since the place had just opened. Anyway, I thought, if it's a dream, I'm not going to bother pinching myself; undoubtedly I will wake again on the morrow, returned to reality.

Meanwhile, Don swam leisurely laps in one of the three outdoor, heated pools—the only person in it, and David and I swam in another, which we also had to ourselves. There were several hot tubs, all sorts of tennis courts, a golf course, and fountains and gardens and—well, too much to take advantage of in one night. Indeed, I thought it was too much, period. But I gave in and enjoyed it anyway.

The following day was Easter and also, by coincidence, the first day of Daylight Saving Time. At long last Otto was back on home time! Now, too, Don would have plenty of daylight for walking and would not have to start so early in the morning if he did not feel like it. He celebrated the very next morning by lingering long enough to swim again in one of the Olympic-sized pools before hitting the sandy trail, which would lead to the last of the Florida beaches on Little Talbot Island by day's end.

While the Walker was making his way inland to Yulee, Florida, the next day, where he would begin following Route 17 north into Georgia, I said goodbye to David at the Jacksonville Airport. It was not really a sad parting, which surprised me.

Something was changing—or had changed. The unknown of the road ahead was certainly still there, but the cutting edge of it was missing. Anything could still happen, and yet, there was more room for confidence than ever. Indeed, almost the minute David was gone, I felt as if I had walked out of one dream only to enter another. I didn't know quite how to explain it to myself. We were still at least a couple of thousand miles from home, but something was already over.

In retrospect, I can see that whatever distance from home was still there—it no longer felt out of reach. It was possible, I realized a little belatedly, that I could get home—I mean, actually drive there from where we were in less than twenty-four hours. Ironically, I seriously began to wonder if I was really ready to *be* home. I could see the journey ending, and I realized, almost with alarm, that I still had some reckoning to do before it did.

In *Travels with Charley*, Steinbeck said, "Who has not known a journey to be over and dead before the traveler returns?" He wrote further: "The reverse is also true: many a trip continues long after movement in time and space have ceased." For Don, I think, the latter statement holds good. I could easily imagine from mere force of habit that Don would continue to walk on into his dreams, happily ever after. Given so many miles underfoot, and given Don's need for physical activity, how could Don not rise, as he was now, with the full consciousness of having to go another thirty miles before the sun set—no matter what he was doing? Steinbeck said about himself, "My journey started long before I left, and was over before I returned."

But for myself, I think, on the last leg north, as we honed in on our starting point—it was the physical journey that faded, while another one—in my head—was just beginning. On the physical plane, I felt like Steinbeck; in many ways, the moment I knew I could get there in a day's drive, I could almost feel the journey was over. But on a mental plane, it was another story—a new and different sense of journeying had just begun.

Part Ten

APRIL

Georgia, South Carolina, North Carolina, Virginia

Chapter 84

And I Would I Could Know

Don's trek through Georgia followed Route 17 north and took barely four days. The Walker made his way striding through Georgia grass, for the most part, since the road was narrow, but at least it was not busy, thanks to Interstate 95 being close by and taking the bulk of the traffic. Though we were no longer within sight of the Atlantic Ocean, we saw plenty of water, in the form of rivers and tidal estuaries. The low, flat land might have recalled the sea prairie on the Texas Gulf if it weren't for the abundance and variety of trees trimming the marsh edges, frequently interrupting a more extensive view.

Early April meant the youngest, tenderest green of spring overtaking the deciduous trees and shrubs just then leafing out, while the green in the marsh was more olive, still mixed as it was with the old, golden-beige of winter. Commonly springing from the wayside grasses were low-growing white lilies, wild sweet Williams in pinks fading to blue, rosy thistles, crimson clover, and bunches of blue-eyed grass. Yet these did not lavish the boldest, gaudiest splashes of color upon the countryside. For that, the azaleas, blossoming in every bright hue, especially in the vicinity of towns, would have to win the prize. At times these showy shrubs were in such profusion and climbed to such heights that their countless corollas seemed to tumble all over themselves in great, frilly cascades—a flower-fall of color. We began to see the feathery-leaved wisteria, too, with its heavy, grape-like clusters of blooms in blue and white, climbing about yards and forest clearings. Now and again the unfamiliar perfumes in the air were so strong as to be mildly obnoxious, yet because of the wayward breeze were difficult to assign to anything in particular. Spring.

Our way through Georgia was mostly quiet and uneventful, yet Don got a thrill when he crossed the bridge over the Altamaha River at Darien and found himself welcomed to McIntosh County. Not long after, Kathleen Russell interviewed the Walker McIntosh for the *Darien News*; and the rest of that same day, we came across the name McIntosh in a variety of settings—from a McIntosh Family Cemetery to a town named McIntosh on the map.

This town, upon closer inspection, proved to have nothing more to it, that we could find, than a small concrete-block building buried in weeds nearly as tall as it, labeled "182cond Court of Justice—8th Voting Precinct." But Don got the biggest kick from meeting George McIntosh. This friendly Black man somehow got wind of the McIntosh Walker coming through and called Don over to his yard for a chat, proudly claiming to be descended from the McIntoshes who originally settled the area.

Our night in Darien, we stayed at a lovely colonial bed and breakfast called "Open Gates," owned and operated by two Middlebury College graduates who also had been expecting that Don might pass through. Phil and Carolyn Hodges graciously welcomed us. And though they were both transplants from other parts of the country, they served up the local history, along with the southern hospitality, in generous portions.

But what I enjoyed most about our visit was the sudden availability of books arranged on quaint, old book shelves and liberally distributed about the house. I stayed up late reading, breaking my vow, at least, for this night. And I felt something inside me come to life as I did. Indeed, on this northward trek, since David's last visit, knowing I was truly headed home, gradually I began to shed that sense I had had for so long—the same that I had communicated to family and friends— of feeling as if I had died and been given permission to correspond with the living.

Maybe the year had long since bottomed out; maybe the spring renewal itself couldn't help having a rejuvenating effect on anyone in the midst of it—whatever, I began to look through the windows of Otto less and more through the windows of my own soul; I began to realize the sense of deadness I had felt was, in reality, merely a kind of dormancy, like that of a seed that awaits the proper conditions to germinate. For me, picking up a tempting book off a shelf was a part of this process of coming to life. One of the books I happened upon fell open to Sidney Lanier's verse immortalizing "The Marshes of Glynn"—marshes that Don had skirted just the day before, near Brunswick, Georgia—marshes very similar in feel to ones we had met before and would meet again further north. Some of the lines haunted me, a Midwestern transplant to the Green Mountains of Vermont, in ways but for the journey, they might not have.

> "Oh, what is abroad in the marsh and the terminal sea?
> Somehow my
> soul seems suddenly free
> From the weighing of fate and the sad discussion of sin,
> By the length and the breadth and the sweep of the
> marshes of Glynn."

April 7, while Don walked McIntosh County, I quietly commemorated a significant childhood anniversary. Thirty-one years ago to the day, my family (mother, father, and six children) was in a car accident that killed my father and youngest sister and partially paralyzed my mother for life. I was eleven at the time and the second-oldest in the family. Needless to say, it was a nightmarish event for all of us— an event each of us struggled by various means and for many years after to recover from. It marked the beginning of an uncertain, almost chaotic, existence in which it was impossible not to flounder, not to doubt, not to despair at times—and for which, excluding the accident itself, no one was to blame.

Earlier in the journey—somewhere in California—I had contrasted our slow, steady movement with that of being "in place"— the difference between being at center, like a sun, or in revolution, like a planet. At home, in place, we are all like suns at the centers of our separate worlds—people and events seeming to revolve about each of us. On a journey like this, like The Walk, I was more conscious of revolving about some other center. And this day in Georgia, as fair and dry as the day thirty-one years ago had not been, I suddenly wondered that the journey, which was taking us to all the edges of the continental U.S., had—as its center—my own place of origin, as well as the place of origin of Don and me as a couple. For me, these two particular, if unremarkable, beginnings were related. There, like a sun, was the great mass of material from which we were spun and thrown off, or escaped—who could say which.

Surely this journey we were on had something to do with our once-upon-a-time marriage, though Don and I had never really discussed it as if it had. However much I felt I might owe Don for sharing his life with David and me these past ten years, so that I could be closer to my children—on this day I recollected an older, deeper source of gratitude to him, one I had hated myself for ever betraying.

Four years after the trauma of my family's accident and all that came with it, loving and being loved by Don was like a gentle, steady, long-falling, life-giving rain following a parching drought. Later, that I had not been true to this love haunted me until…until…?

Well, that was it, I thought, it was to some extent plainly still haunting me. I looked up a passage from Proust that I had recorded in one of the commonplace notebooks I had brought with me. "There is no man…however wise who has not at some period of his youth said things, or lived in a way the consciousness of which is so unpleasant to him in later life that he would gladly, if he could, expunge it from his memory. And yet he ought not entirely to regret it because he cannot be certain that he has indeed become a wise man—unless he passed through all the fatuous or unwholesome incarnations by which that ultimate stage must be preceded." Though I had found solace in these words when I first stumbled upon them, and later practically committed them to memory, I understood that the truth of them hung on whether or not a person had gained a certain wisdom from past errors. Surely I had, yet *if* I had—why was I still haunted?

Later that day, April 7, on Route 17 in Georgia, I came upon a tiny chapel, out of sight of any other buildings, tucked into the shade of an old and magnificent live oak. A sign declared the place to be "the smallest church in America." Ten by fifteen feet, the structure could harbor a dozen people, at most. I was there alone, and because a little, xeroxed brochure mentioned that weddings had been performed there, and since that was what was on my mind already, I sat there and wondered what makes a marriage sacred.

Surely it is not the marriage ceremony itself, I thought, *or any official document, or who actually joins a couple in marriage.* Neither the highest authority in the land nor the Pope himself could ensure that a marriage would last. Outside influences alone obviously cannot make two people take their commitment to one another seriously. What can? Something within those two people, plainly—something within and between—like love. The depth of commitment has to have something to do with the depth of that love—or stubbornness. *Can a love be stubborn?* I wondered. Well, if one could, I guessed that Don's and mine was.

Surely, I continued in my thinking, *it is not the physical union of two people that makes a marriage sacred, because marriages often successfully continue long past any dependence on physical love.* Some marriages have probably never known physical union and yet turned out to be good, if not procreative, marriages; just as physical union alone and by itself far too often falls short of being a tie that binds.

It had often been my hope that Don would marry again. There were some good possibilities in that direction that might have worked out or still could. But more and more, it seemed important to realize that I could not *make* things work out for Don that way. The most it seems I could do is stay out of the way and give my blessing when the time came, as Don so graciously did on my marriage to David.

But then I flushed red and felt my shoulders begin to burn with embarrassment, as I suddenly had to ask myself—*have* I been out of the way? And with the illumination of a lightning flash, for a second, I saw perfectly clearly that I was not. The journey itself was the incontrovertible evidence. Perhaps I had rushed in to become the driver before it was really necessary. Perhaps, if the vacuum had been there even a little bit longer, someone else would have become the driver? Was my "debt paying" only an excuse to stay "in the way," so to speak? Was I haunted by past wrongs because I had never really let go and gone on with my own life? Surely I would have been happy to rearrange Don's life to assuage my own conscience. Hadn't I even tried that at times? Now was I trying something else? Yet surely there was little wisdom in it. Maybe—it struck me again in another blinding flash—maybe Don *was* doing this walk for me—that is, by letting it seem that I was doing it for him?

Oh dear, I puzzled, as a certain darkness returned, *I will never get to the bottom of all of this*. And I recalled the lines of Lanier at the conclusion of my spiraling contemplation:

"And I would I could know what swimmeth below when the
    tide comes in
On the length and breadth of the marvelous marshes of
    Glynn."

Chapter 85

Numbers Are Just Numbers

As for what swimmeth above? *That* Don and I were coming to know rather too well—gnats! One day only in Georgia was not plagued by these creatures—a day the wind blustered so strong out of the north, under a clear sky, that the gnats must have been blasted back to Florida. But like the mosquitoes we met going west in the summer, we were learning gnats also came in more than one variety. In Georgia, people called them "sand gnats," and though these were small and clever enough to penetrate Otto's screens, they gained quite visibly in size once bloated on a person's blood. It was the warmer, more humid weather we ran into, which did not always boast a breeze, that made the gnats bothersome, even by day. Thank goodness weather in the southern spring was not a settled matter. Bouts of rain and cold brought relief; and whatever the trials of a storm, gnats were not one of them.

When the Walker left Georgia behind, he did so by strolling through Savannah, its oldest city. He crossed the Savannah River and set foot on South Carolina soil wondering mainly about one thing—gnats.

That night at our camp site on South Carolina's Combahee River, I wrote to David: "Don't ask me what I am doing—I mean, if you could, that is. I probably look like I have St. Vitus's Dance—but I am only gnat-crazed. The things are everywhere. Today where I bought groceries—even on the asphalt parking lot—they were swarming!

The little boy who helped carry out my groceries was attacked and ran off in the middle of our conversation because of them. Then a swarm got into Otto when I was putting the groceries away. Ugh!

"But at day's end I found what I thought was a good camp site. I sat and played my recorder watching carefully to see if any gnats were about. All seemed okay. But now—now that the sun's down, now that we're all settled, now that Officer Hamilton of the South Carolina State Patrol has put his blessing on our camping here—well, now the gnats are all over the place. I am distressed. We've had to go on a bloody rampage. We are enduring the suffocating stuffiness of being sealed in a can—only every now and then, Don momentarily dares to crack a window for a puff of air. I guess we are lucky it's no warmer.

"Coastal Georgia has bled imperceptibly into what's known as the Low Country of South Carolina—piney backwoods, watery marshes, nasty gnats and all. So far the only difference I've detected is *maybe* the river waters we've crossed are less murky here. Georgia seemed to have a lot of brown water, and places where the banks of mud looked exactly like chocolate pudding—slick, shiny, and dark."

I put down my pen and tried to think of something more cheerful to write.

"I liked Savannah, didn't you, Don?" I called down to the Walker.

"Yeah," Don said without much enthusiasm, as he cracked the window again for a few seconds and turned a page of his magazine.

"All those lovely squares," I went on. "A lot of parks like that make a city more habitable—and it couldn't have been prettier, with all the spring flowers and so many trees blooming—red buds and dogwoods—tons of azaleas. I liked all the Georgian colonial and Greek revival buildings too."

"What?" Don asked, as if he hadn't been listening.

"You know, all the old buildings—the place had character, don't you think, Don?"

"Yes, but it must have had something like a paper mill nearby, too—too bad the flowers couldn't have covered up the stink of that. Didn't you smell it?"

"Yeah," I admitted. "Anyway, suddenly I am just thinking how good it is to move on. It would be pretty tough for any place to make me want to linger now."

"Long as there's these blasted gnats—that's for sure," Don added. "Hey, I forgot to mention a funny thing that happened the other side of Savannah. The sun was beginning to bake me, so I pinned on a few dishtowels and bandannas for shade. A while later a state trooper stopped me to ask what I was doing. I explained about The Walk and offered him my card, which he just waved aside. He didn't want it. He said, 'Know why I really stopped? 'Cuz I ain't never seen nobody dressed like you before.' And then he laughed."

"Well, I guess you are a sight, Don."

"And you know what, Fran?"

"What?"

"I am sick to death of even mentioning The Walk."

"You can say that again. Time to be off this adventure. Funny, but during the first months, every fifty miles or so seemed such an accomplishment—whereas now, well, I don't know—the numbers are just numbers."

"Sixty-three days," Don sighed, turning out his light.

"Sixty-three," I echoed, and went back to writing my letter by flashlight.

Chapter 86

The Big Journey

Don skirted South Carolina marshes along Route 17 all the next day and the day after, approaching Charleston. Swallows and purple martins swooped over low bridges; white egrets, wood storks, and the great blue haunted the far-flung water thickets; fish crows cried; the mockingbird sang; and the gnats endured—or, rather, we endured the gnats. Rain caught the Walker north of Beaufort; and at Ravenel, South Carolina, unsettling news caught up with us both: the serious illnesses in the family and among friends had taken turns for the worse.

I wrote in my journal: "How quickly the world changes. And yet the un-startled blue sky is just that—un-startled. But would I even want the natural world to be in sympathy with my feelings? I think not. Should the birds *not* sing because I am moved by the suffering of others? Or because I suffer myself? No, we are, in a way, cut off from their world—and they, the wild things, are cut off from ours— undoubtedly to spare us a worse catastrophe: the world falling apart because we fall apart. Thank goodness things do go on—there is always the outside chance that we will recover and *want* to catch up later, however much we might not want to now.

"Yes, and Life, while it is ours, is the BIG journey, we think. But maybe not. Maybe it's just a warm up for a bigger journey yet. Most of the time I cannot help thinking this. Most of the time it's not hard to believe that our days here on earth are only a prelude. There is

450

more to come; it is not all right here. It does not quite make sense to me unless I allow that all of it—of Life, is more than so many miles walked, so many places visited, so many friends made, so many deeds done. It is more than the adventure of each one of us—and even more than the adventures of all of us."

From Ravenel, April 12, Don walked thirty miles to Whitehall Terrace, South Carolina, passing Charleston about halfway between, in time for lunch—also in time to be greeted by the Summerville High School Band, playing in honor of the bicentennial of the U.S. Customhouse there.

Charleston seemed, like Savannah, another quaint old corner of paradise bursting with spring. Blossoms of every design crowned trees, crept along vines, tumbled over shrubs, and finally spilled into our path, so that the Walker and I both trampled fallen petals underfoot. Azaleas, wisteria, dogwood, spirea, and a hundred others I couldn't name adorned walkways, courtyards, dooryards, and whole sides of buildings until it seemed the old city itself was nothing but a bower for spring to clamber over and array herself upon and for onlookers to praise.

Before the Walker left Charleston, a cold rain began to fall and hurried him on his way. He crossed the Cooper River and walked past dozens of simple but picturesque lean-tos—basket stands in which a few of the Mt. Pleasant basket makers stayed at work, even in the rain. The traditional basketwork of sweetgrass, bulrush, pine straw, and palmetto, dating back to the early 1700s, was still deftly being made. This called attention to a cultural richness in the area of which I knew we were hardly getting even a taste.

Something of the charm of the basket stands was also reflected in the neat, little, ramshackley cottages and bungalows I'd been noticing, with tiny porches, well-tended flower gardens, and tidily trim yards. Sometimes these houses were gaily painted, sometimes not, but if they ever spoke of a certain poverty, they also spoke of imagination and resourcefulness. I could only wonder about the lives within.

I had worried some before traveling through the South about racial relations and how things would seem. In truth, we were too removed, too much skimming the surface, and too quickly moving on to notice much in the way of how people of one race treated those of another. At times all races seemed almost painfully polite in their manner toward us; at other times, open and friendly. We were tourists, outsiders, northerners—and we were treated, for the most part, like guests.

The only incident perhaps worth mentioning occurred near Waverly, Georgia. I had tucked Otto into the recesses of a small swamp thicket, hoping we could camp there escaping notice. But a Georgia State Trooper discovered Otto. "No, Ma'am," she said to me in a thick Georgia drawl, after I explained about The Walk and that I was waiting for the Walker, "it won't do to camp here—nor anywhere in Camden County along this route—it's too danged red-necky." She didn't explain any further, but recommended a campground over the county border. And though it meant driving over the same route a few extra times, we took her advice.

Between Charleston and the busy South Carolina beach scene was a rare coastal stretch of national forest. Route 17 cut across it. McClellanville, a sleepy little village, nestled within it. Situated on the Intracoastal Waterway, McClellanville, out of sight of the Atlantic, nevertheless harbored fishing, shrimp, and oystering rigs, but because of the forested atmosphere of the surrounding area, did not suggest the sea. The weather had turned cold, so that a break from the gnats gave me leisure to contemplate something I hadn't as yet.

Ever since we had come into the South, I had been drawing back in wonder at the presence of the grand and ancient beauty of the noble live oaks, which stay green throughout the year. Trees in the East do not live as long as trees in the West, but any species of tree that can boast a fourteen-hundred-year-old member is a venerable species indeed. If redwoods and sequoias astound one with their towering stature, a great live oak does so with its tremendous horizontal reach. It's as difficult to capture a live oak in a photo as it is one of the great redwoods. Both defy framing, and take the onlooker's imagination into new dimensions beyond the human scale of things.

There is another world of light beneath an old live oak, and a magnitude of difference still beneath a grove of them. In McClellanville, a great company of these trees spread wide their embrace, inviting all and sundry under the meandering tangle of their limbs. Walking through the green haze beneath one, I felt as if I had at last entered a real Southern mansion. Soft draperies of silvery-gray hanging moss and fronds of resurrection fern, lining the oaken windows through which I peered, waved hypnotically in the passing breeze; wisteria climbed what seemed a spiral oaken stair, infusing the air with perfume.

But while the silence of the live oak is similar in some ways to the silence of all trees, that is, when the wind does not stir their leaves, yet the reach of live oak limbs about their massive trunks creates a sense of movement—of dance, in which the stillness is broken in a different sense. I could feel myself wanting to join hands with these old trees and reach out with them to all other life. And the moment we all connected? Why, maybe then the real dance could begin. "Will you, won't you, will you, won't you, will you join the dance?" (The nearness of oysters always brings to mind at least a line of Lewis Carroll.)

Chapter 87

Being Carried Along

In one respect, I did not particularly appreciate the lay of the map since we had turned north. It was difficult to put aside the nonsensical notion that I would have to bear down on Otto's gas pedal without let up in order to climb the apparent curve of the planet. If I took my foot off the accelerator and did not quickly apply the brake, I could imagine us starting to roll back to Florida. It was the opposite somehow of heading south alongside the Pacific, which had felt almost like coasting. At times the sensation of Don slogging along, exacerbated by our impatience to be home, was impossible to shake off. If there hadn't been a powerful counteractive to all this, our northward push would have been just that—all push.

But frequently, and perhaps when we most needed it, we got a sense that we were being carried by something far greater than ourselves— the tidal wave of spring. At times, like surfers we caught and rode the very crest of this wave and enjoyed the exhilaration of it. But even at less spirited moments, we knew we had become part of the great northward migration, and it felt as if Nature not only had conspired to cheer us on but to escort us home, as well.

"Where do you think we were a month ago, Fran?" Don asked one afternoon after we had been in South Carolina four days.

This sort of question was always a stumper; he might as well have asked what I was doing on this day in another life. "I haven't the vaguest notion, without looking at my notes," I said.

454

"Mobile, Alabama," Don reminded. "Remember? I took the day off."

"Hmph. Mobile seems a lot longer ago than that. So where were we a month before Mobile, Don?"

"You'll have to tell me."

I got out a notebook and flipped through the pages. "San Antonio," I announced.

We were both silent then, as if trying to guess where we were a month before that and a month before that. We couldn't do it. I got out the big map of the U.S. and began to color in our most recent inch of progress.

"Fran," Don said, getting ready to head back out onto Route 17, "I counted fifteen wedges of geese this morning. Did you see any?"

"Not that many, but I have been seeing a most encouraging bird."

"An encouraging bird? What's that?"

"A gnatcatcher—the blue-gray gnatcatcher, to be specific. They're all over these woods."

"Well, that *is* good news," the Walker agreed.

"And swallows, Don. The air these days is full of swallows in places. I'll bet they eat gnats, too."

"Good," Don said, and then changed the subject. "I should begin hitting the beaches again sometime today—might even be some folks from home lying about on them. Quite a few people from Middlebury like to go to the Myrtle Beach area in April, you know."

"Hey, Don, what do you think?" I asked, holding up the big map of the U.S., which showed the yellow line beginning to close in on itself.

"It's looking good," Don said after a summary glance. He stepped onto the road just as another round of honking Canada geese flew over, heading north.

I stepped out, too, to watch them pass—a long, undulating line of silhouetted birds looking like a thread of yarn waving in some lofty breeze high overhead. So high they were, I was amazed we could hear them. I watched the Walker and the skein of geese disappear together—one round the bend, one into the clouds.

The rest of the way through South Carolina led the Walker across the Intracoastal Waterway, past some paper and steel mills at

Georgetown, and out onto Pawley's Island—the beginning of a series of connected beaches, some of which Don walked.

We camped one night at Huntington State Beach, and the next morning two events let me know we were still in an exotic clime. I spotted what I took to be a small parrot—its feathers boasted so many brilliant and contrasting colors; red and blue about the head, gold and green on the back, highlights of orange and purple—but the bird turned out to be a painted bunting, common enough in the area, though something I would never see in Vermont.

Later, at a nearby lagoon, a crowd of people gathered to watch a young girl toss chicken fat and chicken necks, which she had been intending to use to catch crabs, to lure some large alligators within arms' reach. But while one gator was slobbering over the tidbits she threw down a small embankment and into the water at her feet, another crept ever so slowly onto the shore and off to her side, as if to take the girl herself as bait. I was relieved when she ran out of meat and got out of there in plenty of time. Just after the girl retreated, I noticed another big alligator lose interest. It had been sneakily drifting toward the girl, but now, without any apparent effort, it sank like a submarine and disappeared completely into the beery-brown water.

As far north as I thought we had come, it was still the land of the reptile—lizards, alligators, rattlers, water moccasins, and countless other kinds of snakes—all waking to the spring warmth and slithering about among the shadows of cabbage palms and loblolly pines.

April 15, the Walker strode the length of Myrtle Beach and then some, hoping to spot a friendly face from home—without any luck. I thought it more likely someone would spot him, or even Otto, yet that didn't happen, either. The Myrtle Beach area was perhaps too much of a carnival scene, and though it wasn't the busiest season, there was plenty going on and I was not sorry to pass through quickly and leave it behind.

North of Myrtle Beach, Don crossed the border into North Carolina. And if Georgia bled imperceptibly into South Carolina, South Carolina bled imperceptibly into North Carolina, at least for a start. The road led further inland for a time, and at Wilmington,

North Carolina, I wondered again at the luxuriant, cultivated display of spring decking out the city environs. Such a glory of color could be matched only in the far Northeast, I thought, in the flare of autumn foliage.

For a long time now, too, every lawn, yard, and meadow at first glance looked rather like a golf green—and then at second glance *was* a golf green, or blended easily into one. The Walker was pocketing two or three prize golf balls daily to add to his collection, but if he was less particular, he could have had many more. We had never skirted so many golf courses in succession as along this southeast Atlantic stretch.

North of Wilmington, Don decided to leave Route 17 behind at Folkstone, in order to take the shortest route to Cape Hatteras by walking an area known as the Crystal Coast, which included the Carteret Peninsula. He would pick up Route 17 again later, on his way out of North Carolina and into Virginia.

Instead of skirting the marine base of Camp Lejeune, to save more miles, we both got permission to cut across, which was not hard to get. "Just stick to the main drag," the officer warned when we stopped at the gate and got our passes.

At my first base pullover to wait for the Walker, I got a glimpse of tanks on maneuver in and around a forest of pines highlighted with magnificent dogwoods in full bloom. Somehow all that unwieldy and unforgiving metal shaking down the dogwood petals first struck me as ridiculous. Later, when some furious thunderstorms hit, and I thought to drive ahead to offer the Walker some shelter, couldn't find him, got a bit lost, and heard what sounded like gunfire raining down on both sides of me, I suddenly wished Otto *was* a tank. It was impossible to say what was storm and what was not.

I found out afterward, between storms, that Don had hiked into the woods to take shelter from a downpour in a tin lookout, but then, on top of what he knew to be thunder, he heard all sorts of other explosions on either side of him. Don was sure that he had accidentally stumbled into a mock-war. He waited until the storm let up and things quieted down again. When it seemed safe enough to make his escape, he did. On the other side of Camp Lejeune, we gratefully headed for Swansboro, North Carolina. Another storm harassed us as we went, yet seemed only too tame after the gunfire.

Chapter 88

Is It Hard to Keep Up?

Back in Wilmington, North Carolina, I stopped at a Triple-A Office to get the final maps of the journey. Since then, Don had been consulting them on every break he took. The entire journey, we had seldom looked beyond the state we were in, and only to the state ahead when we neared a border. Now the Walker was calculating and counting out the miles clear to the end of The Walk.

"It's April twentieth, Don—that means it was ten months on The Walk two days ago," I said, as I watched the Walker bent in study over a map. "We both forgot even to mention it."

"I thought of it, though," Don said, looking up. "Where's the New Hampshire-Vermont map?"

I handed it to him. After a long while and a look over Don's shoulder at all the familiar place names—all the roads leading to home and tugging at my heart—I sighed and asked, "What do you think?"

"Fran, you won't believe this—I could be walking New York City by May 8. But, well, I'm not going to be able to break ten thousand miles, it doesn't seem. Unless…unless I decide to start walking forty miles a day and do the entire perimeter of Maine and get home sometime well *after* the last day of school."

The thought gave me an involuntary shudder. In theory, Don *could* walk on into the summer months if he really wanted to.

"You're not considering that, are you?"

"No, definitely not. I want to walk in on the last day of school, so that the kids who watched me set out can see me cross the finish line. I think that's important, somehow."

"Right," I said with relief. "By the way, Don, what about this recent batch of student letters? Are you going to answer them now, or do you want to wait and say thanks in the next newsletter?"

"The next newsletter," Don said, putting away the maps and getting ready to head out again.

Periodically, Don received fan letters from classes of students who were following The Walk—many from schools where Don had spoken or from classes around the country whose teachers were friends of ours or had heard about us and thus were on the newsletter mailing list. Mostly the students asked the same questions—everything from "Are you sick of walking?" and "How many pairs of shoes have you worn out?" to "Do your feet hurt when you go to bed at night?" and "Do you ever think of cheating?"

Don answered that he wasn't sick of walking, but he was beginning to be sick of The Walk. He would tell them that, for the entire journey, his feet hurt when he went to sleep at night but usually felt better by morning. He had worn out about ten pairs of shoes getting as far as North Carolina—but "worn out," for Don, meant mainly that the shoes had lost their cushioning and not that they had holes in them. But yes, Don had begun to think of cheating—that is, legitimately.

Don was figuring that if he walked as close to the eastern coastal edge as possible, he could take a few connecting ferries. Also, he was beginning to hear people warn that there was no way he could get permission to *walk* the seventeen-mile-long Chesapeake Bay Bridge-Tunnel, if he chose to go that way. And since that was the way that followed along the easternmost edge of the continent and would be the shortest northward route home and avoid a lot of congested areas around East Coast cities, he was definitely considering taking that route. Don didn't worry about it. He would cross that bridge-tunnel, one way or another, when he came to it.

Occasionally one of the letter writers would ask *me* a question. And the question that struck me the most out of the latest batch was worded thus: "Is it hard to keep up with the Walker?" Whatever the student meant by it, I had to realize that it *was* hard for me to keep up with the Walker.

Don's spirit is definitely lighter and fleeter than mine. In all the years I'd known him, I saw him but rarely grounded, that is, stalled out by anything like depression. He was ever in motion and somehow rode just above the great, oceanic waves of life in a ship crafted and re-crafted, as he went, of some magically buoyant material that kept him out of the dark and the deep. Often I found myself buoyed simply being near Don. It's no wonder I did not let go completely.

David, too, had a spirit less liable to be mired by the muddling tendencies of life. He, too, naturally sailed above the turbulent waters, on a stream of air that never seemed to support the likes of me. What? Did I need the buoyancy of two men simply to keep my head above water? So it surely seemed.

Well, one thing I was learning from the journey—some things are given. It is a given that Don walks more lightly upon the earth than I. I saw this in his easy and graceful adjustment to the demands of life on the road, however widely it varied from the life he was used to at home. Not that this was the first time I had come to such a conclusion, but it was the first time I had had such a powerful example, and it made me recognize more fully, as we came nearer and nearer to home, that my own set of givens must be different, indeed.

It was beginning to come to me, as I looked back upon my life, of which the journey was but an emblem of the whole, that I might forever be trudging along under the weight of something. And though I could be misled into thinking the early trauma of my family's accident could account for my heavy step, I knew too that years earlier—as early as second grade, I could shed tears for no apparent outward reason.

I remember my father taking me aside one November, when I was barely six, to try to get to the bottom of one of my glooms. I hardly knew how to put into words what I was pondering. It had to do with looking ahead and feeling unprepared to deal with events—events that I already knew, simply by the laws of random probability, would often be unpleasant and tough to face. I remember having a terrible time trying to explain to my father that I could somehow see ahead to a lifetime of these sorts of events all at once, yet without quite knowing what it was I really saw. I knew, of course, that good things would happen, too, but I was fearful of the balance and ignorant of what strengths or resources I might have to draw upon. I do not know what my father concluded from what I said then, or if he even understood. He simply sat with me for a long time and listened. My mother told me years later that she and my dad were just plain puzzled by me.

In one of his letters, C. S. Lewis wrote, "It is the rule of the universe that others can do for us what we cannot do for ourselves and one can paddle every canoe *except* one's own." Slowly, it was coming to me on this journey that much of my dread, as a child and an adult, stemmed from the fear that I would have to solve every problem of life completely on my own. But not only that—that I actually *had* been solving every problem of life completely on my own. Indeed, I owed Don and David much more than I ever thought, but not only them. I mean, what does a person ever accomplish alone? What is not built on the efforts of others? What is *not* given?

But my last thought, before it was time to catch up with the Walker again, was how bottomless the pit of my reasoning could be. The truth was that we all owed each other, and that I should begin to take some joy in being grateful and get out from under that *imagined* weight. Was I afraid to admit, even to myself, that I might have come on this journey for other reasons entirely, that is, as much for the adventure of it as Don? It was something to consider.

In the third week of April I learned from David that we had snow at home. Looking about me there in North Carolina, the closest thing to snow that I could see was the white bracts of the dogwood blossoms. Ever since we hit North Carolina, it seemed the dogwood trees were more and more numerous—not only planted as an ornamentals in someone's yard but everywhere growing wild in the woodlands besides. I had seen a few blossoming dogwoods as early as late February in Texas, yet nothing so lovely as what surrounded us now.

I was reminded, as I looked at them, of my maternal grandmother, who grew up in Kentucky, and who asked me when I first moved to Vermont whether we had flowering dogwoods *(Cornus florida)* in the forest there, which we don't. I didn't think to ask her then why she wanted to know. But I was learning. They were an incomparable addition. But, I decided too, their flowers were not really like the snow. They did not weigh down a branch so much as uplift it. The horizontal attitude of the flowers on a limb made them seem weightlessly suspended. They were no burden to their bearer, and I realized then that spring might give up all her gaudy colors, yet keeping the dogwood, would still inspire crowds of onlookers and poems of praise.

Chapter 89

Fear Not

A few days after I learned of snow at home, as Don began walking the Crystal Coast, a cold wave hit, dropping even North Carolina temperatures well into the snow-making range of the low thirties. A hard wind off the Atlantic came with it and seemed to let us know we were indeed getting north. Yet the skies were clearest when it was coldest, so there was little chance of seeing snow. I was reminded of my bet with the Walker, though, and I thought it not entirely unlikely that snow could fall on him yet—perhaps some late spring snow when he was crossing the Appalachians.

The Crystal Coast, a two-day walk for Don, extending from Swansboro, North Carolina, to Ocracoke at the beginning of Cape Hatteras, was a pleasant mix of barrier islands, forest, mudflats, and salt marsh invaded by freshwater creeks and rivers, tidal inlets, and ocean surf. Almost every town had designated itself a bird sanctuary, and Cedar Island, from which we would ride a ferry out to Cape Hatteras, was a national wildlife refuge. Unlike other marshes we had typically skirted from the side, this one was cut in half by the road. The road dead-ended at the ferry landing, and thus was deserted at day's end when Don and I took our separate walks upon it, long after the ferry had closed.

I wrote in my journal: "The wind, on my long walk through the Cedar Island Marsh, was as fierce as the wind I thought was going to blow me off the bridge between Morehead City and Beaufort yesterday. A Louisiana blue heron, several little blue herons, egrets, laughing gulls, terns, and some smaller birds I did not recognize kept me company. Also, of course, fish crows. But what impressed me at first was not the wildlife so much as the lush expanse of marsh itself. So thick and fine were the marsh grasses that they appeared to be the fur of a great hide stretched out over the waters to cure in the air and sun. The lusty wind ran its fingers through it—now this way, now that. In places it looked as if the fur had been permanently matted down—the way it might have over an old wound. I wondered what could have caused these matted swatches—something huge and heavy lying there overnight? Unsolved mysteries of this trip abound.

"Whatever green I saw coming to the marshes further south has not yet penetrated these. I could not help but wish for a little kayak or coracle to go paddling about the small streams riddling the marsh like a maze. One feels fenced out to be confined to the edge.

"Later, twice, I watched ospreys make spectacular splashing catches—flying off with fair-sized wriggling fish in their talons, plucked rather dramatically from steep swooping dives out of shallow marsh waters. The second catch a kingfisher and I witnessed together. And afterwards, the kingfisher fluffed out his feathers some, adjusted his grip on the twig he was on, and cackled a bit—as if to say, 'Well, yes, that was a fine catch, but I can do it too.' And not long after he did—spearing a big minnow in a headlong dive, which he then thwacked against a branch he flew to, and after giving it a moment to go limp, juggled it about and swallowed it whole.

"Later still, I spied the great blue. And this great blue was quite a ragtag moth-eaten affair—as if he were very old, or in the middle of a molt, or—I finally concluded—as if he had been on a long journey. I felt as he looked. When the wind rudely ruffled his feathers the wrong way, he hunkered down—as if to say, 'This too will pass.' And before he went off to see about supper, he stood like that for a long, long time—pondering, I had to think, the fishy realities of this world."

The next morning, on the two-and-a-half-hour ferry ride to Ocracoke Island, the first of the barrier islands forming Cape Hatteras, also known as the Outer Banks of North Carolina, I wrote to David: "It just doesn't seem possible that Don can walk to New York City by the eighth of May. Oh, but I am hoping it's true. This ferry ride feels as if it is helping, though we are leaving the continent for a thin elbow-strip of land it doesn't look wide enough to walk on the map. This feeling is probably not real—I haven't a leaf, or a twig, or a rock, or a shell to prove it by—but I have a feeling we are making a great leap north. Only a feeling. The view of the grey-green sea under woolly blue cloud cover is a fine and restful sight. It's the twenty-second of April and north we go."

It was a three-day walk for Don from Ocracoke to Buxton to Rodanthe to Nags Head rounding the Outer Banks. I was thankful we did not encounter any storms, caught as we were between the sound and the sea. At one point we were as much as forty miles distant across Pamlico Sound from the mainland. Once we were out there with the shifting sands beneath our feet, we knew there was no easy exit. While ships may go down, a walker may be washed away, or swept from sea to sound and back again.

As it was, the ocean looked rather riled and threatening, even with no storm to stir it up. Don only occasionally walked the beach itself— once to look out upon what the towering Cape Hatteras Light warned against—Diamond Shoals, the graveyard of the Atlantic.

There, the Labrador Current coming down out of the Arctic meets the warm waters of the northward-flowing Gulf Stream—and these, with the offshore shallows, have combined to treacherous effect for many a luckless ship over the years. Markers testified to where famous ships went down or where old life-saving stations were once manned year-round to rescue passengers and crew from foundering vessels. Tales of pirates, battles at sea, and world-record fish catches were still told.

The same waters that sink so many ships were just as famous for great fishing. Yet when we were there, fishermen were few, and sunbathers or swimmers entirely absent. At a few places, well-seasoned, wet-suited surfers did take to the waves, and windsurfers to the more protected sound. Otherwise, for company, it was the rare leap of Atlantic blue marlin, a pod of bottle-nosed porpoises, or a phalanx of flying fish. And, too—of course, the continuing northward migration of spring and all her entourage, of which we were a part.

Two migrants surprised me, though. One spoke of home, and one of the journey itself. Both somehow reminded of all that is good which comes to a person unasked.

The first was a flock of songbirds I saw three times—one bird of which would surely nest in the thickets near my home on the mountain. I had even lured this bird to my window feeder more than once in early spring, when the weather had turned chill and made the insects scarce. But I saw on Cape Hatteras what I never have seen at home—a flock of male indigo buntings. One male indigo alone has enough blue to slightly stun a person. It is the blue of all blues— ranging from indigo at the head to royal to peacock, finally shading to the slightest suggestion of turquoise above the tail. All this set off by a sterling-silver beak—the whole bird not much bigger than a goldfinch. One of these would arrive at home about the time Don was claiming he could make it to New York City.

The other migrant woke me one morning with the thrilling phrases that conjured up first the prairie, then the Plains, then the coastal meadows along the Pacific, and finally even, the desert. It had been a while since I had heard a meadowlark sing, and now, when I listened, it seemed to sing of a journey entire. So why should it sing so sweetly? It must know something I didn't yet know. I felt sure it did, but it wasn't until a meadowlark flushed from the grass and I got a glimpse of that dark "V" against the bright yellow breast that I believed my ears.

How many days when a note or two, or a flash of its tail alone, carried me through to the next! I considered the hardest day ever so much less so for even the smallest hint of this bird's company. Who could have said to me then when I was leaving home, "Fear not; you will nearly always have the meadowlark—and when you least expect it, the great blue." "What?" I would have answered. "What are you saying?" Surely I would not have understood. Surely I could have only said then what I wouldn't have, and what I was leaving behind.

Chapter 90

F-N-N-A-A-A-R-R-K

While the Walker set out from Nags Head, North Carolina, in quest of his eight-thousandth mile on the morning of April 25, I began the day by climbing the great sand dunes at Jockey's Ridge State Park. Otto was the only vehicle in the parking lot there, and, for a time, I could see nothing but unruffled blue sky and wind-rippled mountains of beige sand. I could suddenly imagine myself back in the desert sand hills of southeastern California. While thinking this as I climbed, I realized that nearly everything I saw from here on out would, in all likelihood, conjure up some place on the journey we had already been. Soon, too, we would be coming upon familiar territory replete with various former associations, and the only thing new about it would be the unique way we would be passing through—that is, at the Walker's pace of thirty miles a day.

Since the wind had firmly consolidated the sand in many places underfoot on the mountainous dunes I climbed, I was surprised to find the grainy going easier than I anticipated. At first the only evidence of man was the track I knew I was leaving behind me—one that the wind was hurrying to cover, even so. But once a hundred feet up and more above the sea, all illusions of being in a deserted place were dispelled—the view below displayed the junkier aspects of civilization encroaching on every hand. More picturesque were the colorful kites gracefully flown in formation from another high ridge, and hang-gliders making beginners' hops off a lesser peak and into a soft, sandy valley.

Climbing down again, I took my time and enjoyed the illusion of being alone with the land. How little of that sensation lay before us, I could easily guess. Still, we had the wondrous company of spring and all the continuing small surprises of our way of life upon the road.

"Look, Don, I've found the culprits. I knew it—I just knew that "f-narking" sound had to actually *be* on top of us! Hurry up, Don, you won't believe this!"

"I'm coming, I'm coming, just tying my shoes."

I stood malignantly surveying our campsite near Gandy, North Carolina, which we had found after dark the night before. I was thinking that its three-dollar price ought to have given me a clue beforehand that it wasn't going to be ideal.

Here, I saw a kennel of dogs that at long last seemed ready to rest their weary lungs after rousing themselves, and every other dog in the realm, from the midnight moonrise on. And there, yes, there, was a pen of squawking geese alongside a pen of other noisy game fowl who had had to chime into the night chorus from time to time. And somewhere nearby, but hidden from sight, I know was a barred owl who tried in the wee hours to calm the neighborhood down, at last giving up completely with a long, exasperated, sighing coo. But the loudest, most disturbing cries, regularly intermittent throughout the night, were shrieked by what I pointed out to the Walker now in the tree limbs directly above Otto.

"What? What *are* those things—looks like a couple of wet mop heads hanging down," Don said blandly, squinting into the morning light.

"Peacocks, Don—two peacocks and one peahen. One or the other screams 'f-n-n-a-a-a-r-r-k,'" which I now screamed out with gusto, bringing a confirming f-narking shriek out of one of the peacocks above.

"Jeez, Fran, you've really got it down. How'd you learn to do that?"

"Don't tell me you didn't hear these things a hundred or more times in the night?"

"Oh, I guess I heard them—but I slept, too."

"This," I said more to myself than to Don, "is the real secret of the Walker's good cheer: he sleeps through *everything*!"

"At least we don't have gnats anymore, Fran. Gnats are worse than peacocks."

"Maybe," I grumbled, wondering which could drive a person madder quicker.

"But damn these mosquitoes," Don said, "let's get back into Otto and finish breakfast. I sure hope we get a good wind or enough sun today to burn them up."

"Right," I agreed, slamming Otto's door and waving away a cloud of mosquitoes at the same time.

Don made Elizabeth City, North Carolina, on the Pasquotank River off Albemarle Sound by day's end. We were making another cut inland and away from the sea in order to pay a promised visit to Chuck and Dee Dee, a retired couple—the brother and sister-in-law of Pete, our nearest neighbor back home on the mountain. Had our timing been better, we might have met our neighbor Pete and his wife Dottie at his brother's place; as it was, we even somehow missed Pete and Dottie on the road when they were deliberately searching for us as they came closer and closer to North Carolina. They couldn't know Don would temporarily forsake his proposed route on the Delmarva Peninsula for a quieter back road, and we had no way of knowing exactly when or where they would be looking for us.

I waited for the Walker at Mariner's Wharf in Elizabeth City, a small, waterfront area made available by the town for visiting pleasure boats. I mused at the sailboats and cabin cruisers gently bobbing in the water, boats that had come from as far off as Alaska and the Caribbean. I watched a handsome-looking couple—young, tanned, blonde, fit—ride up on bicycles, collapse their bikes, and neatly tuck them away into bags, then disappear with them below deck on one of the sailboats. I recalled Don's earlier dream of a sailing adventure and thought how glamorous such a seagoing life looked just now—how romantic, even.

But not long after I had settled into my nautical daydreams, and mere moments before Don came trekking along, I was awakened by the arrival of an energetic and enthusiastic, self-appointed welcome committee—a committee of one white-haired, spectacled, retired postman named Fred Fearing—driving up the wharf sidewalk in a golf cart loaded with goodies for the visiting voyagers. When Fred later learned of Don's walk, he graciously included the Walker and me in his goodwill gestures (not officially sponsored by the town), bestowing on us and all—chips, dip, beer, North Carolina wine, visors and gym bags, a button proclaiming "I Love Elizabeth City," seeds from his own garden, and a good deal of information on the town and the area—not to mention a flyer about himself and his welcoming tradition, subtitled "a living legend."

Fred easily lived up to his reputation and soon had all the sailors and us landlubbers visiting merrily with one another and him. I was surprised to find the young couple I had been musing about suddenly looking at the Walker's and my life upon the road with admiring eyes. Apparently they were tiring of the great and petty hazards of two years at sea and wondered perhaps if what Don and I were up to wasn't more fun. We just laughed.

Our brief get-together with Fred and all included a photo session against a brick backdrop sporting the town's name—and for the footsore Walker, a ride in Fred's golf cart. We might have stayed longer, but we were expected at Chuck and Dee Dee's for dinner. As it was, we nearly missed it—a home-cooked meal, and the wonderful feeling of somehow being part of their family. We hadn't had a treat like this since Cross-Check Ranch in Texas. And though initially we had been shy about imposing (since Chuck and Dee Dee had other family visiting), we were immediately made to feel entirely at home and were glad we stopped.

The next day, after the Walker hit the road, I lingered over morning tea with Dee Dee. And then, when we were talking about the territory back on the mountain in Vermont, she suddenly thought to get a picture she had taken on a visit a few winters back.

"This will probably make you a little homesick," she said, when she came back with a photo of two figures skating on Pete's pond, which was less than fifty yards from our house. "I didn't know who was skating—just thought it made a lovely picture," Dee Dee commented.

"Why, that's David and me!" I laughed with surprise. And it did make me homesick to look back on what suddenly seemed a bygone era. What were we skating on but borrowed time? Did we have any inkling in our heads then of this year of journey?

Chapter 91

Those That Love a Pilgrim's Life

Later that day, April 27, the Walker made a new state—Virginia. Don might have walked other roads, but he chose to get back onto Route 17 because it skirted the great Dismal Swamp and followed directly alongside the Dismal Swamp Canal, the oldest man-made waterway in the U.S., connecting the Chesapeake Bay with Albemarle Sound. But the minute Don crossed the border into Virginia, the road narrowed to dangerous proportions and the traffic was suddenly too thick and too close for walking with any peace of mind, much less letting one's gaze drift off across the canal and into the swamp. Don let me know as soon as he could that he intended to take the first road leading east, which did not turn out to be any time soon. But at the intersection of Route 104 and 17, the Walker headed away from the swamp and toward Great Bridge, Virginia.

I had come to love swamps, and while waiting for the Walker at one point, I liked what I could see of the great Dismal Swamp. But looking at it led me into a round of thinking that put the emphasis on the word "dismal."

I recollected that the poet Robert Frost, thanks to an unhappy love affair, had once thought of seeking oblivion in this swamp, which reminded me of many of my own adventures I'd had running away from home as a child after my father died, which reminded me of the train I had ridden on some of these adventures and how often I had heard the train's hoots and whistles and rumblings on this journey, which then made me ask myself again if there wasn't something I was running away from at home, even now.

Well, it wasn't an unhappy love affair—unless it was an unhappy love affair with my work? Was that it? Five years earlier I had quit teaching to write. Of course, I had been writing for many years before that—but as long as I was teaching, I seemed to have plenty of excuses to explain away my failures at writing. And if I was recognized as a good teacher, what difference did it make that I was not recognized as a good writer? But once I had made the leap to put most of my energy into writing, I found I was embarrassed after a few years to still have nothing published and have little to report, as far as any measurable success.

It wasn't the money, I told myself, even if Samuel Johnson did say "no man but a blockhead ever wrote except for money." I was at least that much of a blockhead, I knew. *Then what did I want?* I asked myself, as I looked off into the murky regions of the swamp.

In response to this question, a great feeling of nausea came over me, leading me to believe that it was entirely possible I had been running away from my work—or from having to answer to no one for the time at my desk—or from having nothing to report in terms of worldly success—or from the uninterrupted stream of rejection slips. Alas, a rejection had even pursued me on the road early in the journey.

Still, I hadn't answered the question. What did I want to come of my writing, anyway? If not money—must be fame, huh? I mean, if I simply enjoyed writing for the sake of writing and to please no one but myself, why would a rejection bother? Why even bother to submit? So many submissions—so many rejections. The words themselves: "submission" "rejection"…like the great "Dismal" Swamp reminded me of places in John Bunyan's *A Pilgrim's Progress:* "This is a Valley that nobody walks in, but those that love a pilgrim's life"—that is the Valley of Humiliation. Had I not been walking my own thirty miles a day in this Valley for five long years?

In his preface to *An Inland Voyage*, Robert Louis Stevenson wrote, "It occurred to me that I might not only be the first to read these pages, but the last as well; that I might have pioneered this very smiling tract of country all in vain, and find not a soul to follow in my footsteps." I knew the lonely feeling.

I wasn't sure I wanted fame or not, but it did seem to me then that to want fame to come of writing the sorts of things I wrote was to be wishing on a star—and an extremely faint one at that. Closer to home, I mused that it would certainly be nice to get a little praise now and then, or have reason to think that one had at least sometimes done a good job at writing somewhere along the way. But most of all, I realized, it could be wonderful somehow to connect with kindred souls—as I so often felt I did through reading. Yet if no one can read one's work because it is never published to the light of day? How can it happen?

I got out of Otto and climbed down the bank of the Dismal Swamp Canal. I sat down, stared into the swamp, and then into the sluggish water at my feet. For the life of me I could not tell which way it flowed. For the moment, the swampy waters seemed to be the perfect reflection of the blood in my veins, the ink in my pen, and the career in my writing—hidden and self-circulating.

Still, I liked swamps—and if there was something stagnant about them to the superficial penetration of the eye, yet they were rich in their own way. Couldn't I be, in mine? Isn't it a success of sorts to be able to persevere, even when you have none of the obvious reasons to do so? If I had run away from my desk, I certainly had not quit writing. Chiefly, I thought, watching a fish momentarily swirl to the surface, it is the stagnating appearance of things that hurts—having to face the world with nothing to report. And I *might not ever* have something to report, I realized. So? I asked myself, the real question is, *Can I keep on writing regardless?*

A cardinal darted from one thicket to another, leaving what seemed a streak of brilliant red lingering in the air behind. A kingfisher cackled. Only, I decided, answering my own question, only as long as there are swamps, and miry places in the world, and dark, still waters. Yes, I thought I could do it—I could love a pilgrim's life.

Part Eleven

MAY

Maryland, Delaware, New Jersey, New York, Connecticut, Rhode Island, Massachusetts, New Hampshire, Maine

Chapter 92

For a Million Dollars?

Don walked Virginia Beach and then rounded Cape Henry on the morning of April 28 and met me at the Chesapeake Bay Bridge-Tunnel. He did not waste much time trying to change people's minds to get permission to walk the bridge-tunnel, and soon I was driving him the 17.6 miles across. Even if I had driven him often enough to and from campsites, this felt a bit strange. We stopped once at a rest area on Thimble Shoals. Don had to get out and do *some* walking—the breakwater, at least.

I stayed behind and watched sea swallows perform an aerial ballet. A dozen or so terns were diving on a school of fish—two, three, four terns would dive at once. In an instant they would be into, under, and out of the water so fast my eye could hardly follow. The gleaming white of them and their keen-edged wings cut as easily into the purpling dark sea below as into the purpling dark clouds above.

Don walked to Cheriton on Virginia's eastern shore, putting in a thirty-three-mile day, which did not include the seventeen he rode. I got mail at the little post office in Cheriton—the only place of the entire journey where, when I said I was expecting mail general delivery, they didn't ask my name. They simply said, "Oh, you must be Fran. We were wondering when you'd be by." This gave me a lift, and when the news contained in the letters was full of happier turns in the health of family and friends, my heart fairly soared.

Finally too, David's letters reported some long-awaited milestones of spring back home—wood frogs clacking in the thawed wet lands, hepaticas blooming in the valley, and the first big showing of spring bulbs. In the more immediate vicinity of home—the phoebe was busy building her nest, forsaking the porch light for our eaves, and the hermit thrush was singing forth its otherworldly songs from the dark hemlock woods all round. Yet what made my heart really take off like a hot-air balloon heaving its ballast overboard, was learning David was planning to meet us again near New York City.

Monday, May 2, at Bethany Beach, Delaware, I wrote in my journal: "Yesterday was Maryland, the day before—Virginia, and today already—Delaware! Tomorrow we will ferry from Cape Henlopen, Delaware,to Cape May, New Jersey! Sometime yesterday unbeknownst to us we must have crossed the Mason-Dixon Line— which supposedly bisects the state of Maryland. We have suddenly gotten north—not very far north, but north,even so. It's all kind of dizzying—five states in one week! I can't begin to keep track of it all.

"Yet, when I think about it, I did feel as if we came into a new and more northerly kind of light the minute we arrived on Virginia's eastern shore from the bridge-tunnel. Something about the light was recognizably different then, though I am hard-pressed to put it into words. Here too, we began seeing the first lilacs. Azaleas are less extravagant here—smaller blooms, though maybe even more intense in color. Little wisteria anymore—not like there was—and no palm trees at all, and no more Spanish moss. Hurrah! I am cheering not because I do not love these things but merely because to leave them behind is to make visible progress towards home.

"Don walked from Berlin to Ocean City, Maryland this morning and ever since we have been beside a great deal of beach development. At the moment I am near a stretch of 'Private—no public beach access' signs. Such beach areas are, for the most part, the least interesting areas to pass through, however fine it is to see the sea. One compensation—I can hear willets. Their 'pill-will-willet' call, with something of the timbre of the whippoorwill, is common along the East Coast and I have come to love it.

"But what was truly lovely while it lasted in Virginia and Maryland was the farm country Don walked through. Seemed like a long time since we'd seen anything like it—quiet, rural, at peace with itself. Old stately farmhouses, a few in rather grand settings like mansions upon beautifully groomed estates; tiny, sleepy villages with tidy houses, trim lawns, lots of churches, and few restaurants. Freshly plowed fields, a few with seedlings just up, but others lush with mature crops of winter wheat and rye. The wind was the making of them—wild and raw, but what else could have shown them to such advantage? In Maryland, in addition to the tilled fields, we passed all manner of chicken farms— that is, until we hit the beach areas again. Yet this even is good—helps to sober me up. My spirit might otherwise lose contact with the earth even more than it has."

What also seemed to speed us on our way from south to north and add to the general delirium of these days were two visitors. Debbie, who had driven up from Virginia to meet Don in Long Lake, New York, in June, staying to accompany Don for a few days in the Adirondacks—caught up with us again in Atlantic, Virginia, and stayed to hike into Maryland with Don. The day she left, Bruce Canaga, another former swim buddy of Don's, caught up with him to hike an eight-mile section of road and wish us both well.

"I don't know, Don, I just can't believe I'm looking at New Jersey up ahead," I yelled into the wind, as we both leaned upon the Twin-Capes Ferry railing the morning of May 3. The wind—stiff, chill, and salty in our faces—was almost too much to bear.

"It's not over yet, of course," Don yelled back, "but I've been thinking, for a million dollars would you set out on the road the next day after we're home to do it all again—you know, for a million dollars?"

Don's favorite unanswerable questions often had the phrase "for a million dollars" in them. I looked at him to see if he was even the least little bit serious. We both turned to put the wind at our back.

"Don, how can you even ask such a question. Would you?"

He actually seemed to be considering it. I laughed—an on-the-edge-of-going-crazy laugh. Don laughed.

"Hey, did you see the sign welcoming us to Maryland, Don? What a contrast, huh, like with the sign back in Hondo, Texas? One says, 'Welcome to Maryland, please drive gently'—the other says 'Welcome to God's country, don't drive through it like hell.' Do you miss the West?"

"Not when I'm thinking about home. Hey, the sign that I remember best in Maryland was on a church and it said, 'The main thing is that the main thing remains the main thing.'"

"You made that up, Don."

"No, I swear—I saw it."

"Anyway, Don what do you think—can that really be New Jersey up ahead?"

"It better be, because I'm counting on it—and anyway, for a million dollars, Fran would you…"

Chapter 93

No More Elevens

"Every day is at least a year complete with four seasons. Morning is the spring full of hope and rejuvenation when I am somehow pleasantly surprised that it is a new day—that is, an advanced day on the calendar and thus a day closer to home. Summer is the afternoon when the sun reaches its peak and there is typically lots to be done—whatever the work and challenge of the hour. Autumn is the late afternoon of diminishing light, diminishing energy—when the drag of the journey pulls heavily on one, and it begins to seem again as if The Walk will take forever, and the day is long. Winter is the night when the date I put on my letter is the same as what I used that very morning, when the optimism of the earlier hours has faded, and when one restlessly suspects that whatever is missing at that point may well be lost and irreplaceable—something vital, extravagant, real." Such an entry in my journal of early May as we entered the Northeast, I realize now, might have been written almost anywhere on the journey.

May 3, Don walked the South Jersey shore from Cape May to Sea Isle City, putting in thirty-four miles and passing through the Wildwoods, Stone Harbor, and Avalon. This was a stretch like no other ocean stretch we'd come upon. Here was no typical beach development, but instead suburban cities of dense networks of streets and housing, sidewalks, town halls, banks, libraries, fire departments, shopping centers, traffic lights—and all of it eerily empty when Don and I passed through, as if a plague had just swept the area of any living inhabitants. Each of these towns seemed far too developed and well established to be merely deserted summer resorts. We could not shake the sense we had that some disaster had mysteriously cleared the places before we came through or that the entire populace watched us secretly from hidden vantage points. Indeed, the feeling was so unsettling that Don decided to forsake the coast after Sea Isle City and head north, and a little inland, on Route 9.

But meanwhile at Stone Harbor, before Don forsook this well-paved path, we came upon another odd setting. Smack in the middle of a densely populated (if also deserted) residential setting of homes, neatly trimmed by a sidewalk and protected by tall, chain-link fencing all round was twenty-one acres of bird sanctuary and heron rookery. No human entry was allowed into this squared-off jungle of tangly vines, creepers, shrubs, and miscellaneous undergrowth climbing all over itself, studded here and there with a few mudflats dotted with grasses and reeds and dampened by a little water flowing through. I walked the sidewalk round and was amazed at all the activity within.

Dozens of flights of glossy ibises came and went—the sunlight throwing a ruby light about their heads and necks, and setting their wing and back feathers agleam with green and bronze highlights. Their strange, long, de-curved bills led them off on a search for snails, perhaps among the miles of marsh and tidal flats that served as feeding grounds for the rookery at some distance. Black-crowned night herons fussily fluffed out their feathers as they squatted over their nests. Various other herons and egrets were perched and preening and offering nesting materials to one another in and around them. A pair of great egrets gracefully mated in a tall, twisty shrub, the male atop the female, keeping his balance with wings outspread and making what seemed like figure-eight movements with them as he did. Fish crows were everywhere, red wings, and warblers—not to mention much going on out of sight.

But one yellow-crowned night heron I watched was on the hunt in the sanctuary just behind the fence—creeping with painstakingly careful steps over a small mudflat. Indeed, its motion was so excruciatingly slow I almost could not watch. And yet, I sensed its moment was at hand, so I held my breath and waited. At last it bent, with considerable care, over some small prey and began swaying its head gently back and forth, back and forth, back and forth, until… boom! It had the mesmerized creature in its beak—a mud-caked frog. I swallowed hard, more than once, when the heron swallowed, feeling a lump stick in my throat even as I watched the lump in the heron's seem to struggle as it was slowly and gradually forced down.

When we turned inland, we saw more clearly that we had again set spring *back* in the most recent ferry ride north. Dogwoods, beginning to go by on the Delmarva Peninsula, here had not yet reached their prime—tulips were reopening, cherries just underway, and the early, bright, yellow cascades of forsythia not yet gone by.

One of my first impressions of New Jersey-ites was that they were not shy and loved to talk. I was suddenly reminded of Montana and the western cafes where friendly people didn't think twice about saying hello or asking me what I was writing. Here, too, for the first time on the journey, when people met Don and learned of The Walk and how far he'd already come, they expressed their wonder by sometimes asking him for his autograph.

I figured Otto's license would at least not raise eyebrows anymore, but actually more than one New Jersey gas station attendant noticed it and let out a small, serious gasp saying, "Jeez, man, you're a long way from home!" *If you only knew*, I would smile to myself.

From Sea Isle City to Port Republic, a spring rain came down hard and cold upon the Walker all thirty-three miles. The next day, when he cut through the pine barrens via Route 539 to just west of Whiting, the rains came down harder and colder yet, while Don sloshed through some thirty-four miles. And the following day, when it was more drenching still, the Walker waded wearily through thirty puddling miles getting to Freehold, New Jersey. But we came up with a new standard of wetness—what came to be known as a three-laundromat day.

The best place for a break in this kind of weather was a laundromat where the Walker could luxuriate a brief while in the warm and dry, watching his tumbling rain gear do much the same. But the Walker's clothes did not stay dry for long. The closer Don walked to New York City, the wetter he seemed to get—the rain soaking him thoroughly not only on the down stroke but again and again in the outward-flaring spray of speeding cars and trucks.

Cold and damp as it was in Otto these forty-degree days, I did not mind the laundromat breaks myself. I was thankful there were so many of these conveniences when we were needing them most. But I was amazed, when I checked my records, to discover that as wet as a few other places on the journey had seemed, like Mississippi and Louisiana, this was the first full, unbroken, three-day stretch of heavy rains. And though I was disappointed not to be able to go further afield in the pine barrens because of the soggy weather, the increasingly urban territory that followed was not hard to resist. Besides, other buoyant hopes were helping to keep us afloat these days.

May 5, in Lakehurst, New Jersey, I wrote in my journal: "Well, the laundry is done—Don has caught up again, dried out again, and gone on again—and the rains continue. I somehow do not even care. I just called David's brother's place in Roseland, New Jersey—and David answered the phone himself! Hurrah! He's now on his way to this very laundromat. I am just sitting here waiting—watching the cars go by. If a navy blue one does, my heart jumps.

"Don's excited too. He can't wait to walk New York City. Some of the swimmers he coached at Middlebury who live and work in the city are going to meet him, walk with him, and put him up while he's there. I'm thrilled Otto doesn't have to scramble for parking spots and lurk in the shadows of that place. We'll meet three days from tomorrow out on Long Island after David heads home again. This time is going to fly—rain or no rain, I just know it."

And so it did. And to Don's delight and mine—without the rains. Three days later, on Route 25-A, near East Norwich, Long Island, I leaned out of Otto from a restaurant parking lot to hail the Walker.

"Over here, Don," I called, and then watched him approach in the rearview mirror by way of a crosswalk at a traffic light.

"Horrible traffic all morning through Queens, Fran," Don said, as he took the pack he'd been carrying and gratefully flung it to the floor in Otto.

"I can well imagine," I commiserated. "So how was the Big Apple?" I asked, preparing for a grim report.

"Absolutely fantastic—could not have been better, really," Don answered, surprising me with his enthusiasm as he untied his shoes. "My one mistake, though, was forgetting to take any extra shoes. I've got a lot of sore spots on my feet and new blisters. But New York City was the greatest," Don reiterated. He rummaged about for some blister-tending equipment.

"The greatest?" I asked. I was recalling my own rattling passage following David through the city by way of the George Washington and Throg's Neck Bridges, where the results of flying high-speed over junk-strewn, pot-holed roads had jarred Otto's fire extinguisher loose and flung books and jars out of cabinets for the first time on the journey.

"Yeah, the greatest," Don repeated. "Every bridge even had a place for me to walk—some fantastic bridges, and what views! So much going on everywhere. I loved it." And then, putting his feet up and forgetting his blisters for a while, the Walker went on.

"Let's see, Bill and Val walked twenty-three miles or so with me on Sunday—which was most of Staten Island, including the boardwalk along the beaches there. We took the ferry past the Statue of Liberty with the sunlight shining on her torch—just perfect. We walked along the south Street Pier, which was full of all kinds of street entertainments—magicians, musicians, I don't know what all. From there I walked the Brooklyn Bridge and down into Brooklyn Heights and on to Greenpoint alone. I went back to Val's for supper and then to Bills' to spend the night.

"Yesterday, Monday, I was on my own—took the subway back to the Fifty-Ninth Street Bridges. Well, but I got temped by the Tramway to Roosevelt Island in the East River—hiked around there. Walked up Broadway to Madison Avenue to Central Park—went all around the park. Took one break to watch the end of an exciting softball game. And ended my day walking Fifth Avenue back downtown to

Hunter College, where I met the swimmers and even had a swim with them."

"Wait a minute, Don." I said, handing him a mug of juice, "wasn't some of that out of your way?"

"Yeah, a whole lot of it—probably made up those miles I cheated on the Chesapeake Bay Bridge-Tunnel. But—what I forgot to say was—I first hiked out to Flushing in Queens from the Fifty-Ninth Street Bridge along Northern Boulevard. I don't know, I just felt great. The weather was gorgeous and I just wanted to walk Manhattan. I saw the greatest street musicians—an Aztec Indian group on recorder, guitar, and drum. You would have loved them, Fran."

"So this morning you started walking in Flushing, right?"

"Right. I just wish I'd remembered to take some changes of shoes. My feet are killing me. Still, I'm not quitting here. I should at least be able to make Centerport—though that won't be breaking thirty miles. Really, Fran, the city and all the bridges and all the interesting neighborhoods—I just had the best time. Maybe it was being with friends again, too, and having beautiful weather after all that rain— and such a crazy scene. How 'bout you and David?"

"Well, it was a nice break," I said, feeling by contrast that I hadn't much to report. "We spent a little time at his brother's and camped two nights—but it was hard to say goodbye, as always."

"Won't be much longer, you know," Don said. "One month exactly from today, I will walk back into school. And anyway, after tomorrow there'll be no more elevens."

"No more elevens? What are you talking about?" I asked, watching the Walker gear up to get back on the road.

"You know," Don said, leaping out of Otto as if his feet were not the least bit sore, "tomorrow is the last eleventh day of the month I'll have to walk. The next day's the last twelfth, and so on."

"Oh," I said. I really had to marvel at the way Don's mind worked. I watched him run a red stoplight to get back on the other side of the busy thoroughfare. *No more elevens*, I repeated to myself, *good enough*.

Chapter 94

Methinks It Is No Journey

Don's second full day on Long Island began in a heavy downpour on roads that were temporarily flooded, in traffic as bad as any we had seen, reminding us of other congested places on the journey and making us both feel somehow out of place. In *The Old Patagonian Express*, Paul Theroux says, "Travelers do not belong in the suburbs, and the most civilized places tire the eye quickest; in such places, the traveler is an intruder..." and, I might add, feels a bit ridiculous.

Something about the proximity of so many backyards reduces an adventure like The Walk, at least temporarily, to a kind of stroll. Not that Don or Otto or I didn't easily blend in; nevertheless, parking on busy, crowded streets of residential areas, I often felt as conspicuous as if I was pitching a tent—perhaps because of the distances already crossed and what stretched out behind us in our mind's eye. Or perhaps it was the affront of seeing so many homes—yet none of them our own home. Or perhaps it was simply too many reminders of business as usual—and what we were only prepared to take up again when we were in our own backyard.

But the following morning the sun came on strong, and Don's last day-long walk along the north shore of Long Island brought us into a surprisingly quiet and more rural setting. Don hiked beside turf and potato farms, luxuriant nurseries, and the serenely bright but almost milky-blue Long Island Sound. It was a country of nesting

489

ospreys, nesting swans, and blood-sucking ticks by the dozens. But there was spring again—always somehow managing to come to a fresh peak—here with more pine and white blossoming dogwoods, cherries and crab apples, and, for the first time, to remind me of the mountain back home—the flowering shad.

For a long while now, as long as the rather prolonged sense of spring had been with us, I would begin the day trying to sort through the morning bird song—always listening for the kind of chorus I might hear at home. Yet not only was I never awakened with a precisely homelike mix—I was never awakened with a blend of voices I had heard exactly so before—even on the journey.

I supposed it was because our nightly habitat was never in the same place, and often not even in the same type of place. One morning it would seem all robins and orioles, the next all of these overlaid or underlaid by the familiar and mysterious warblings of other lesser known spring singers—insects and frogs, among them.

On Long Island I woke one morning to a song that stood out among robin voices like a flute among banjos—but it was not flute-like. A little like the soft musical whir of the woodcock's wings; a little like the soft drumming of a woodpecker—but upon a strange wood of the finest quality; and a little like the low notes I might blow vibrato very softly from my recorder—I had never heard anything like it. One of these singers called to another not far away, and called so strongly to something in me that I crept out of Otto to see if I could discover what it was. I never found it in the dusky twilight, but I watched the moon set and was not sorry to be out.

The evening before Don would walk from Greenpoint to Orient Point, where we would ferry from Long Island to New London, Connecticut, I talked the Walker into an evening's short drive and a couple of short ferry hops to get from our campground to Sag Harbor. I was looking for the point of origin and the point of return of John Steinbeck's journey in *Travels with Charley*—what he called his "little fishing place at Sag Harbor."

Thanks to a helpful couple we ran into who were headed to a nearby cottage, Don and I were able to find the Steinbeck place. It was still boarded up for the winter season, but I stood and looked over and down on the harboring cove below, where Steinbeck himself must have often stood. Don waited in Otto.

"There was a time," Steinbeck wrote, "not too long ago when a man put out to sea and ceased to exist for two or three years or forever." And standing there, I understood yet again how my own journey had been a time when I had somehow ceased to exist. Even in the newsletter I was not myself—never Fran—always "the driver."

I watched a big, glorious, azalea-red sun hovering over the horizon. I felt myself hovering—holding back—resisting the very thing I longed for—home.

"Come on, Fran," Don called. "We'll miss the last ferry."

Don hiked early the next morning to meet Otto and me at Orient Point in typically good cheer, anxious to board the ferry for Connecticut. As for me, I didn't know it yet, but I was about to be swamped by a virus. My journal entries chart the progress of it—every night I am thinking I will have to be over it by the morrow. Periods of briefly feeling well keep me from taking it too seriously, but I am less and less myself. I am instead—dizzy, feverish, achy, and dog-tired—trying to flush out my system with juices, and constantly on the lookout for bathrooms.

We were one day in Connecticut and one day in Rhode Island. The weekend traffic, out for spring rides along the coast, was so bad the scenic route was rather spoiled for us both. At some point, May 16, I noticed we were on the Moby Dick Trail coming into New Bedford, Massachusetts; but it was morning rush hour at the time, I was feeling sick and beginning to worry that I was not going to be able to shake whatever I had, and I hardly knew what to do for myself. My notes of these days are correspondingly thin and record the up-and-down terrain of my illness more than anything else.

May 17, at North Falmouth, Massachusetts, I wrote in my journal: "Here I am in New England and I feel as if I am limping home. What little I saw or noticed of Connecticut was pretty, Rhode Island too—especially with all its bridges, spanning rocky ocean inlets; but the traffic and my throbbing head made these places impossible to enjoy. I haven't taken a picture of anything in days; I just cannot find the energy. I think, when I look back upon this section of the journey, it will be a blur and a hum. Last night the dizziness came on me with a vengeance. Today my ear aches. Tomorrow, well, tomorrow I hope the worst passes or this thing turns into something reassuring like a common cold. Maybe the worst has passed?! But meanwhile, my head feels weird. I was surprised not to feel any great excitement on reaching land at Connecticut, but now I'm certain it's because this virus was already on me.

"But it *is* New England—and if nothing else shouted it out from the countryside—these things were immediate notices: hills with twisty, winding roads—and stones, and stone walls, and the stony solidity of the continent underfoot—and yes, the postcard's trademark—white church steeples against a northern sky.

"Strange to say, I have not yet this spring truly heard the wind in the leaves. Just as the leaves begin to get full enough for the wind to work them, we take another giant step north and they get small again. Spring is not unfolding, it is folding and unfolding and folding and unfolding. But whatever it is right now—I am numb to it. I almost feel as if I am still on a ferry and the states are going by me and not me by the states. I have the strangest visions and thoughts in this fever—and frankly, have to concentrate to remain sane. I am Fran O'Bedlam—as in the seventeenth century verse about Tom:

'With a host of furious fancies
Whereof I am commander,
With a burning spear, and a horse of air,
To the wilderness I wander.
By a knight of ghosts and shadows
I summoned am to tourney
Ten leagues beyond the wide world's end
Methinks it is no journey.'"

Chapter 95

Does the Road Wind Uphill All the Way?

From the moment the Walker stepped onto Cape Cod until he was well out of Massachusetts, a great deal of the territory Don traversed was as familiar as his own face, however much time had intervened to add its wrinkles and blemishes. Having grown up outside Boston, Don still had relatives and friends in the area. He spent idyllic summers as a child at a camp his family owned and shared with two other families on College Pond near Plymouth, Massachusetts. Indeed, one summer, twenty-seven years earlier, his family took me with them from St. Louis to visit these places for the first of many times.

In certain ways, then, we were both going home, yet for various reasons, some of the friends and relatives still knew little or nothing about what changes had come about between Don and me. Many times these days I wished I had written a book containing our history, so that I could refer people to it who might want to know our story better than I could explain on the spot and under the circumstances of the journey.

Yet perhaps people weren't *that* curious; it was just that I rarely felt I did the story justice, and since we seldom had, or would have, the opportunity to bring people up to date in person, it seemed important to do so while we could. What I didn't realize until much later was

493

that some friends and relatives thought, perhaps even hoped, that maybe the journey was going to bring Don and me back together again.

To complicate matters, my illness, which was not as readily apparent as, say, a cold, was still feverishly burning away inside of me as we made our way through this territory, frequently punctuated by visitors and nightly visits catching up on the years. At almost every day's end, for a while, was a friend or relative or familiar haunt to take us in. There was Aunt Phyllis and Uncle Jim, and Ruth and Dave, at Yarmouth Port; Bud and Phyl at Weymouth; Grandma Mac at Braintree; Chris and Gail at Ipswich (having driven up from Philadelphia); and finally, Uncle Bob and Aunt Barbara and cousins and spouses, not far north of Boston at Dover, New Hampshire.

Of course, it was a blessing that there were home-cooked meals, and hot showers, and warm hugs, and good advice about roads and short cuts, and cousins dropping by. And yet, the days were still thirty-mile days with weather, and traffic, and crazy roads I managed to get lost on; in spite of studying maps and mostly knowing our way and getting good directions from people who knew the best roads to take.

May 19, I wrote to David from a cafe in Pembroke, Massachusetts: "It is cold, blustery, wet, and miserable out there—reminiscent of the New Jersey rain that first day you came to visit. I have taken two aspirin, but I'm looking for a drugstore with a sympathetic pharmacist—which is why I am a long way from where Don is walking at the moment. I hope he's faring better than I am. There must be some sort of medicine I could take?! I have got to shake this thing somehow; the world is going by in a fog.

"In a way, in these more familiar places, Don's pace seems faster. I'm not exactly sure why—maybe because in strange places nothing much stands out as a milestone—whereas here—there are so many milestones and so quickly gone. I can't believe College Pond has come and gone already.

"Yesterday on 6-A, coming off the Cape, the walking was not too bad—more like the old Cape, still picturesque and somewhat peaceful. But the day before, going out to Yarmouth Port along Route

28, the traffic was like rush hour all day long—and such development and congestion!

"I can't remember if I told you, but Aunt Phyllis and Uncle Jim arranged for the *Cape Cod Times* to interview and photograph Don. And I know it will be great for Don to have the clippings later, but such things are also exhausting and take more time than you think.

"But I guess everything's exhausting when one is ill. Tonight we'll be at Bud and Phyl's; we are anxious to see them. Supposedly a northeaster is stalled over this part of the world; a bed out of the cold and wet will not be unwelcome. Don't worry. I am trying to get well. I'm sure I'm not *very* sick. At least I'm not out in the middle of the desert. I'm in New England moving north. Reel me on in. That gossamer ball of thread must be breaking its own record. I'm sure to be better tomorrow."

But the next day I wrote: "Oh dear, I am still on the way down. I feel swamped. I am sick of being sick. And I did spend the dark, rainy, traffic, complicated road day yesterday trying unsuccessfully to get some medicine or help at various drugstores. But Phyl kindly gave me a bottle of vitamin C tablets this morning and maybe those will help. I am drowning myself with juices, yet finding bathrooms is a pain. Boston is looming ahead, and I am supposed to meet up with Don before the Callahan Tunnel on Atlantic Avenue—to ferry him through.

"But I keep getting lost—or I go out of my way for a bathroom and because of all the one-way streets can't easily find my way back. I am used to a snail's pace and a snail's pace of decision—and my head is spinning even when the crazy rotary intersections are not. Otto and I have had enough narrow escapes from broad catastrophe to rival Mr. Magoo. I hope the gossamer thread is still attached. I barely know what I am doing. Anyway, don't worry—this is the last big city we have to bother with. Onward."

But while I made my way through the suburbs and the city and the fog in my aching head—Don was meandering through a fog of his own—the misty land of lost childhood. The Walker revisited old neighborhoods on foot, resting briefly on the porch steps of houses once lived in, looking up into the high branches of trees once climbed, and examining the flotsam and jetsam on beaches once roamed. Don loved returning to the scenes of his childhood crimes, especially in the wake of reminiscences with all the relatives and friends over old photograph albums.

One particular triumph for the Walker was his hike from his old house on Hovey Street, near Wollaston Beach, to downtown Boston. Some forty years earlier Don had set out to make this very trek, stiffly decked out in his new snowsuit after a half day in kindergarten. He climbed over the back fence of his yard and headed for the tall buildings of the big city, which he could just make out on the horizon from Wollaston Beach. He was off to find Santa Claus, whom his kindergarten teacher mentioned had just arrived in downtown Boston that day. Though he wanted to be the first in his class to see Santa, after a few hours the police found him, swept him up, and delivered him home. And, as Don tells it to this day, the humiliating thing about it was not that he didn't reach his goal (because his mother took him downtown to see Santa that very night); but that he had wet himself and his snowsuit—which made him figure the policemen would never let him grow up to become one of them, that is, once they discovered the big wet spot he left behind him in the squad car.

"Fran, I might as well just walk," Don said impatiently as Otto crawled on all fours, inch by inch, through the traffic-stalled Callahan Tunnel.

"Don, the fumes alone from all these cars and trucks would kill you," I argued.

"I could have already walked the tunnel three times over by now. I'm probably breathing more fumes just sitting here," he complained.

"Well, that's true enough," I said, "it has to be our luck to be held up by some guy's engine breakdown. But we've got to be almost through this place by now, don't you think?"

"I guess," Don sighed.

"So how far do you think you'll get by tonight?"

"Somewhere around Lynn—I think. We'll just stick to 1-A. I hope the traffic thins out. By the way, Fran, are you feeling at all better? Are those vitamin C tablets helping?"

"Maybe. But I guess I'm afraid to say they are, because just when I think I am feeling better the bottom drops out from under me again. I keep thinking I'm dreaming all of this—all the people we've seen, all the places we know and don't know. I'm behind in my journal, my letters—"

"Skip the letters, Fran," Don interrupted. "It's not that long until we're home." And then, more sympathetically, he advised, "Fran, why don't you rest up some—take some naps—concentrate on just getting well."

"Well, I guess I really should."

"Say, when you called David, did he mention whether the boys were home?"

"Oh yes—you mean I didn't tell you? They're both home and both college graduates. Don't you wish we could have been there—to see them graduate, Don?"

"Well, yes, but I don't see how it could have worked out, since they were both graduating the same day at different colleges. We'll celebrate when we get home—hey, you can pull over now. We're out of the dark—here's a good place. See you up the road. Now, get some rest."

And with a leap and a slam of Otto's door, Don was off and walking—heading north, leaving me to sigh wearily and to recite a familiar verse of Christina Rossetti's that kept playing in my head of late:

"Does the road wind uphill all the way?
Yes, to the very end.
Will the day's journey take the whole long day?
From morn to night, my friend."

Chapter 96

Masquerade

Don walked thirty-one miles to Lynn, thirty-two miles to Newburyport near the Massachusetts border, and then thirty-three miles to Dover, New Hampshire, where we stayed with his Uncle Bob, one of our most faithful correspondents and an enthusiastic fan of the newsletters from the first.

From Uncle Bob's in New Hampshire, it was very tempting, at least to me, to make a beeline home heading west. Instead, Don had to angle back a bit to the east and away from Vermont to hit the coast of Maine and keep to the perimeter for a while longer as he headed north. If I hadn't begun at last to feel better, this turn away from home would have been a lot harder to take. But slowly and steadily, in spite of another nasty turn in the weather, bringing more cold and more rain, my ears and head quit aching, my lymph glands deflated, and my energy returned. Whatever it was I had, it never did turn into a cold.

Our first two full days in Maine it rained—both of them "three laundromat" days. We were lucky to have a dry haven at night in Yarmouth, staying with a former swimmer and good friend of Don's—

Scott Davison. Scott took us out to dinner and gave us good steers as to the better walking routes around and through Portland; but the cold rain was almost the Walker's undoing, when he stopped to help an elderly woman who had a flat tire. By the time he changed the tire in the pelting downpour and caught up to me anxiously pacing in a laundromat, wondering what might have happened to him, he was bluer than his royal blue rain suit. This was the third time on the journey Don had changed a tire for an elderly motorist, but the only one under such adverse conditions. Somewhere in the vicinity of that woman's flat tire, Don had walked his 9,000[th] mile.

Meanwhile, about the time the sun decided to come out in full shining dress over a well-scrubbed and dazzling green earth, Don loaded and took up his pack again to hike some of the Maine Coast alone—or at least until Luke caught up with him on his motorcycle for the third time on the journey (after Long Lake, New York, and Bena, Minnesota). Don was continuing on alone, so that David could whisk me home for a special concert he didn't want me to miss—a live broadcast of Prairie Home Companion from the campus of Middlebury College. David saw no reason he couldn't drive the ten-hour round trip to pick me up, and then, after a day— drive the ten-hour round-trip again to take me back to The Walk and get himself back home again.

But, since it was so close to the time The Walk would be ending anyway, and since I would be home such a brief amount of time, I did not want to attend the concert as myself. I wanted to go in disguise. I just did not want to suddenly be home and have to answer a lot of questions about the journey, more or less eclipsing Don's final grand entry. I had agreed to this visit only as long as I could wear a disguise while attending the concert in public.

If the journey through familiar territory in Massachusetts, while I was ill, had seemed bizarre and dreamlike, this whirlwind visit home as someone else was even more so. I had only the five-hour car ride to dream up a new identity—and a quick stop at a drugstore to acquire a little makeup, an ugly pair of glasses, and a bra five times larger than I would normally wear. I already had a convincing wig that dramatically altered my hairline.

I practiced a new voice in the car, padded myself in a hippyish and matronly dress in the few moments I had at home before the pre-concert picnic, and wrapped an air brace around my ankle, so that I could have an excuse to limp and thus disguise my walk. I also proceeded to adopt a somewhat bullying and obnoxious personality. The few friends we were attending the concert with were in on it—except for my friend Michael.

The object was to fool Michael—and no matter what happened, to carry on as if we were fooling him. David and I did not go together to the concert. Nor did we go together to the picnic on the campus lawn beforehand, so we were not really associated with one another during this outing, which obviously helped keep the cat in the bag. I joined the party on my own.

To everyone's immense and lasting delight—that is, to all who were in on the joke—we succeeded royally in fooling Michael. We also, as it turned out, fooled a lot of other people inadvertently. But Michael fell for the whole masquerade and did not find out how badly he had been bamboozled until six months later at a Halloween party, when this strange person known as Edith Kimball turned up again and was rather dramatically unmasked. Indeed, I myself did not know how absolutely fooled Michael had been until the moment of my unmasking. Had I known for certain, I might have enjoyed the joke even more, but I always had a tiny, niggling doubt that maybe Michael really knew, or at least suspected, and was thus playing the greater trick on me.

Despite the fun of the joke, not seeing dear friends for a full year, and then being suddenly among them without being able to be myself, was actually a rather painful and jarring experience. I knew lots of people and saw other friends at the concert, and something inside me reached out to each one of them, while at the same time eliciting never so much as a glance of recognition in return. I had buried my true self under layers of painted makeup and un-Fran-like dress—but the effect on me was closer to being invisible than merely disguised, or even of looking out at a familiar world of sunshine from a cold cave that light could not penetrate.

By the time the concert started, I wanted to throw the whole thing over—but by then it was too late.

A day later, May 29, David drove me to Hallowell, Maine, where we met up with more friends—Judy and Fred of Aloha Camp days—and with Don. Luke dropped off Don's pack for him at Judy and Fred's and had to hightail it home. David followed soon after. But first there was a lobster feast and more reminiscing.

Judy and Fred knew every inch of the back roads Don wanted to walk through Maine and on into New Hampshire—including great little stops for ice cream, swimming, and camping. We would never be on a major highway again.

Looking at the map of Maine, I thought the place names along the route strangely exotic for where we were—South Paris, Norway, South China. If Don wanted, he might have taken walks through Poland, Sweden, Denmark, or Peru before leaving Maine. Were we really heading home?

"So, Don, I forgot to write this down in all the recent excitement. How far up the coast of Maine did you say you got before turning west?"

"Belfast," Don reported back from below me on his bunk.

I had the big map of the U.S. out and was tracing the yellow mark of our perimeter trail with the yellow beam of my flashlight. "Gosh, Don—that doesn't come close to equaling the northern limit of your walk out west. You hit your northernmost point near Bonner's Ferry in Idaho, but you would have to walk up to somewhere above the Canadian Province of New Brunswick to do that on this end."

"No, thanks," Don said simply. "Tomorrow we'll be out of the state of Maine, Fran."

"Tomorrow is June first, Don."

"Ten more days—it's the final countdown—and I hope this right foot of mine hangs on. The little toenail came off this afternoon, my ankle is swollen, and there was plenty of blood in my sock when I took it off tonight."

"Don, you're the one who's going to be limping home."

"No, I'm not. It'll get better when I take those couple of days off for that meeting I have to attend at camp in Fairlee."

"Oh, for a moment I forgot about that break. Well, that's good—and David's going to try to come over to visit then, too, if he can. Hmmm. Looking at the numbers here—by the time you get to Fairlee, Vermont, on June 4, you will have walked seventy-four days in a row without a break. Your last break was March 21, near Apalachicola, Florida, when Patty was visiting. And let's see now," I said, doing some more figuring, "that's almost three-thousand miles straight, walking at a thirty-one-mile-a-day average."

"But I won't be breaking my 10,000-mile goal."

"No, you won't be doing that—but considering all the luck of the journey, good and bad—"

"I know, Fran," Don said, interrupting and turning out his light, "we've been damn lucky. Except for a few mosquitoes in Montana, a scare or two on the West Coast, some cold and some car trouble, a few gnats down south, and some rain in the Northeast—I mean, of all the things that might have gone wrong…" Don paused, as if searching for something. "Hey, Fran, if you knew it wouldn't be any worse than it was the first time around—for a million dollars, would you—"

"Goodnight, Don," I cut the Walker off. "And shut up about your million dollars," I added. "I'm listening for coyotes."

Part Twelve

JUNE 1988

New Hampshire, Vermont

Chapter 97

After All You've Seen

My mother asked me one day toward the end of The Walk, "Now, Francie, after all you've seen, how are you going to go back to little old Vermont?"

"Well, Mom," I told her, "by foot and by Otto, I guess."

Reflecting on what she asked, I later wrote in my journal, "In spite of all the wonderful places along the way—and in spite of all the places that did pull at my heart and say 'Stay,' home is the place you go when the adventure has ended. And though you may set out again, like a sailor for the sea, you might also sit beside the fire and tell the tales of where you've been and make up stories (you never intend to come true) about where you might be going next."

At the end of the day on June 1, in Conway, New Hampshire, the Walker folded the last map of the journey for the last time. It was easy to see now to the journey's end, but until this symbolic moment, I had never really let myself think with perfect confidence that we *would* actually come full circle. Yet now, as I looked at the map with the Walker, I did. It was impossible not to. Earlier that day I had put the last on-the-road newsletter into the mail. The next and final newsletter I knew I would be writing at home, at my desk, in place, on the mountain.

Of the raw materials given to the eye, when I looked out of Otto's windows now, every detail cried "home." It took little rearranging of the landscape to conjure up familiar settings with stream or river,

505

pond or lake, field, stone, or forest. The crest of every green hill opened on a view of other, more distant hills, with mountains piled in ridges behind these, shading by subtle turns from green to blue. The peaked and rumpled land was speckled with tiny towns and villages. And every wayside flower, from blue flag to daisy—and every spring songbird, from white-throated sparrow to hermit thrush—sang openly of secrets I once knew but had somehow forgotten, the way one forgets each year the glories of autumn foliage, or the stirring sound of the wind in the leaves after the barren winter, or the stunning sight of naked branches scraping against sky, caught and shimmering in a net of stars after the brief, misty nights of summer. Indeed, it seems that one *must* forget, in order to have the joy of remembrance, recovery, and recreation.

Even so, this was not yet our home state. The way through New Hampshire led the Walker across the White Mountains via the Kancamagus Trail, Route 112. Don climbed to the Kancamagus Pass at 2,860 feet, which was far lower in elevation than the mountain passes he had climbed out west; but because of the consistent roller-coaster nature of the terrain, these eastern hills seemed far harder climbs to the Walker's legs, and even to Otto, than did the western ones.

Don was reminded more of his trek through the Adirondacks than his traverse of the Rockies and the Cascades. His muscles ached on the long hills up, and his joints ached on the long hills down; only the cold, fast mountain streams, in which he soaked his feet and legs from time to time, could numb the pain and get him marching again.

After the Kancamagus, Don wound his way about more of the White Mountains, passing through Lincoln, Warren, Wentworth, and Gilman's Corner. At Orford, New Hampshire, the Walker crossed the Connecticut River to Fairlee, Vermont. Here Don took his last break of the journey, spending a weekend round of meetings at Camp Lanakila on Lake Morey, making plans with the director and other counselors for the approaching summer-camp sessions.

Two days later, Don would begin his somewhat circuitous route through Vermont, timing his arrival in Middlebury to coincide with the last hour of the school day on Friday, June 10. It was not going to be precisely the last day of school as Don had once thought, but it would be very close to it.

In the meantime, I had the weekend to rendezvous with David. But instead of the idyllic interlude I had pictured ahead of time before the final push home, something else occurred—perhaps just to let us know that we were not yet home free.

Otto snapped. Or something *in* Otto snapped. Just as I was parking at dusk in front of a restaurant in Bradford, Vermont, I heard it—a distinctive, twangy plunk, as if some inner stretch of piano-wire nerve had finally let go. When I tried to get him into gear, I couldn't. I went into the restaurant to wait for David, thinking maybe Otto would be okay when we came out later, but I had a sick feeling inside that he wouldn't.

While I sipped a glass of wine, I racked my brain for what might be ailing Otto. His last oil change had been in Dover, New Hampshire. All had seemed okay then. Of course, there was that certain, very occasional, odd noise Otto had been making ever since we had begun pressing north along the East Coast. Come to think of it, it could almost have been a lesser version of that final plunk. Still, I had no idea what *that* signified. Maybe Otto had simply had enough of this journey—maybe he didn't know how close we were to being home— or maybe, I thought, as I drained my glass of its last drop—Otto doesn't like being taken for granted.

When David arrived, full of fresh excitement about our nearness to home, I tried to put Otto's troubles out of mind and enjoy our dinner. But when I climbed into Otto later, the sickening feeling returned— and I still could not get him into gear.

What to do? We were told the nearest place to service VWs and that had a good supply of parts, was thirty miles away in Lebanon, New Hampshire. But how to get Otto there? I put him into neutral, and David rolled him out into the street, facing a downhill stretch. If I could force him into gear, the plan was to strike out immediately for the interstate and head south for the garage in Lebanon, with David following close behind. When Otto started rolling on his own, I managed to find third gear. We were off and running.

Unfortunately, the garage was closed for the weekend, but we parked Otto there anyway and left his keys with the night watchman. It was a time of nervous suspense. I knew The Walk was not really in jeopardy, but I did not want to entertain the thought of Otto being unable to finish the journey with us.

Early Monday morning, Don headed out on the road alone while David dropped me off at the garage. Eight-and-a-half hours later, I drove Otto out of the place. I was exhausted from the long, nerve-racking wait, but thankful to learn that Otto seemed to have needed only a minor adjustment in his clutch cable. Apparently the lengthy wait was only because the garage was short that day on mechanics.

Chapter 98

Would Someone Have to Wake Us?

South of Waits River, Vermont, on June 7, I wrote in my journal: "The Walk continues on home ground. This is, so to speak, our own backyard. Suddenly, nothing about this country feels anything like other places on the journey. It doesn't even feel like New Hampshire. It feels like home. But as I wrote to David this morning, I see my own sadness somehow inscribed upon these hills—of when I left them behind one long year ago. I feel this even as I am filling up with joy to be coming back. I *am* back. I have to keep reminding myself. And yes, it does seem sillier and sillier to be writing to David. It's just that the journey and its routines and rhythms are oddly in place even this close to home.

"I don't know—probably some of the sadness I feel is for all the faraway places I fell in love with—for having to let them go—for having to let the journey go—for the beauty and mystery and craziness of traveling at the pace we did—and for having to let that go. There is sadness too in knowing that it is not a way that one will ever be going again—million dollars or no million dollars."

"Fran," Don called as he approached Otto, interrupting my melancholy reverie on the page. "Here's another dime—also a golf ball—and look at this." The Walker climbed into Otto and handed me a rainbow-ribboned windsock. He added the golf ball to his plentiful collection.

"Great, Don; Otto can wear this on the final day home," I said. But for the moment, I added it to the upper layer of junk under one of Otto's seats—a collection that now included a giant Clint Eastwood poster; three dinosaurs, a cow, and a tiny hand—all made of green plastic; two bandannas—one with the stars and stripes, and one with the union jack; a black satin bow tie; an MG insignia; a hand-woven Guatemalan purse; an inspection tag for a shellfish container; a man's fake gold ring with a fake blue stone; a pocket knife with a picture of a leopard on it; a fishing lure and sinker; two pounds of bagged white sand; assorted pizza tokens; a few odd tools; a sign embossed with a state seal saying, "Maine Dept. of Transportation, Traffic Survey Car"; and one tiny, pink, plastic pig dressed up as a Viking in triumphant pose.

"Well," I sighed, closing the lid on these treasures, "I know I'm going to hate myself when I get home and survey the entire pile of road finds. And," I continued, bringing up another matter, "I suppose I really am going to lose the bet about the snow. Plenty of frost this morning, but these powder-puff clouds look entirely innocent.

"Good grief, Don," I interrupted my own train of thoughts, "what in the world are you constructing there?"

I was watching the Walker pile globs of cold spaghetti on a slice of bread, which he then proceeded to cover with corn chips, each of which had already been plastered with peanut butter.

Don did not answer. He simply closed the concoction with another slice of bread, gave it a solid pat to mash it together, and sank his teeth into it.

I said, "We will not be arriving home too soon. Your tastes, Don, are getting a little weird."

Don only nodded with his mouth full, grabbed a banana, and signaled for me to open Otto's door. He then leaped out and continued on his merry way. I noticed that a certain bounce in his step, which had been missing for some time, had returned. And I realized, too, as I watched him disappear over a hill, that I had never once tired of such a sight—that I felt even now some of the same wonder and joy for him that I had felt in the very first miles of the journey—and that I couldn't help but count it a blessing to be witness to the indomitable spirit of this man.

Retracing Don's rather circuitous route in the Green Mountain State now, I find it looks as if the Walker was in no hurry to get home. He wandered here; he wandered there. "I know I am dreaming this now, Fran," he commented in a daze at one point. I knew what he meant. Even so, The Walk in Vermont amounted to a mere 112 miles, or a hike of three-and-a-half days.

The Walker first wound his way north toward the state capital. A few miles outside of it, the shadow of a creature with a six-foot wingspan crossed his path, causing Don to look up and follow it with his eyes. He watched it join a throng of others in a sprawling stick nest among other stick nests situated in a stand of tall trees high above the Winooski River on a bank opposite him. Later, Don had me drive him back to this spot, so that I could focus my field glasses on the spectacle of these birds. He thought they might be eagles.

"You won't believe this, Don," I said excitedly. "It's a great blue heron rookery! What you thought were eagles are a bunch of gangly juveniles waiting to be fed. Here, look."

And while there must be great blue heron rookeries in many parts of the country, seeing just this one, and in our home state, and at the end of the long journey, after we had been befriended so often by one of these stellar creatures—well, it seemed surprisingly grand and fitting. I took it as a good omen. I knew if we didn't happen to notice the great blue on the homestretch ahead, it was only because we needed it no longer: nothing could keep us from the goal now.

After Montpelier, Don began tending south, toward home. He strolled through Middlesex, Moretown, and Waitsfield, then climbed up and over the Green Mountains by way of the Appalachian Gap. After the gap, Don climbed up many a hill and down many a dale, but he never had to exert himself again on steeper terrain. He rambled through the villages of Jerusalem, Lincoln, Bristol, New Haven, Waltham, and Weybridge, enjoying a rapidly mounting sense of accomplishment as he gained on his goal.

The closer to home we came, the more glorious the weather—the more gold the shining sun, the more blue the stunning sky. We both knew that mosquitoes and black flies, which were commonly part of the season, could easily have subtracted from the pleasantness of these days. Yet some beneficent wind continuously blew fresh breezes and intoxicating smells of spring at the Walker's face, inadvertently keeping any pests at bay. There was something unreal about these days. Don might have been sleepwalking. I might have been sleep-driving. I wondered whether someone would have to wake us to tell us we were finally home.

"Oh no! Don, did you hear that—that—that plunk? It's happened again! Darn it all, I can't get Otto into gear!" I shouted just as we were pulling into our campsite in the shadow of Elephant Mountain on our very last night on the road.

"Well, calm down, Fran. It's not the end of the world. It can't matter much now. Home's just around the corner. Put Otto in neutral and I'll push him into place."

"Oh, Don," I groaned. "It does matter." It mattered to me because I knew there was going to be a parade the following day—something Don didn't know. The parade was going to be a surprise for the Walker. I wanted Otto to be in the parade, too, and I knew that Don would be just as disappointed as I was not to have him there.

Early the next morning I managed to drive Otto, crippled and ailing, to the very same garage that had done all they could, over a year earlier, to fix Otto up for the journey. The mechanics remembered him, and in spite of his injury, even thought Otto was in great shape. He needed a *new* clutch cable, that's all—something he undoubtedly had needed earlier.

The next thing I knew, Otto was rolling his tires through downtown Middlebury to the tune of "The Magnificent Seven" in the "welcome home" parade. Don led the way, wearing a red, white, and blue plastic lei that a friend had made for him. He walked behind a police escort. A student bearing the U.S. flag walked just behind Don. A flurry of backyard-hopping cameramen and news people buzzed in and out and around the Walker. The Middlebury Union Junior High Band blasted out marching tunes from behind the flag bearer. Otto and I followed behind the marching band. Otto sported two new magnetic signs on both his front doors (which David had thoughtfully made for him) identifying him as "Otto," and he proudly waved the rainbow-ribboned windsock from his antenna. I was now wearing a pink plastic lei I had been given, and I felt like some sort of homecoming queen on a float. On every corner, the same small collection of loyal friends from my writers group waved and cheered me on. Bringing up the rear, just behind Otto, were two children carrying a banner welcoming us back.

This was, without a doubt, the longest, slowest mile of the journey for the Walker, the Driver, and Otto—not because of any pain we were feeling, but for all the attention we were getting. Indeed, I laughed my head off later, when I watched Don on the news that night being filmed and interviewed as he led the parade. He kept looking down at his feet and picking them up as if there was something wrong with them, while he tried to explain to the newscaster how awkward it felt for him to suddenly be walking such a slow pace.

The parade ended triumphantly at the high school, where several hundred people were gathered, including students, faculty, family, and friends—some of whom had flown in from around the country—all waiting to cheer the Walker's last steps with a welcoming roar. It was a moment I was completely unprepared for. The Walker and the band marched right on into the gym, followed by the crowd—everyone eager to hear what Don would have to say about The Walk.

I still don't know how Don could face such a huge and admiring throng and find words to equal the situation. But he did. First he had a moment to collect his thoughts while he was presented with some gargantuan orange sneakers and a framed caricature of himself striding across the U.S.

But then the Walker reported, in clear and convincing terms, how utterly thrilled he was to see everyone and how inexpressibly glad he was to be back. I was surprised to learn, for the very first time, that even early in the journey Don had imagined himself like Dorothy in the Wizard of Oz—occasionally clicking his heels together, saying to himself, "There's no place like home. There's no place like home."

And then, after introducing me as his best friend, he called me up to join him and thanked me profusely before one and all. He then described a few outstanding highlights and lowlights of the long road, fielded a round of questions, and closed his presentation by reading a prayer of thanksgiving—something we had worked on together. At the conclusion, the Walker got a spectacular and uproarious standing ovation, which must have echoed pleasantly in his dreams for a long time after.

The Walker's Prayer
Thank you.
Thank you for the fantastic walks that made up a 9,450 mile year…
Thank you for the people who believed in me, who gave me this opportunity,
who cheered me on, and now welcome me home…
Thank you for Fran and Otto, who helped make it possible and shared the good
and the bad of a very long road…
Thank you for David who worked hard for us behind the scenes and kept the
home fires burning bright…
Thank you for letting me walk so many bridges— especially the bridge to the
U.S.A. from Sault Ste. Marie, Canada…
Thank you for swimming holes on hot days and for Nathan who showed me the
best one of all near Trout Creek, Michigan…
Thank you for a hot, home-made cinnamon bun big as a birthday cake, and for
boiled crawfish in Cajun country, Louisiana…
Thank you for helping me cross prairies and plains, mountains and deserts,
swamps, and marshes—and for the beauty of each…
Thank you for the serenades by loons and coyotes and other strange creatures
of the night…

Thank you for stars and moon and planets and for Montana's big sky…

Thank you for all the people who stopped to offer me a ride or who wondered

what I was doing—and for Thelma, the waitress in North Dakota, who

drove her whole family out to wave at me on the road…

Thank you for the wonder of clear waters from Lake Superior to Santa Rosa

Island on the Gulf of Mexico…

Thank you for all the wild animals still in the wild— black bears and grizzlies,

seals and sea otters, the deer and the antelope, alligators too…

Thank you for the Great Blue Heron who seemed to turn up everywhere,

watching to see if I could really do what I set out to do…

Thank you for safe places to camp and to walk…

Thank you for good cafes, home-cooked meals, and cold spaghetti out of a jar…

Thank you for laundromats on rainy days and hot showers on cold ones…

Thank you for my good health…

Thank you for newsletters and letters…

Thank you for family and friends along the way, and for family and friends who

came to walk with me on the road…

Thank you for the road—it was long and varied and always led me to where I

wanted to go—especially here…

Thank you for being there, for listening to me, and for your company throughout the day…

Thank you, Lord, thank you.

Epilogue

The welcome-home celebration on June 10 carried on into the wee hours of the morning at a cookout and reception organized by David and open to all family, friends, and well-wishers. The party took place at the great Bread Loaf Barn on the mountain— exactly where the big farewell party had taken place a year earlier. A steady stream of people came and went, but the Walker seemed to have a small crowd continually gathered round him. Energized by all the attention, Don laughed, told stories, and answered questions, miraculously staying on his feet the entire time, about as animated as I have ever seen him.

I had long since collapsed in a comfortable chair beside the bright fire, watching it dance over a stack of logs in a great, fieldstone fireplace. I chatted with whomever happened along, feeling deliriously numb and exhausted, while caught in a happy stupor of disbelief to be on home ground at last.

Not far from me in the great barn where we were all gathered, a huge paper banner, which David had made, stretched across a wall congratulating the Walker, the Driver, and Otto. This was hanging above some banquet tables that had been pushed together to display the complete collection of Don's road finds. Well, it was as complete as we could make it, in the little time we had to unpack boxes and round everything up before the party got underway.

It was an impressive array of material—no longer looking exactly like junk. Certain objects managed to speak to me from across the crowded room of very particular places—of prairie and mountain and desert and marsh and beach—tangible symbols of our year on the road. Not that we meant to keep everything. Some of it was already gone, namely the $91.70 which Don had collected in road moneys and which we spent along the way. Except for a small pile of treasures, such as the javelina skull, the tail of a black-tailed jackrabbit, the riding whip, the pajamas that our mascot Bubba was wearing, the magnetic Montana dealer's license, and a few other things—people were invited to take home from the party whatever might strike their fancy. I saw some children walking off with plastic dinosaurs and other toys, our own two sons scoffing up the mardi gras beads, and a few people examining and asking about the tools; but I had a sinking feeling there was going to be a lot left over to be swept out with the party debris. And there was.

Homecoming week was punctuated by waves of congratulatory cards, flowers, telegrams, and phone calls from all around the country. None of this went to Don's head. He was already packing up for camp. He also got a thorough checkup by the team of doctors who had examined him before he left. This included certain performance tests, such as how many push-ups he could do in a minute, how many sit-ups, etc. In every category he now far exceeded what he had done before he set out. He was down to ten percent body fat. Otherwise, the Walker seemed none the worse for trekking 9,450 miles in a year, at an overall average of slightly better than thirty miles per day, with a grand total of forty-eight days off. Just a week-and-a-half after coming home, Don left for camp. I did not expect to hear that he was having a hard time adjusting to his new old life. And I didn't.

As for myself? I doubt the reader will be surprised to learn that I did not, in spite of my longing for home the entire way, make a graceful adjustment. I felt a jolt. I was disoriented in my own house. Sitting at my own desk, surrounded by precarious stacks of maps, and notebooks, and newsletters, and journals, and boxes of slides and photographs, and a year's worth of letters to David—

not to mention booklets, and brochures, and newspaper clippings collected from the entire journey—I didn't know where or how to begin digging out. It took me two weeks simply to get around to unpacking Otto.

Otto. Whenever I looked at him in our driveway, I didn't know what to think or feel. I didn't like him just sitting there, somehow—looking back at me with what seemed a reproachful stance. Neither did I feel like jumping aboard and driving off in him. Did I think if he stuck around I would be tempted? Finally I put an ad in the paper. A few days later, Pam and Rob, a young couple from the other side of the mountain, were driving him off.

But at the very moment Rob drove off in Otto, I had a change of heart. I had not appreciated the way Rob drove Otto on the test drives—so hard! I had never once gunned Otto the way his new owner did. And when Rob had trouble with Otto stalling—again and again, as he was trying to maneuver him out of our driveway to take him home, I felt certain that Otto was never going to make it up and over the mountain.

Indeed, when Otto had been gone a half hour, I felt compelled to follow in his tracks. I actually drove up to the mountain gap, expecting to find Otto abandoned and broken down by the wayside.

But no…Otto was gone. And at that moment I finally let go and knew that this machine, which I had invested with a life and personality of its own, was going to be all right.

Besides, I told myself, Rob and Pam seemed thrilled to have Otto: when they heard I was going to write a book in which Otto was one of the chief characters, they promised to write a sequel celebrating his further adventures. And I knew Otto was going to have more escapades, since Pam and Rob had gone off to follow The Grateful Dead.

About this same time, in reading a small book a friend loaned me called *The Traveler's Key to Sacred England*, by Jon Michell, I came upon these words in the introduction: "Settlement involves guilt. In the exchange of the delights and hardships of the road for the more even life of domestic comfort, certain things were lost." Michell was discussing some of the consequences of the change from nomadic to settled life that followed the beginning of agriculture in England about 5,000 BC. I, too, was adjusting to a change from nomadic to settled life. But the statement I just quoted sent such a shock wave of recognition through me that I had to ask *Why?*

Two weeks home from the journey, I wrote: "Why does settlement involve guilt? What is lost in exchanging the delights and hardships of the road for the more even life of domestic comfort? Do we lose our sense of what life really is? A journey? When we are wanderers, pilgrims, explorers are we closer to the true intent of why we are on this earth? In other words, to be settled is to be deluded into thinking that this life on earth is more permanent—less transient than it really is. And since we are merely passing through, to encumber ourselves with possessions and to occupy ourselves with establishing a stationary way of life is somehow false, even absurd. We focus all our efforts on 'staying'—something we were never meant to do." Strange—this was a truth I kept coming to "on the journey"; now I had to learn it again, "at home."

The journey, I saw more clearly than I ever had yet, had been a gift—a gift I was only beginning to be able to receive. The journey's end was but the lifting of a very thin veil, a first awakening, a glimpse of treasures we had only partly unearthed and had yet to fully appreciate. And, too, it was a gift evoking response.

In *The Songlines*, by Bruce Chatwin, among other places, I have read of Aboriginal "walkabouts"—dream journeys taken, both inwardly and outwardly, for the purposes of spiritual renewal—journeys recreating those of totemic ancestors who once sang the entire world into existence, including themselves, by singing the names of all who crossed their path. Surely, the story I would be writing—sharing would be my attempt to "sing" our own journey and the names of all who crossed our path.

The *Dhammapada* says, "Wakefulness is the way to life—The fool sleeps as if he were already dead." And that is the main problem, I was learning, with a settled way of life: How to stay awake? The object somehow is to stay on the journey. The Chinese sage, Lao Tsu, says, "Without going outside, you may know the whole world. Without looking through the window, you may see the ways of heaven. The further you go, the less you know." In other words, the journey need not be taken in actuality, if one knows how to live.

Yet where is the journey tending, if not home? In a strange way, as long as I was on the journey I knew where home was. But once home? But that is just the point: I truly believe our place of refuge here on earth is not our true home. Accepting this, and accepting that there are no shortcuts to that place we long for—then, as the proverb says, the longest way round *is* the shortest way home—even, perhaps, the only way home. Divas in Deo.

Afterword:
"The Forgotten Manuscript"

When our continental roundabout ended, I gradually established a new writing routine. On the edges of family life and other distractions, I carved out the time I needed, as often as I could, to tackle the narrative. A local publisher/editor advised me not to try to write the entire book, but rather just a few chapters. Then I could send them out and see if any publisher would be interested. I saw the wisdom of this, and the mountain of material I had to work with: letters, newsletters, journals, notebooks. On the other hand, I wanted a vision of the *whole*. I ended up with many false starts and retreats. *Twice*, after getting us all the way to California—I realized that at the pace of my words, I was literally writing volumes and not a single book. In the end, the writing of the whole book (but not the fine tuning) took three years and then some. Meanwhile, I did send early chapters out and about to see if there was any interest. There really wasn't. Nevertheless, I kept at the task, hoping.

At last, the finished manuscript was some six-hundred pages. The 1987–88 year, though, was itself fading from public memory. Big life events took over: cancer for me, heart disease for David, marriage for Don and our two sons, grandchildren arriving one after the other, etc. At some point, for safe keeping, I placed the typewritten manuscript on a shelf—but I kept writing: letters, journals, a novel, essays, stories, and piano music for stories and songs.

Thirty-three years later, during the covid pandemic, wanting to read something fireside to David (an evening tradition), I picked up my journals of Don's walk and began reading them aloud. As soon as we finished them, we started searching for the manuscript of the book. We really didn't know where it was. Since we had physically moved (downsized) in the past ten years, we wondered if, indeed, the manuscript was still with us. We never did locate the digital copy we had put somewhere for safekeeping. However, we did find the bulky manuscript.

The journals were, of course, like written letters to myself. Valuable in their own way, but not a "story," so to speak. The manuscript told the story and swept us both up in it, as we read, remembered, and relived the ongoing tales of trials and triumphs. We were both surprised by how it spoke to us.

Soon, other members of the family expressed interest in reading the story, even in its unwieldy form. Beth, the Walker's younger sister in California, surprised me with written and enthusiastic praise, to say the least. Others were also appreciative. David and I thought we might as well try again to find a publisher. And now, we can both say, we are so happy we did (a story for another time).

Acknowledgments

First, I want to thank a man who shuns the stage to work behind the scenes and thus helps to make possible what otherwise might never come to be. Thank you, dear David, husband of nearly fifty years. You know my heart the best and you are so much that I am not—especially patient.

My thanks also to Beth, the Walker's younger sister, and one of the first of our extended family to read the book in its most cumbersome form. Beth wrote notes that I saved and read and reread—making me feel as if I somehow had written a prizewinning bestseller.

My thanks to Laurene, dear friend, who retyped the entire manuscript (in record time) so we could have a digital copy to submit to publishers and editors. And, as she worked, she made this tedious project seem like fun, a task that would have taken me months, if not years, to complete. Laurene also encouraged me with her enthusiasm for what she was working on—sometimes staying at the keyboard late into the night just to see how things turned out.

I thank my son, Dan, for his faith in the book and his ideas for the cover. His skill in executing these ideas on the computer was remarkable.

Last and most importantly, I thank Rick Cooper, my brilliant editor. I choose the word "brilliant" because his many encouraging words were like sunbeams breaking through my dark clouds of self-doubt. Furthermore, his suggestions in the editing and proofreading process were brilliant because he clearly understood my original intent and could help me make choices and changes that gracefully improved the text. I might not have connected with Rick except for some lucky coincidences. Or maybe, as I tend to think, the stars and planets realigned to make it so. I shall be forever grateful.

Don McIntosh, the Walker, is a retired physical education teacher, coach, trainer, camp counselor, and masters swimmer. He lives in Middlebury, Vermont, with his wife Carol. Don is active in various men's groups and regularly enjoys a good walk and a good swim workout. He and Carol love traveling together and cheering on their seven grandchildren.

Fran McIntosh, the Driver, is still very much the writer, as well as a musician and composer. She plays jazz piano and is also a fiddler with the Champlain Valley Scottish Fiddle Club.

David Disque, Fran's husband of forty-nine years as of this writing, is semi-retired from retail sales in the family store, The Middlebury Shop. Fran and David love cross-country skiing together, traveling, dancing, exploring nature, and keeping up with the grandchildren.